Peter Blake

peter blake a retrospective

First published 2007 by order of the
Tate Trustees by Tate Liverpool, Albert Dock,
Liverpool L3 4BB

in association with Tate Publishing,
a division of Tate Enterprises Ltd, Millbank,
London SW1P 4RG www.tate.org.uk/publishing
on the occasion of the exhibition

Peter Blake: A Retrospective
Tate Liverpool 29 June – 23 September 2007

British Library Cataloguing in Publication Data

A catalogue record for this book is available from the British Library

ISBN 978 185437 717 3

Distributed in the United States and Canada by Harry N. Abrams, Inc., New York

Library of Congress Cataloging in Publication Data
Library of Congress Control Number: 2006937947

Designed by Valle Walkley
Printed by Die Keure

Cover: *Drum Majorette*, 1957 (detail)

Liverpool 08
EUROPEAN CAPITAL OF CULTURE

The exhibition at Tate Liverpool is supported by the Liverpool Culture Company as part of the city's preparations for European Capital of Culture 2008.

peter blake a retrospective

edited by christoph grunenberg and laurence sillars

tate publishing

Foreword and Acknowledgements

Peter Blake's reputation as 'the godfather of British Pop art' is truly deserved. His innate fascination, manifest in his work, with all streams of popular culture and entertainment has defined a specifically British Pop aesthetic. Blake's pioneering images of the 1950s and 1960s have long been seen as iconic, not only within art history but as more popular recordings of the social preoccupations of that time. Yet, as this exhibition shows, his work goes far beyond this. From his earliest work of the 1950s, Blake's paintings and drawings have been fundamental to the traditions of figurative realism in this country and abroad. His engagement with the Victorian imagination, myth and folklore during the 1970s as a Ruralist continued his nostalgic pursuit of a dream world while introducing a new cast of characters and themes. Since the 1980s, a substantial body of work has developed out of an increasingly conceptual and self-evaluative practice which has not been given the critical attention or exposure it deserves. I am delighted that, nearly 25 years after Peter Blake's first major retrospective was held at the Tate Gallery in London, Tate Liverpool has the opportunity to present such a comprehensive body of his work from the last sixty years. Following the exploration of Blake's fascination with the technique and aesthetics of collage in the exhibition *About Collage*, which he curated for Tate Liverpool in 2000, we are pleased to present here an inclusive survey of his oeuvre concentrating on the media of painting, drawing and printmaking. What emerges is an extraordinarily rich and diverse body of work, exploring a wide range of themes drawn as much from the world of popular culture, literature and myth as from his personal life and passions. The enduring appeal of Blake's art is testament to its continuing significance, fascinating fans for more than half a century and inspiring generations of artists.

It has been a pleasure and an inspiration to work with Peter Blake, and we at Tate Liverpool would especially like to express our heartfelt gratitude to the artist and his wife Chrissy for their tireless and long-standing enthusiasm for the realisation of this exhibition. The show would not have been possible were it not for the support and encouragement of a great many people both within and beyond the organisation. I would like to thank Leslie Waddington and his staff at Waddington Galleries, especially Louise Kybert, who have not only provided extensive help and advice throughout all stages of the exhibition's planning but have lent a number of important works and facilitated the loan of a great many others from private collections around the world. Similarly, I would like to thank Galerie Claude Bernard, Paris; Wetterling Gallery, Stockholm; Nishimura Gallery, Tokyo; Hazlitt-Holland Hibbert, London; and all of the other lenders who have so generously supported the exhibition by allowing us to borrow works from their collections.

At Tate Liverpool, I am most grateful for the productive collaboration with the co-curator of the exhibition, Laurence Sillars. We were ably assisted by Darren Pih, who managed the complex research and organisation of this ambitious show. I would, as ever, like to thank all the staff at the gallery for their invaluable contributions and, in particular, Wendy Lothian, Ken Simons and Barry Bentley for their meticulous care of shipping and the exhibition's installation. I am grateful to the catalogue authors for their insightful and illuminating essays, which add fresh perspectives to Blake's work. I would also like to thank Daniella Valle and Richard Walkley for their wonderful design, Helen Tookey for her quick and efficient editing, Anna Gorse for the picture research, and Larissa Kolstein for producing the book with her customary skill.

The exhibition has been generously supported by the Liverpool Culture Company and we are grateful for their help in making this show possible in Liverpool.

Christoph Grunenberg
DIRECTOR, TATE LIVERPOOL

the 1950s

painting like a fan?

simon faulkner

Peter Blake has often been discussed in terms of the apparent directness of his artistic approach to his subjects. For example, Robert Melville stated in 1962 that '[Blake's] work is a declaration of his interests, intransigent to the point of naïvety',[1] while Michael Compton observed in the catalogue to the Blake retrospective at the Tate Gallery in 1983 that 'Blake is an artist whose work seems to spring in the most direct way from his interests and affections'.[2] In a similar vein, Blake has also been described as a painter who is a 'fan'.[3] In 1960 Lawrence Alloway declared: 'Blake works as a fan'. This declaration was reworked by Roger Coleman in the catalogue for Blake's first retrospective in 1969 and repeated by Natalie Rudd as the last sentence in her 2003 monograph on the artist.[4] As a fan, Blake is meant to be someone who takes a straightforward pleasure in the cultural forms he chooses as the subjects for his paintings. Thus his approach to popular imagery is presumed to be 'natural' and a matter of uncomplicated appreciation, because Blake and his subjects 'have simply grown up together'.[5] In Rudd's words, Blake's work is defined by an 'honest simplicity'.[6]

Can Blake's art be as straightforward as these commentaries suggest? Is the relationship between Blake's work and his consumption of popular culture[7] as uncomplicated and organic as described in the existing literature on the artist? This essay will suggest that the answer to these questions is no. But to understand why this is the case we do not need to dismiss out of hand the notion that Blake's approach to art is driven by his genuine interests in popular culture. Nor does the idea that his art has been structured by his desire to approach his subjects in as direct a way as possible need to be rejected. However, a distinction needs to be made between such desires and the means Blake has employed to achieve them.

Directness, simplicity and the enthusiasms of fandom are themes within Blake's art, but this does not mean that his representational practices are direct, in the sense of having an unmediated relationship to their subject, or simple, or really akin to the practices of cultural consumption involved with being a circus, cinema, or pop music fan. The experience of popular culture is itself far from simple, involving complex forms of knowledge and institutional contexts, but this needs to be distinguished from the specific forms of art-making and spectatorship which are defined by their own conventions and institutions. It is not enough to

1
Robert Melville, 'The Durable Expendables of Peter Blake', first published in *Motif*, no. 10, Winter 1962–63, reprinted in *Peter Blake*, exh. cat., London, Tate Gallery, 1983, p. 36.

2
Michael Compton, 'Peter Blake', in *Peter Blake*, exh. cat., London, Tate Gallery, 1983, p. 14.

3
See Lawrence Alloway, 'Introduction', in *Theo Crosby Sculpture, Peter Blake Objects, John Latham Libraries*, exh. cat., London, Institute of Contemporary Arts, 1960.

4
Roger Coleman, 'Introduction', in *Peter Blake*, exh. cat., Bristol, Bristol City Art Gallery, 1969, p. 4; Natalie Rudd, *Peter Blake*, London, Tate Publishing, 2003, p. 121.

5
Compton, 'Peter Blake', p. 16; Coleman, 'Introduction', p. 5.

6
Rudd, *Peter Blake*, p. 7.

7
It should be noted that I use the phrase 'popular culture' as a convenient catch-all category for a wide range of cultural practices, without assuming that it defines anything other than a collective distinction from those cultural forms conventionally defined as 'high culture', including fine art. The historical nature of the 'high/low' cultural divide remains a matter for research and debate. See John Frow, Cultural Studies and Cultural Value, Oxford, Oxford University Press, 1995, Chapter 2, 'The Concept of the Popular', pp. 60–88.

suggest, as Roger Coleman did in 1969, that Blake's 'period as an art student did not change or modify the direction of his thought or weaken his ability to remain himself, it simply enabled him to develop and refine his skills for saying what he already wanted to say'.[8] Becoming an artist by going to art school and entering the art world is a quite specific social experience. Similarly, developing an artistic practice involves adapting pre-existing ways of making art that are quite different from other forms of cultural expression no matter how similar artworks might appear to the subjects they appropriate from other areas of society.

Although Blake appears to be an exception in certain ways to these conditions, Coleman was ill-advised to state that his art was the equivalent of fans celebrating their heroes by 'pasting them into scrapbooks or pinning them to [their] bedroom wall'.[9] But it is precisely the appearance of exceptionality on Blake's part that defines the power and quality of his art. That his work appears to be simple, direct and natural in its approach to popular culture is an effect of the sophisticated pictorial practices Blake has developed, not the result of his naivety and innocence as an artist. It is in these terms that we can understand Coleman's definition of Blake's work as encapsulating 'a kind of innocence, albeit a very sophisticated innocence'.[10] In a sense, Blake does paint like a fan – his passion for his subjects informs the choices he makes – but making a painting involves the re-presentation of a subject to create something new and separate from the original. Blake makes pictures of innocence and fandom, rather than directly embodying these things in his work. What this means is that his objectives as a painter are different from the more intellectual approach to popular culture found in the work of Richard Hamilton, but both artists create work that is necessarily distanced from its subjects by the very fact that it involves artistic representation and by their positions as artists. Artists make choices, but, like all of us, never under conditions they entirely control. Artists make art, but not without utilising the precedents of past art; they have intentions, but these intentions are always shaped in one way or another by the existing forms and contexts of art.[11]

We can explore this issue further by considering Blake's work from the 1950s. The painting Children Reading Comics 1954 appears to represent innocent childhood pleasures, despite the sombre look of the boy and the medical patch

8
Coleman, 'Introduction', p. 5.

9
Ibid., p. 4.

10
Ibid.

11
See Michael Baxandall, *Patterns of Intention: On the Historical Explanation Pictures*, New Haven and London, Yale University Press, 1985.

Children Reading Comics
1954
Oil on hardboard

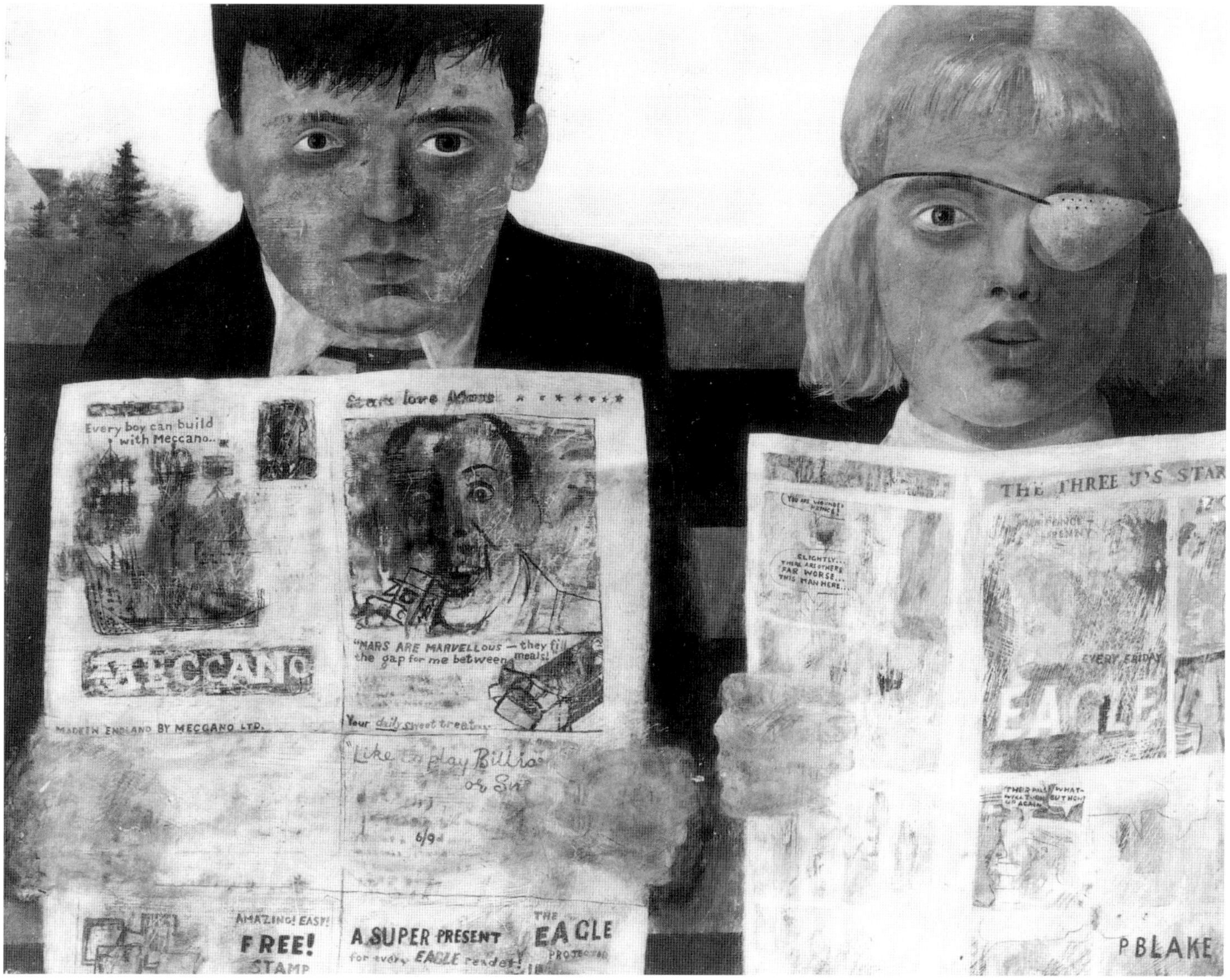

Children Reading Comics
1956
Oil on hardboard

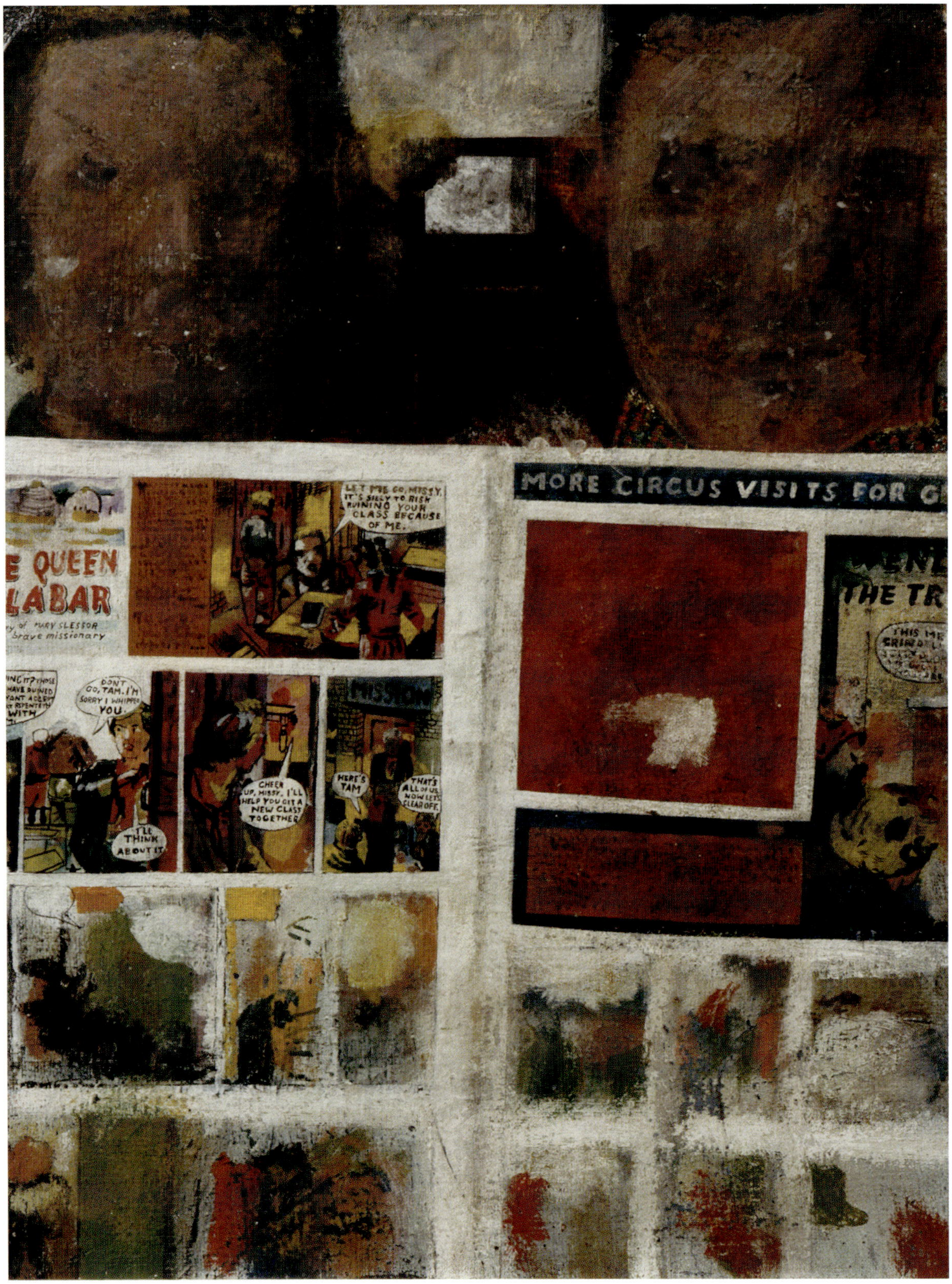

over the girl's left eye. The scene suggests that the children have been pictured at the moment when their reading has been interrupted – perhaps they have been asked a question by someone outside the space of the painting and have lowered their comics in response. The children and the comics are pictured as if they are close to the literal surface of the work and almost in the space of the viewer. The uncovered eye of the girl also stares at the spectator, creating an impression of direct visual contact between the two. Moreover, the form of the picture as a whole positions the spectator at the level of the children. The work creates a dual sense of visual directness through the close relationship between the children and their comics within the pictorial space of the painting and through the relationship set up between the children, the comics and the spectator. But what needs to be stressed is that these impressions of directness are the result of compositional choices. Blake could have chosen to depict a scene of children reading comics in other ways. We might compare Children Reading Comics to another painting, *World's Greatest Comics* 1946 by the American artist Ben Shahn,[12] which is of a very similar subject and may well have been one of the sources for Blake's work. Shahn's picture shows two boys reading comics in a playground. The boy in the foreground crouches to read a comic that lies on the ground, his pose suggesting the excitement of this experience. Yet despite his location in the foreground, this figure is diminutive in contrast to the space around him and in comparison to the scale of the children in Blake's painting. This comparison suggests that the choice to picture the children and their comics up close to the picture plane was made by Blake to create the sense of a direct relationship between the viewer and the subject of the work. We are distanced from Shahn's children by their small scale within the expansive pictorial space of his painting, thus we see them from a position outside their world, whereas in Children Reading Comics the viewer is a spatial counterpart to the children.

The photographic historian John Tagg has argued that during the nineteenth century the head-on stare in photographs was sometimes taken as a sign of the 'bluntness and "naturalness" of a culturally unsophisticated class', in contrast to side-on poses, which were associated with people higher up the social hierarchy.[13] Frontality in portraiture implied simplicity and the lack of sophistication of the

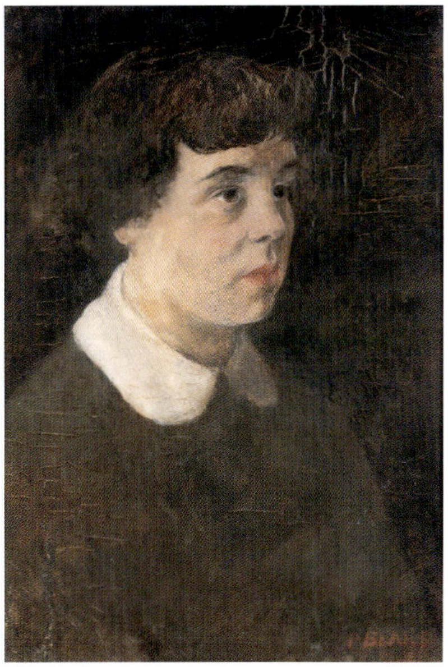

Portrait of Shirley Blake
1950
Oil on cardboard

12
See Frances K. Pohl, *Ben Shahn*, San Francisco, Pomegranate Artbooks, 1993, p. 89.

13
John Tagg, *The Burden of Representation: Essays on Photographies and Histories*, Basingstoke and London, Macmillan, 1988, pp. 36–7.

The Deluge
1953–4
Oil on board

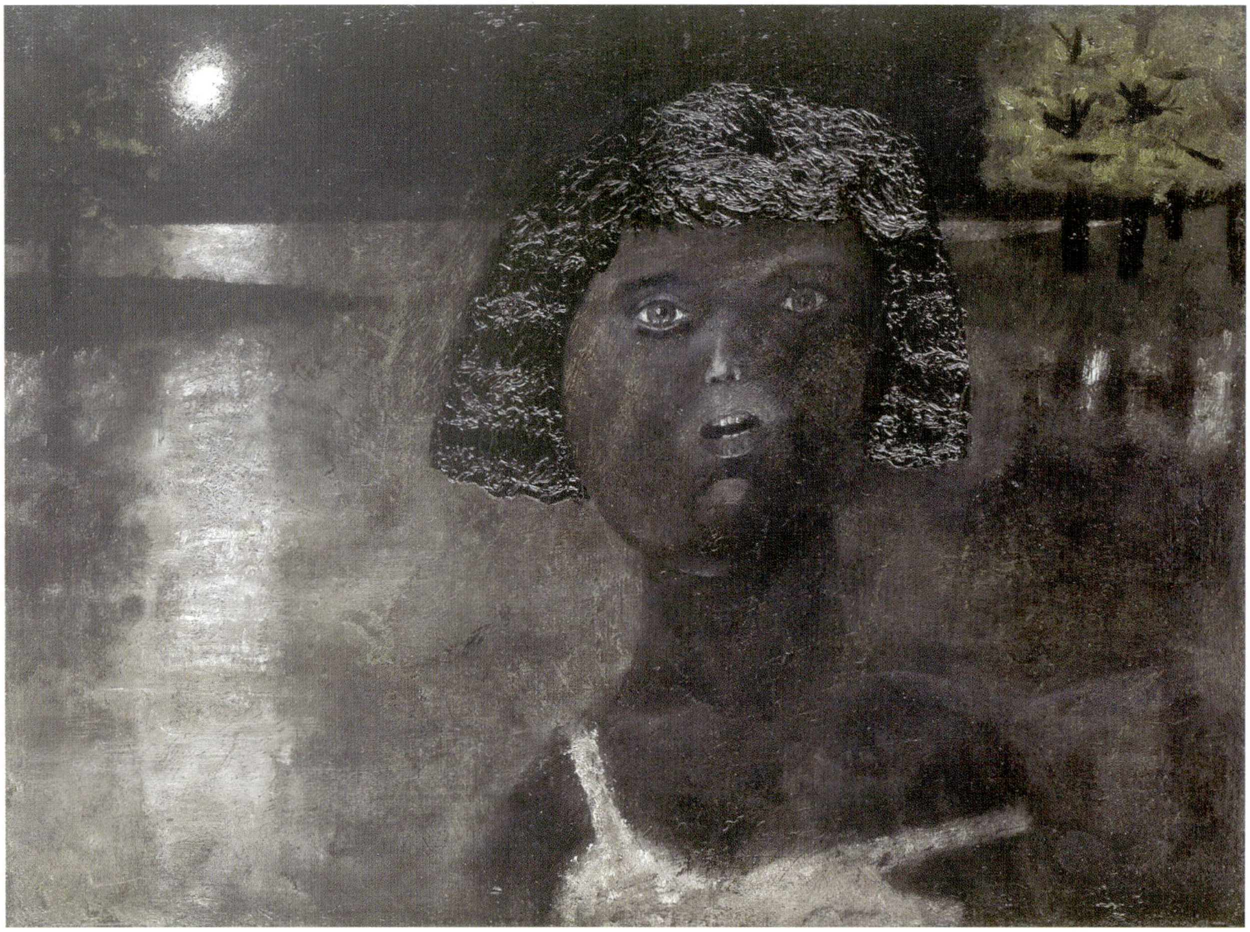

Self Portrait
1949
Oil on hardboard

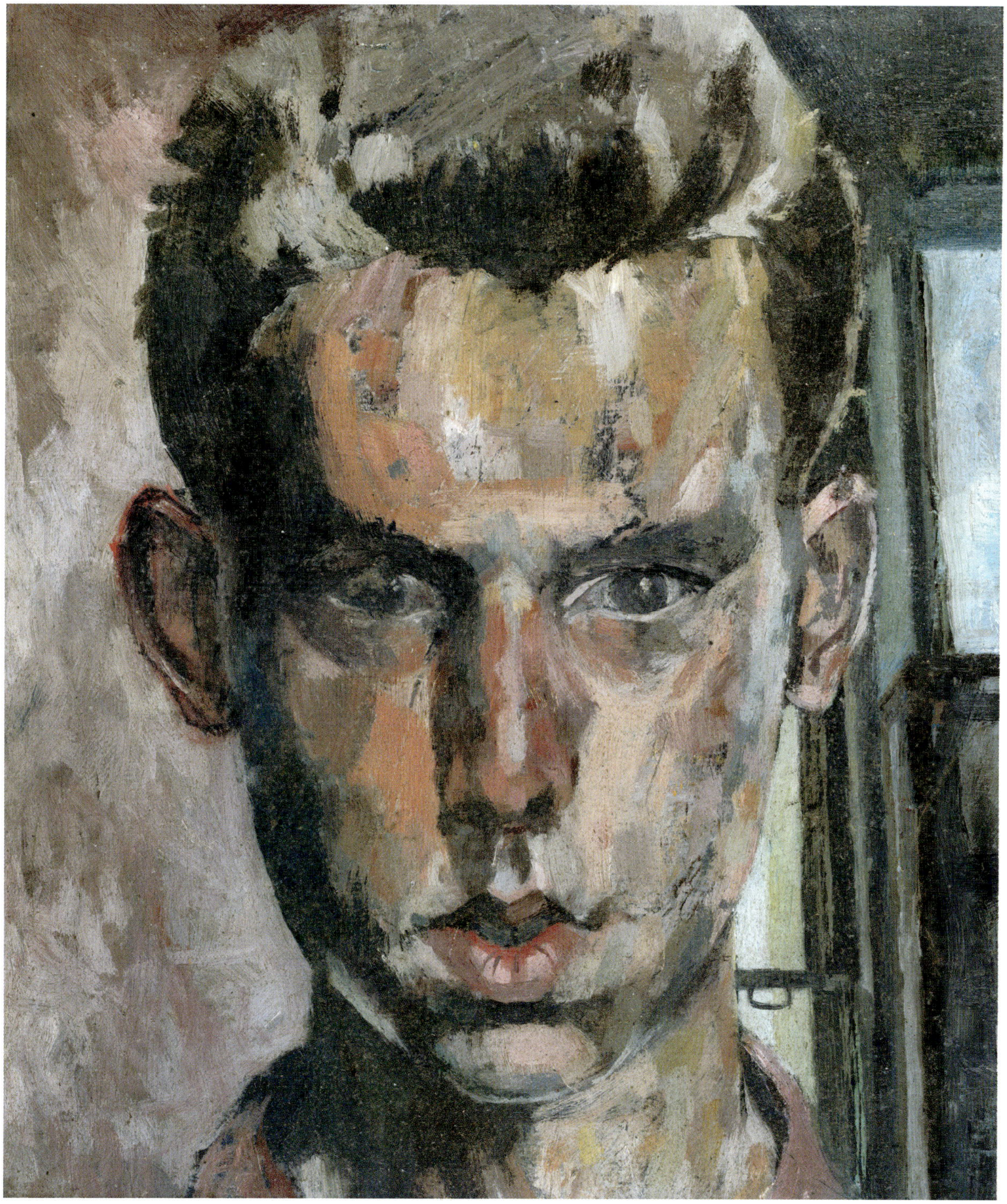

Still Life of Apples
1958
Oil on wood panel

Shoe on the Beach at Nice
1956
Oil on hardboard

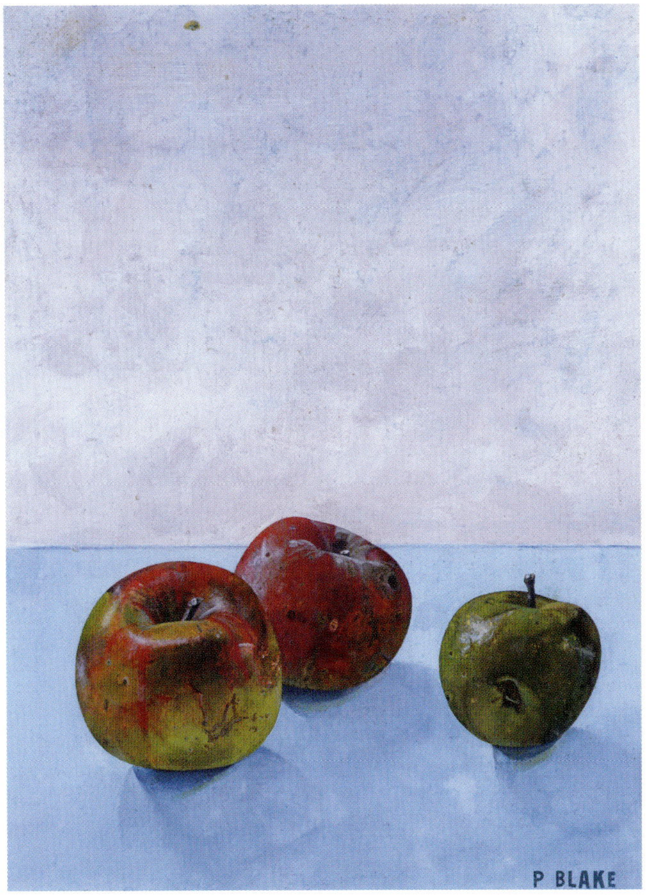

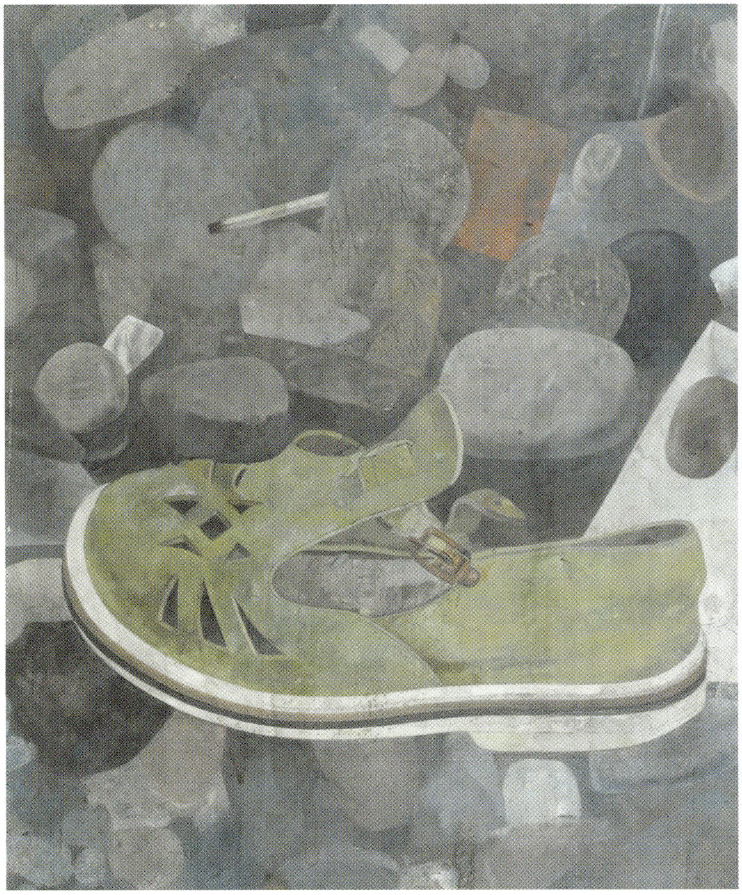

Boy and Pigeons
c.1954
Oil on hardboard

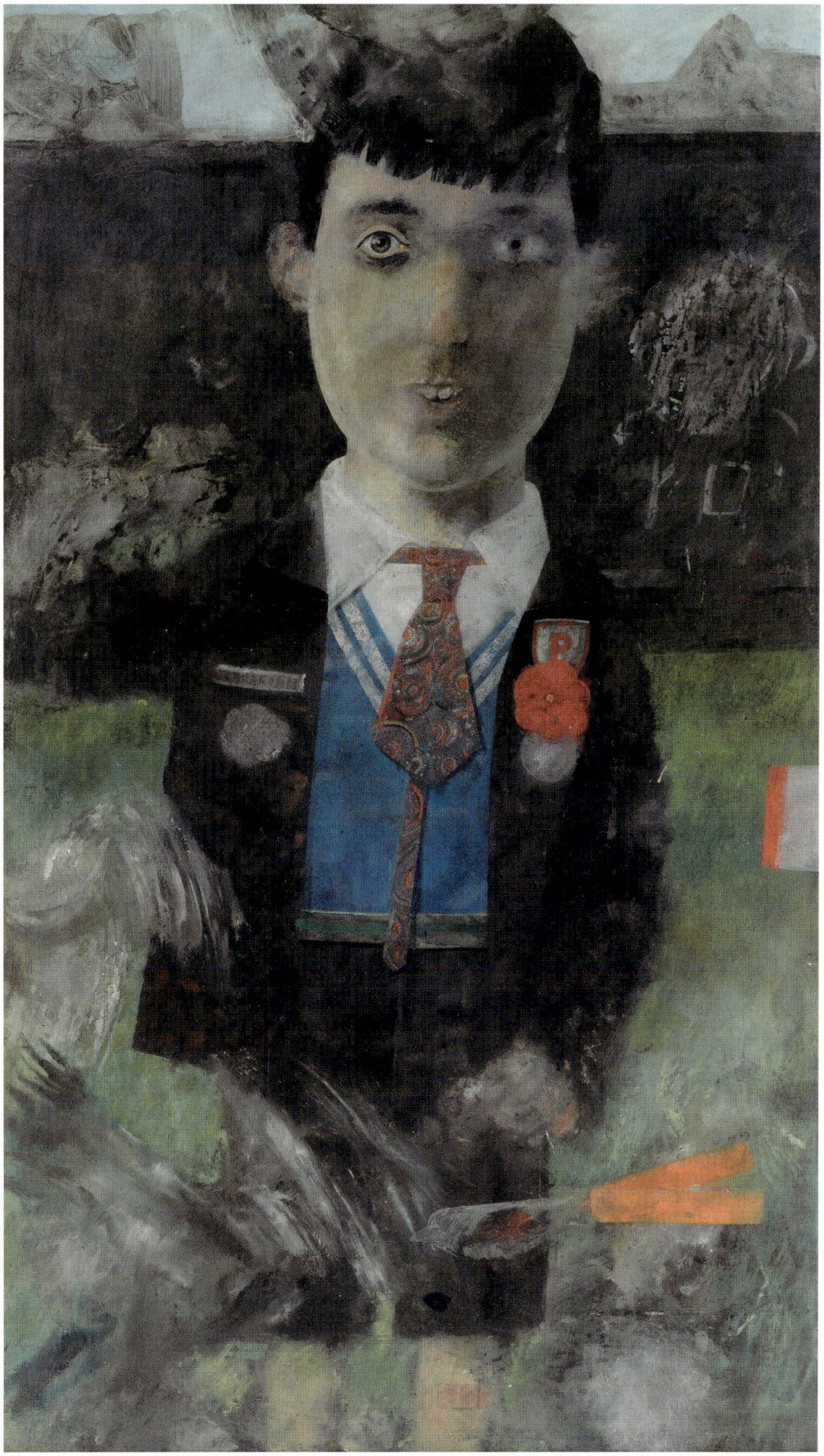

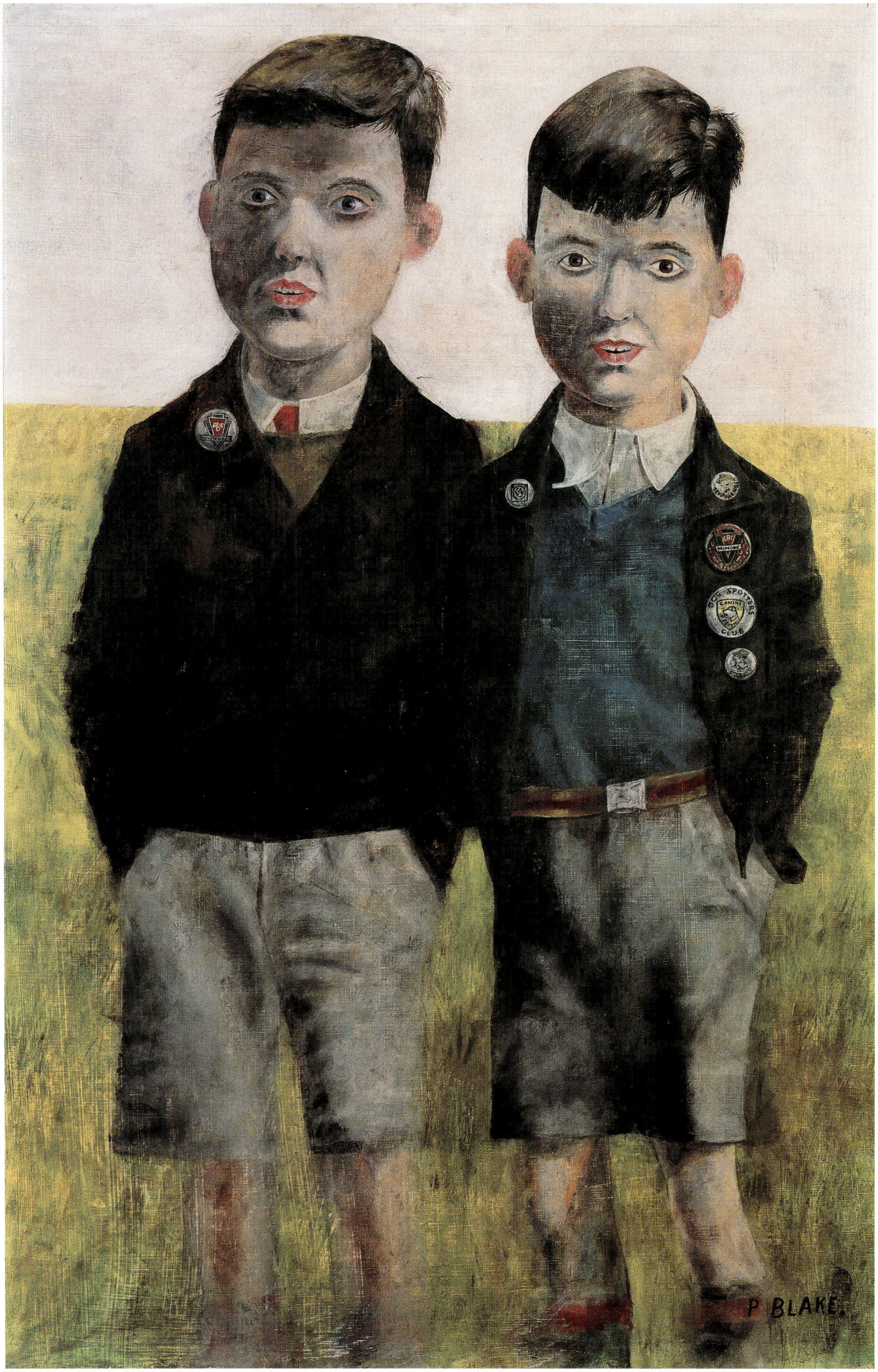
DOG SPOTTERS CLUB
P BLAKE.

ABC Minors
1955
Oil on hardboard

person represented. Blake's Children Reading Comics was derived from family photographs of him and his sister when they were children,[14] and although the painting was not about any sense of lack on the part of its subjects, the composition may well have been informed by long-standing notions of the association of frontal portraiture with simplicity and naturalness. With this in mind we might also note that frontal portraits are characteristic of Blake's art throughout the 1950s and into the 1960s. These works include **Self Portrait in RAF Jacket** c. 1952–53, **ABC Minors** 1955, **The Preparation for the Entry into Jerusalem** 1955–56, **On the Balcony** 1955–57, some of the circus paintings, and **Self Portrait with Badges** 1961.

While discussing the relationship between Children Reading Comics and possible pictorial precedents we might also consider other instances within art history when pictorial closeness has implied a sense of directness, immediacy and transparency of relationship between picture and viewer. T. J. Clark has suggested that this is the case with Jacques-Louis David's *Death of Marat* 1793, in which Marat's corpse, the bath in which he was murdered, and other objects were painted as if in very close proximity to the beholder.[15] We might also consider certain paintings by Shahn in which it is not only the large scale of figures within the picture space but also their incompleteness that creates the impression of closeness. The same goes for Children Reading Comics: the heads and legs of the children are cut off, implying that the viewer is too close to see their whole bodies. What all of this suggests is that the format of Blake's painting was the result of compositional choices and an awareness of certain artistic and cultural conventions. It was through these choices and the reworking of pictorial conventions that an idea of directness was represented in the painting.

Blake's work from the 1950s is also steeped in a sense of nostalgia for childhood. But this does not mean that Blake was focused on experiences in the past. He had a double focus on the past and the present that was shown through his interest in both old and new forms of popular culture. In line with this, Blake has stated: 'I paint about the life I knew. It isn't Victoriana, it's nostalgia, or rather a sentimentality, for my childhood, but it's also a feeling for what's going on now – an emotion.'[16] He has also observed: 'For me, pop art is often rooted in nostalgia: the nostalgia of old, popular things. And although I'm also continually trying to

14
Peter Blake, exh. cat., London, Tate Gallery, 1983, p. 74.

15
T. J. Clark, *Farewell to an Idea: Episodes from the History of Modernism*, New Haven and London, Yale University Press, 1999, p. 34.

16
Quoted in *Peter Blake, Patrick Caulfield, Howard Hodgkin: Paintings from the 60s and 70s*, exh. cat., London, Waddington Galleries, 1995, p. 8.

Boy with Hot Dog
1960–5
Acrylic on hardboard

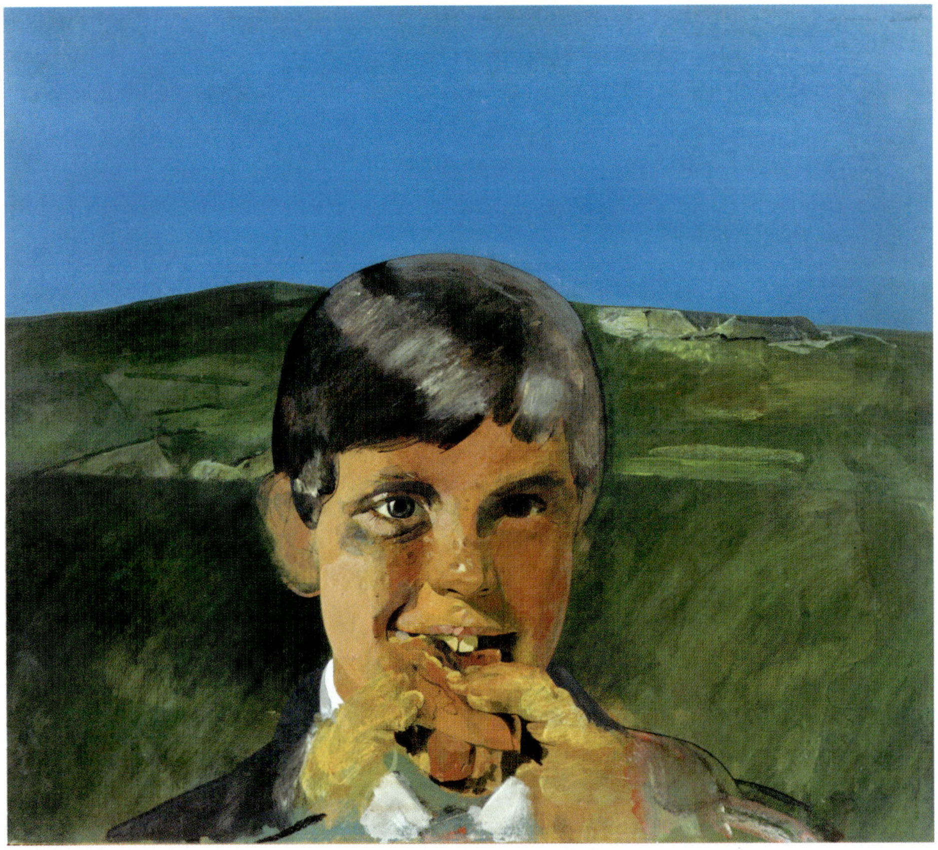

Self Portrait in RAF Jacket
c.1952–3
Pen and ink and gouache on paper

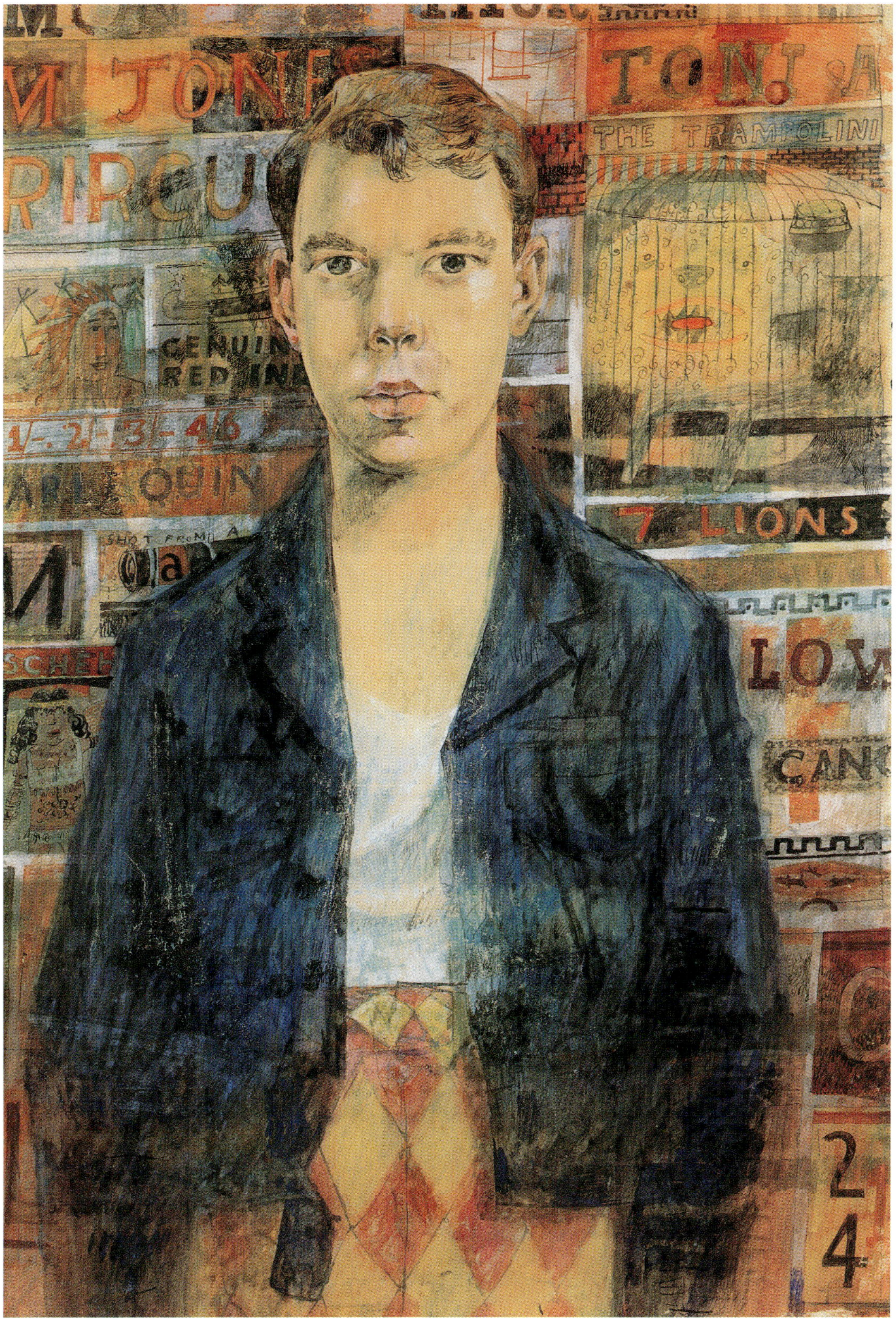

establish a new pop art, one which stems directly from our own time, I'm always looking back at the sources of the idiom and trying to find the technical forms that will best recapture the authentic feel of folk pop.'[17] Such a relationship between past and present informs Children Reading Comics. The *Eagle* comic pictured in the painting began publication in 1950, so even at its earliest date of availability this comic could only have featured in Blake's life when he was eighteen and a student at Gravesend School of Art. Therefore Blake used a contemporary comic to symbolise pleasures of childhood that might have been his own in the 1930s and 1940s, and equally might be those of children in the present. Here mid-1950s' popular culture functioned as a vehicle for nostalgia, interweaving the past and the present.

Knife Thrower's Board 1957 is another picture that both suggests the visual pleasures of 1950s' popular culture and harks back to older forms of popular entertainment that were part of the artist's childhood. The knife thrower's assistant is a figure from a circus tradition that was established as a staple of working-class 'organised entertainment' in the last quarter of the nineteenth century.[18] However, the image that Blake used as the basis for his picture was a life-size pin-up of the contemporary French film star Brigitte Bardot derived in weekly sections from the 'gentleman's magazine' *Reveille*. This pin-up was an example of the increase in 'cheesecake' (the female equivalent of 'beefcake') imagery in the British print media during the 1950s. Reveille was itself a significant element within this development, having been taken over by the *Daily Mirror* in 1947 and given a weekly front page displaying what Harry Hopkins described as 'a "Luscious Lovely", posed "provocatively"'.[19] The image Blake used displayed characteristics of 1950s' 'cheesecake' imagery, identified by Richard Hoggart in 1957 as differing from pre-war images, which were 'fairly simple', involving a 'comparatively "straight" photograph of a girl's legs, or of her body in a bathing costume'. In contrast, contemporary photographers 'specializing in the pin-up business' knew they had to 'produce photographs sailing as nearly as possible to the laws of indecency and carrying a powerful charge of that sort of suggestion which it is difficult to bring within the orbit of any regulations, simply because it does not depend primarily on the amount of body exposed, but makes its point by suggestion, by the turn of a

17
Originally quoted in *Studio International*, November 1963, reprinted in *Peter Blake*, exh. cat., Bristol, Bristol City Art Gallery, 1969, p. 26.

18
See Raymond Williams, *Communications*, London, Chatto and Windus, second edition, 1966, p. 25.

19
Harry Hopkins, *The New Look: A Social History of the Forties and Fifties in Britain*, London, Secker and Warburg, 1964, p. 225.

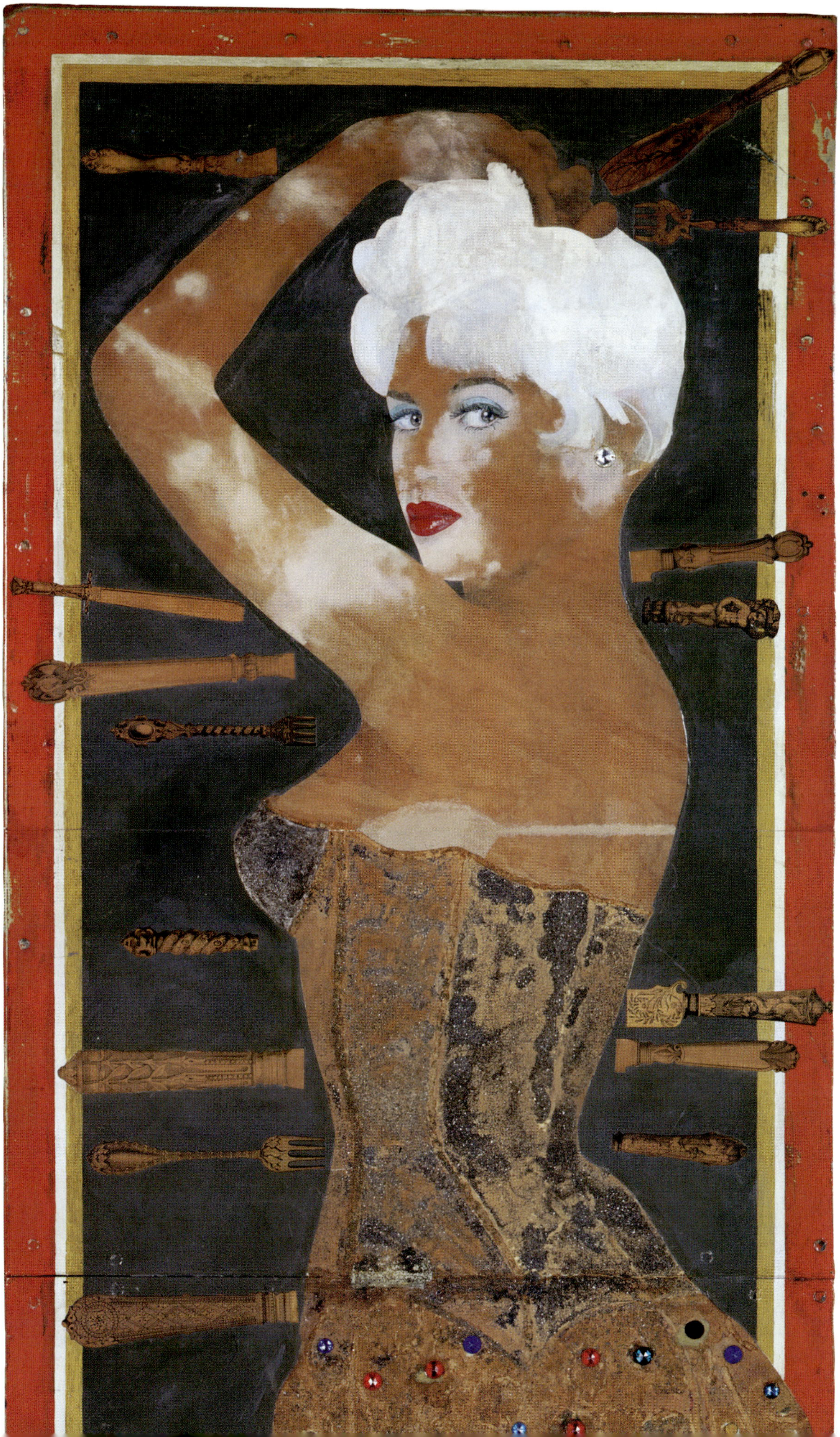

Knife Throwers Board (detail)
1957
Oil and collage on hardboard

leg or the bend of a shoulder'.[20] In this context Bardot's pose can be contrasted to the frontal poses of the female circus performers in Loelia, World's Most Tattooed Lady 1955 and Siriol, She-Devil of Naked Madness 1957.[21] The point to be made here is that Knife Thrower's Board uses the most contemporary way of representing women's bodies for male visual pleasure to reinvent the visual culture of the circus tradition. In this case the circus is not only the subject of nostalgia, it is also the context for the mixing of different forms of eroticised representation and looking.

Knife Thrower's Board, along with the other mixed media works *Locker* 1959 and Girlie Door 1959, with their collaged pin-ups, can be located within contemporary debates over erotic imagery, morality, and cultural values. The British Press Council stated as early as October 1953 that it was 'deeply concerned about the unwholesome exploitation of sex by certain newspapers and periodicals'.[22] By contrast, Hoggart felt that the 'sex [had] been machined out' of contemporary pin-ups, meaning they could have few harmful sexual effects. Instead his fear was that working people were 'exchanging their birthright' of traditional working-class culture for 'a mass of pin-ups'.[23] This links Blake's work to concerns about the expansion of image culture during the 1950s and 1960s, and a sense that 'image', as something manufactured and artificial, was replacing direct experience.[24] The development of more sexually suggestive images of women within mainstream commercial culture enabled Blake's 'girlie' pictures, but despite the apparent simplicity of the pleasure he found in 'cheesecake' images, we cannot assume that all the viewers of his work were able to divorce these pictures from wider anxieties. From this perspective we can begin to understand that the 'innocence' of vision associated with Blake's work could only exist when framed in particular ways.

As we can see from the above discussion of Children Reading Comics and Knife Thrower's Board, there were continuities between Blake's interests in older forms of popular culture and new forms of visual experience. In particular pictures circus imagery was reworked using images derived from magazines, while other works linked the circus to the world of popular music. The figure in Siriol, She-Devil of Naked Madness sports an 'Elvis' tattoo on her left leg. Here the relationship between past and present cultural forms was not simply defined by nostalgia for

20
Richard Hoggart, *The Uses of Literacy*, Harmondsworth, Penguin, 1958, p. 175.

21
This contrast is also suggested in Rudd, *Peter Blake*, p. 23.

22
Quoted in Hopkins, *The New Look*, pp. 225–6.

23
Hoggart, *The Uses of Literacy*, pp. 191 and 175.

24
See Williams, *Communications*, p. 33; Daniel J. Boorstin, *The Image*, Harmondsworth, Penguin, 1963.

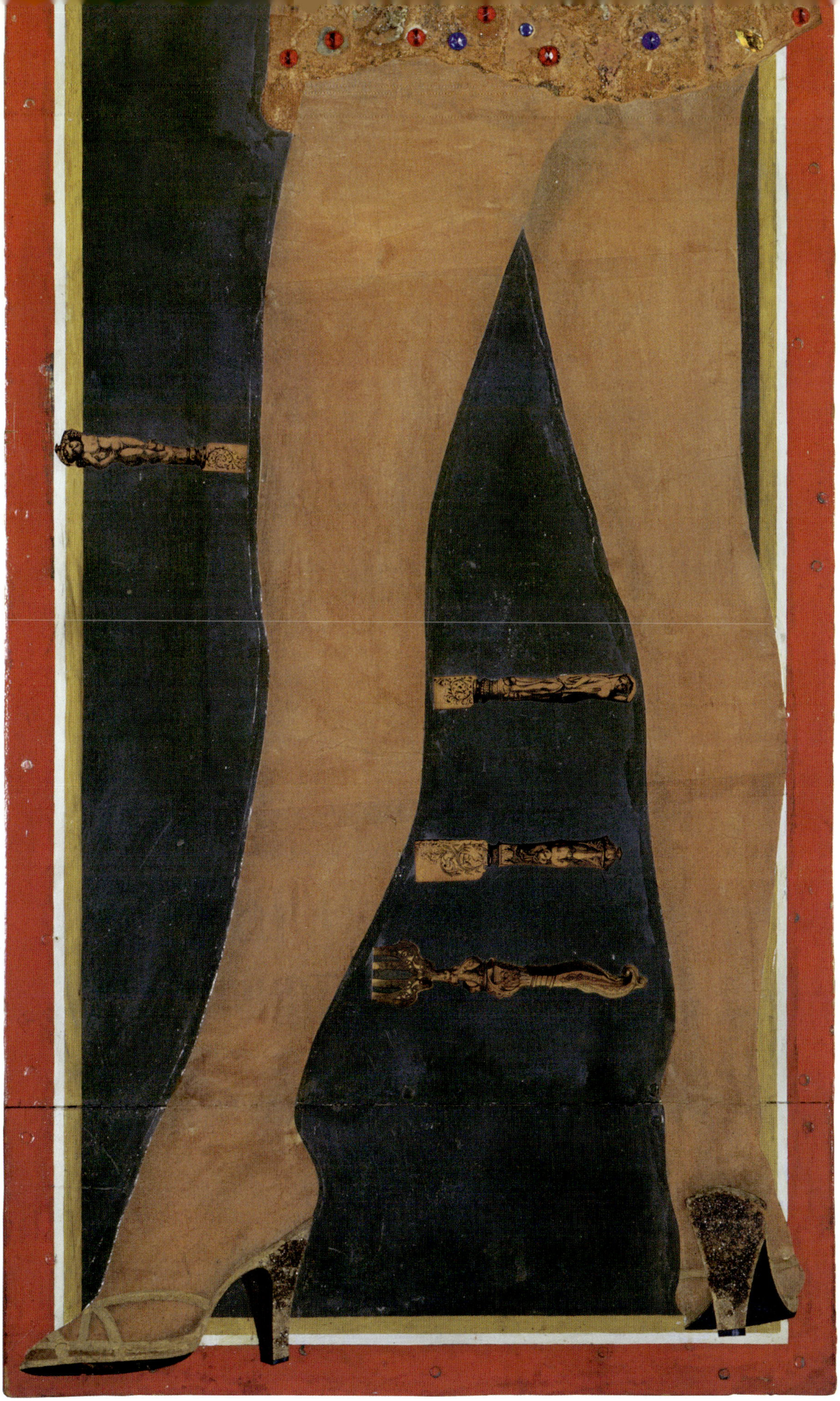

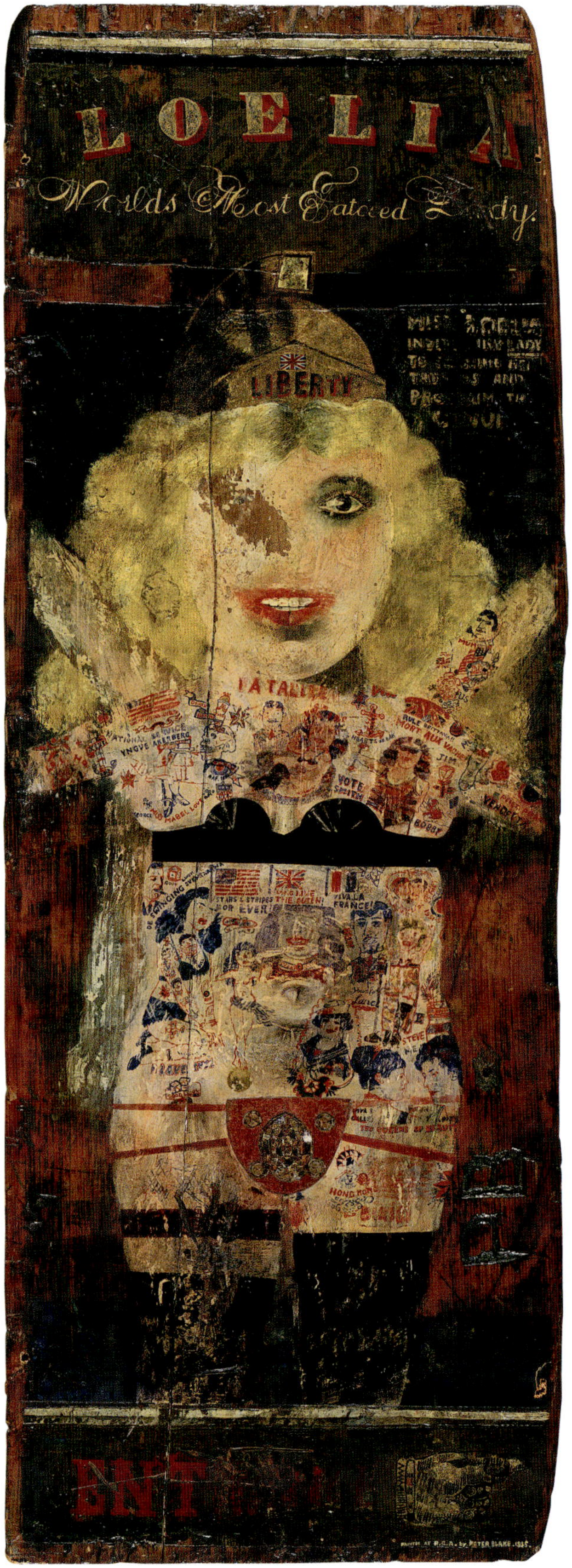
LOELIA
Worlds Most Tattooed Lady.
LIBERTY
ENT

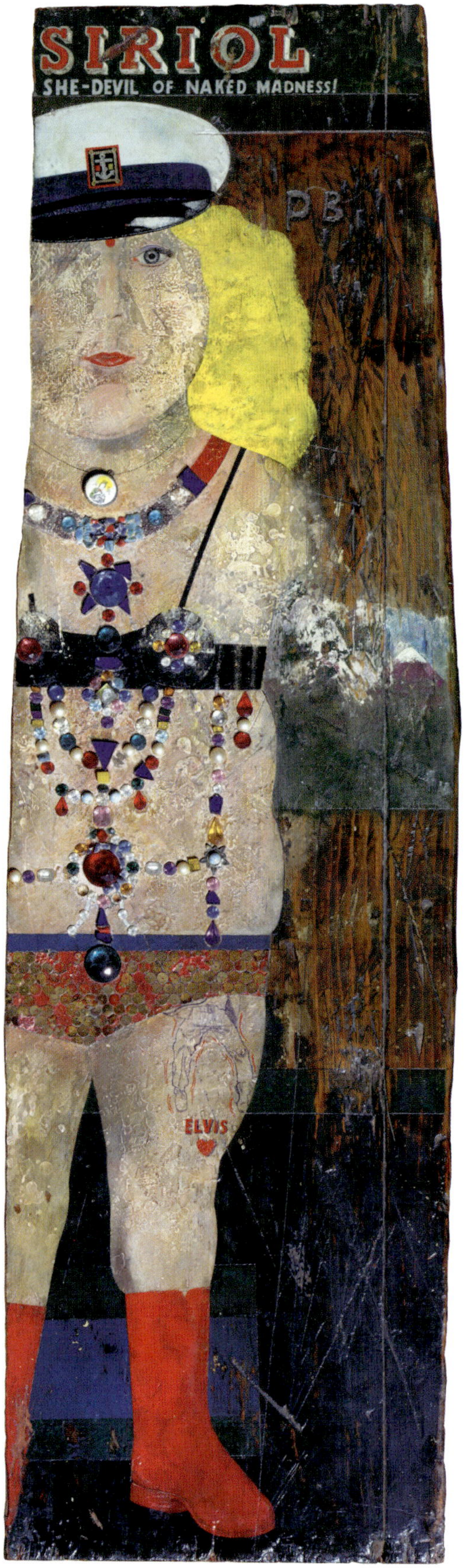
SIRIOL
SHE-DEVIL OF NAKED MADNESS!
PB
ELVIS

Loelia, World's Most Tattooed Lady
1955
Oil and collage on panel

Siriol, She-Devil of Naked Madness
1957
Oil and collage on panel

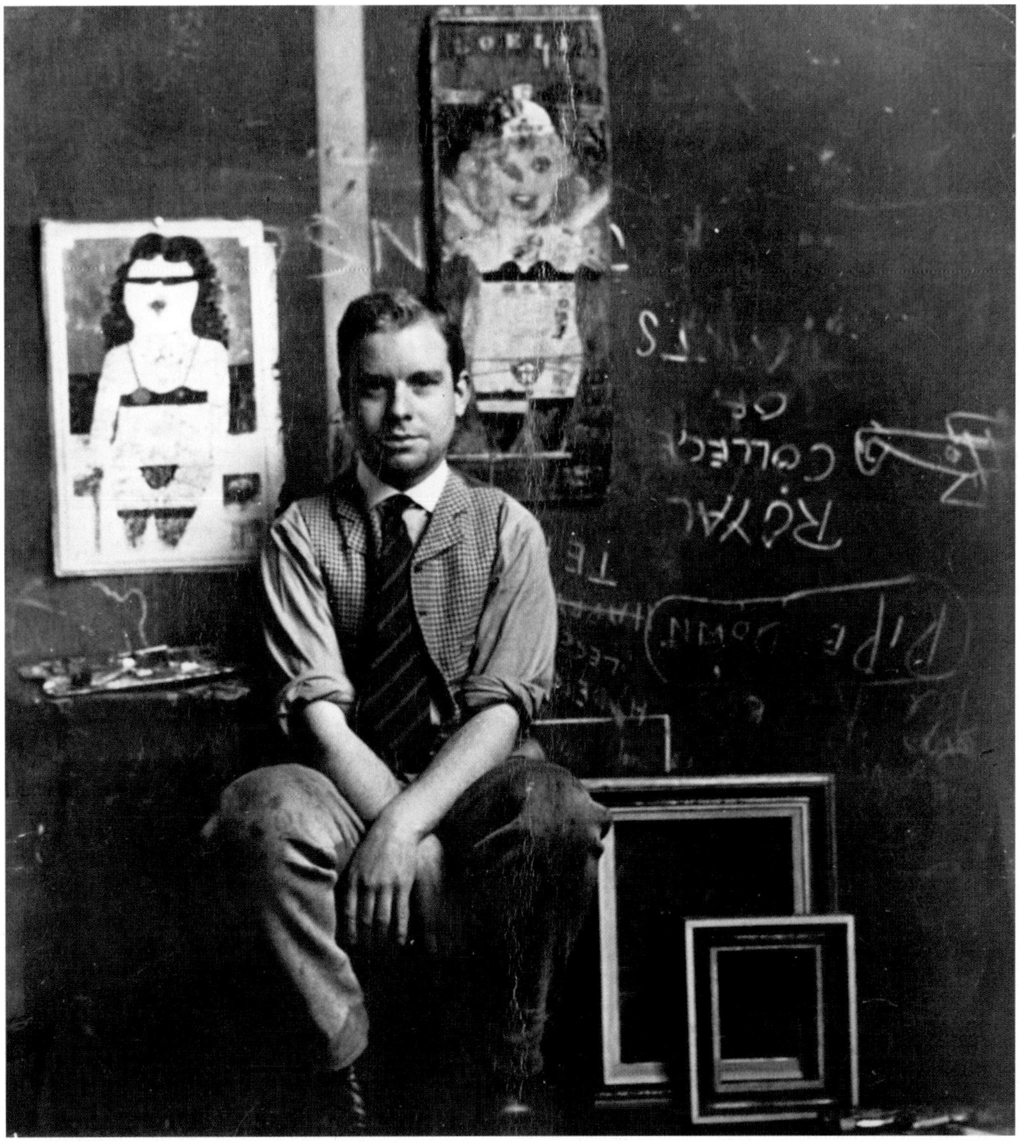

Peter Blake at the painting school,
Royal College of Art
London 1956

Tattooed Lady with Collage
1958
Gouache and collage

pre-1950s' popular culture, even when that nostalgia was represented through contemporary images, but also in terms of the circus being understood as the forerunner of contemporary rock and roll, pin-ups and glossy magazines. In Blake's work old and new popular culture were not easily separable. This is shown by the way he continued to take elements from both in his work during the early 1960s, for example in Got a Girl 1960–61, which depicts a row of rock and roll stars along the top over a large area constituted by an apparently abstract configuration, which was in fact derived from the funfair and is pocked with shooting gallery bullet holes. The dialogue between past and present in all these works suggests that Blake was more than just a simple consumer of popular culture, if there can ever be such a thing. Blake's paintings and mixed media works of the 1950s presented viewers with new ways of looking at familiar cultural forms. Blake used the accumulated forms of art – *trompe l'oeil*, modernist flatness and frontality, and collage – to create commentaries on the consumption of popular culture, bringing different forms of cultural artefact together and combining them in new ways.

Elvis's performances during the mid-1950s were often seen as sexually suggestive, while rock and roll in general was understood to be sexualised music.[25] Perhaps the linking of the figure in Siriol, She-Devil of Naked Madness to Elvis through the tattoo was meant to conjure up comparable risqué associations, something reinforced by the title of the painting. But despite the sexual image of Elvis, Blake's references to the American performer are varied. One of the children in On the Balcony wears an 'I LOVE ELVIS' badge as if it were something unknowingly picked up to add to a collection. We should bear in mind that the images and objects seemingly presented by the children in this painting are things that interested Blake, hence the mixing of a *Life* magazine cover with a painting by Manet, and works by Richard Smith and Robyn Denny, who were contemporaries of Blake at the Royal College of Art in the mid-1950s. In Girls with their Hero 1959–62 the Elvis phenomenon is the primary subject of the work, rather than an incidental element. The canvas is divided into three horizontal bands: the upper third of the painting is defined by a space in which four female fans are visible, while the lower two thirds of the work are filled with images of the star. Some sense of the excitement created by the singer is implied by a

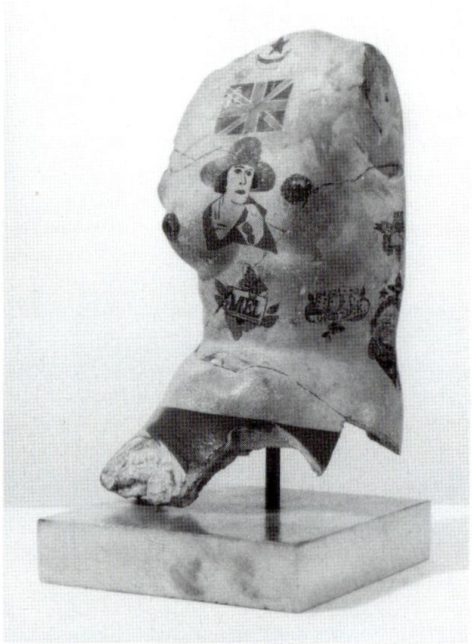

Fragments from 'Crazy said Snow White' (detail)
1959
Gouache on bust

25
See Dominic Sandbrook, *Never Had it So Good: A History of Britain from Suez to the Beatles*, London, Abacus, 2005, p. 461.

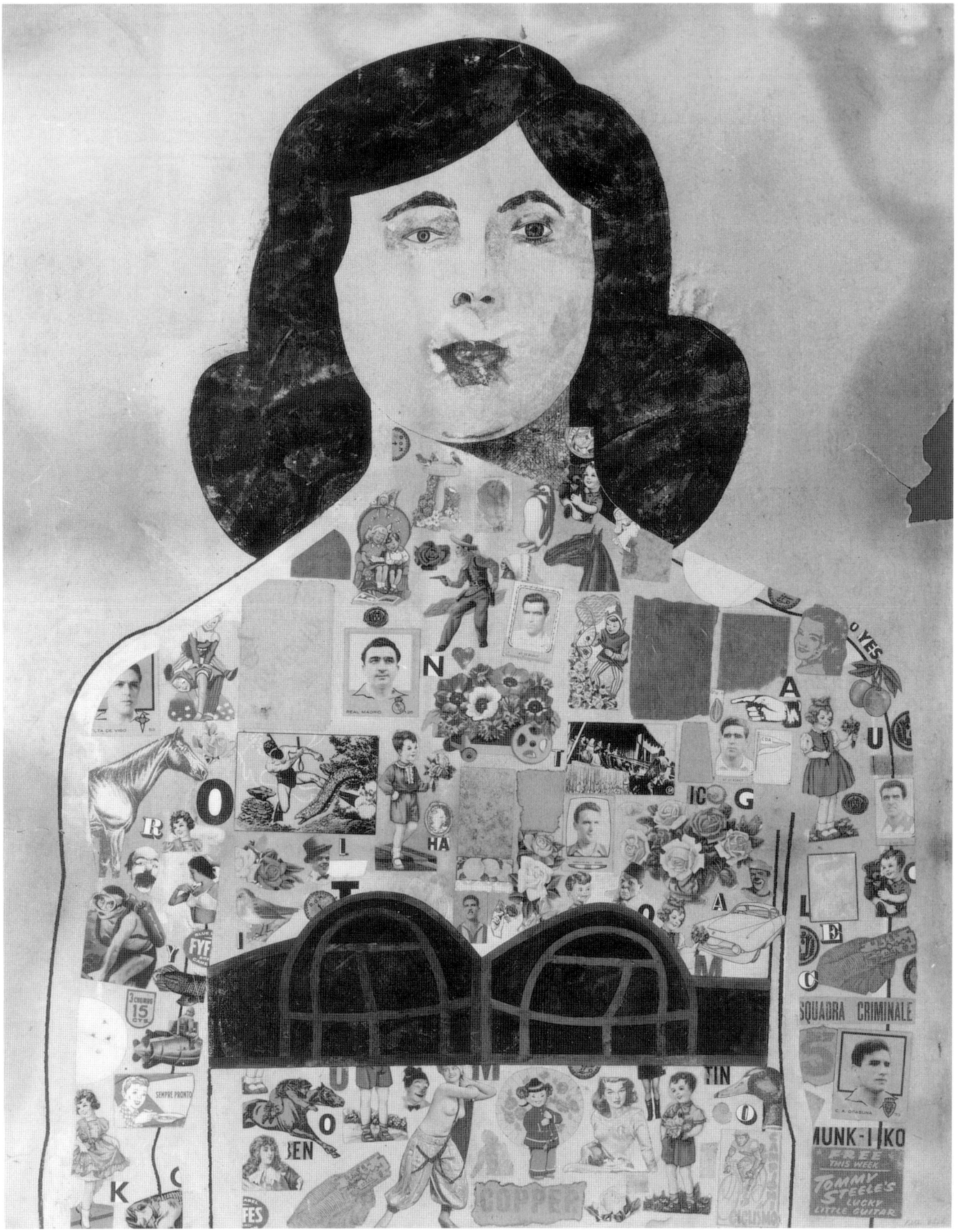
SQUADRA CRIMINALE
MUNK-I-KO
FREE THIS WEEK
TOMMY STEELE'S LUCKY LITTLE GUITAR
SEMPRE PRONTO
REAL MADRID
O YES
COPPER

Drum Majorette
1957
Oil and collage on hardboard

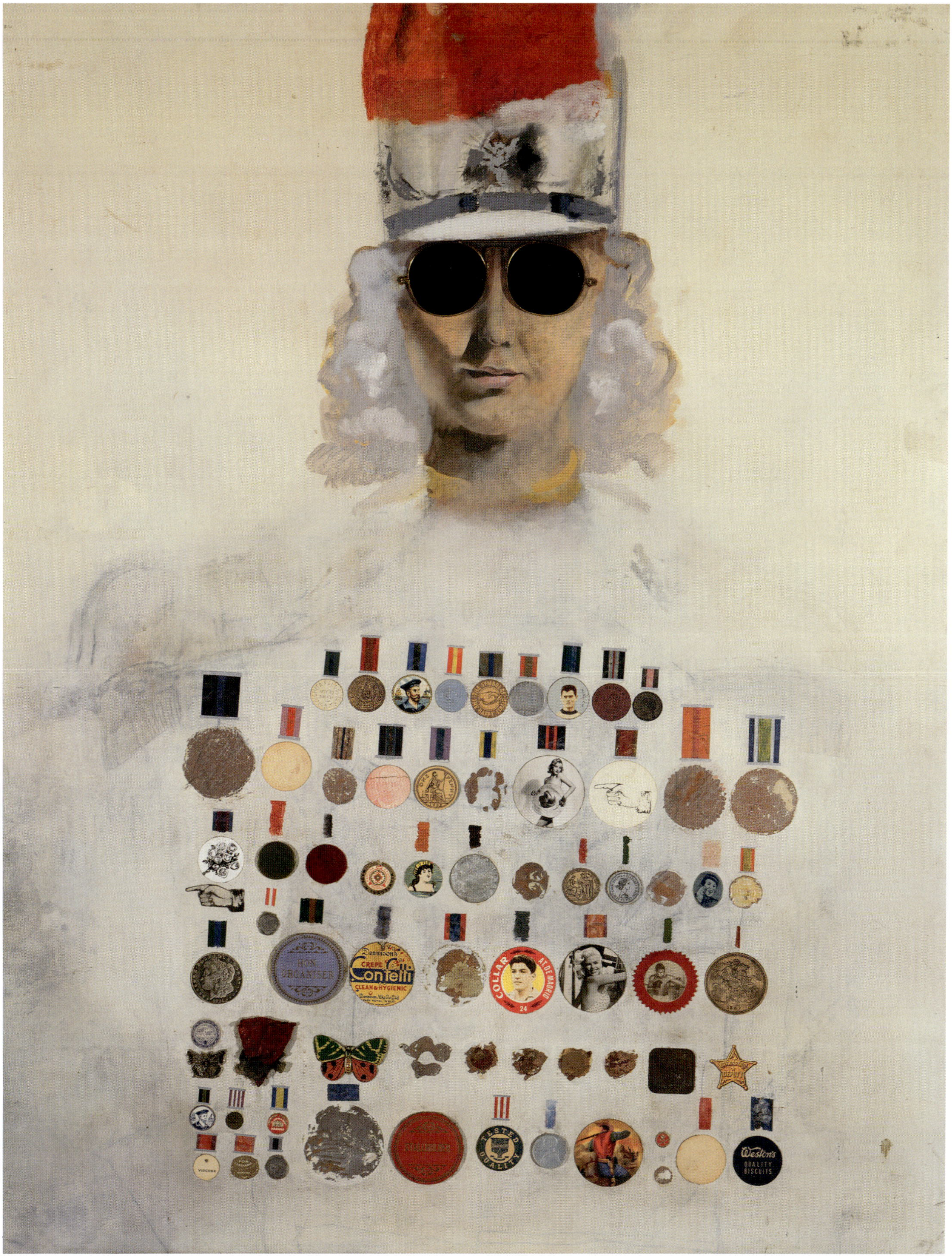
HON ORGANISER
Dennison's
CREPE
Confetti
CLEAN & HYGIENIC
COLLAR
TESTED QUALITY
Weston's
QUALITY BISCUITS

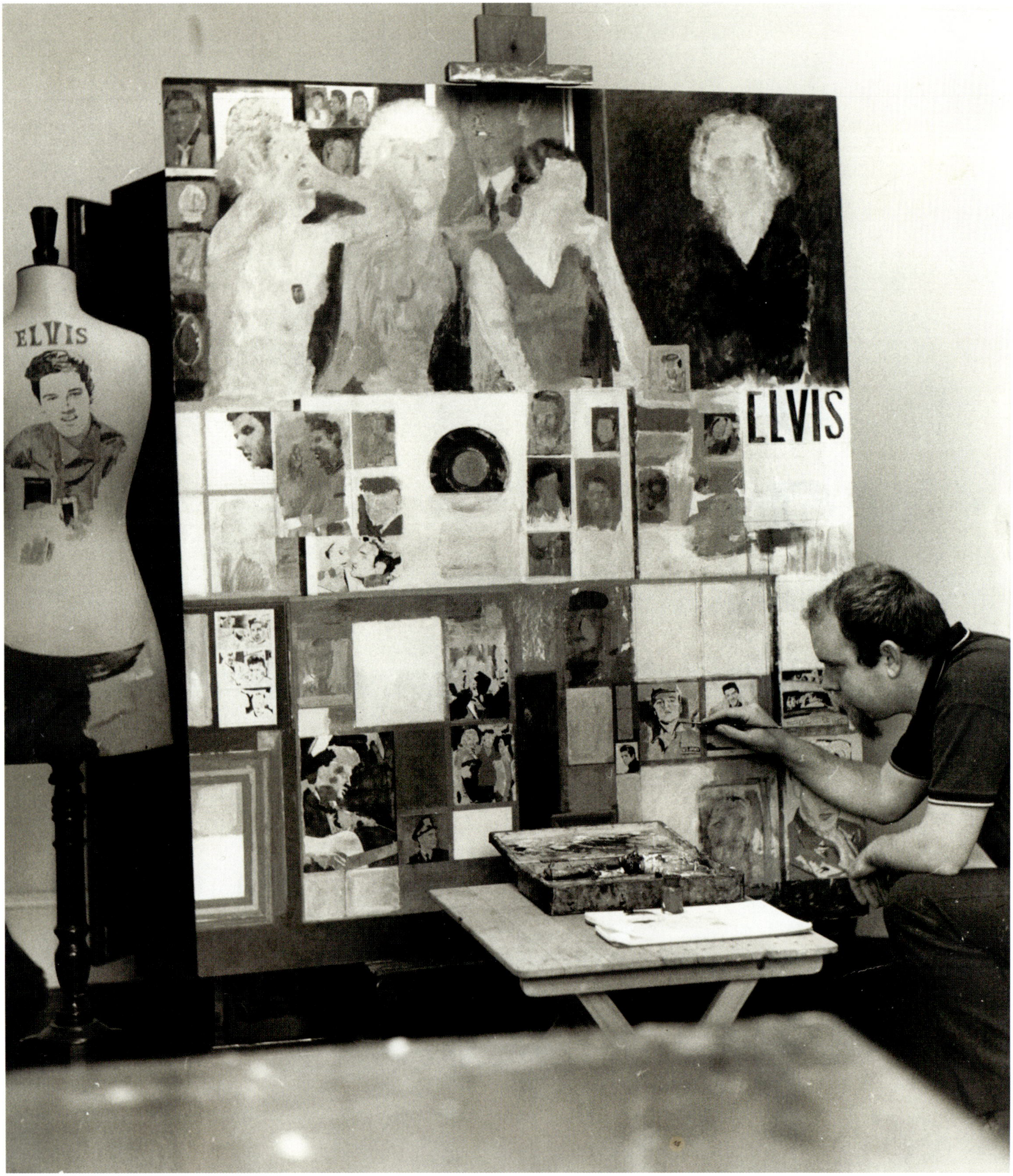
ELVIS
ELVIS

Blake in the studio working on
Girls with their Hero
London 1961

shrieking fan in the upper left corner, and the conjunction of the fans with pictures of Elvis, rather than with the star himself, suggests that images alone were enough to produce an erotic charge.

This discussion brings us back to the sophistication of Blake's pictorial strategies. The upper third of Girls with their Hero defines an illusionistic space within which the fans are positioned, but the lower two thirds involve the depiction of flat surfaces. The panels of Elvis pictures positioned at the bottom of the painting appear to be attached to pin-boards leaning up against the legs of a table, while above them the tabletop, displaying other Elvis paraphernalia, is depicted as if seen from above. The impression presented by the combination of the pin-boards and the tabletop is of a continuous vertical or horizontal surface, albeit made up of different panels. In effect all the flat images of Elvis are viewed as if they resided on the literal picture surface. Seen in this way, much of Girls with their Hero is compatible with the American critic Leo Steinberg's conception of the 'flatbed picture plane', which he understood to be 'the characteristic picture plane of the 1960s'.[26] For Steinberg, '[the] flatbed picture plane makes its symbolic allusion to hard surfaces such as table tops, studio floors, charts, bulletin boards – any receptor surface on which objects are scattered'.[27] Richard Smith used similar terms to describe the work of Derek Boshier in the RCA student magazine *Ark* in 1962, stating that Boshier organised his paintings 'rather like a table littered with consciously or casually collected expendibilia'.[28] The horizontally oriented surface of the flatbed picture plane existed in contrast to the traditional picture plane, oriented towards the visual field of an upright human being. With the flatbed picture the eye of the viewer stopped at the surface of the painting, as if looking at the floor or another impenetrable surface, rather than going into the space of painting as if it were a window. Yet in Girls with their Hero, Blake combines a flatbed mode with a more traditional picture space at the top, a strategy that he also used in different ways in Children Reading Comics and **Portrait of Sammy Davis Jr** 1960. In these works the flatbed aspect of the painting is often defined by an illusionistic ploy involving a person holding up a flat surface so that it is congruent with the surface of the painting's support. We might also note that at the top of The Preparation for the Entry into Jerusalem and in the top right corner

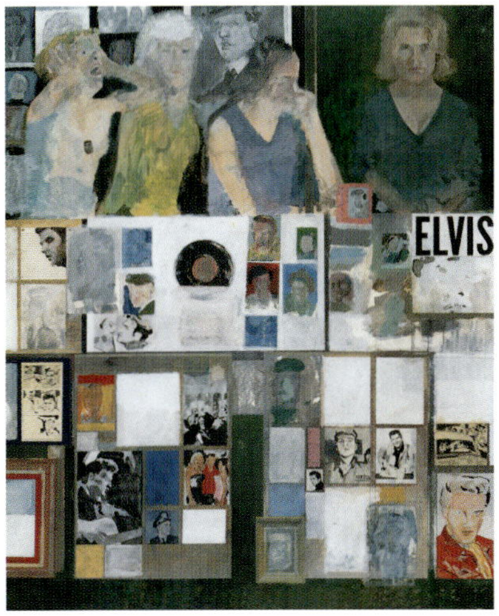

Girls with their Hero
1959–62
Oil on hardboard

26
Leo Steinberg, 'Other Criteria', in Steinberg, *Other Criteria: Confrontations with Twentieth-Century Art*, New York, Oxford University Press, 1972, p. 82.

27
Ibid., p. 84.

28
Richard Smith, 'New Readers Start Here', *Ark*, no. 32, Summer 1962, p. 40.

Only Sixteen
1960
Cartoon strip, published in the Royal College of Art magazine *Ark*, no. 25

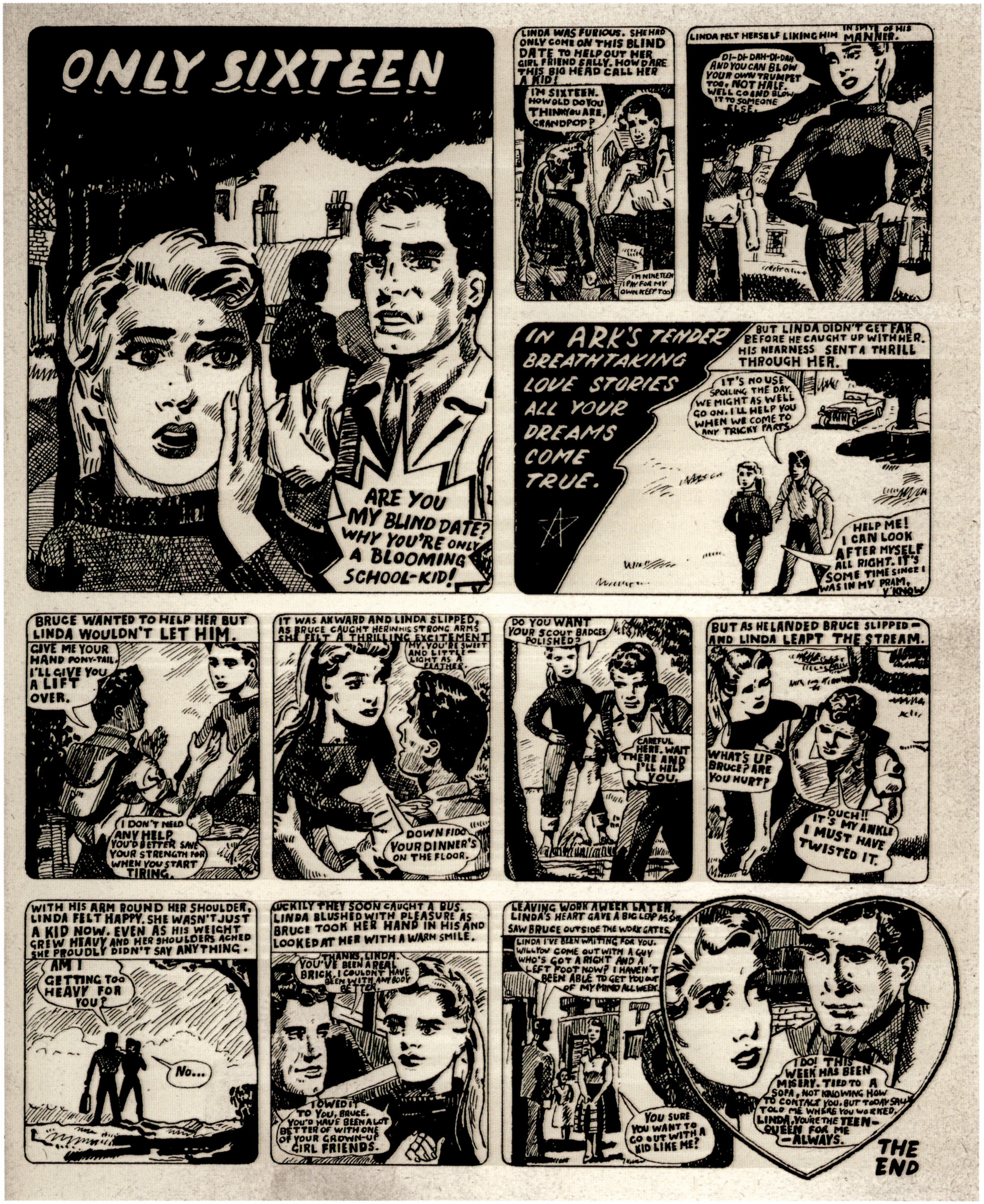

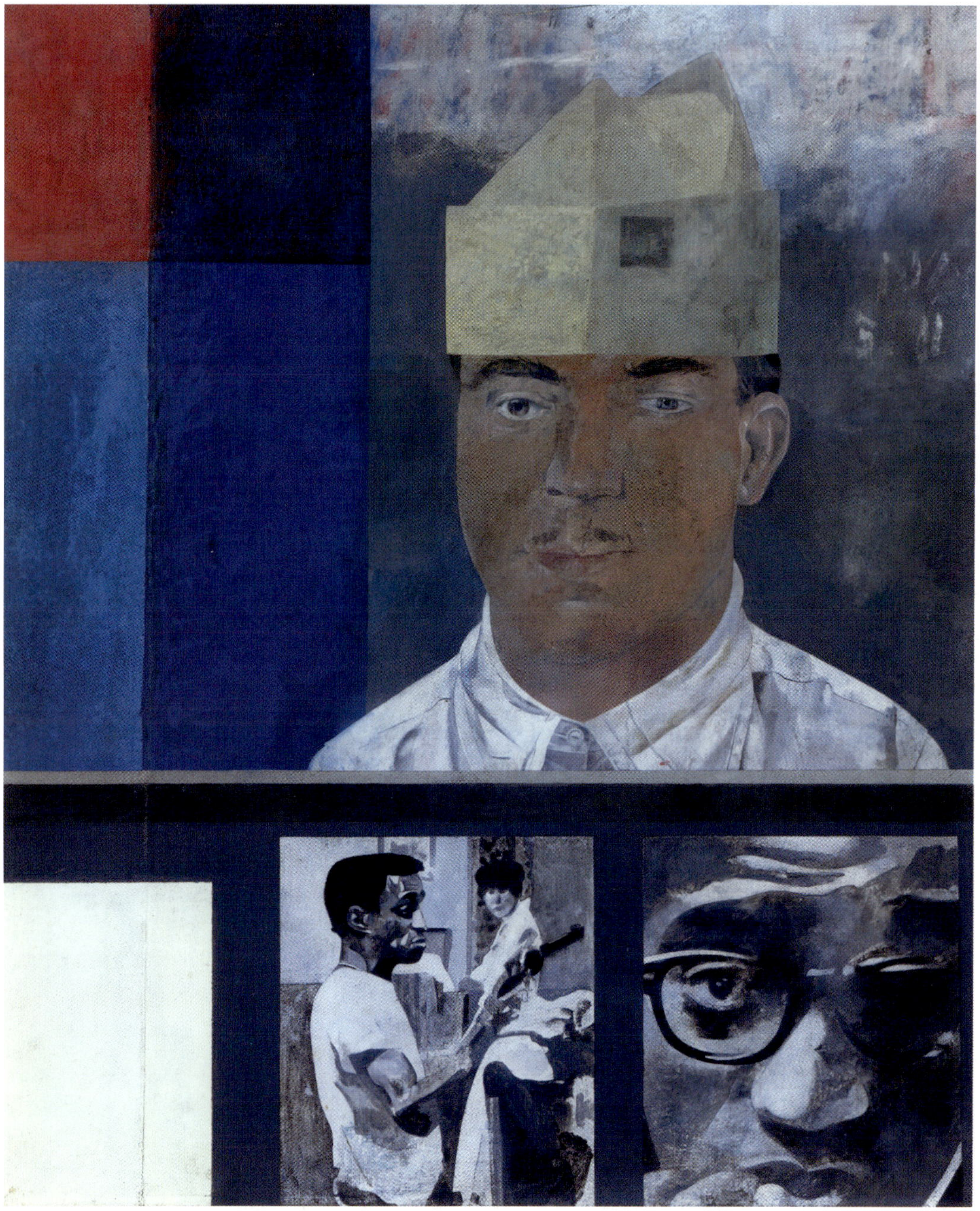

Portrait of Sammy Davis Jr
1960
Oil on hardboard

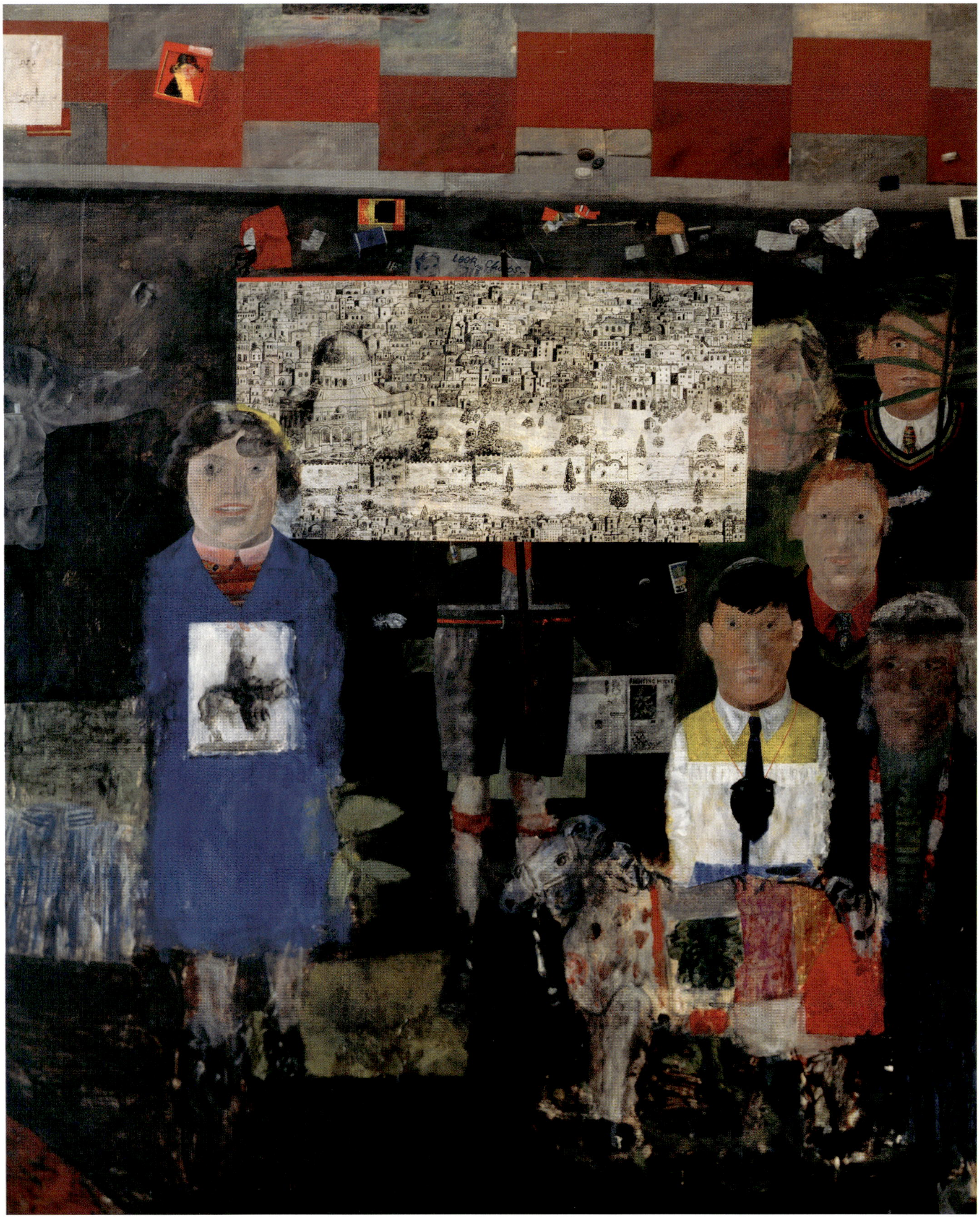

The Preparation for the Entry into Jerusalem
1955–6
Oil on hardboard

of On the Balcony there are areas where the recessive space of the painting is replaced by a representation of a flat surface, the pavement and gutter in the former, and the green lawn in the latter. Both of these areas are strewn with images and objects. In On the Balcony the pictorial flatness of the lawn at the top right also seems to continue down and across the painting in the form of the frontally presented images of the cover of *Life* magazine, the royal family, John Minton (Blake's deceased tutor at the RCA), and so on. Some of these images overlap each other, but they retain a sense of residing on the literal surface of the work. These images flatten the painting in contrast to the recessive space around them.

Shifts in picture plane within Blake's paintings from the 1950s and early 1960s indicate his acute awareness of developments in art, whether the 'personal' or 'magic' realism of Shahn during the 1930s and 1940s, or the emphatic flatness of different types of more recent American and British painting. This diversity of pictorial approaches reveals Blake's sense of a need for eclecticism when it came to the representation of his diverse interests. There is a knowingness to all of this that suggests something rather different from the idea of the painter's 'innocent eye', however qualified this notion might be in some writing on Blake. His paintings are often pictures of pictures: pictures within which other pictures are held up to the viewer, pictures in which other visual images are attached to the bodies of figures, either as badges or tattoos, pictures in which pictures are laid on the floor or attached to boards. Much of Blake's work from the 1950s could therefore be understood in terms of W.J.T. Mitchell's theory of 'metapictures' – pictures that are about picturing, about what pictures are, and what they do.[29] Blake's paintings are about the excitement of looking at pictures, about how we collect them, display them, and treat them as objects. Overall his practice during the 1950s was about the pleasures of looking and picturing in a society saturated with visual images.

These considerations extend to the picturing of words in Blake's work. His paintings present verbal texts as parts of visual images, making manifest the notion of writing as 'visible language'.[30] In works such as ABC Minors, *Litter* 1955, and On the Balcony, words are depicted on badges, paintings, magazines, comic books, and packages. As has been noted by other writers, these words are like the graffiti on the wall in the American painter Bernard Perlin's work *Orthodox*

29
W.J.T. Mitchell, *Picture Theory: Essays on Verbal and Visual Representation*, Chicago and London, University of Chicago Press, 1994, pp. 35–82.

30
Ibid., pp. 109, 111–14.

On the Balcony
1955–7
Oil on canvas

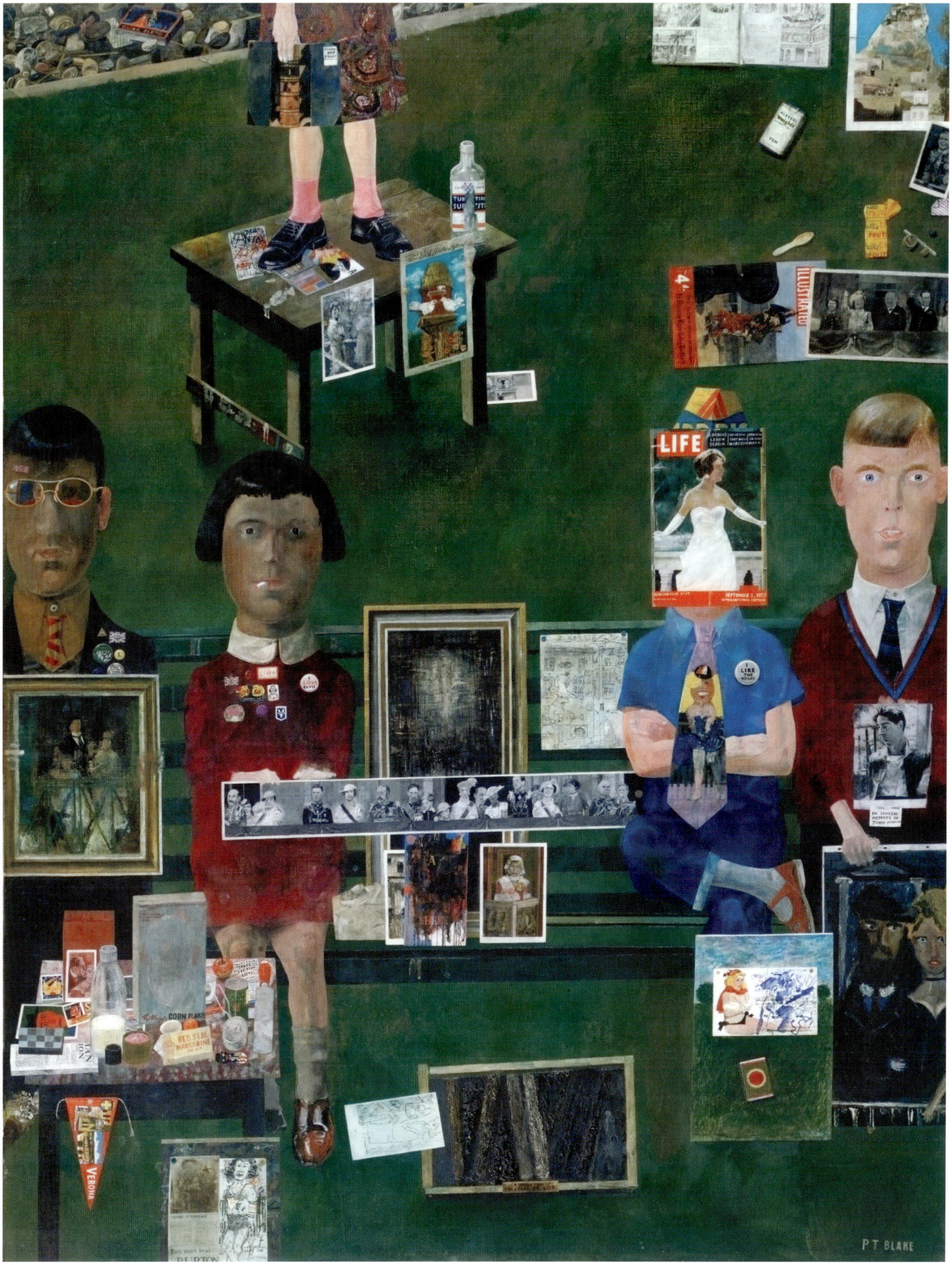
LIFE
ILLUSTRATED
CORN FLAKES
RED SEAL MARGARINE
VERONA
P T BLAKE

Peter in his London studio
c.1960

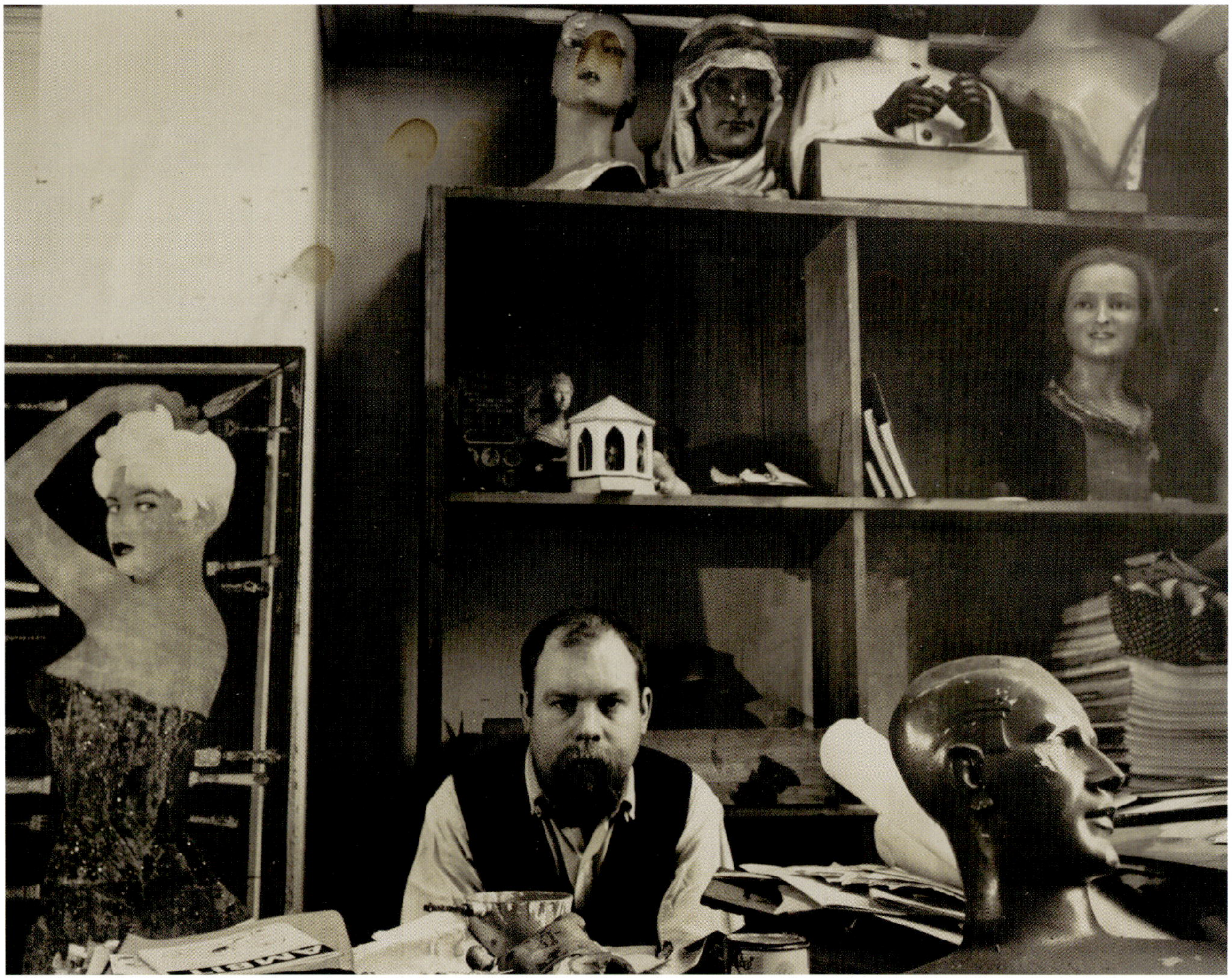

Boys 1948.[31] Another comparison might be to the seventeenth-century Dutch paintings discussed by Svetlana Alpers that present words, not to supply 'underlying meaning', but to 'give us more to look at'.[32] In Dutch art of this period and Blake's work from the 1950s, words need to be depicted because they are an important element of the visual world. In Loelia, World's Most Tattooed Lady words are depicted in a number of different ways, creating a complex interplay of text and image. Words are included as an element of the depicted scene as parts of the tattoos all over the body of the circus performer and in the form of the word 'LIBERTY' on her helmet. Here the flattened body of the woman becomes one of Steinberg's 'receptor surfaces' for pictures and texts. The title of the painting also has an ambiguous presence as a text that is either part of the depicted scene or a label on the painting itself. In addition to this, Blake has scratched his initials into the wooden support of the painting, creating another level of interaction between the visual and the verbal, and another level of ambiguity between the literal surface of the painting and its depicted content.

Seen both individually and as a whole, what Blake's work from the 1950s presents us with is a sense of seemingly opposing things coming together: the old meets the new, fine art meets popular culture, the visual mixes with the verbal, pictorial depth meets flatness, and childhood innocence mixes with erotic fantasy. None of these meetings was resolved into a singular thing, and happily so, for the complexity of Blake's practice is what makes it interesting. This seems particularly fitting for a decade such as the 1950s, when British culture and society involved a complex mix of tradition and change, and of the reinvention of tradition in reaction to new developments, as it had at earlier points in the twentieth century.[33] The Festival of Britain in 1951 presented both futurist visions in the Dome of Discovery and images of tradition in the Lion and the Unicorn Pavilion. The Coronation ceremony in 1953 was watched by almost half the population on nearly three million television sets.[34] Even in the commercial sector, modernisation in the post-war period was, as Frank Mort has observed, 'piecemeal and ad hoc'.[35] Large areas of cultural and social life were left relatively unchanged, while radical transformation occurred in others. With its combination of English gardens and mass-produced images, royalty and modern art, circus performers and Elvis, nostalgia and media-

31
See Rudd, *Peter Blake*, p. 12.

32
Svetlana Alpers, *The Art of Describing: Dutch Art in the Seventeenth Century*, London, Penguin Books, 1989, p. 187.

33
See Alan O'Shea, 'English Subjects of Modernity', in Mica Nava and Alan O'Shea (eds), *Modern Times: Reflections on a Century of English Modernity*, London and New York, Routledge, 1996, pp. 26–33.

34
See Hopkins, *The New Look*, p. 295.

35
Frank Mort, 'The Commercial Domain: Advertising and the Cultural Management of Demand', in Becky Conekin, Frank Mort and Chris Waters (eds), *Moments of Modernity: Reconstructing Britain 1945–1964*, London and New York, Rivers Oran Press, 1999, p. 75.

Self Portrait with Badges
1961
Oil on board

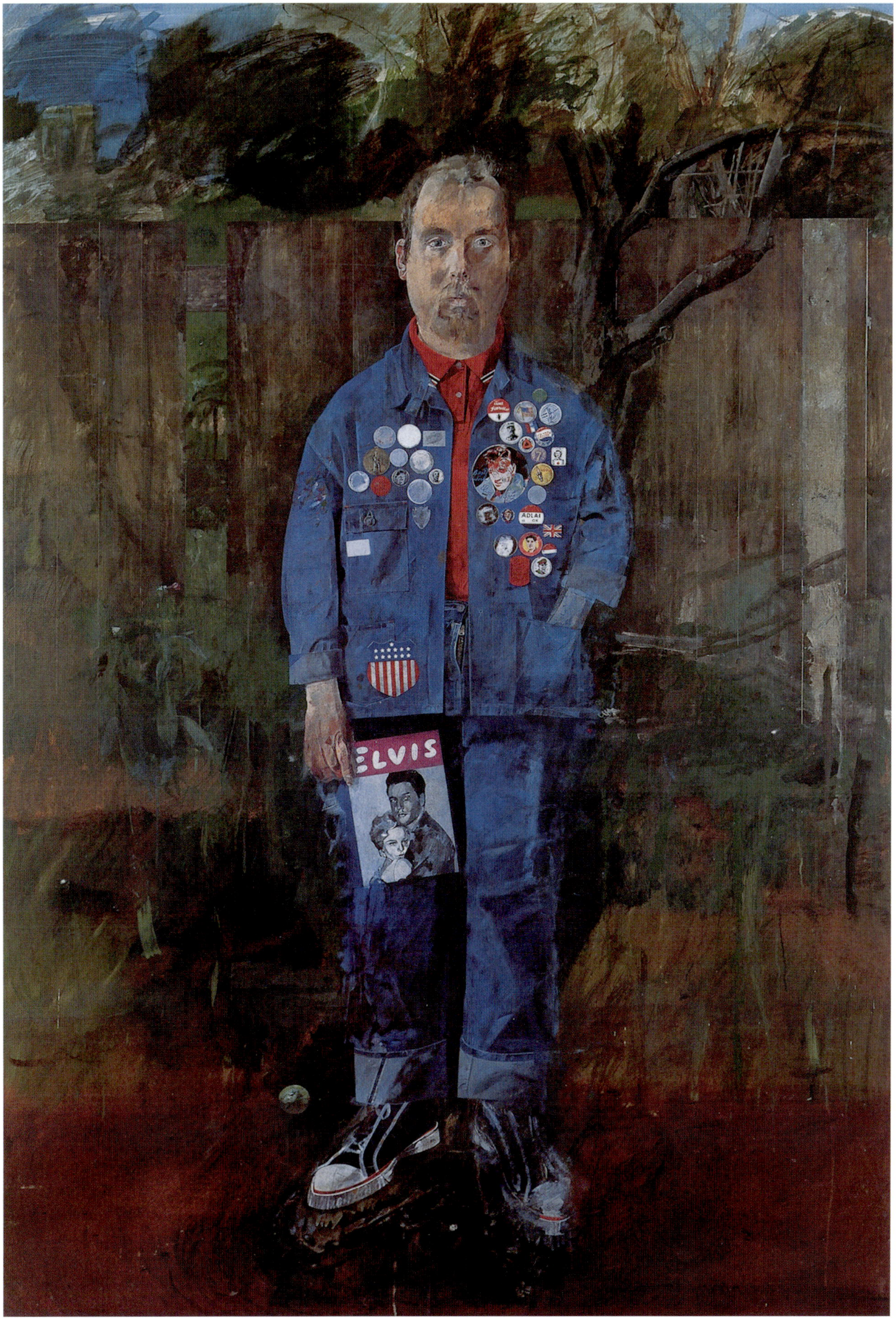
ADLAI
ELVIS

Postcard
1962
Oil on hardboard

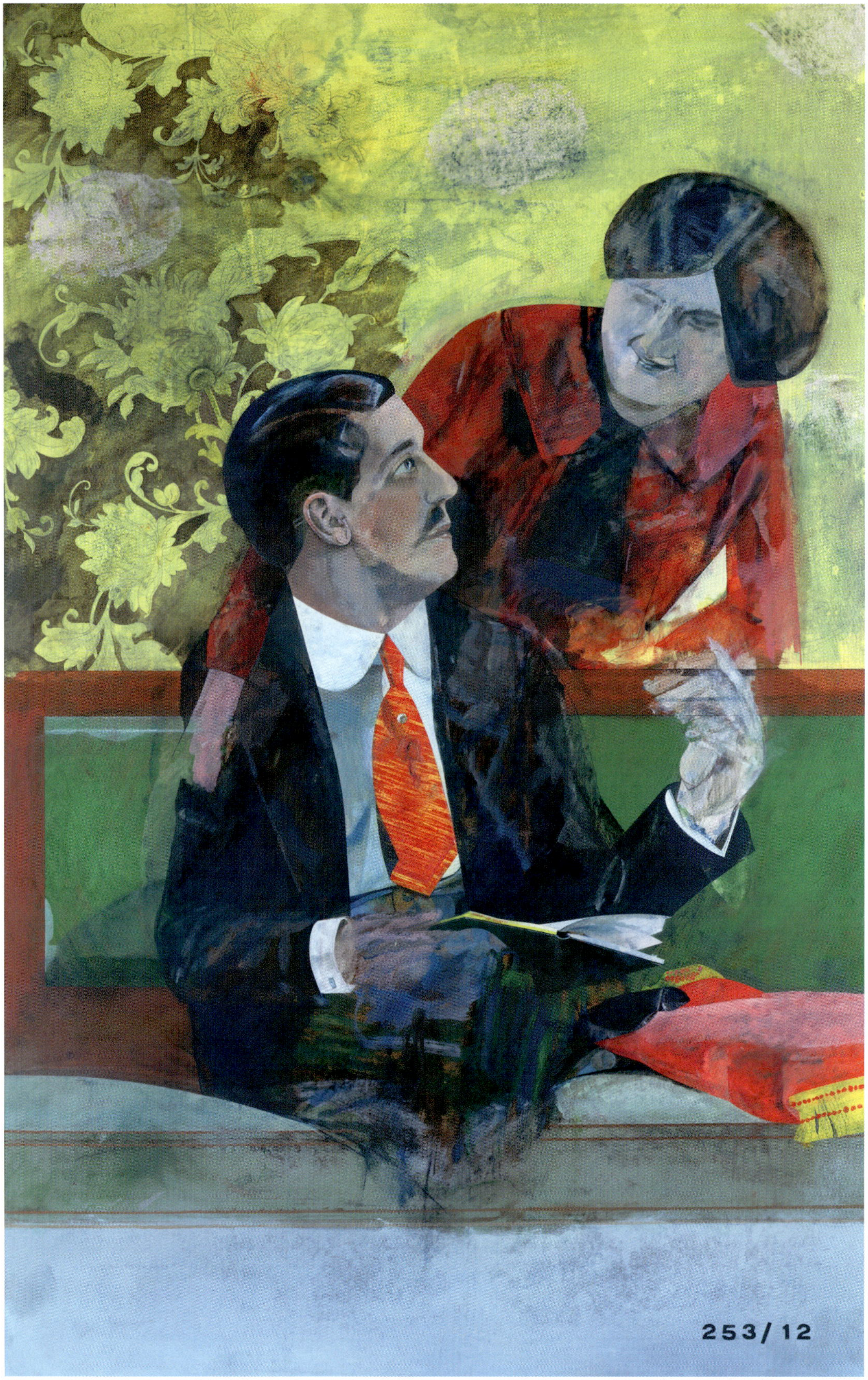

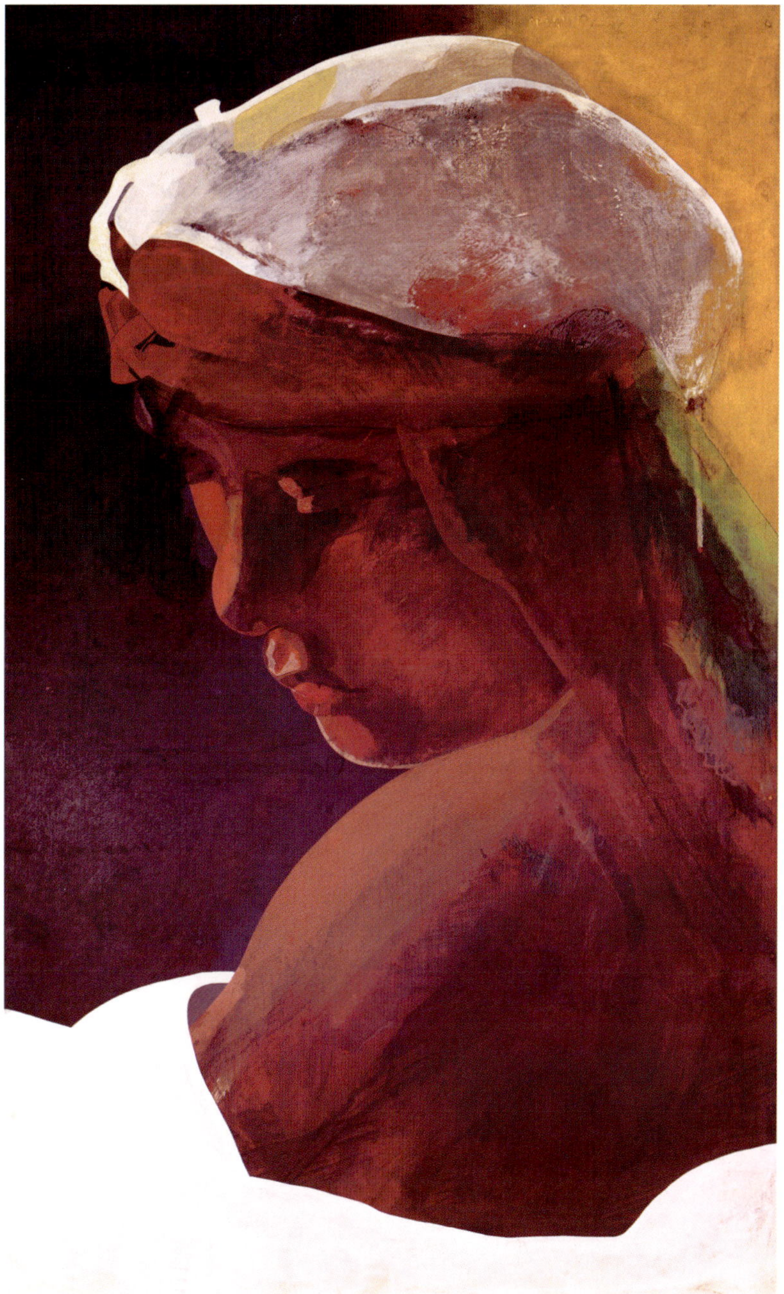

Bedouin
1964–5
Cryla on hardboard

Gold Painting
1959
Gold leaf on canvas

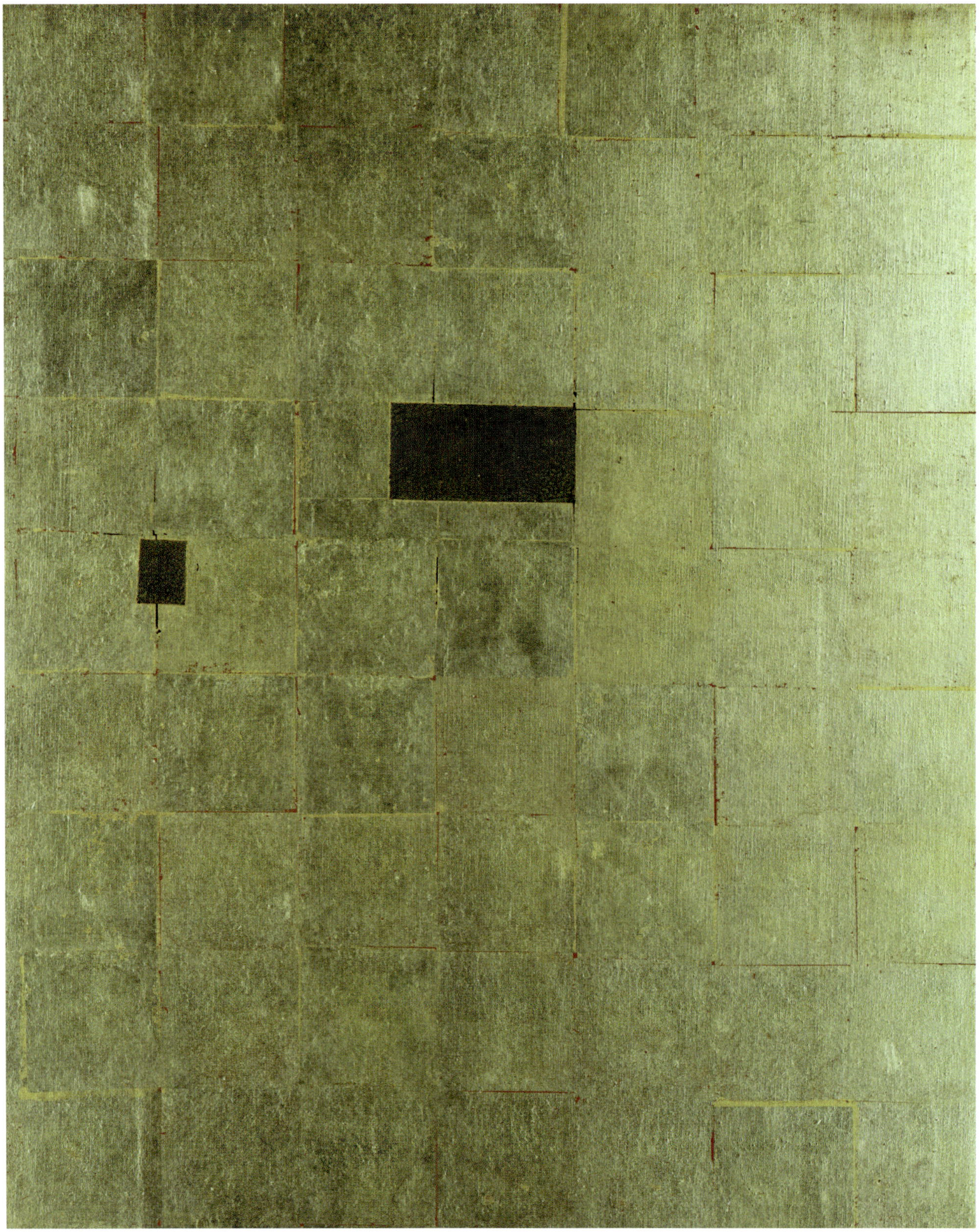

savvy up-to-date-ness, Blake's art can be read as symptomatic and representative of this historical moment. To observe this is not to argue that art mirrors the wider contours of society. Many young artists during the 1950s attempted to negotiate the social contradictions of the period by abandoning all signs of traditional Englishness in their work. In contrast, Blake seems to have been open to the different aspects of 1950s' Britain.

If Blake was a fan, when it came to his art, he was an artist-fan. This was a different cultural figure altogether, though one that was enabled by the new forms of popular and media culture which, during the 1950s, seemed to be breaking up old cultural hierarchies into what Alloway called the 'long front of culture'.[36] In retrospect, there was no such sea change from a cultural hierarchy to a cultural continuum within British culture during that decade; nevertheless, new cultural forms were emerging that changed the experiences of artists such as Blake and placed a new demand upon them to develop new forms of artistic representation.

36
Lawrence Alloway, 'The Long Front of Culture', 1959, reprinted in David Robins (ed.), *The Independent Group: Postwar Britain and the Aesthetics of Plenty*, exh. cat., Cambridge, MA, and London, MIT Press, 1990, pp. 165–6.

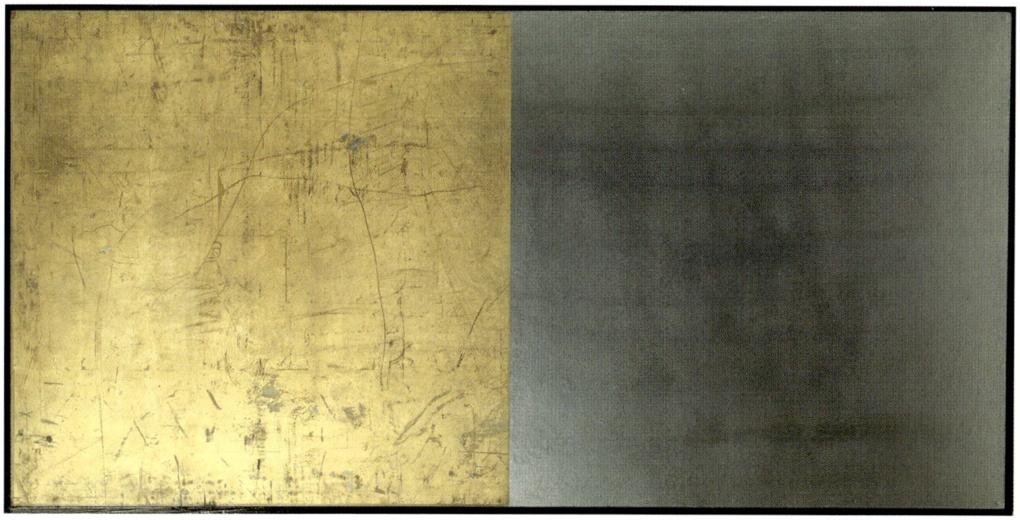

Gold and Silver
1959 and 87
Gold leaf and silver paint
on hardboard

The Fine Art Bit
1959
Enamel, wood relief and collage on board

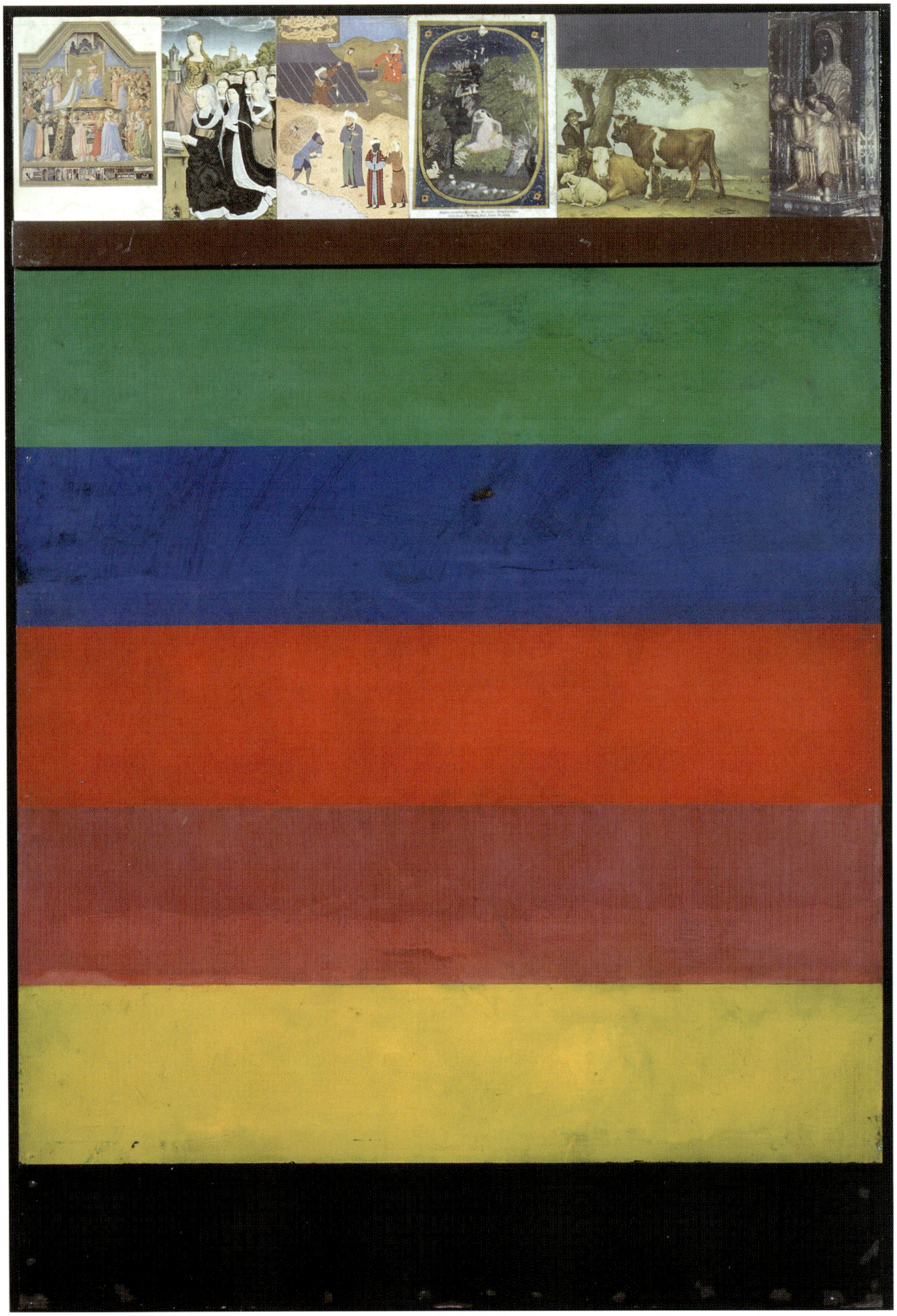

the 1960s

the first real pop artist?

marco livingstone

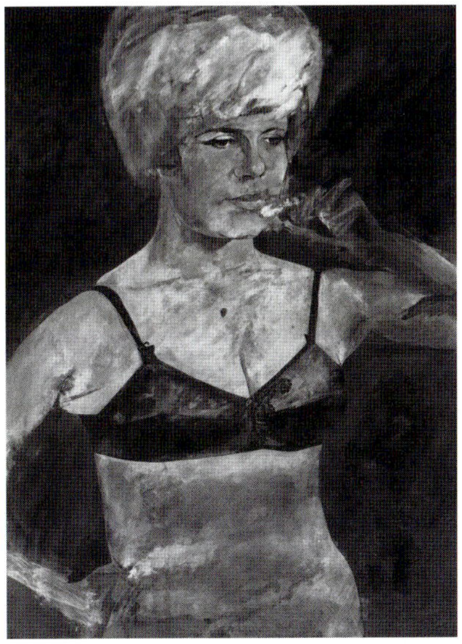

Pin-up Girl
1962
Oil on hardboard

The 1960s now exist in the popular imagination as one long, wild party – a glamorous, cool, taboo-breaking binge of sex, drugs, stylish fashion and ear-piercing rock music. Pop art, of which Peter Blake was undoubtedly one of the pioneers and leading lights, was the movement that gave lasting artistic form to this vision of youthful exuberance and excess. But there were many kinds of Pop, just as there were many conflicting experiences of what life was really like at that time. In spite of their shared enthusiasms for celebrity culture, pop music and commercial packaging, Peter Blake's take on the 1960s in London was very different from the manifestations of that decade in Andy Warhol's art in New York. This is as it should be, for if that period stood for anything, it was for the openness of possibilities, the freedom to 'do your own thing' rather than to remain confined to old prescriptions. For the 27-year-old working-class Englishman who woke up still shy and virginal on New Year's Day 1960, that freedom was to be exercised by continuing to build on the very personal artistic vision he had begun to articulate in the early 1950s, much of it framed in a language that was deliberately out of time. Blithely unconcerned about being of the moment except when this was dictated naturally by his tastes and interests – notably for the newly emerged rock'n'roll music that began to share turntable space with the jazz he had been listening to for years – Blake set out a case for an art that transcends its period and that privileges private, intimate experience, even when celebrating the creativity and energy within mass culture.

Blake's sexual inexperience as a young man might seem an indelicate matter to bring into a discussion of his art, were it not for the fact that he himself has alluded to it and that it helps explain the atmosphere of innocence and arrested childhood that flavours his art and that imbues even his sexiest Pop-period images with a sincerity, vulnerability and humanity at odds with much of the work alongside which it was exhibited. There is a huge difference of intent between the provocatively fetishised image of pure sex in paintings by his friend and colleague Allen Jones, such as *Perfect Match* of 1966–67, in which a virtually faceless female body is portrayed as a succession of equally exaggerated parts tuned to a high pitch of excitement, and Blake's clearly individualised 1965 portrait of an attractive but imperfect Pin-up Girl; though unnamed, this young woman in a bra is presented

The Beatles
1963–8
Acrylic emulsion on board

as an ordinary person, perhaps not quite the girl next door but somebody real in spite of having been glimpsed only in a photograph. Blake's picture, though conveying a young man's thwarted desire, also exhibits an almost fraternal protectiveness towards a young woman stripped bare for the delectation of others.

In an interview with Hunter Davies published in *The Independent* on 19 May 1992, Blake commented on how closely his experience paralleled that of Philip Larkin, who in his oft-quoted poem 'Annus Mirabilis' wrote:

> *Sexual intercourse began*
> *In nineteen sixty-three*
> *(Which was rather late for me) –*
> *Between the end of the* Chatterley *ban*
> *And the Beatles' first LP.*

How appropriate that the arrival of the Fab Four should also be so closely entwined with Blake's initiation into the pleasures of the flesh. The Beatles, portrayed in one of the most memorable of Blake's series of paintings of favourite pop musicians, were to become his collaborators – along with his then wife, Jann Haworth, and photographer Michael Cooper – in the making of the most famous album cover of the decade, Sgt Pepper's Lonely Hearts Club Band from the 1967 'summer of love', forever confirming Blake's credentials as one of the defining artists of the period and as one of the most adept in bridging fine art and popular culture. While the Beatles themselves had long shed the innocence proclaimed in early songs such as 'I Want To Hold Your Hand', Blake's art remained much closer in spirit to that original fresh-faced incarnation than to their later, more rebellious, drug-induced and at times sardonic *personae*.

If sex arrived rather late for Blake, he arrived unusually early, by contrast, at a pictorial realisation of what was later to be termed – however inaccurately – the 'swinging sixties'. Though he was never a swinger either in the sexual sense or as a drug-taker, he was acutely alert to the new atmosphere of permissiveness and to the sensuously indulgent mood that was finally taking hold in Britain after the long privations of post-war austerity. The collage paintings that he had begun

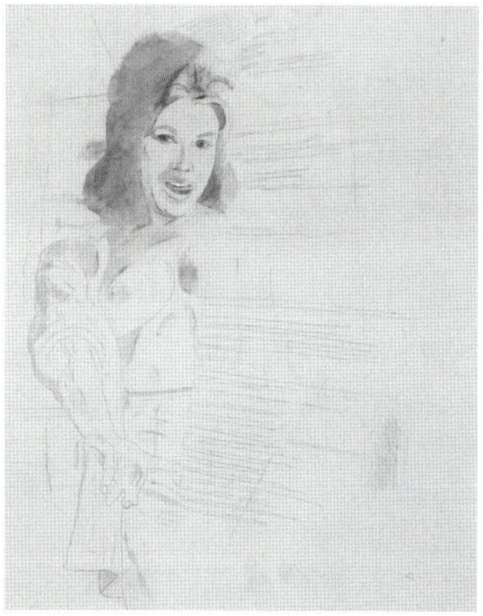

Pin-up Girl
1962
Drawing on paper

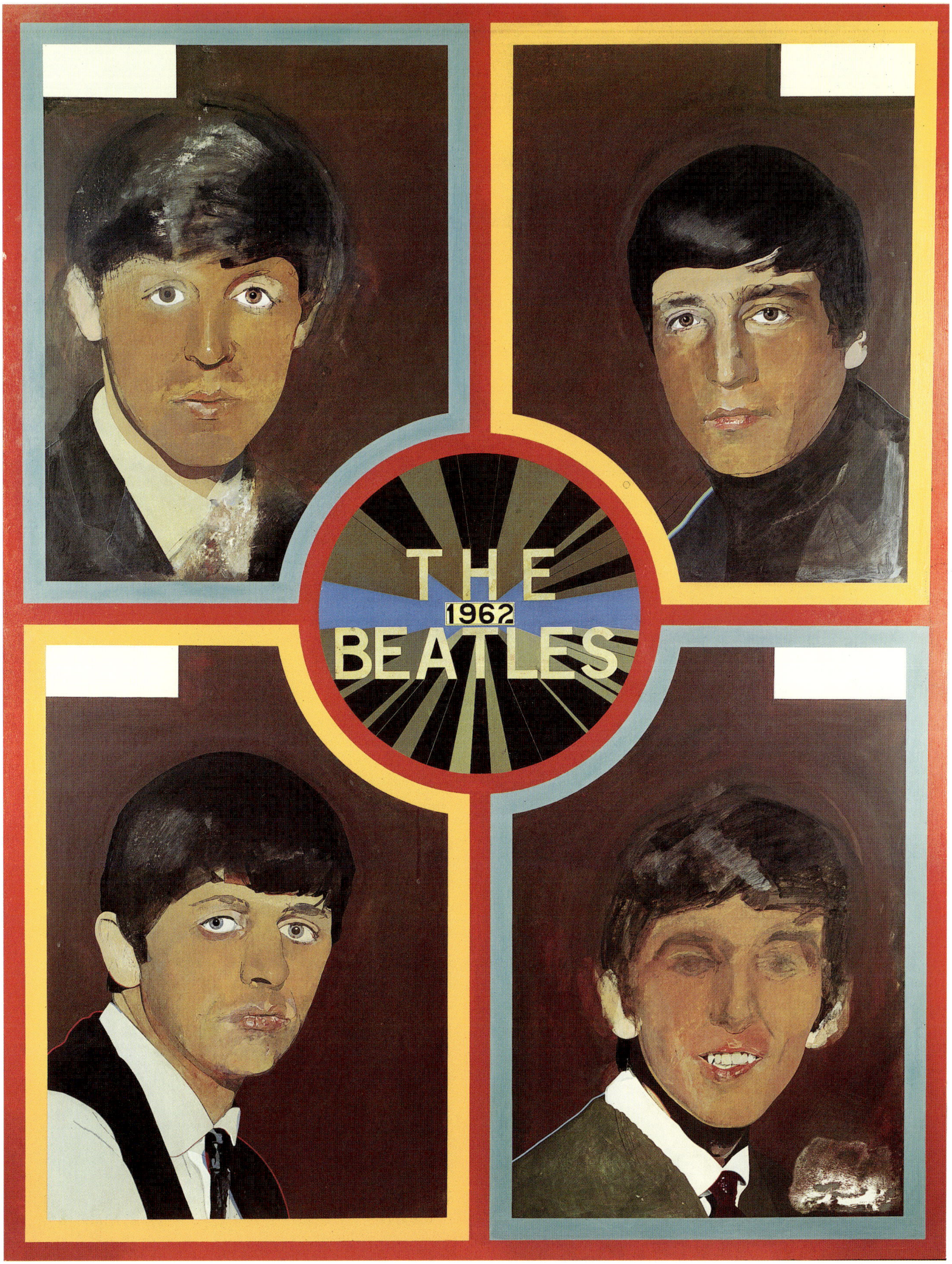
THE
1962
BEATLES

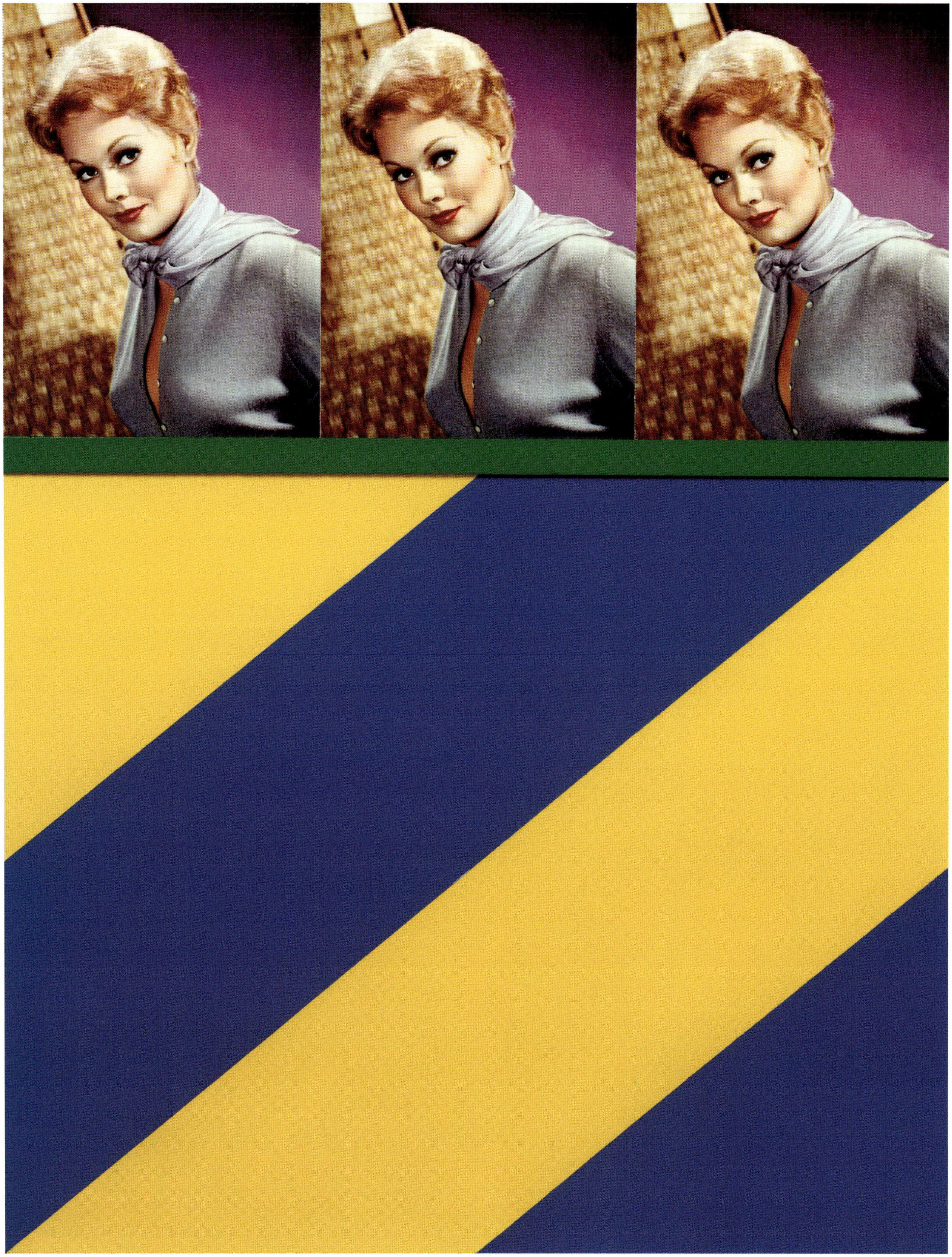

Kim Novak
1960 and 1987
Postcards and enamel print on hardboard

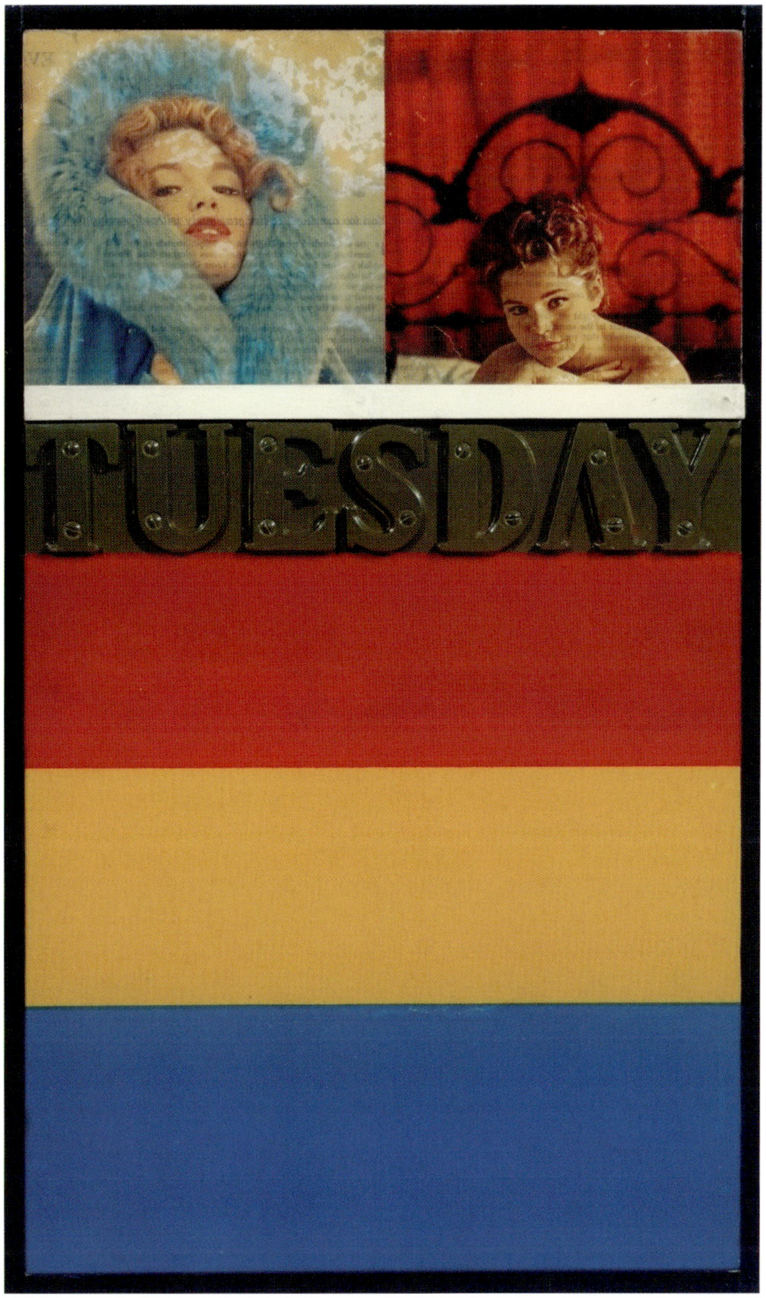

Tuesday
1961
Enamel, wood relief and collage on board

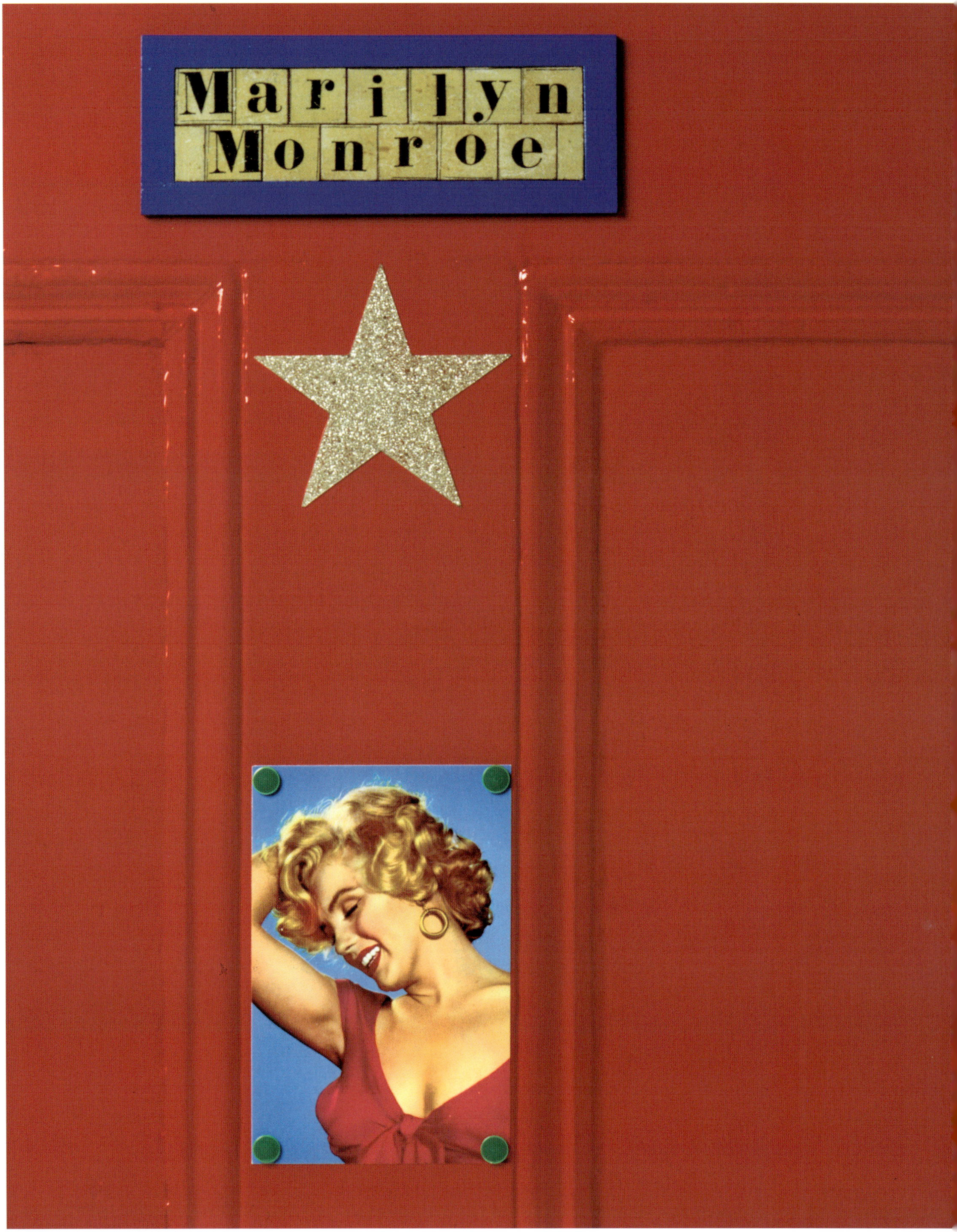
Marilyn
Monroe

Piece of Marilyn Monroe's Dressing Room Door
1962, reworked 1987
Enamel paint on piece of a real door with postcard, letters and silver star

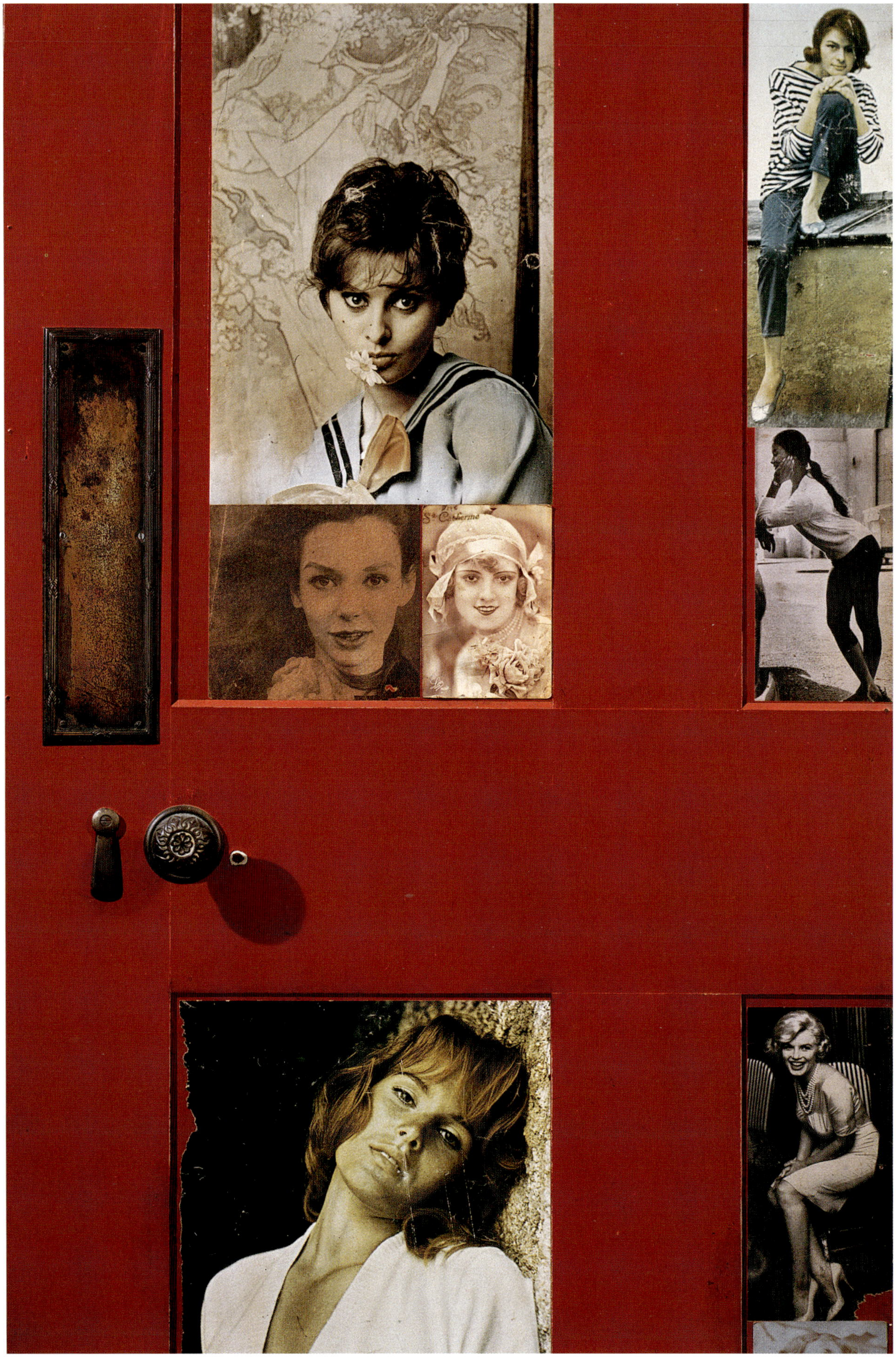

Girlie Door (detail)
1959
Collage and assemblage on hardboard

making in 1959, such as Girlie Door, *Everly Wall* and The Fine Art Bit were a radical and even insolent reformulation of the terms of painting. Nearly half a century later, they still come across as a dramatic declaration of intent and as a determined and deliberate release from the academic naturalism that he had employed for important early paintings, such as On the Balcony 1955–57, and which continued to animate his more traditionally handmade figurative pictures throughout his career.

With their shiny surfaces, bright primary colours, dazzling geometric patterns and formal simplicity, the collage paintings anticipated many of the most radical qualities of the art made by Blake and his colleagues during the 1960s and beyond. Their uninflected surfaces, painted flat in ordinary household gloss paint so as not to show any brushmarks, dispensed with the conventional insistence on personal 'touch' to which Blake himself had attached – and would continue to attach – such importance. Following the example of the target and American flag paintings first exhibited by the American artist Jasper Johns only a year earlier, Blake equated the subject of the painting with its physical manifestation as an object. Conceptually these painting-sculptures operate simultaneously on a metaphorical and literal level and are understood not just as representations, but as actual fragments, of walls or doors. Younger artists associated with the advent of Pop in Britain, such as Patrick Caulfield and Peter Phillips, were quick to follow Blake's lead in using such brash, unsubtle but visually alluring commercial paints, as was to be the case three decades later with a new generation of painters (notably Gary Hume), who in 1959 were yet to be born; that Hume first came to notice with paintings representing gloss-surfaced hospital doors reinforces this link with Blake's highly influential early Pop pictures.

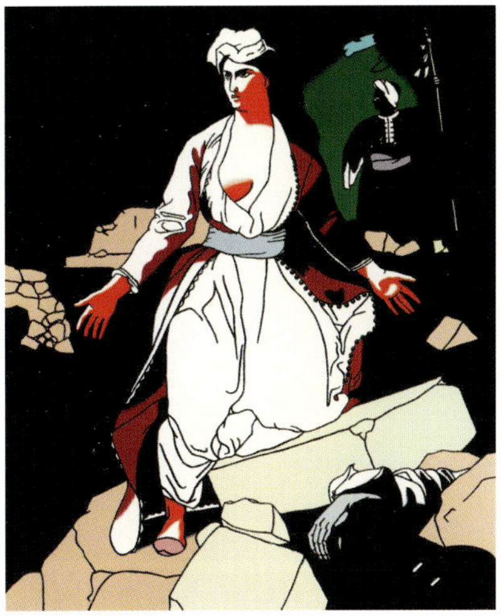

Patrick Caulfield
Greece Expiring on the Ruins of Missolonghi, after Delacroix 1963
Oil on board

Yet what can easily be seen as an affront to the fine-art tradition, particularly given the incorporation of imagery in these and related works exclusively in the form of collaged found printed material and photographs and appended three-dimensional objects, was for Blake also a straightforward and affectionate way of alluding to the beauty he found in his surroundings. Many of these paintings are explicitly named as fragments of unremarkable domestic architecture – doors, walls, cupboards, windows, shop fronts – and they are constructed and painted with the same materials, and using the same techniques, as those functional

Peter Blake and *Locker*
Institute of Contemporary Arts
London 1960

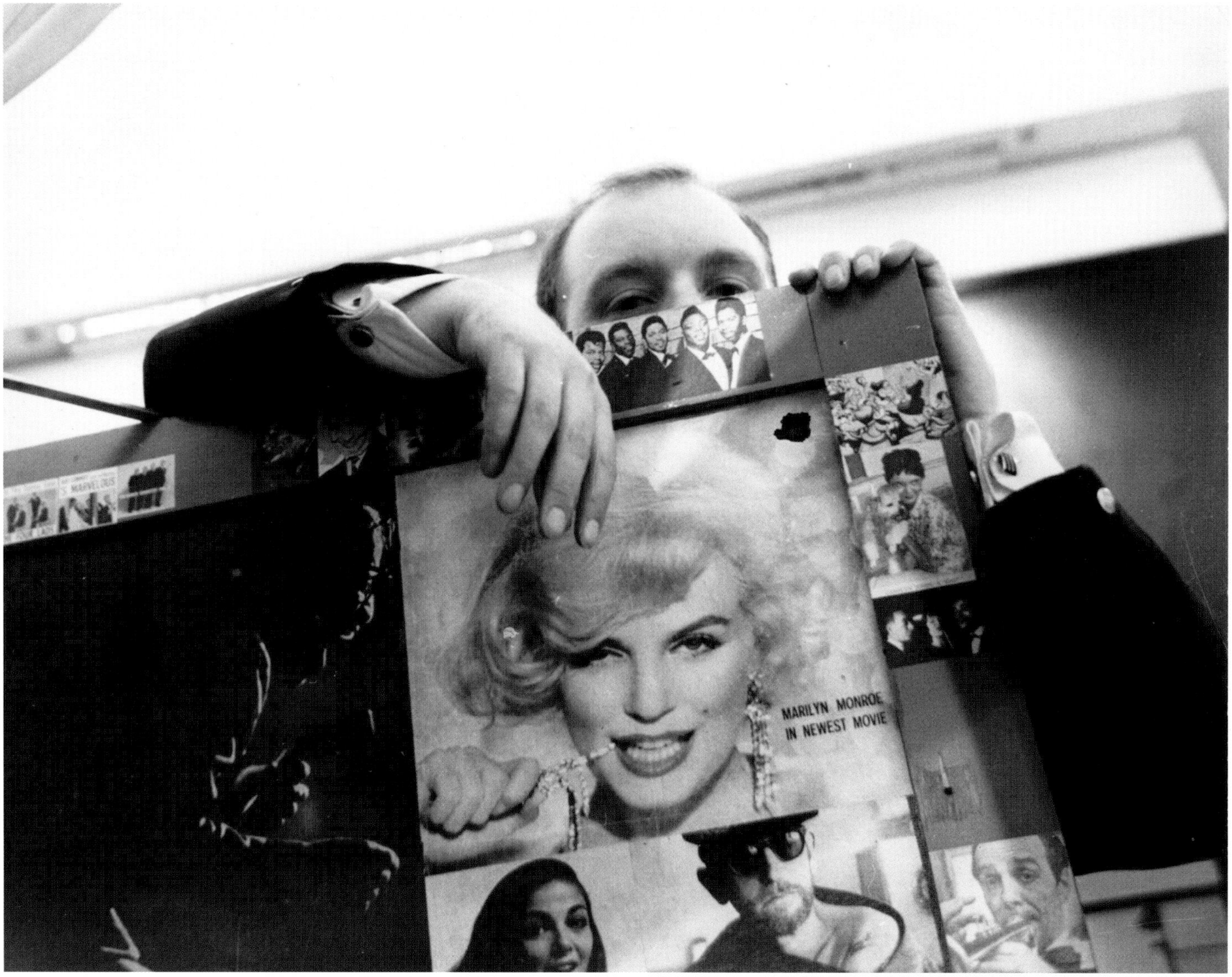

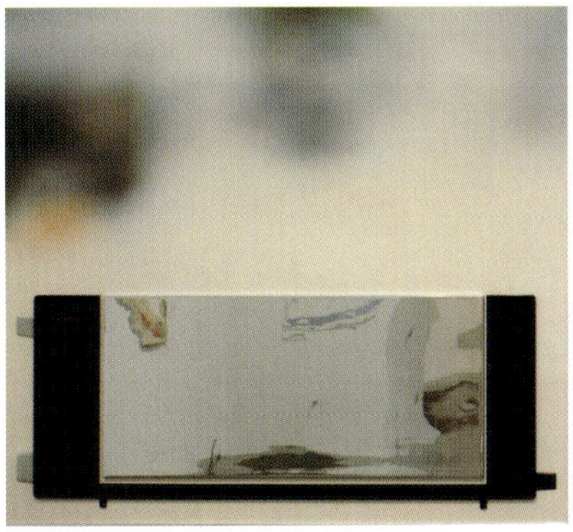

Richard Hamilton
Toaster 1966–7
Chromed steel and perspex on colour photograph

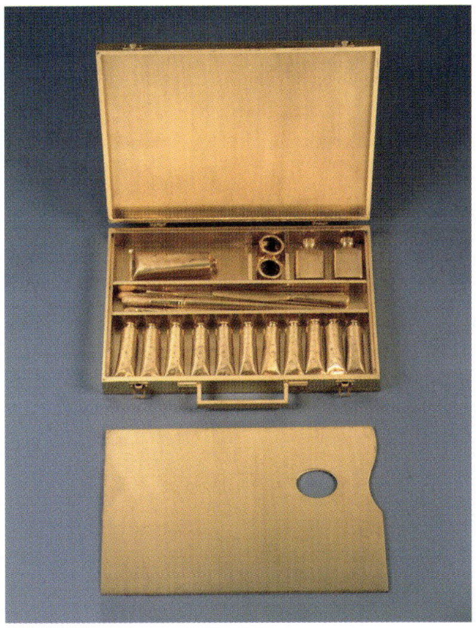

Clive Barker
Art Box II 1967
Gold-plated brass and gold-plated bronze

objects from the everyday environment. Even the blunt application of the collage elements, so brutally direct when compared to the delicately modulated and layered techniques of Cubist and Dada precedents earlier in the century, announces the artist's intention to align himself with the simple acts by which we all decorate our private spaces or create shrines to the ones we love, desire or admire. *Locker* 1959 is made from a real locker that Blake had bought in a local antique shop near his home in Chiswick because it reminded him of the lockers that he and other young men had used while doing their National Service in the Royal Air Force. This mundane object for housing clothes and possessions was both a home from home and a place for escapism and daydreaming, almost a definition for Blake's emerging art. The very fact that the cupboard was redolent of his own recent experiences, at a not particularly happy time in his life, increased its appeal as an object that would have strong personal associations for many people but from which the artist himself could derive a particular emotional intensity by reference to his own life.

The importance attached in Blake's work to memory, and to a nostalgia not just for childhood but for events so recent as to be still fresh in one's mind, was to continue to distinguish his art from that of many of his Pop colleagues. Others often sought to make works that looked as new, perfect and impersonal as manufactured items, as in the case of the chrome- or gold-plated sculptural casts by Blake's friend Clive Barker, or Richard Hamilton's paeans to the sophisticated design and perfect workmanship of upmarket manufactured items. Blake by contrast remained more attached to things that looked worn, weathered and lived-in, as pockmarked, defenceless and knocked around by life as the people who possess them. This is as true of the cheap and second-hand toys incorporated into his Toyshop of 1962 or appended to his painted portraits of wrestlers, such as Kamikaze 1965, as it is of his handmade facsimiles of architectural features or enlarged depictions in two or three dimensions of late Victorian postcards and other ordinary objects such as a *Captain Webb Matchbox*.

Blake's handling of objects and his insistence on their human connotations is absolutely consistent with his approach to people, who continued to provide him with his most urgent subject matter. There is a poignancy and tenderness to

Girl in a Window
1962
Collage construction

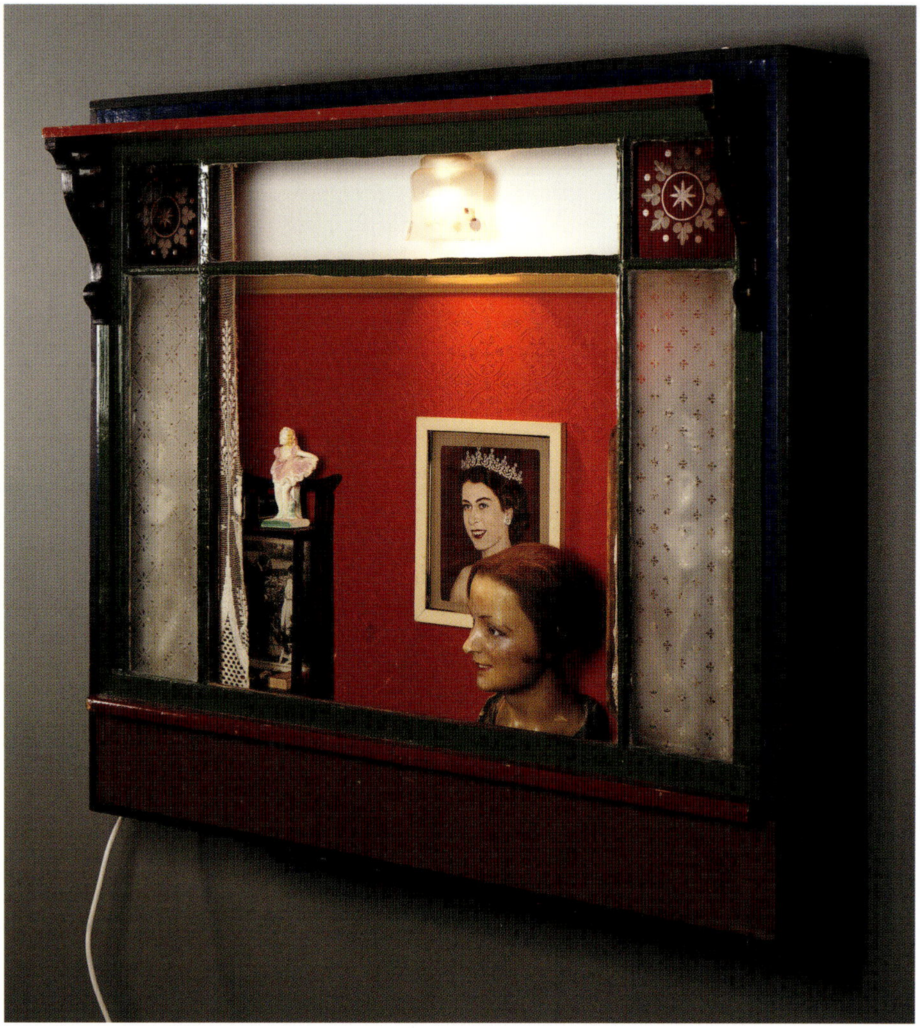

The Toy Shop
1962
Mixed media, glass and painted wood

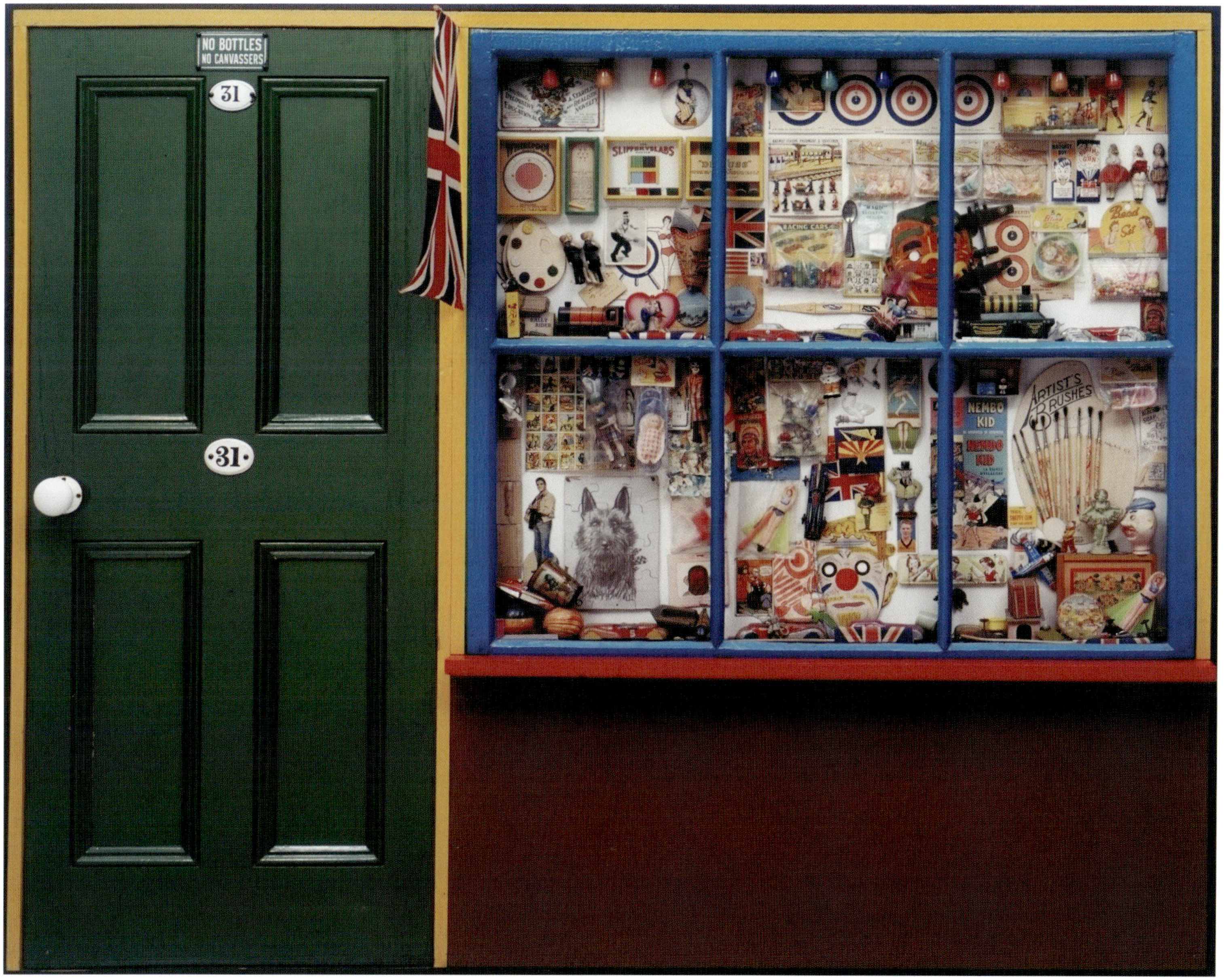

The First Real Target
1961
Enamel on canvas and collage
on board

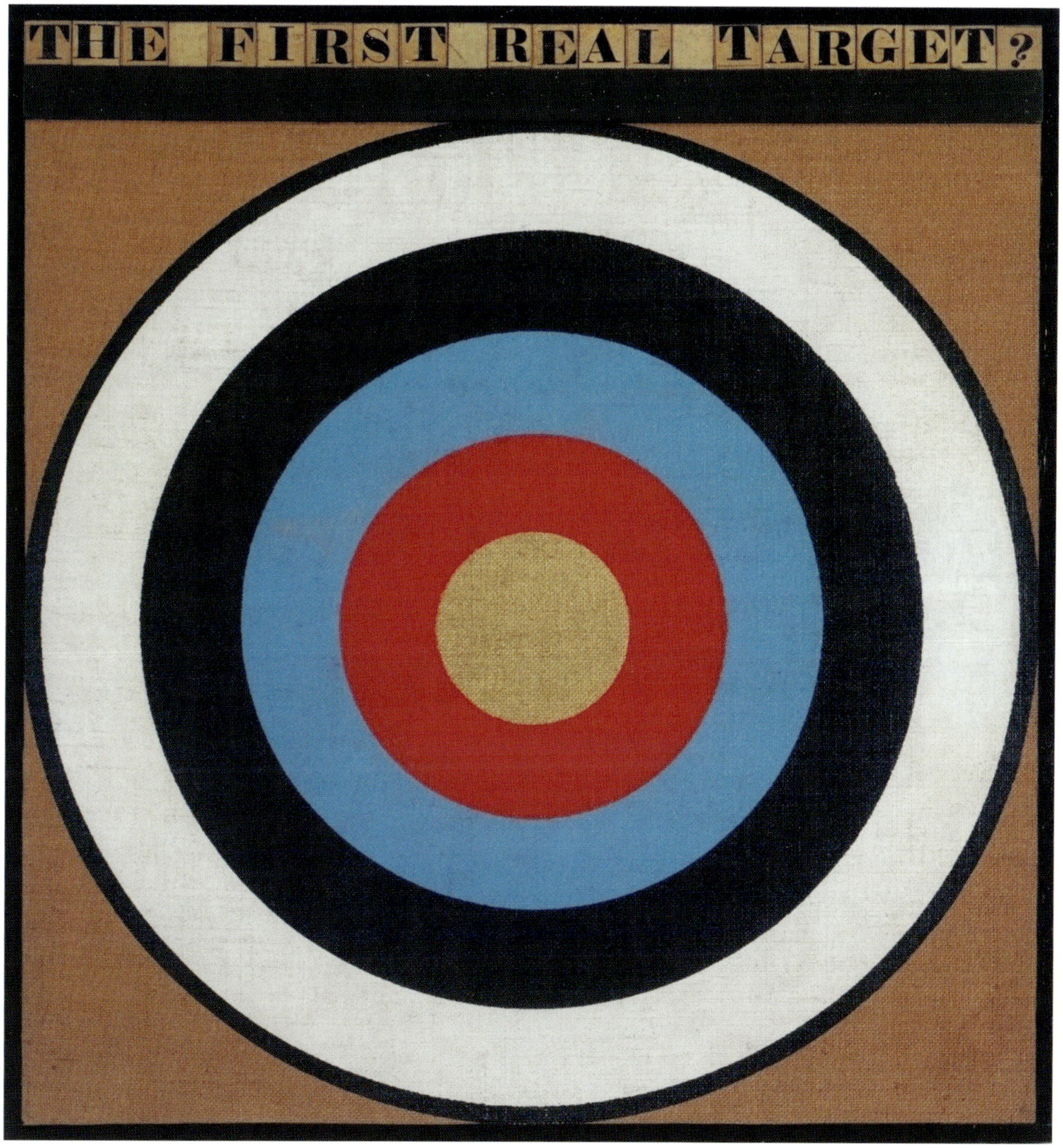
THE FIRST REAL TARGET?

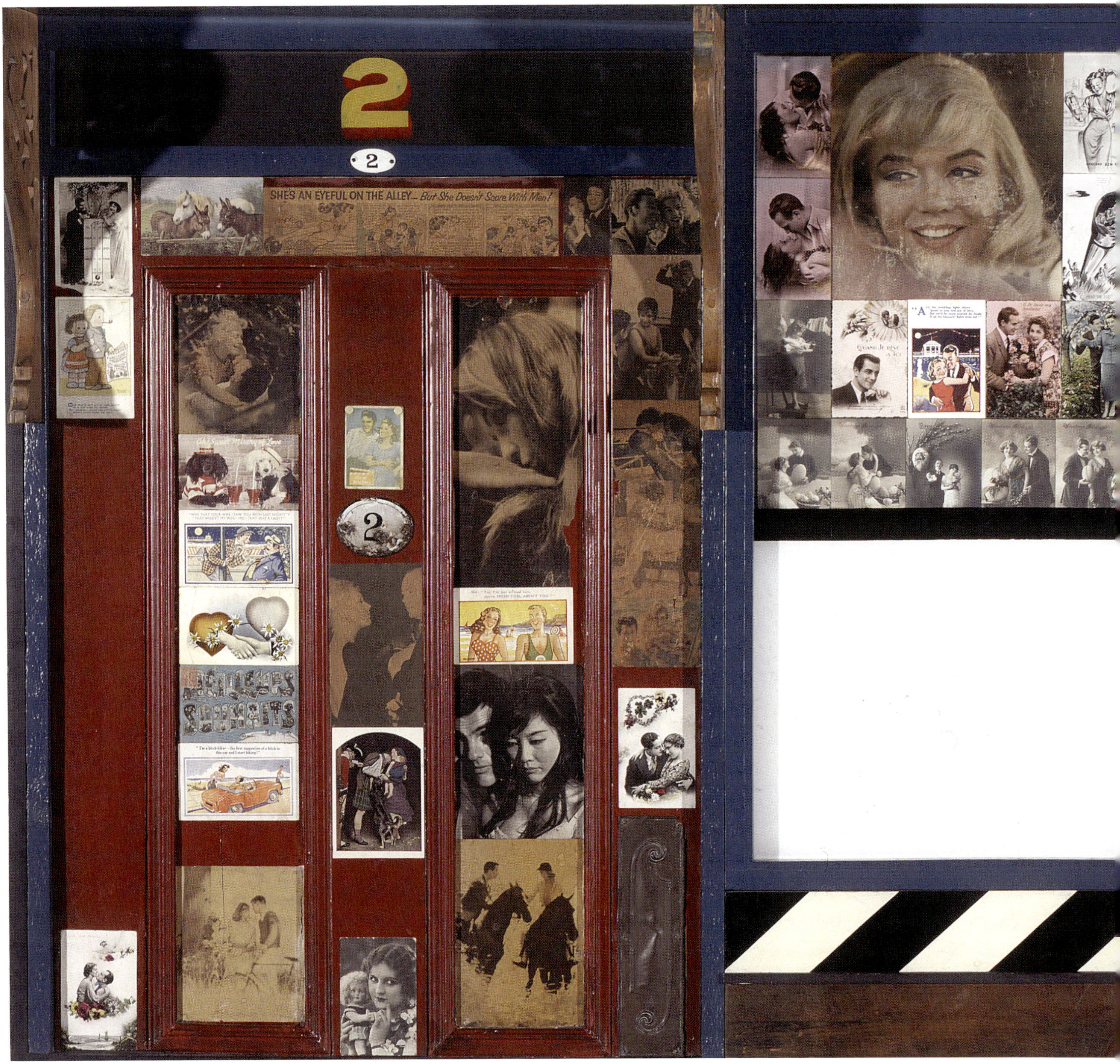
2
2
SHE'S AN EYEFUL ON THE ALLEY— But She Doesn't Score With Men!
Oh! Sweet Misery of Love
2
MEILLEURS SOUVENIRS

Love Wall
1961
Collage construction

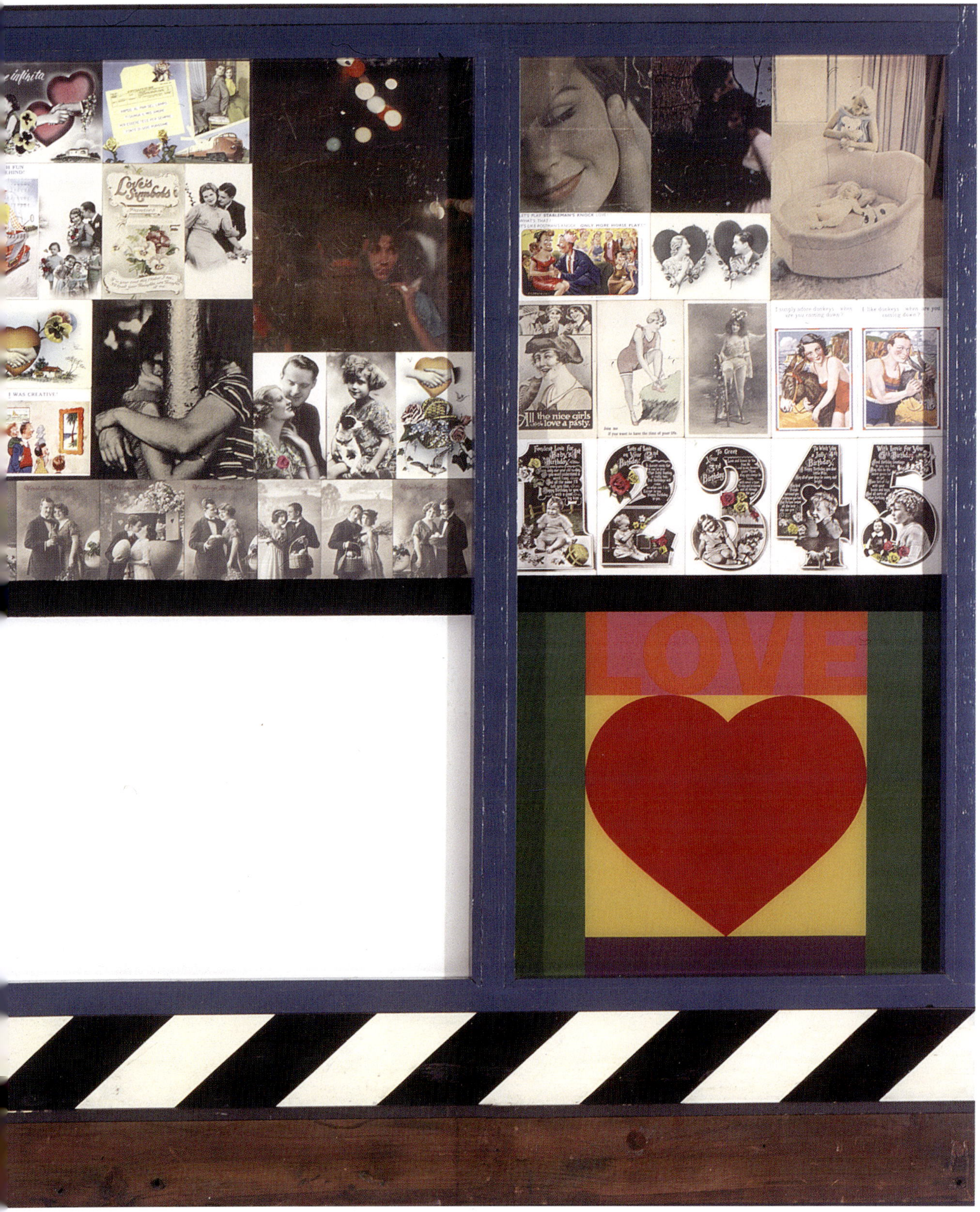

his portrayals even of those who present themselves as hard-bitten, tough and worldly: the female strippers and the male and female wrestlers who populate two of the extended series of paintings on which Blake was engaged during much of the 1960s. The women he had displayed as objects of unrequited desire in the collage paintings – unapproachable film stars and sex goddesses – are separated from mere mortals not just by their fame and wealth, but also by their habitation of a make-believe world that we can never expect to penetrate. The strippers and pin-up girls to whom he turned his attention in the early 1960s, just before his marriage to the American sculptor Jann Haworth, are painted as flesh and blood, but we understand them, too, to be materialisations of fantasy brought to life from photographs printed in the pages of men's magazines. Kandy and *Nudina*, and later on Babe Rainbow, are among the fancifully named beauties with improbably perfect bodies and large breasts that we know we can never meet, even though some of them may have counterparts in the real world. They are forbidden fruit as much to married men as to pubescent boys, but as objects of desire – like the 'Pictures of Lily' in the Who's hit single of 1967 – they can still have 'made my life so wonderful'. Are they soiled by this objectification? For some feminists, that may be so. But there is too much tenderness in these pictures for them to be seen as merely lewd, too much strength in these women for them to be dismissed as passive victims, too much personality for them to be dismissed as empty vessels. What comes across, to me at least, is the fullness of their humanity.

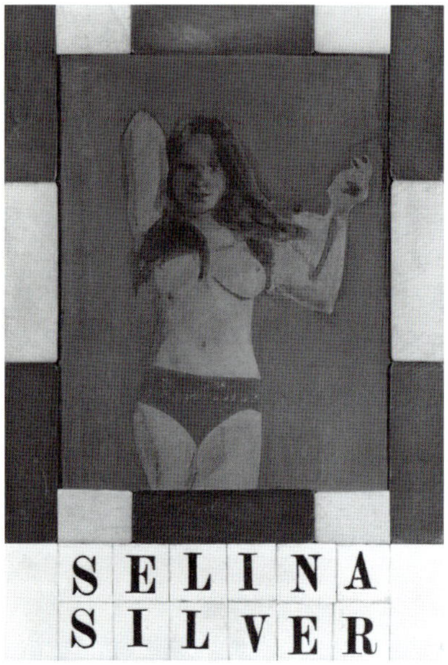

Selina Silver
1968–77
Oil and assemblage on panel

The wrestlers that Blake began painting in 1961, as a continuation of the vein of escapist entertainment celebrated in his circus pictures of the previous decade, provide an aggressively male counterpart to the cast of characters of the stripper and pin-up paintings. With the exception of one wrestler, Masked Zebra Kid, whose real autograph appears as a trophy item in the centre of collaged photographs, and one boxer, Kid McCoy, these larger-than-life figures are all inventions of the artist. In flaunting their toughness and masculinity to the point of self-parody, they play on boyhood fantasies of super-heroes and super-villains. Their often brutish appearance, like their hilariously over-the-top stage names redolent of power, evil and outlaw status – Baron Adolf Kaiser, Doktor K. Tortur, or Franck and Jesse, the James Brothers – masks the suspicion that they are really just big

Kandy
1963–5
Acrylic and collage on hardboard

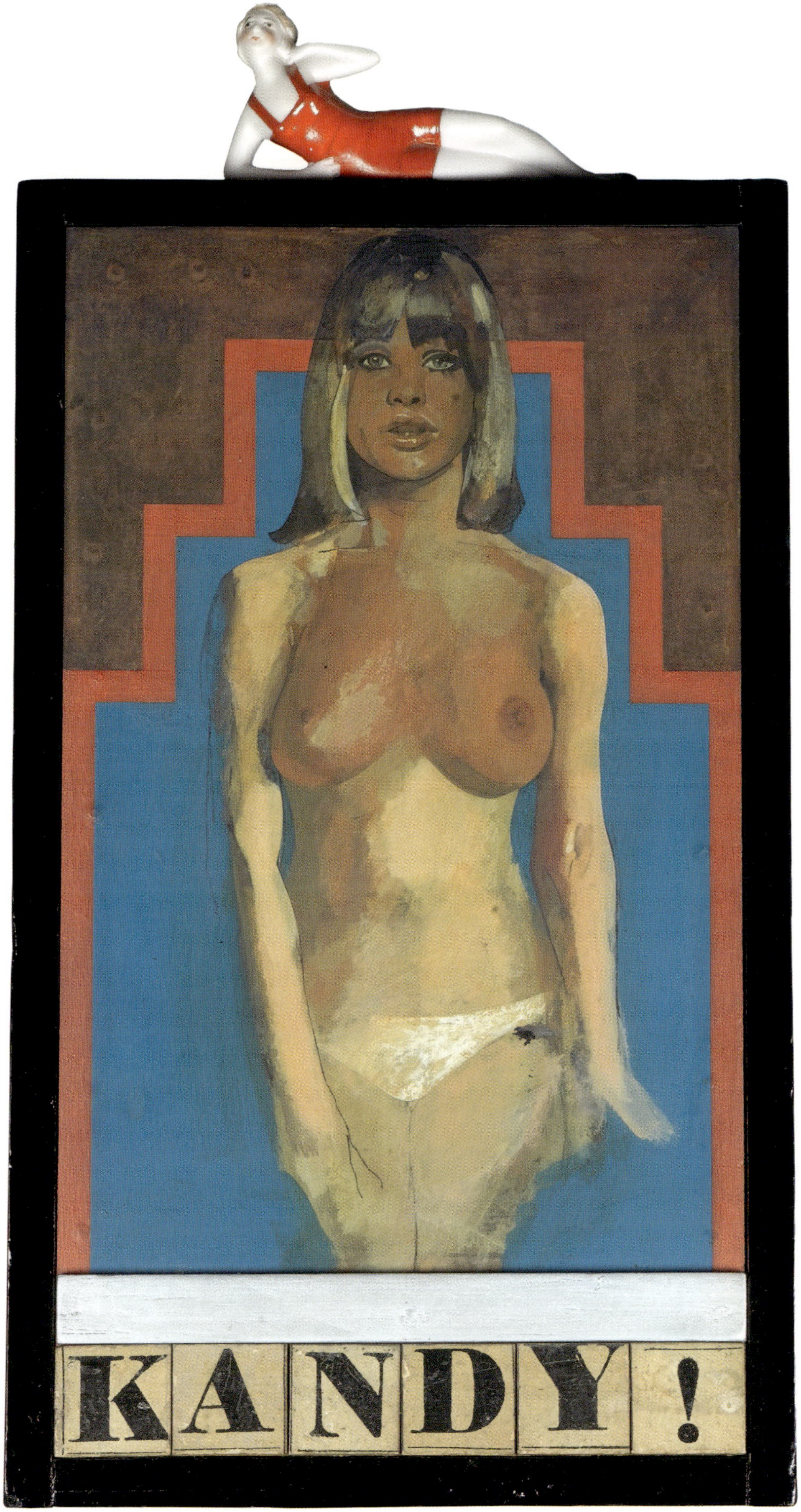

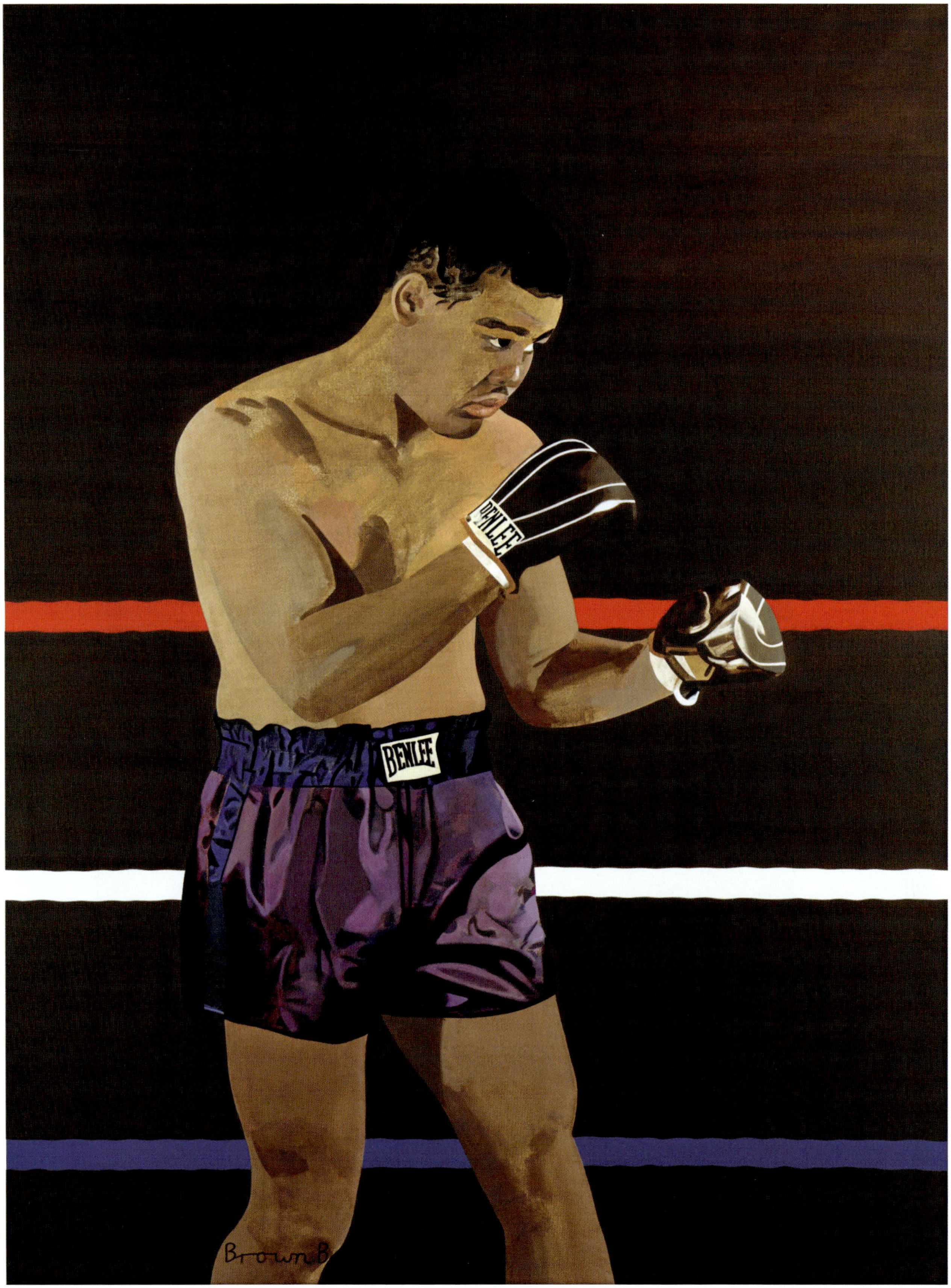
BENLEE
BENLEE

Joe Louis – The Brown Bomber
2001–6
Oil on canvas

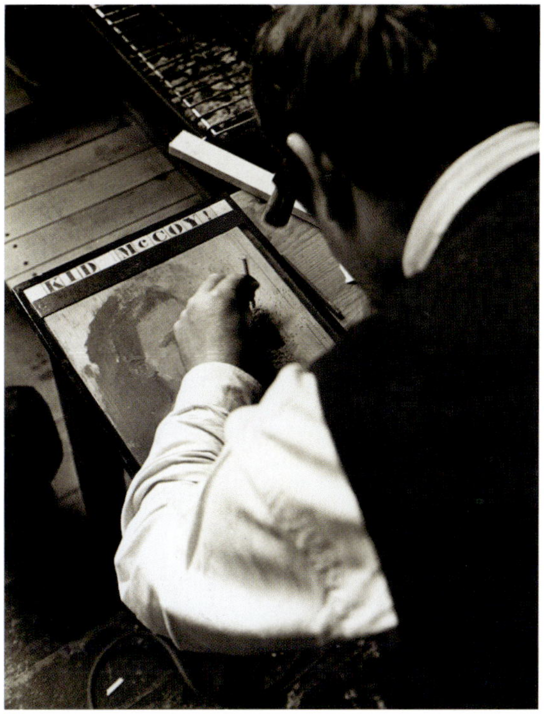

Peter working on *Kid McCoy*
London 1964

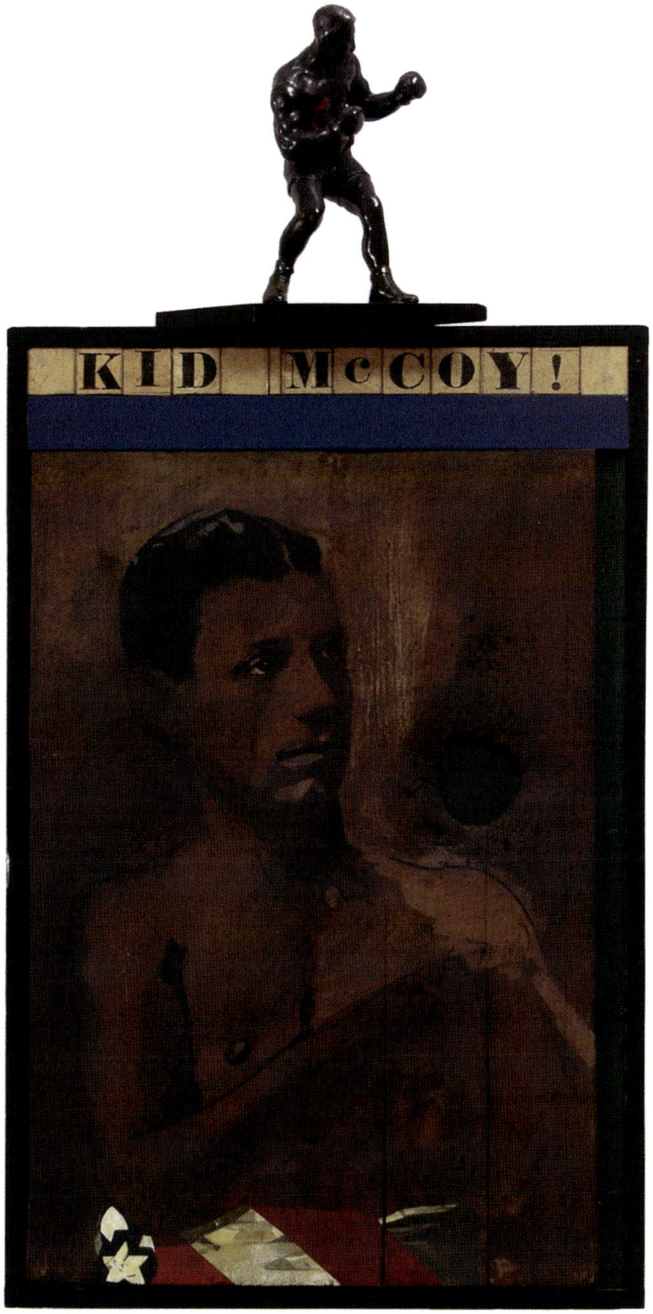

Kid McCoy
1961–5
Cryla and collage on hardboard

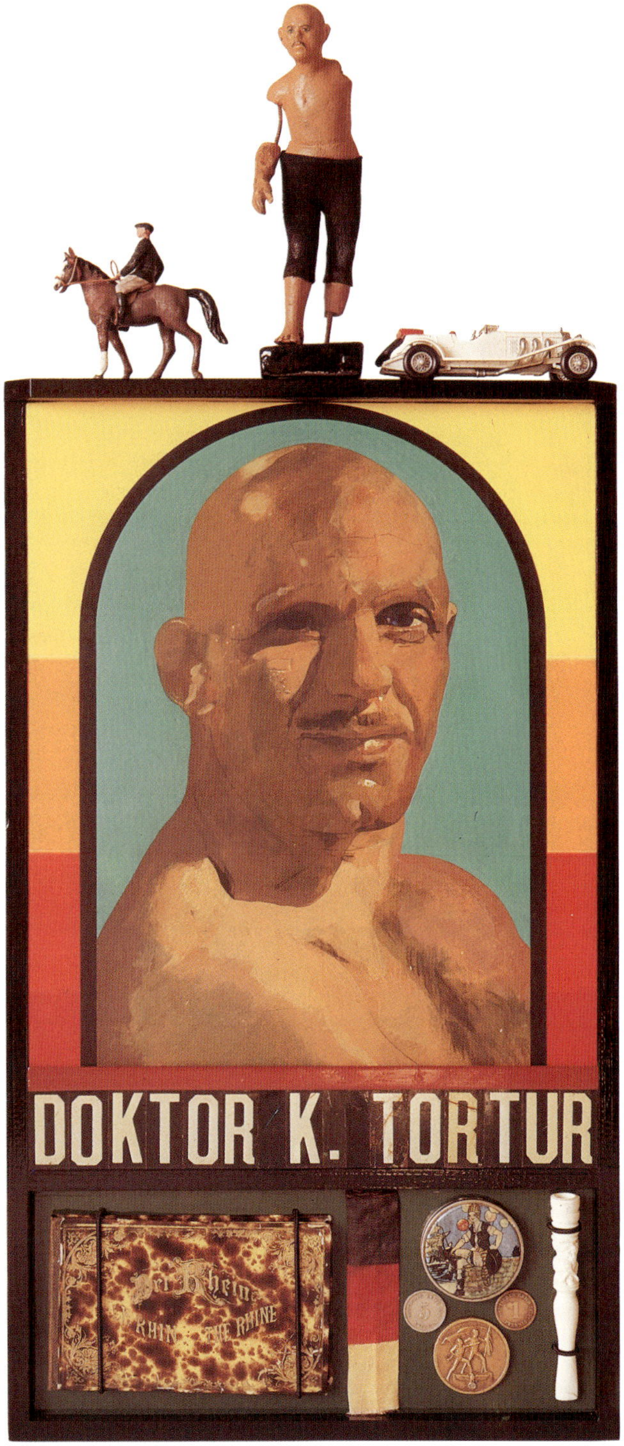

Doktor K. Tortur
1965
Acrylic, collage and hardboard

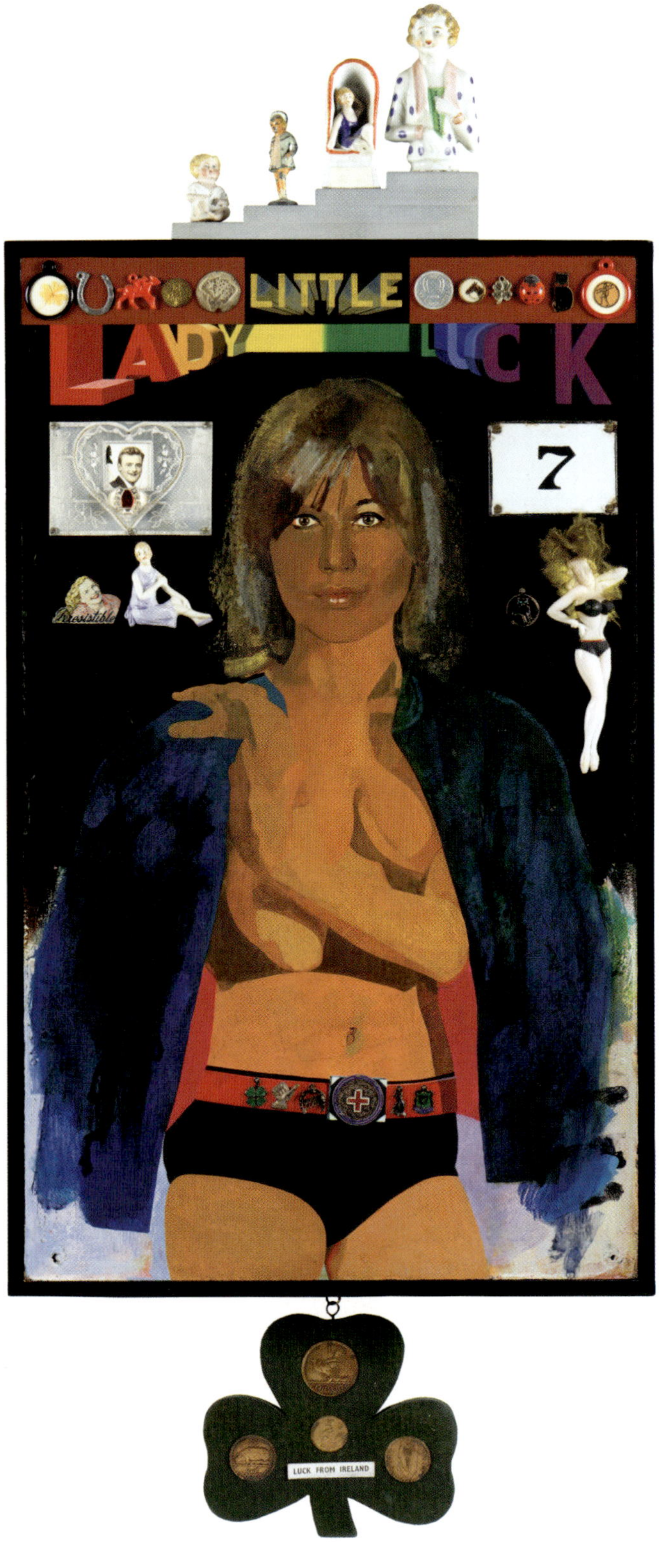

Little Lady Luck
1965
Acrylic and collage on hardboard

Babe Rainbow
1968
Silkscreen on tin

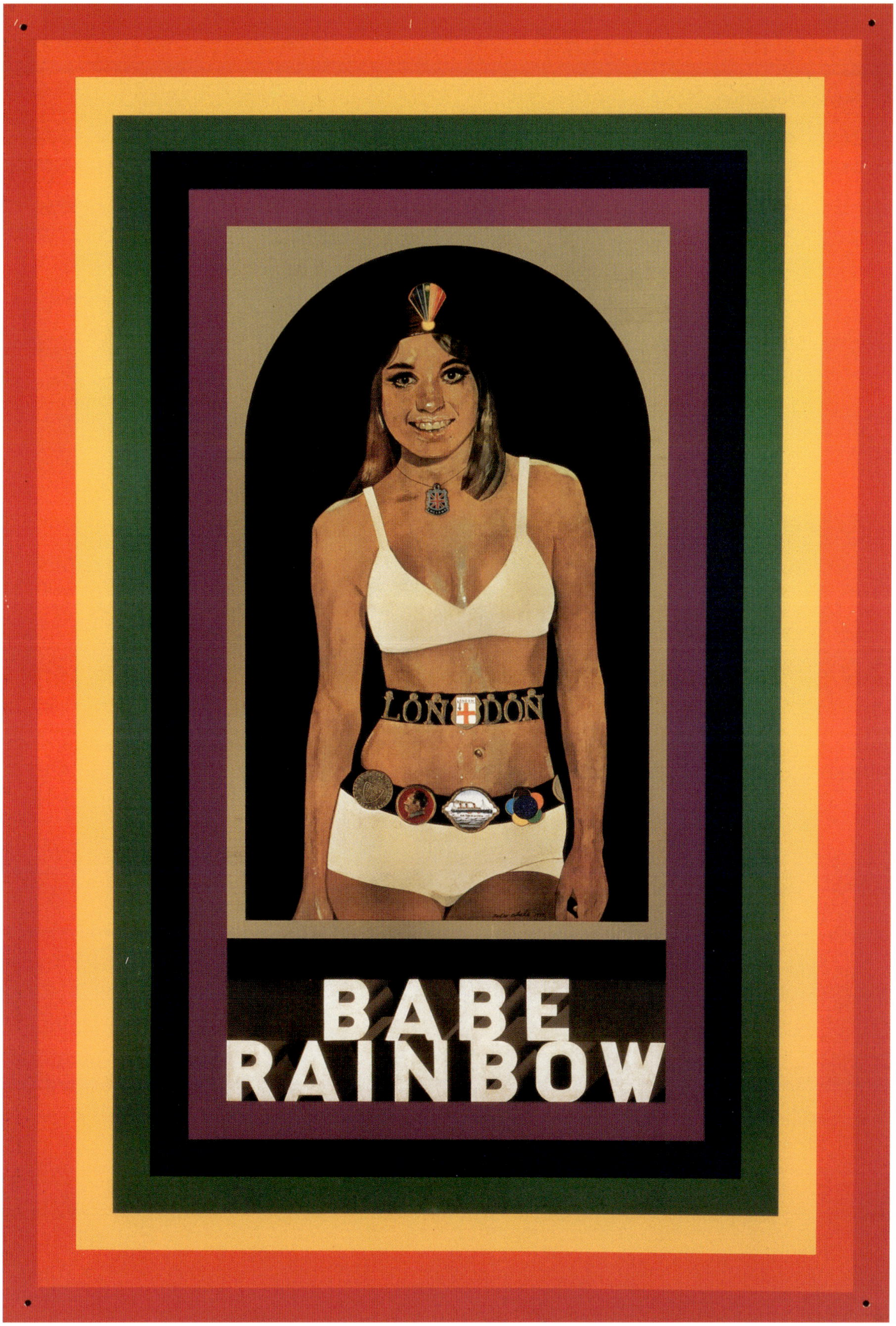

Baron Adolf Kaiser
1961–3
Oil on panel

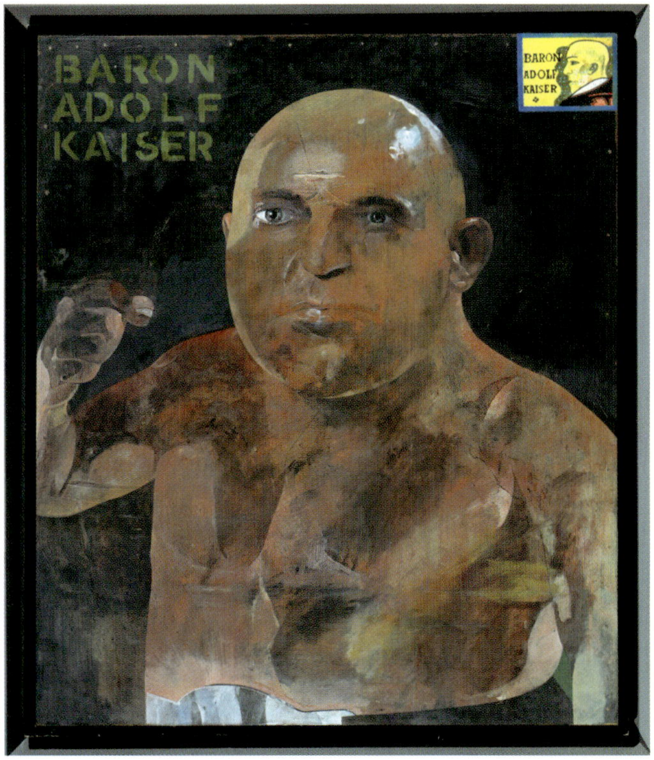

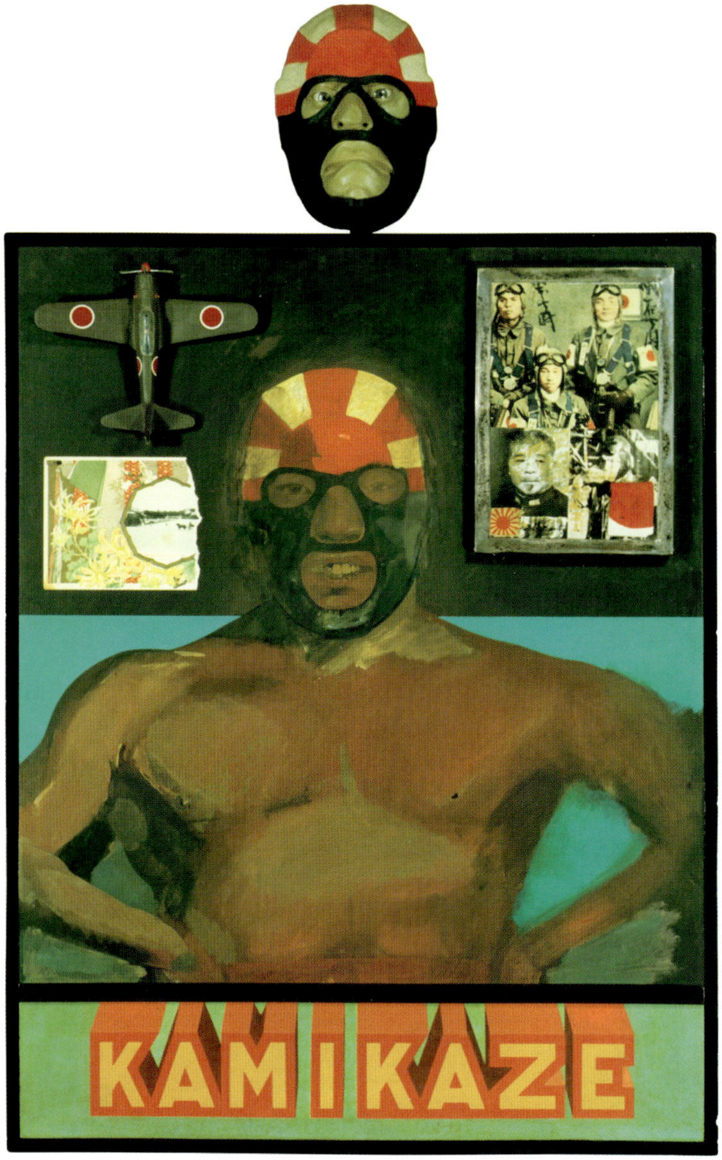

Kamikaze
1965
Acrylic and collage on hardboard

Masked Zebra Kid
1965
Acrylic, enamel, collage and assemblage on wood

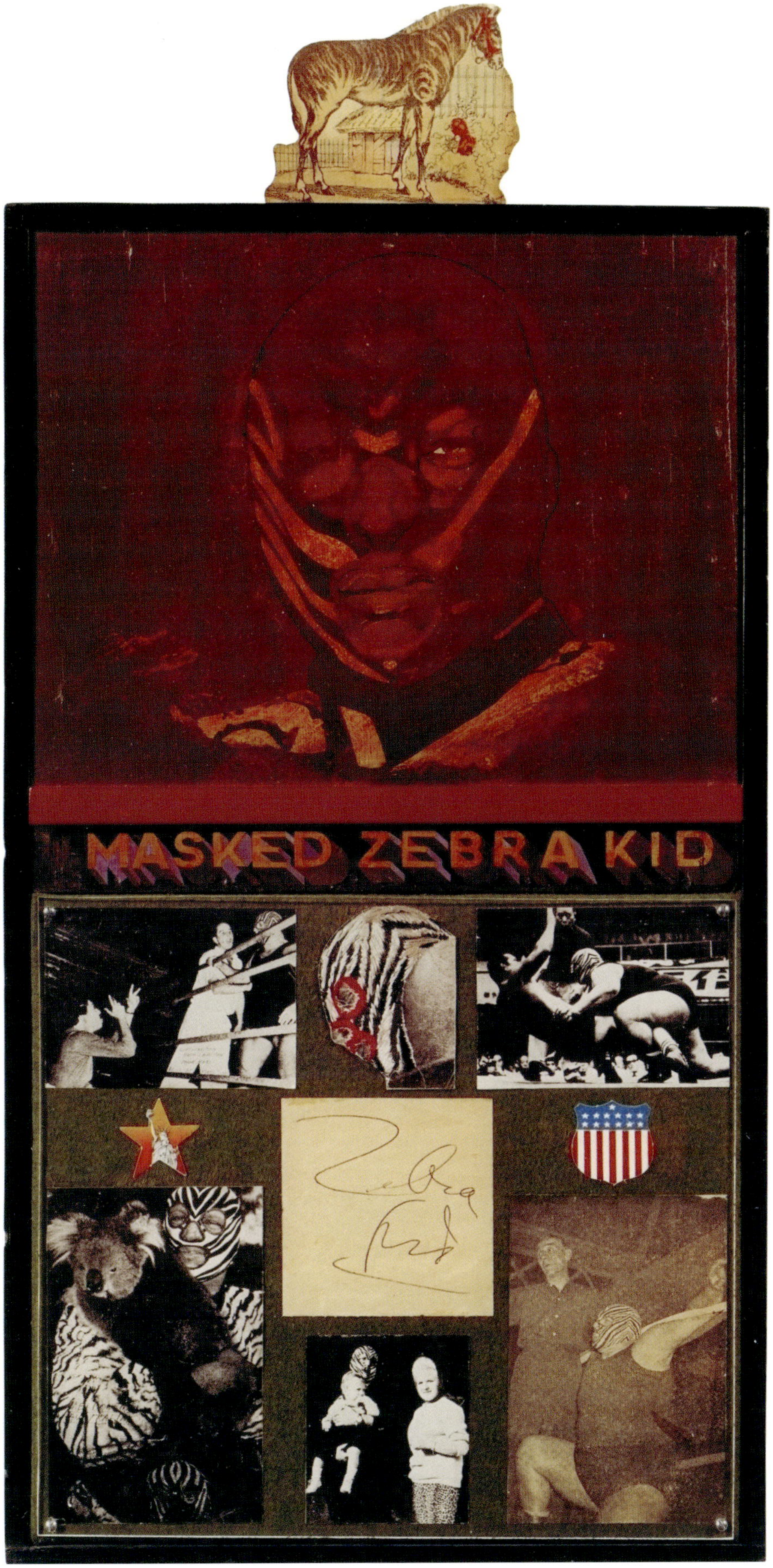

Big Do-Nut Drive-In
1963
Coloured pencil on paper

softies underneath, acting out an assumed identity just as they choreograph their acts of combat in the ring for the entertainment of us mortals. Blake had begun going to wrestling matches as a child in the company of his mother, so he understood that the deception was carried out in full view of the audience and with their tacit collusion. He also appreciated the essentially comic thrust of the whole spectacle, the sending up of masculine stereotypes, that brought these burly men back to earth with a mighty thump. Blake had a lot of fun inventing preposterous names and identities, such as the *Da Vinci Brothers*, presumed Italian mafiosi named preposterously in honour of the painter of the Mona Lisa. In spite of their masks, their muscles and their threatening demeanour, there is nothing very frightening about any of these men. It is more tempting to smile at their posturing than to find them intimidating. They are all, moreover, painted with the greatest delicacy of touch that the artist could muster, and on a small, intimate scale that emphasises that behind their costumes they are just human beings. One could go so far as to say that these *Übermenschen*, through being painted in this way, have been tamed and to some extent even feminised.

Like the wrestler paintings, the more straightforward portraits painted by Blake of film stars, actors and pop musicians during the 1960s are saturated in the adulation of the true fan. How could it be otherwise for an artist who in Self Portrait with Badges 1961 depicts himself guilelessly and without self-flattery as an unassuming young man in thrall to Elvis Presley and popular culture? In his portrayals of others he celebrates the spirit, personality and achievements of individuals he admires. The same respect is afforded to those he knew personally, as in the large portrait of his younger and already internationally celebrated colleague David Hockney, begun in 1965 but not completed until several decades later, as to those he knew only at second-hand from photographs or filmed footage. The Outsider Artist Simon Rodia, whose monumental Gaudí-like Watts Towers Blake had visited on a trip to Los Angeles in November 1963, is commemorated in a finely delineated portrait of 1965, the year of his death, that looks as though it could have been painted from life even though it was based on a magazine photograph. The fictional Tarzan and his family, the subject of two large paintings begun in the mid-1960s and worked on intermittently for years, also appear in

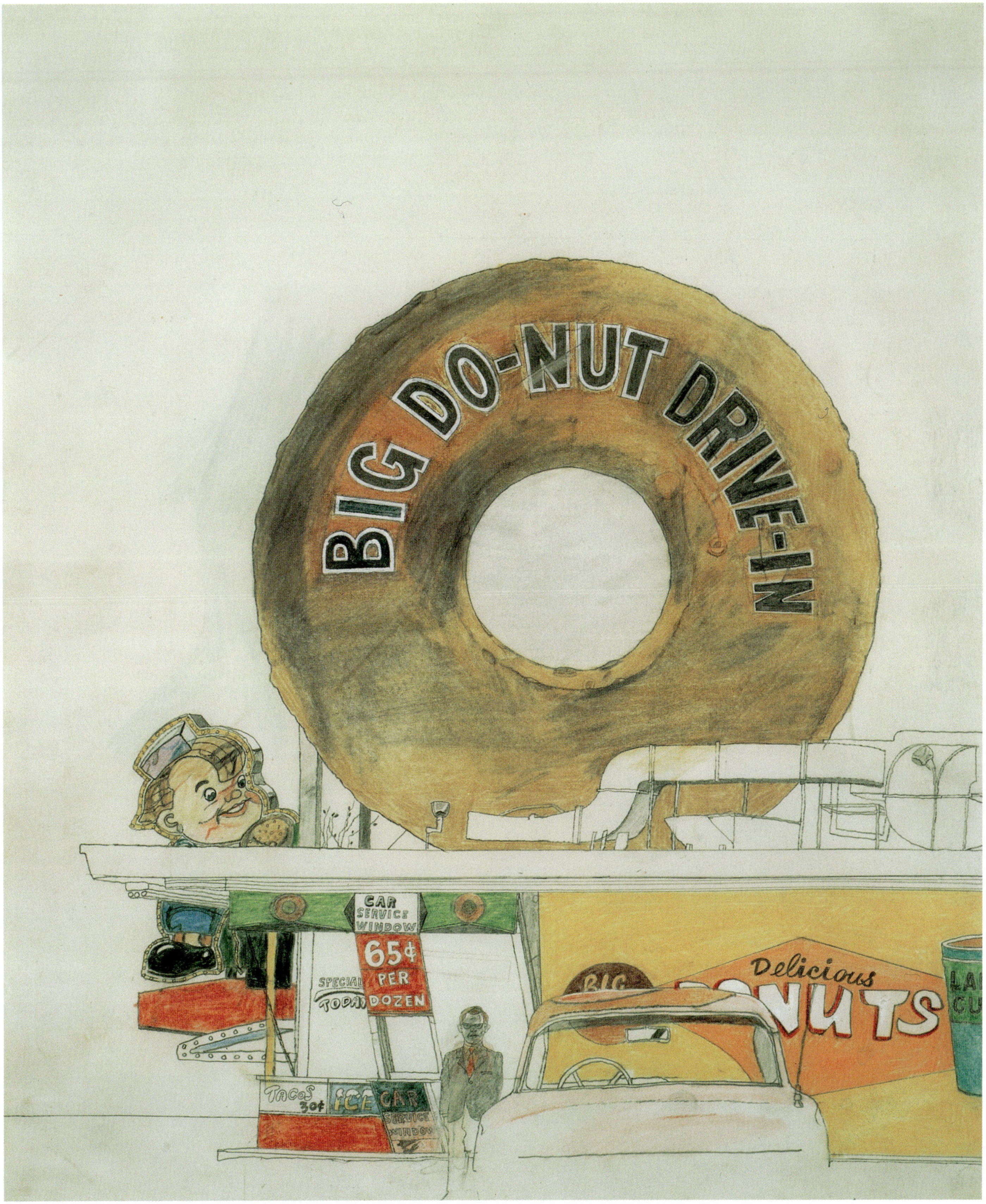
BIG DO-NUT DRIVE-IN
CAR SERVICE WINDOW
65¢ PER DOZEN
Delicious
NUTS
BIG
TACOS 30¢
ICE
CAR SERVICE WINDOW

Portrait of David Hockney in a Hollywood Spanish Interior
1965
Acrylic on canvas

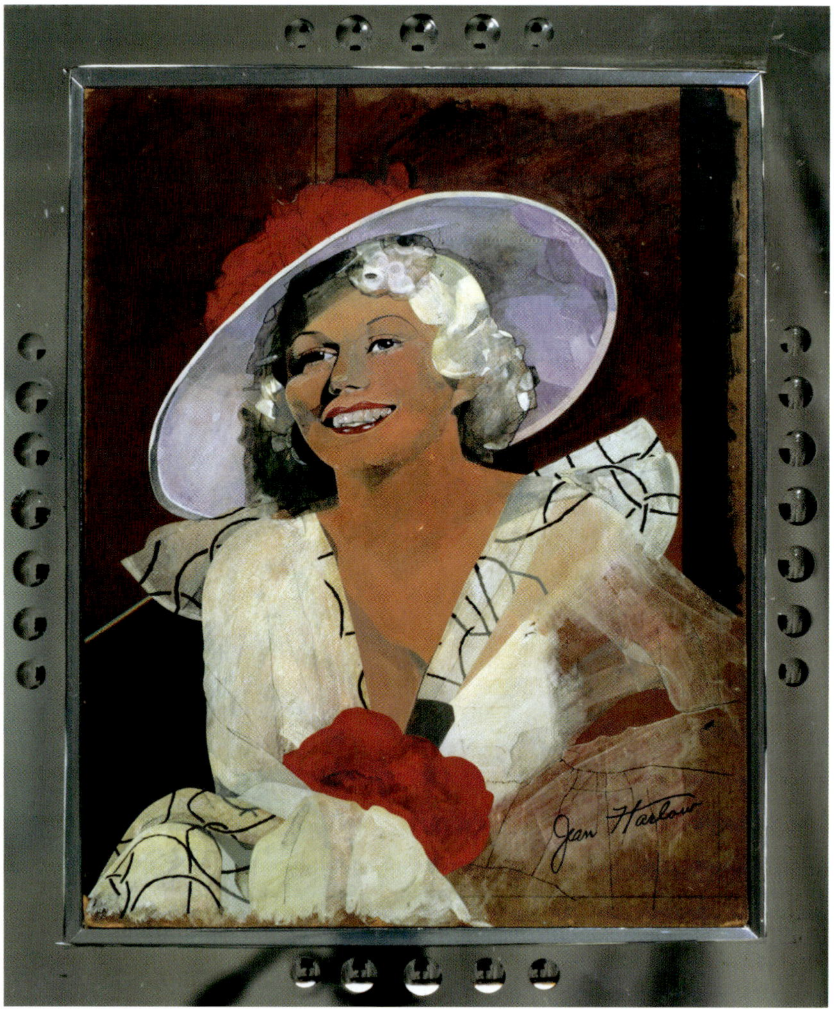

Jean Harlow
1964
Acrylic on hardboard

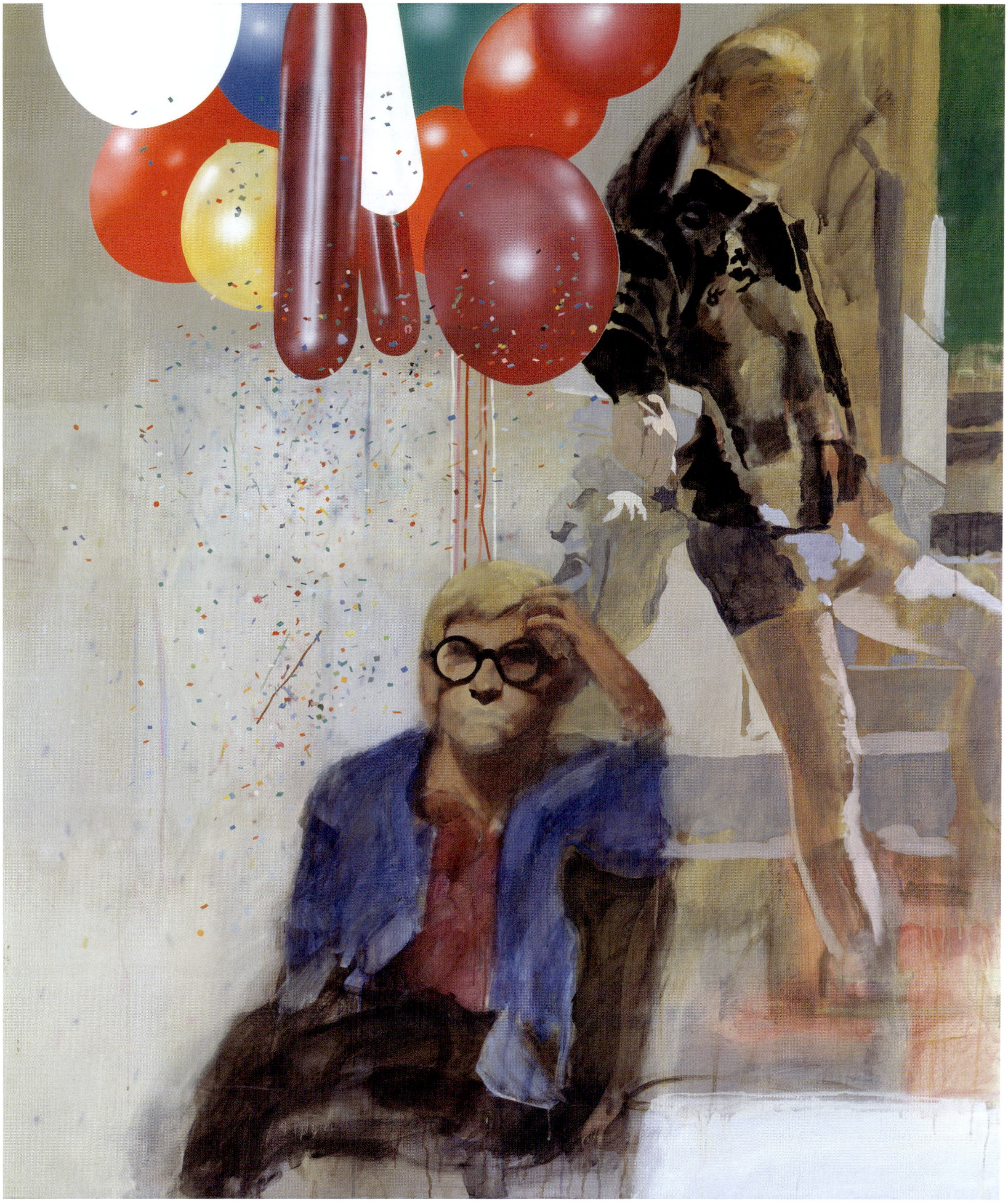

Tarzan, Jane, Boy and Cheeta
1966–75
Acrylic on canvas

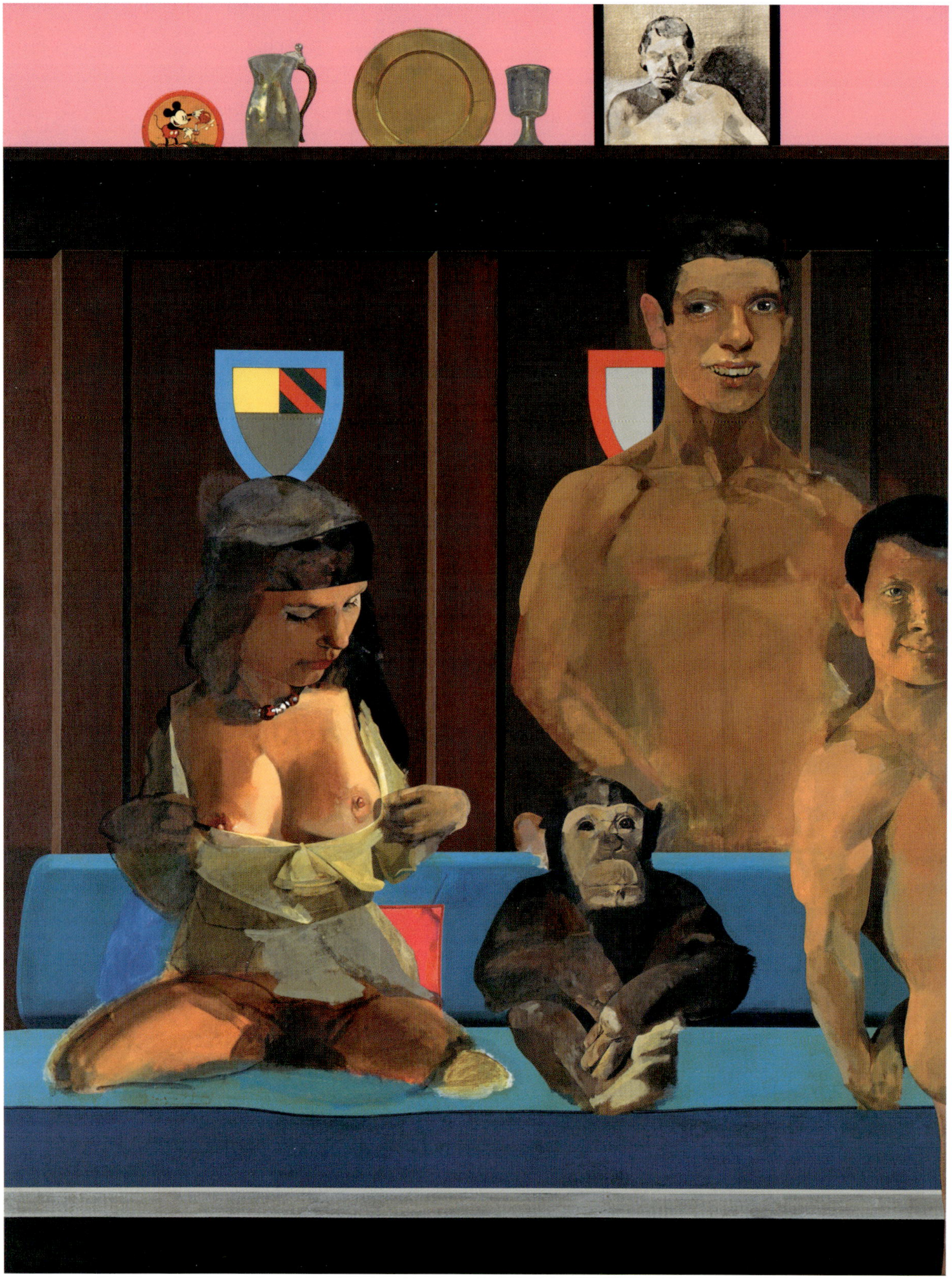

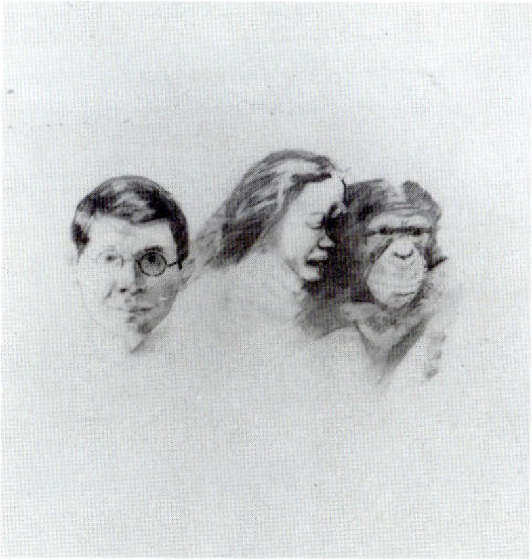

Boy, Jane and Cheeta
1968
Watercolour

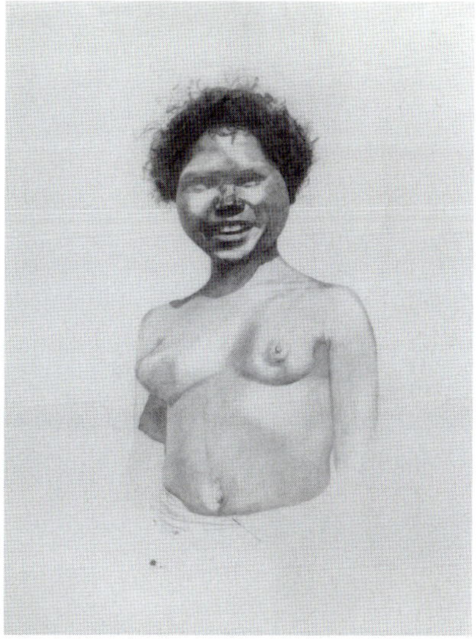

Study for 'Tarzan Meets the Jungle Goddess'
1968
Watercolour

sculptural form in *Tarzan Box* of c.1965 and in other paintings, each time reimagined by reference to different sources but in the paintings depicted with the same verisimilitude Blake brought to portraits of real people; a hand-painted rendering of a black-and-white photograph of the most famous Hollywood Tarzan, Johnny Weissmuller, appears amusingly as a family snapshot propped up on a shelf behind the naked family in Tarzan, Jane, Boy and Cheeta, thus not only acknowledging his use of photographic sources but also incorporating a further layer of play-acting to a 'conversation piece' already teeming with assumed identities and steeped in make-believe.

Blake's portraits of pop musicians, which are central to his contribution to Pop art, were conceived specifically in a spirit of homage by a true fan and as such they share much of the mythologising quality of his paintings of wrestlers, strippers, actors and other entertainers. Among the collage paintings of 1959–61 are several depicting American pop singers – including the vocal harmony duo the Everly Brothers, later to become friends of the artist, and Elvis Presley – through the simple expedient of gluing photographs of them into the top register of a surface whose boldly coloured geometric design was the visual equivalent of this new and vibrant music: loud, elemental, fresh, direct and intensely rhythmic. The zigzag pattern that flows across Got a Girl of 1960–61, with its crisply differentiated stripes of even width, is as brutally to the point as the 4/4 rhythm that animated rock'n'roll. The various heart-throbs whose photographs appear along the top are those referred to in the narrative of the Four Preps single appended to the upper-left corner, from which the painting takes its title. Crooning away in a style already fading fast under the onslaught of the more boisterous new music, the harmony singers lament that they can no longer hold the girl's attention, because she is swooning to the sound of others:

> *There was Fabian, Avalon, Ricky Nelson*
> *Yeah, yeah, yeah, yeah,*
> *Bobby Rydell and I know darned well*
> *Presley's in there too*

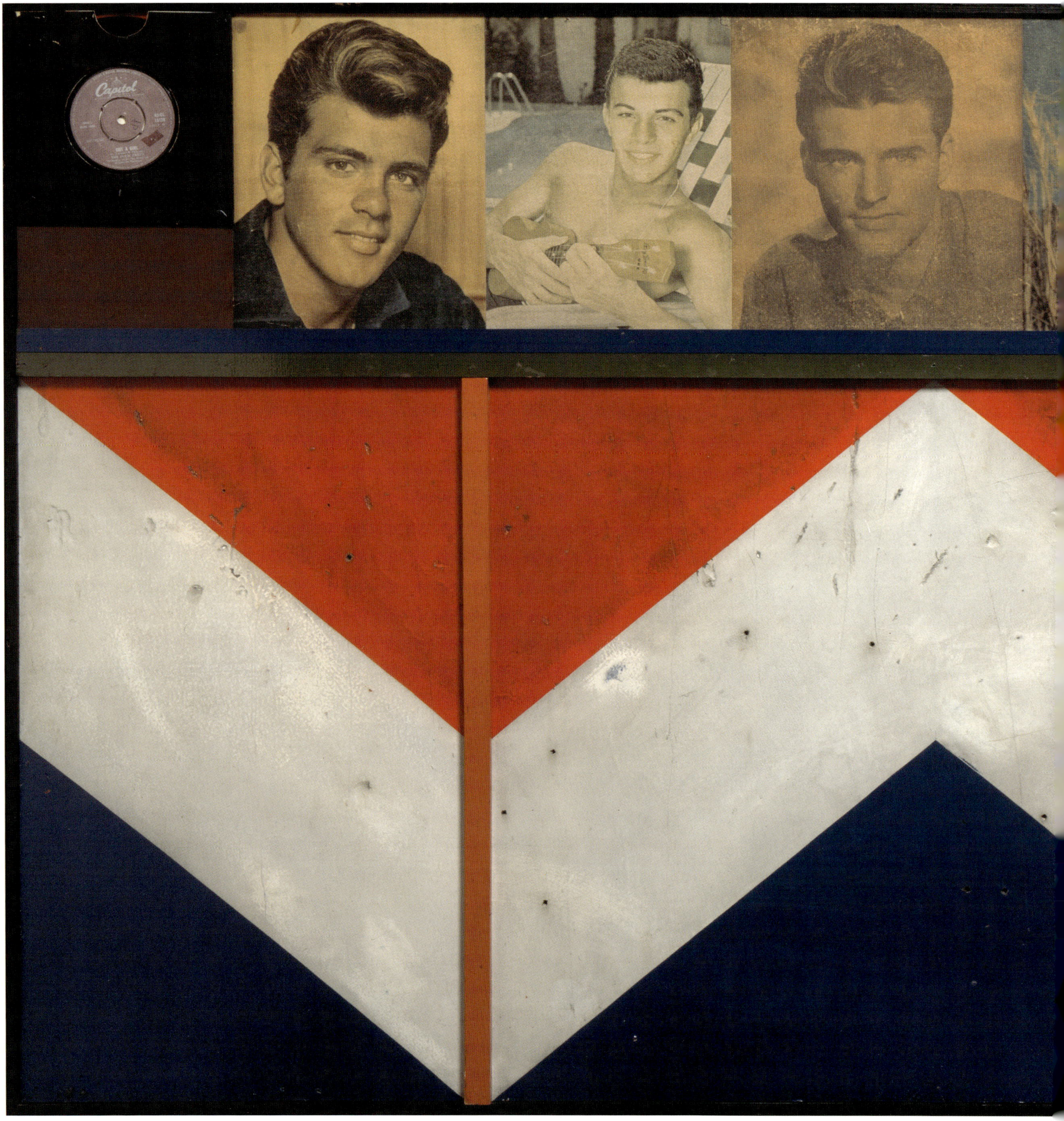
Capitol

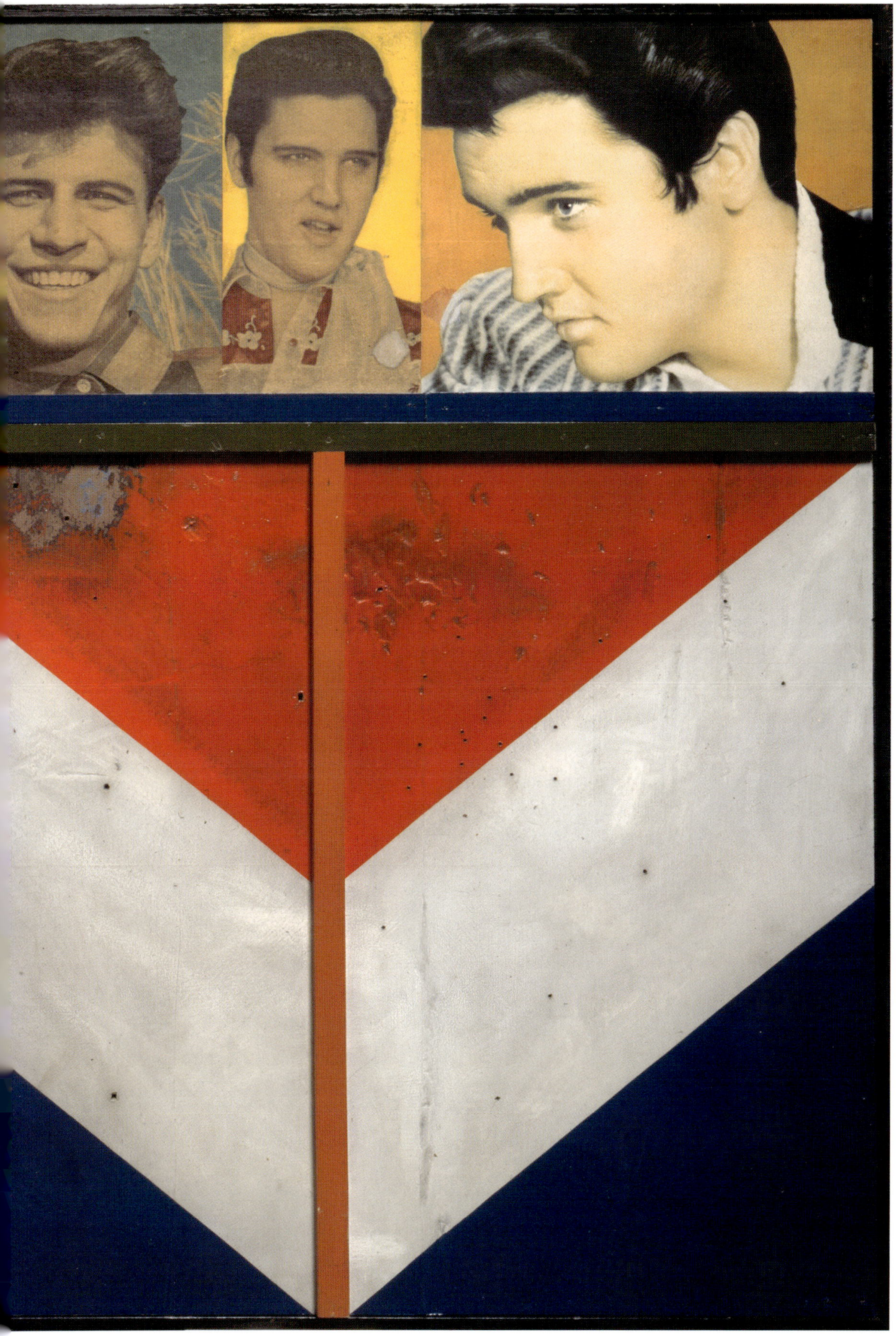

Got a Girl
1960–1
Oil paint, wood, photo-collage and record on hardboard

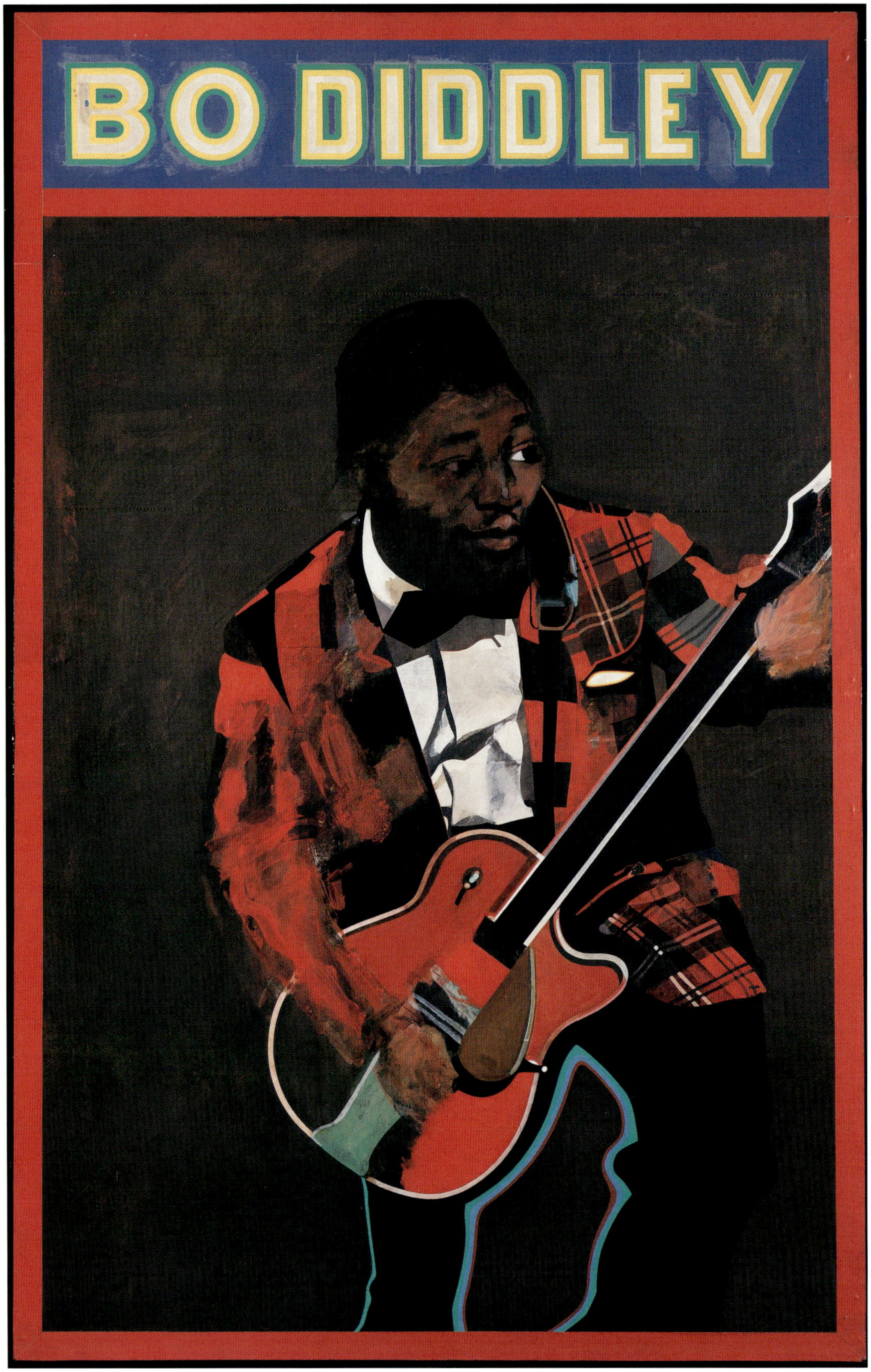
BO DIDDLEY

La Vern Baker
1961–2
Oil and collage on panel

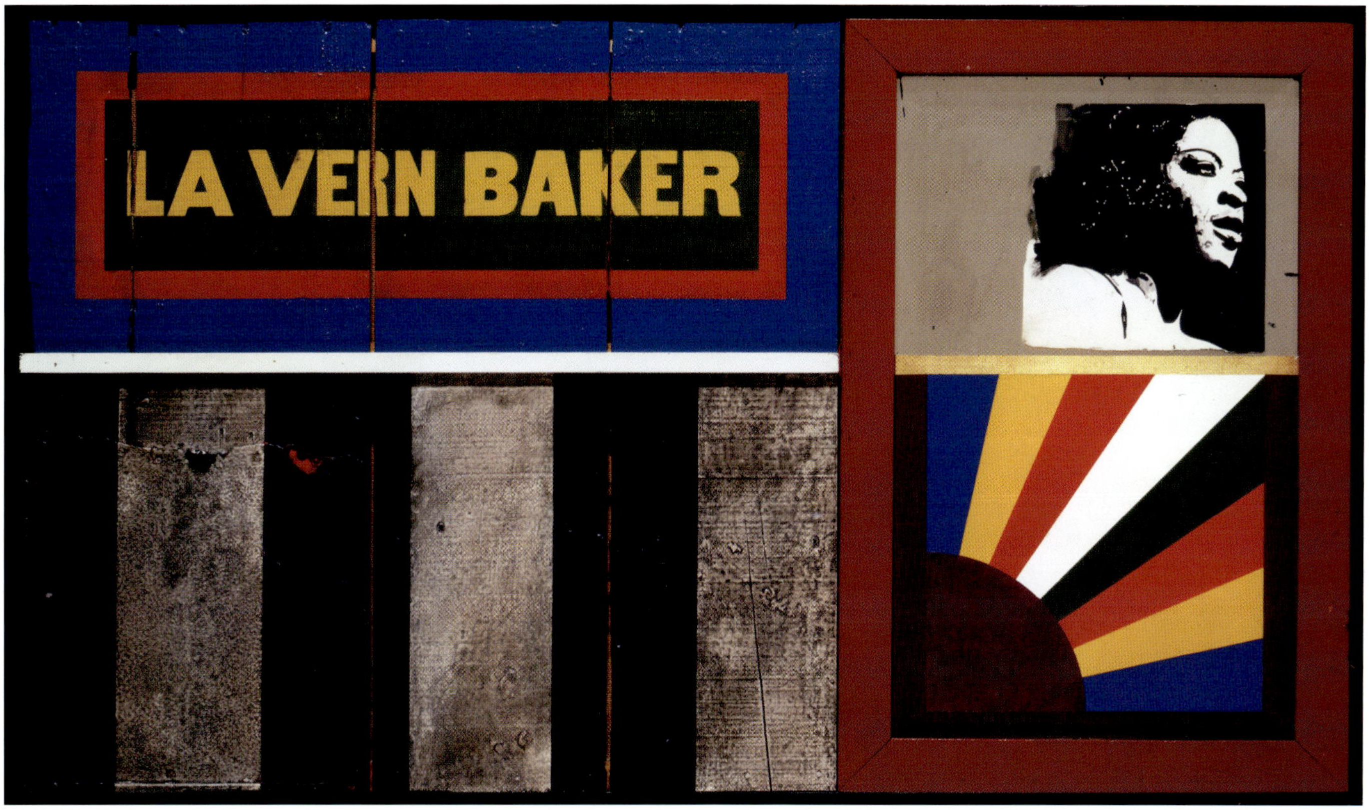

Bo Diddley
1963
Acrylic on hardboard

The Lettermen
1963
Oil on hardboard

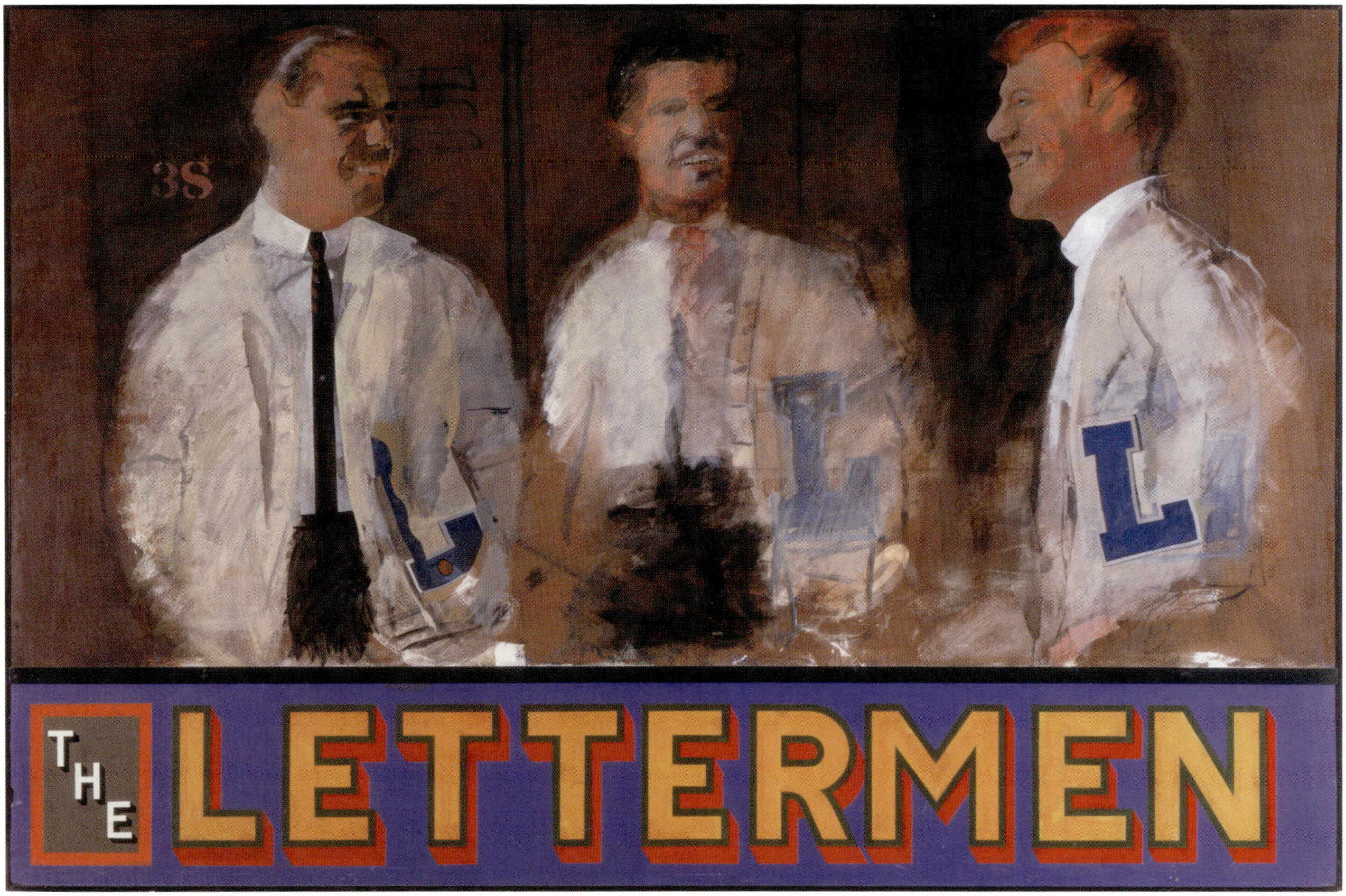

Beach Boys
1964
Screen-print on paper

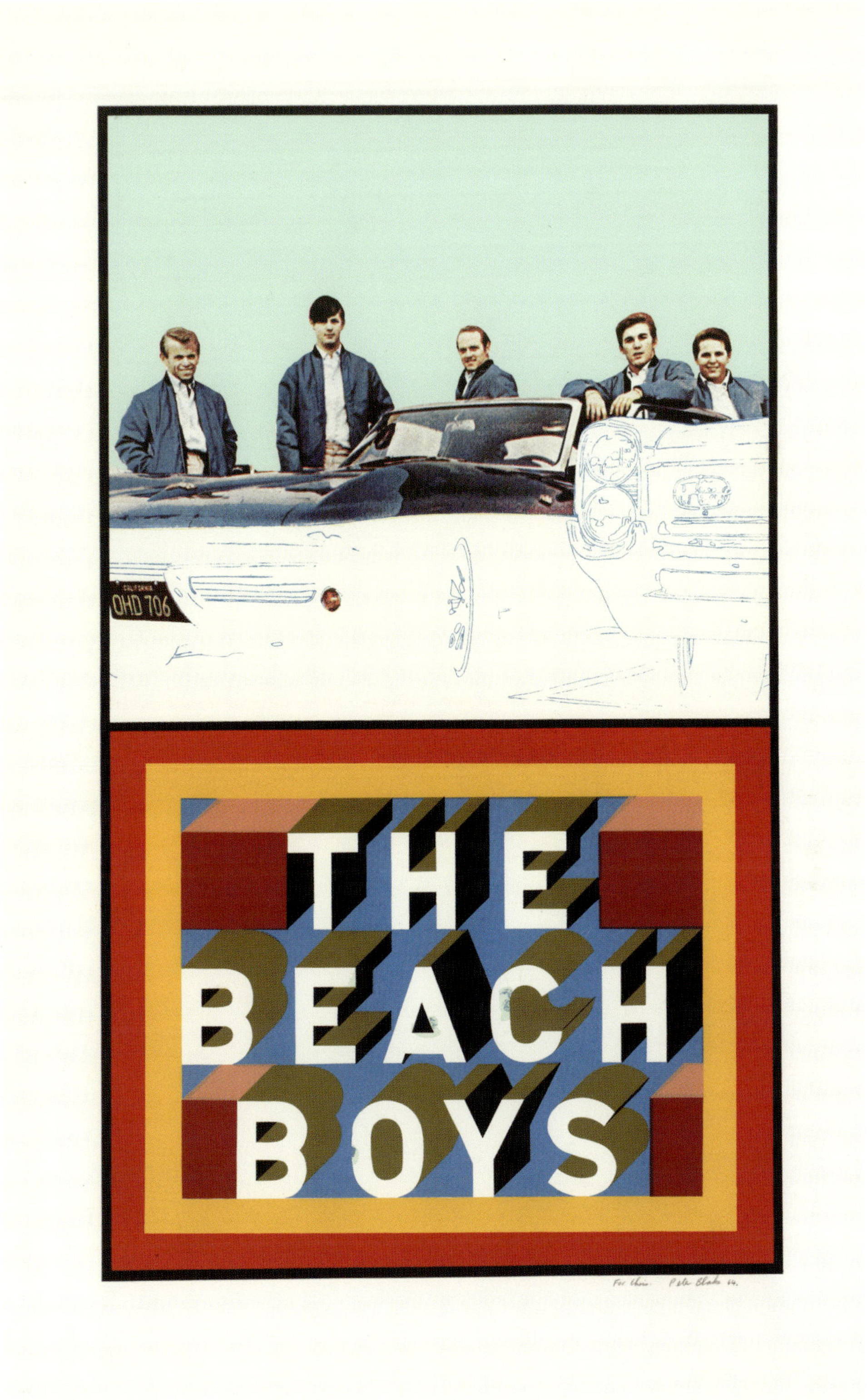

In Blake's picture, these men appear in precisely the order in which they are listed in the song's refrain. Though Blake was fond of such easy-listening pop music, as attested to by the large painting he made in 1963 of The Lettermen, the dynamic pictorial language he employs in these works has much more in common with the aggression and rebellion of the nascent rock music, the dangerous side that had British teenagers rioting in cinemas when the 1955 film *Blackboard Jungle*, with its rock'n'roll soundtrack, was first shown.

Just as Blake portrayed sex goddesses in two contrasting modes – that of photographic collage and that of hand-painted photographically derived portraits in a naturalistic idiom – so he also explored these two methods in his pop music pictures. One of the first of these more traditionally made music-inspired figure paintings was Girls with their Hero 1959–62. Painted when rock'n'roll was in its infancy, it is as much about the frenzied enthusiasm of a pop star's followers as it is about the star himself, in this case Elvis. Abandoned in an unfinished state, and therefore unusually free and sketchy in technique, it nevertheless heralds later painted portraits of Bo Diddley, The Lettermen, The Beatles and other favoured musicians, as well as an equally arresting screenprint of The Beach Boys, all of them based closely on record covers or on other photographs in the public domain. Blake's ambition was to make art for consumption by the same young mass audience that was buying these new records. He has since judged the experiment a failure, as far as securing such a huge audience is concerned: an inevitability given that the sophistication of Blake's pictorial solutions would have been lost on such visually untutored spectators, for whom such pictures probably would not even have conformed to their definitions of art. By 1967, however, a year before completing work on the portrait of the Beatles in their 1962 incarnation as loveable moptops, Blake sold his key pop music multiple – the cover of their Sgt Pepper album – to a world-wide audience numbered in millions. At that moment, as consumers avidly scanned the star-studded crowd on that sleeve and argued about the significance of each person elbowing his or her way to our attention, Blake's mission of reaching and really communicating with the masses was achieved.

Retiring and diffident in manner, Blake entered the mythical decade-long party of the 1960s as something of a wallflower, watching and commenting on the action from the margins. By the time that he and his young family took leave of London in 1969 for a life of rural tranquillity in the village of Wellow in Avon, he had transformed himself into one of the chief chroniclers and architects of that optimistic and celebratory period, without once sacrificing the essential humanity and intense intimacy of his vision.

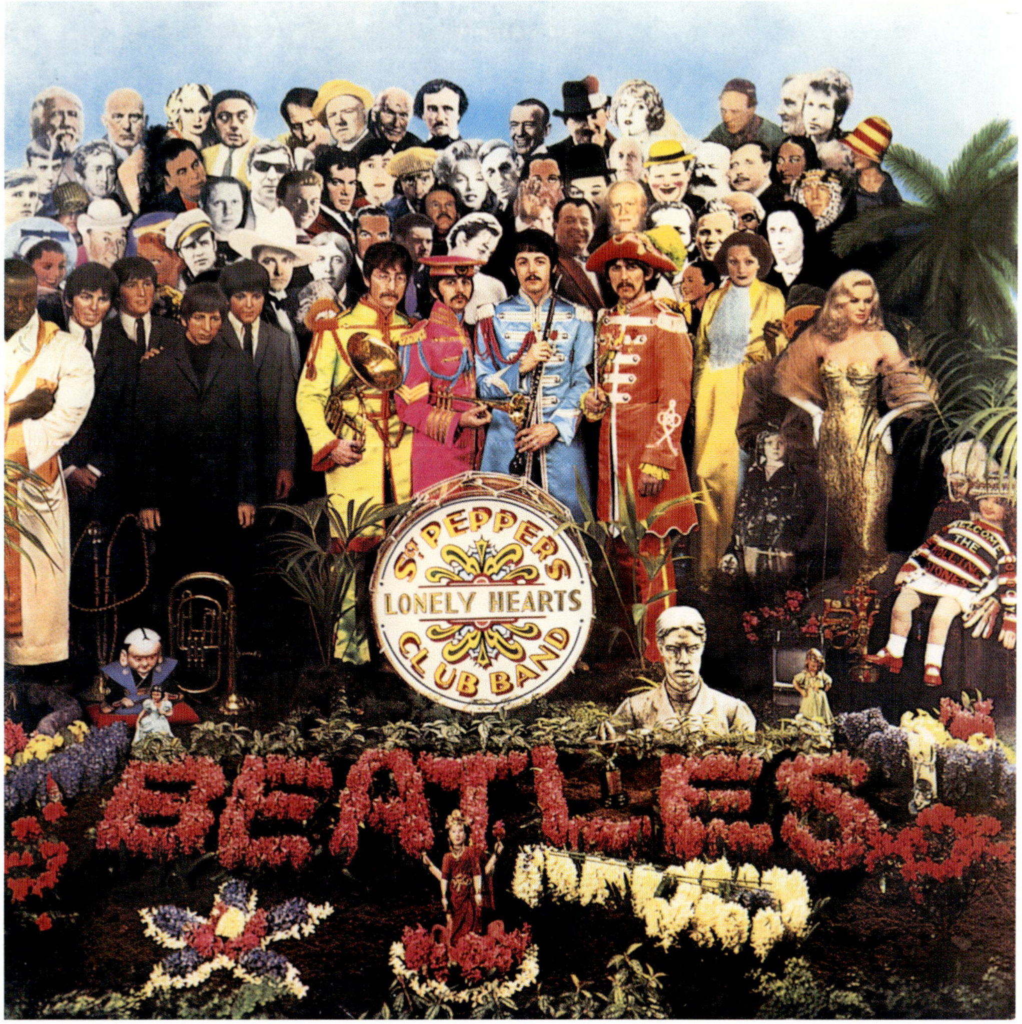

Cover design for 'Sgt Pepper's Lonely Hearts Club Band'
1967

Monarch of the Glen
1965–8
Acrylic on canvas

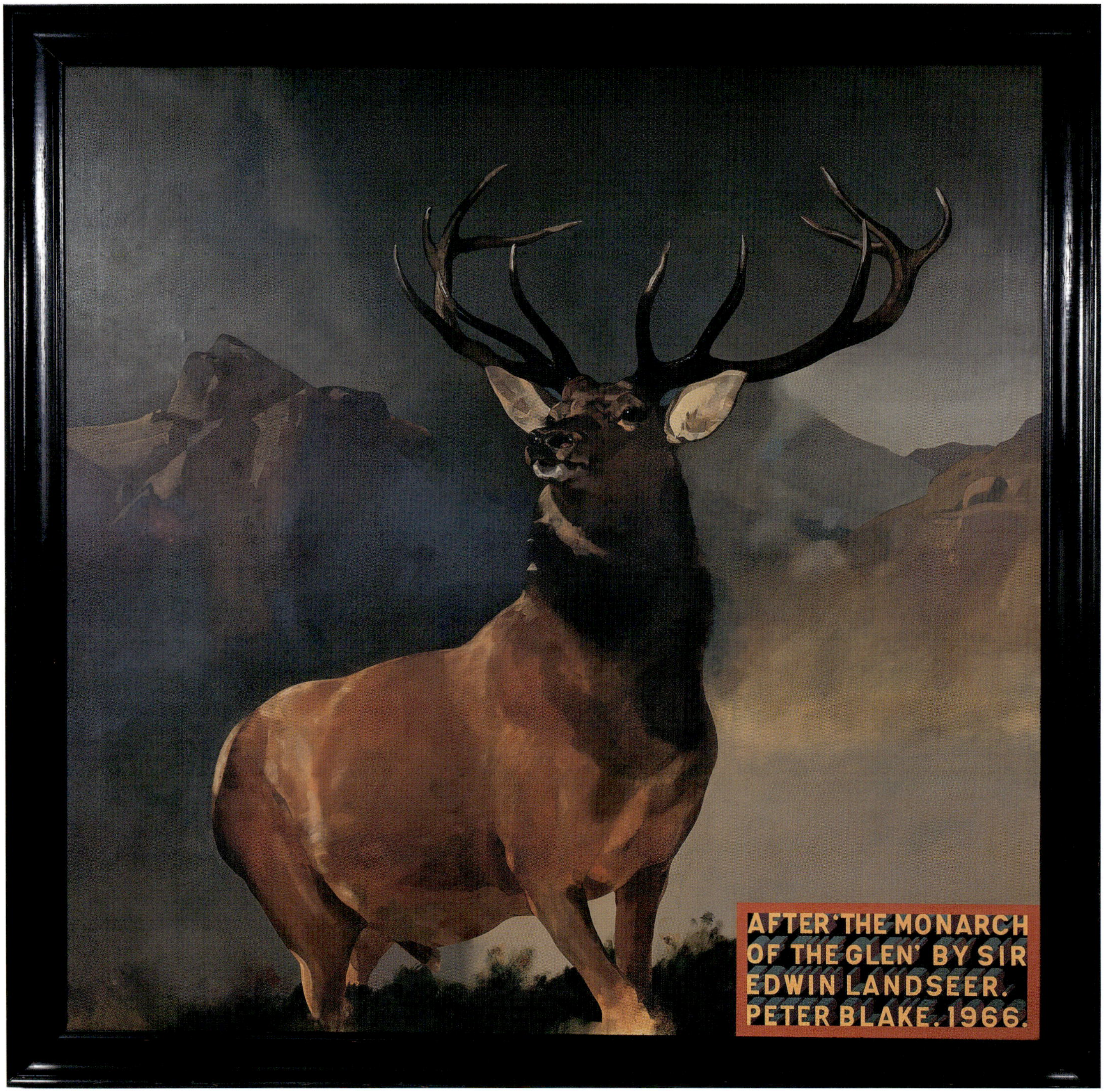

the 1970s

la mode rétro: the ruralist years

christoph grunenberg

In a 1971 lecture, Ernst Gombrich declared 'We are in the middle of a crisis of belief in progress. Nevertheless, we cannot imagine our life without the concept of progress'.[1] At a moment in history when the notion of progress in art itself appeared reactionary, the art world nevertheless seemed to be propelled by a determined forward thrust and a belief, if not in 'progress', at least in change, reacting against a recent past that had to be contested and improved. The radical critique at the time of the modes of artistic production and distribution implicitly aspired to an iconoclastic challenge to established art and order. Those artists, on the other hand, who consciously turned backwards and dared to celebrate the art of an earlier period, adopt traditional styles and embrace established values were, at best, met with mild derision and ironic mockery or, most frequently, just ignored. The Brotherhood of Ruralists belonged to this group of artists who, through their creative practice, lifestyles and pronouncements, wilfully removed themselves from the dominant creative discourse of the time and thus from the historical, institutional and economic mainstream. If there was a group of artists in the twentieth century whose choice of artistic style, subject matter and inspiration seemed to signal reckless career suicide, the Brotherhood is without doubt a prime candidate. To the sophisticated London intelligentsia and critical establishment, nothing could seem less relevant and more eccentric than the Ruralists' celebration of a mythical Albion, devotion to legends and fairy tales and adherence to the techniques of the Old Masters. In comparison with the clever allusions, historical references and moral and philosophical relativisms of the so-called avant-garde, primarily mediated through photography, collage, found objects, documents and texts and most definitely not through painting, the Ruralists' practice necessarily appeared an anachronistic anomaly. Nearly forty years since Blake's escape from London and more than thirty years since the foundation of the Brotherhood of Ruralists, a more objective re-evaluation of this critical period in his work should be possible.

The Sixties did not just draw to a close but crashed spectacularly as the utopian illusions and countercultural hopes of a generation collapsed like a fragile house of cards. It was a short decade that drew to a close in 1968 as Martin Luther King and Robert Kennedy were assassinated, global economic crisis loomed and

1
Ernst H. Gombrich, *Kunst und Fortschritt. Wirkung und Wandlung einer Idee*, Cologne, DuMont, 1978, p.8.

political opposition drifted into increasing radicalisation. As artist and designer Nigel Waymouth observed of Britain: 'I think the whole movement, the psychedelic era, was finished by the end of '68. Politics came into it, Dany the Rouge, Street-Fightin' Man, and everything began to get quite heavy.'[2] It was at this moment, at the very fag-end of the decade (in November 1969 to be precise), that Blake and his wife, artist Jann Haworth, and their daughter moved to Wellow, Avon, a small village near Bath. There was a poignant feeling that an era was drawing to a close and it was time either to despair, turn to radical politics or descend into drug abuse (none of which Blake ever had any interest in), or to move on. Blake and Haworth were part of a wider exodus of a generation of artists and intellectuals tired of 'Swinging London' and looking for a new beginning.[3] To some degree, their motives for abandoning London were personal: they were in search of a better and quieter life following the birth of their daughter Juliette Liberty in November 1968. Howard Hodgkin, Richard Smith and Joe Tilson joined the migration to the West Country and lived nearby, relocating at least a small part of the London art world to the countryside. A sympathetic community developed that was soon to include a wider group of artists, including future members of the Brotherhood of Ruralists.

Following a suggestion of Peter Blake, the Brotherhood of Ruralists was founded on 21 March 1975 (the spring solstice) at a social gathering of its founding members, who included, besides Blake and Haworth, Ann and Graham Arnold, David Inshaw and Annie and Graham Ovenden.[4] Most of the artists had known each other for several years and mostly lived in close proximity (though the Ovendens resided in Cornwall). Graham Ovenden had been one of Blake's students at the Royal College of Art, where he taught during the late 1960s and early 1970s. Blake encountered David Inshaw's work in his research for an exhibition he was invited to curate for the Festival Gallery in Bath in 1974. Inshaw had been taught by Graham Arnold, who lived nearby and whom Blake had also known from his time as a student at the Royal College. As Blake once remarked, the unifying factor of the Ruralists was 'the fact that we were all in the country', rather than a particular devotion to a pastoral agenda, though a fascination with the myths and realities of the English countryside figured strongly in their work.[5] The group grew as much out of a shared interest in figurative painting and certain forgotten or discredited

2
Jonathon Green, *Days in the Life: Voices from the English Underground 1961–1971*, London, Heinemann, 1988, p. 239.

3
I am grateful to Peter Blake for sharing his memories of the period with me and answering many of my questions. Statements by Peter Blake, if not otherwise attributed, are from an interview on 13 March 2007.

4
On the history of the Ruralist movement see Nicholas Usherwood, *The Brotherhood of Ruralists*, London, Lund Humphries, 1981; Christopher Martin, *The Ruralists*, special issue of *Art & Design*, no. 23, 1991; Jerrold Northrop Moore, Peter Nahum and Laurie Lee, *The Brotherhood of Ruralists: A Celebration*, Bodmin, Cornwall, Ruralist Fine Art, 2003; and the Brotherhood of Ruralists information website at www.ruralists.com.

5
Nicholas Usherwood, 'Peter Blake & the Ruralists', in *Peter Blake*, exh. cat., London, Tate Gallery, 1983, p. 32.

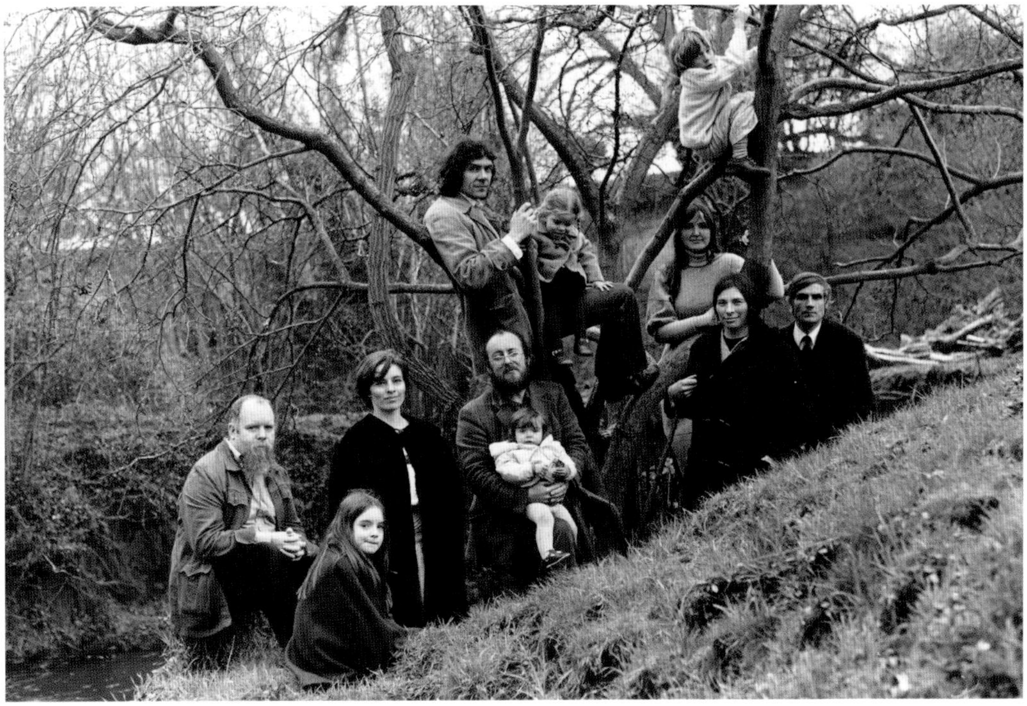

The Brotherhood of Ruralists, from left to right, front: Peter Blake, Liberty Blake, Jann Haworth, Graham Ovenden, Emily Alice Ovenden, Annie Ovenden, Graham Arnold; back: David Inshaw, Daisy Blake, Ann Arnold, Edmund Dante Ovenden. Cornwall 1977

traditions as out of an opposition to the ruling minimalist and conceptual practices of the avant-garde. Defining their group as a 'Brotherhood' made obvious programmatic references to the Brotherhood of Ancients (including William Blake, Samuel Palmer and Edward Calvert) and the Pre-Raphaelite Brotherhood (founded in 1848), with whom they shared a passion for unfashionable art of a previous era. It did, however, also allude to the more recent association of the Broadheath Brotherhood (in reverence to the birthplace of Sir Edward Elgar, a Ruralist hero), which had been founded in 1971 and included, besides Arnold and Inshaw, the artist John Morley, who was an important associate member of the Brotherhood of Ruralists.

The driving force of the Ruralists seems to have been less political than essentially artistic, creating a refuge of a small community of like-minded artists who felt the need to break away from an increasingly alien and hostile environment. A well-known group photograph of its members and their children shows them in the countryside, assembled behind a grassy mound and posing informally around a tree. The image (which also featured on the cover of an early exhibition leaflet) functions as a manifesto as much as any written declaration of their artistic intent might do, perfectly capturing their devotion to nature and their obvious withdrawal from the avant-garde agenda of the metropolitan elite. It is a distinctly casual assembly of individuals with their children and partners, mostly in informal attire (with only Graham Arnold donning a suit and tie), coming together as much for a common love of countryside and in search for a simpler lifestyle as for a shared artistic purpose. As they stated themselves in 1981, the Brotherhood of Ruralists 'is quite simply an association of friends who share strongly-held views on the nature of art… it is a group of friends and not a commune'.[6] There were, however, also political imperatives for their move to the country, and Haworth in particular was committed to the burgeoning green movement and the pursuit of self-sufficiency and autarkic living.

While there was never a manifesto (despite several attempts to draft one), Blake probably summarised the Brotherhood's mission best:

> Simply, our aims are the continuation of a certain kind of English painting; we admire Samuel Palmer, Stanley Spencer, Thomas Hardy, Elgar, cricket, English Landscape, the Pre-Raphaelites, etc… Our aims are to paint about love, beauty, joy, sentiment and magic. We still believe in painting with oil paint on canvas, putting the picture in the frame and hopefully, that someone will like it, buy it and hang it on their wall to enjoy it.[7]

The Brotherhood's philosophy, as so emphatically expressed by Blake, seems so closely aligned with the early- to mid-1970s' turn towards conservative values, politically as well as morally, that one cannot read it today as other than a clever provocation directed at the gatekeepers of avant-garde culture. It appears to be tinged by the wilful naivety of artists who celebrate a dreamy notion of art and Englishness that is deliberately retrogressive and hopelessly romantic in the face of the realities of social and political decay. As a matter of fact, it was a genuinely felt expression of the Brotherhood's artistic philosophy and political convictions – 'a *positive* decision…to live and work in the country' – and not primarily intended as a provocation.[8] They did feel, however, that they also

6
Quoted in Nicholas Usherwood, 'Introduction', in *The Ruralists: An Exhibition of Works by the Brotherhood of Ruralists and their Circle*, exh. cat., Bristol, Arnolfini Gallery, 1981, n.p.

7
Peter Blake, 'Contrariwise', *Aspects*, no. 3, Summer 1978, pp. 1–2. A planned magazine titled 'The Briar Rose' (after the celebrated series of paintings by Edward Burne-Jones) which would have functioned as manifesto and voice piece never came to full fruition.

8
The Brotherhood of Ruralists, Gainsborough House, Sudbury, 18 August to 30 September 1979, p. 1 (emphasis added). Interview with Peter Blake, London, 13 March 2007.

Costume Life Drawing
1971
Screenprint on paper

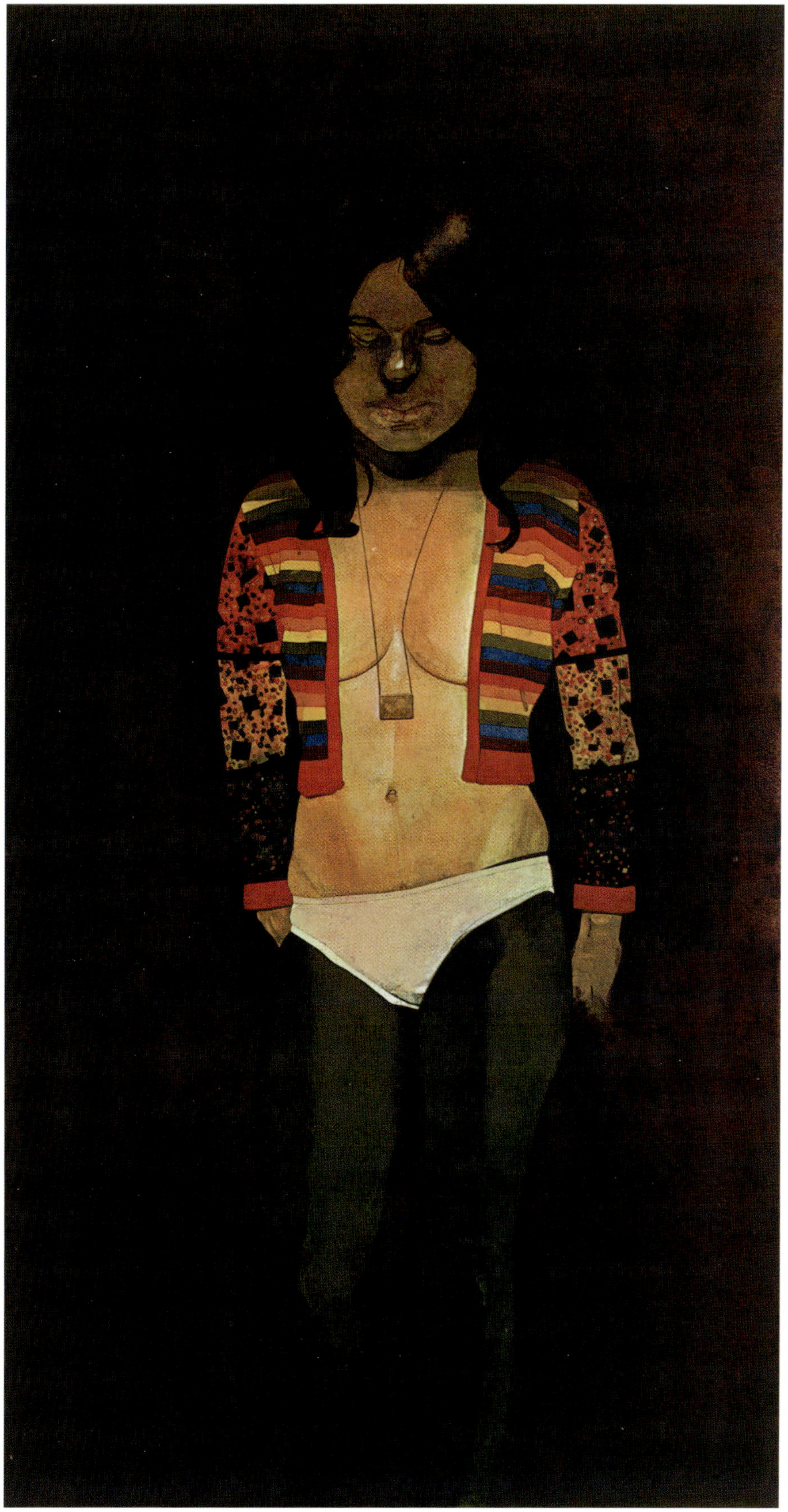

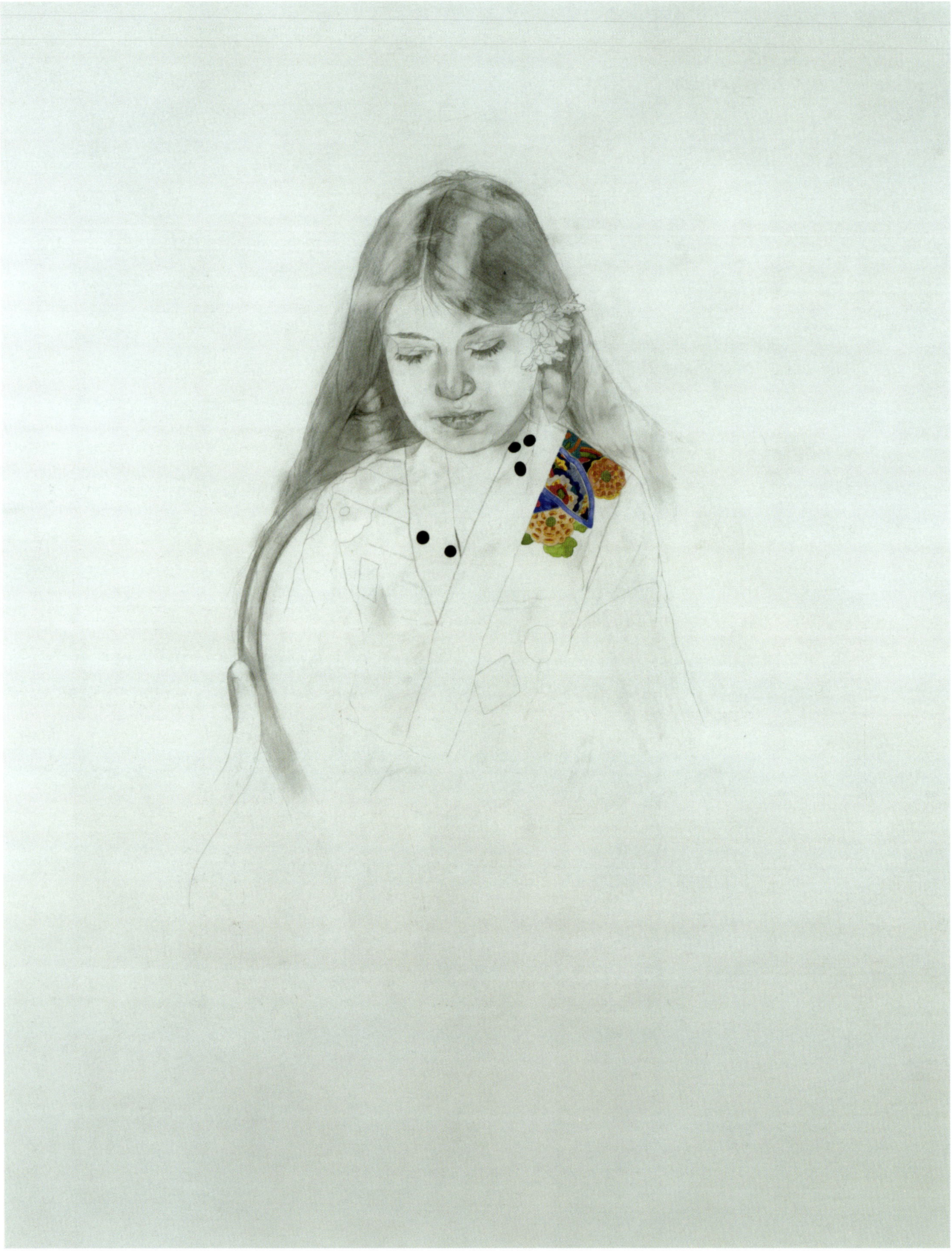

April in a Kimono
1968
Watercolour

had to take 'a positive stand against the emptiness and conformity of so much contemporary thought and art', following the vitriolic critical reception that, to their surprise, the group received.[9]

The Brotherhood had formed, as Blake explained, 'gently and innocently', and they countered the critical negativity that was an inherent force in the arts of the 1970s, based on radical theory and political activism challenging the very foundations of the institutions of art, with a disarmingly affirmative message. The battle between the more militant factions of the self-declared avant-garde and the Ruralists culminated in a very public spat in the pages of the *Guardian*, sparked by Blake's inclusion in the 1977 *Hayward Annual*, featuring the poignant juxtaposition of one his large, typically unfinished canvases with Michael Craig-Martin's conceptual icon *An Oak Tree* 1973 and a similarly reductive Barry Flanagan work.[10] Blake retrospectively accused the 'staid Four', as he labelled the leading critics Richard Cork, Paul Overy and Caroline Tisdall, with Peter Fuller a later addition, of being 'destructive and negative about almost all the art they reviewed', writing from 'the safety of their establishment newspapers, *The Times*, the *Guardian* and the *Evening Standard*'.[11] He identified a preoccupation with what he called 'Art-politics' at the core of the problem, while the art on display was usually ignored.[12] Richard Cork's robust reply claimed to discover an art-political conspiracy in 'a cosy establishment choosing itself and its friends', pointing to the presence of some of the artist-curators in the show and the high representation of artists from two major West End galleries.[13] Cork saved his most acerbic criticism, however, for Blake's work and Titania in particular, labelling his 'revivalism' as a 'retreat into salacious cloud-cuckoo-land', coming 'as a sad decline'.[14]

The 1970s remain one of the most divisive periods in art, full of breaks and ruptures, a pluralistic decade of highly charged political battles that allowed surprisingly little room for variety beyond the clearly drawn ideological battle lines. The almost wholesale critical rejection of the Ruralist Blake is hard to comprehend today, since elements of his work seem to fit easily into the context of the rise of a postmodernist aesthetic with its challenge to the idea of artistic progress, play with narrative traditions, calculated avoidance of originality, skilful blending of historical and contemporary elements and the resurrection of discredited styles

9
The Brotherhood of Ruralists: Paintings and Drawings, 23 June to 15 July 1979, n.p.

10
The painting was *Sword Fight*, begun 1965. The fact that all illustrated works were captioned 'still in progress' in the catalogue and that the process of successive reworking of works, sometimes over decades and without conclusion, constituted a 'conceptual' project for Blake, escaped the critics. Interview with Peter Blake, 13 March 2007.

11
Blake, 'Contrariwise', p. 1.

12
Letter to the Editor, *Guardian*, 20 July 1977, p. 20.

13
Guardian, 20 July 1977, p. 20. The debate filled the letters pages of the *Guardian* for the next week, with replies and contributions from Patrick Heron, David Hockney, John Hoyland, Norbert Lynton, Paul Overy and others on 21, 23, 25, 27 and 28 July 1977.

14
Ibid.

Liberty as a 'Suffolk Child by John Constable R.A.'
from *For John Constable*
1976
Print and mixed media on paper

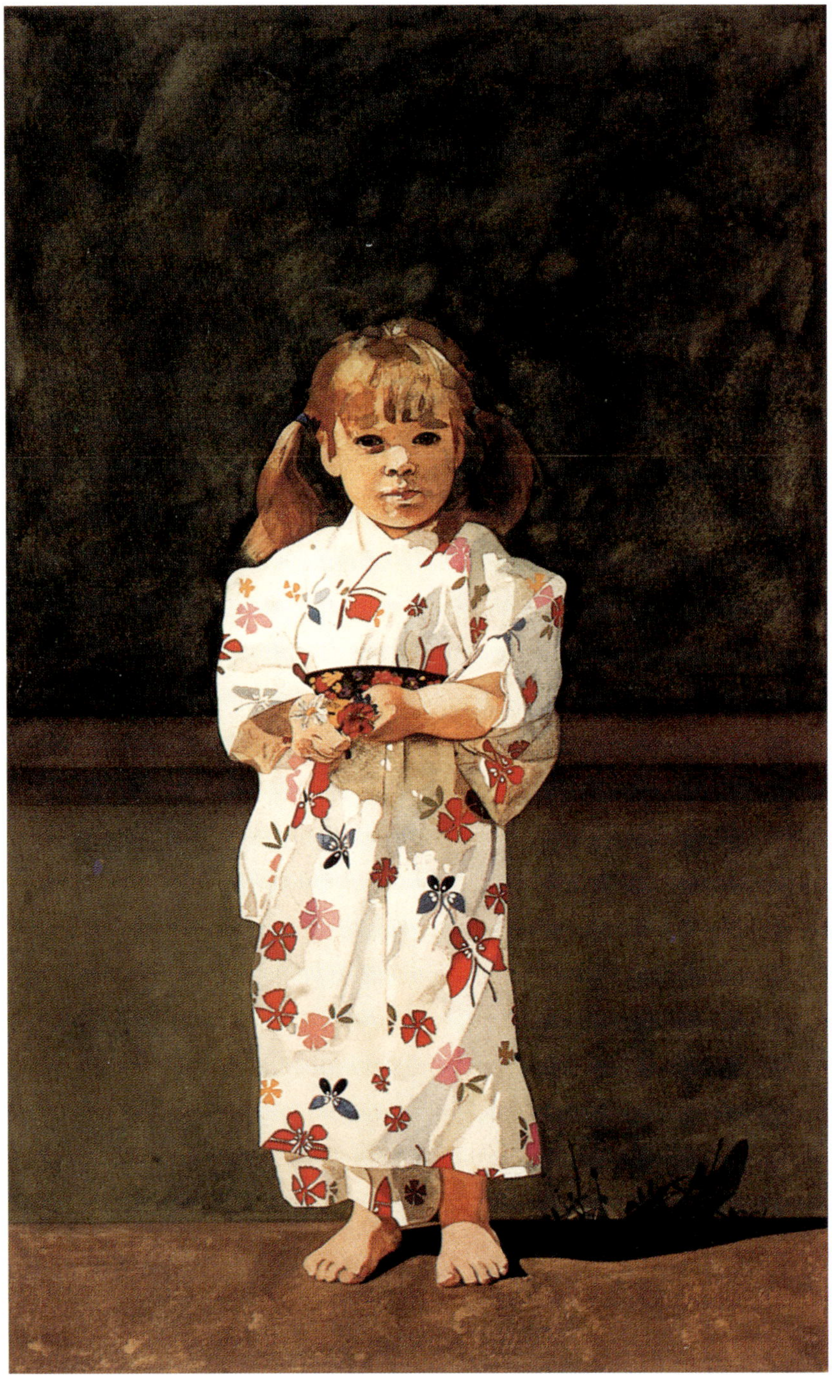

Liberty Blake in a Kimono
1971
Watercolour

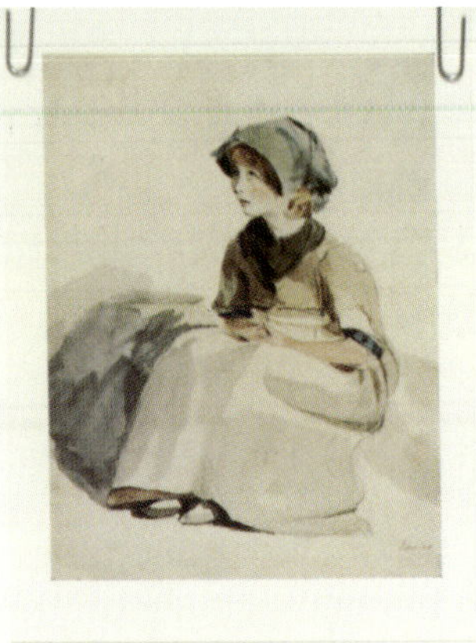
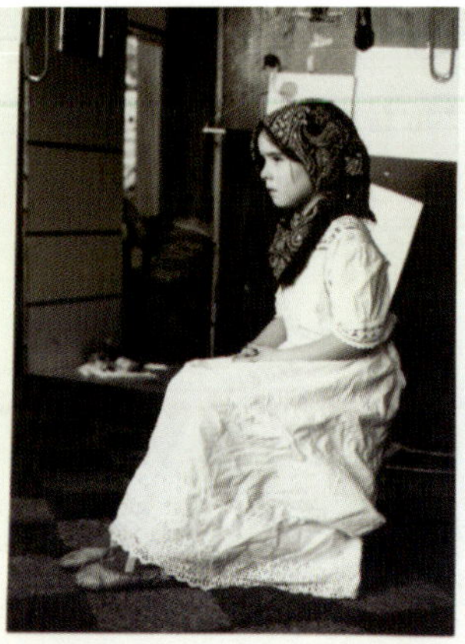
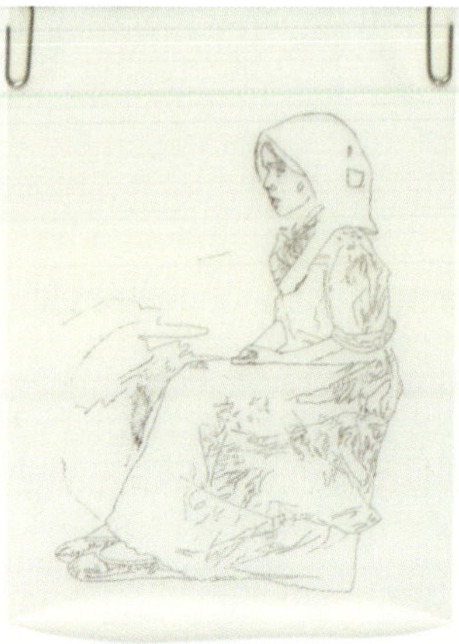

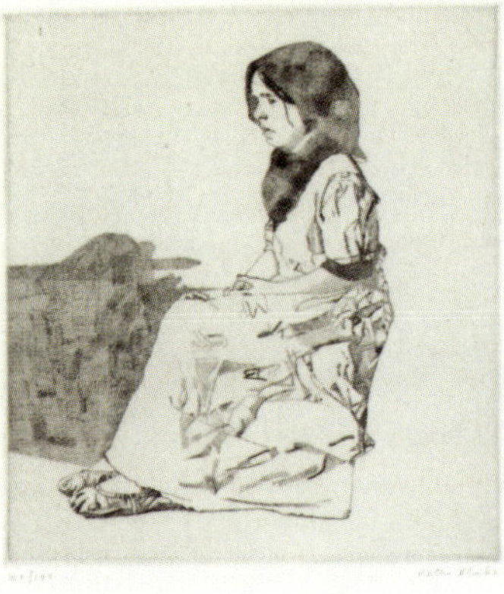

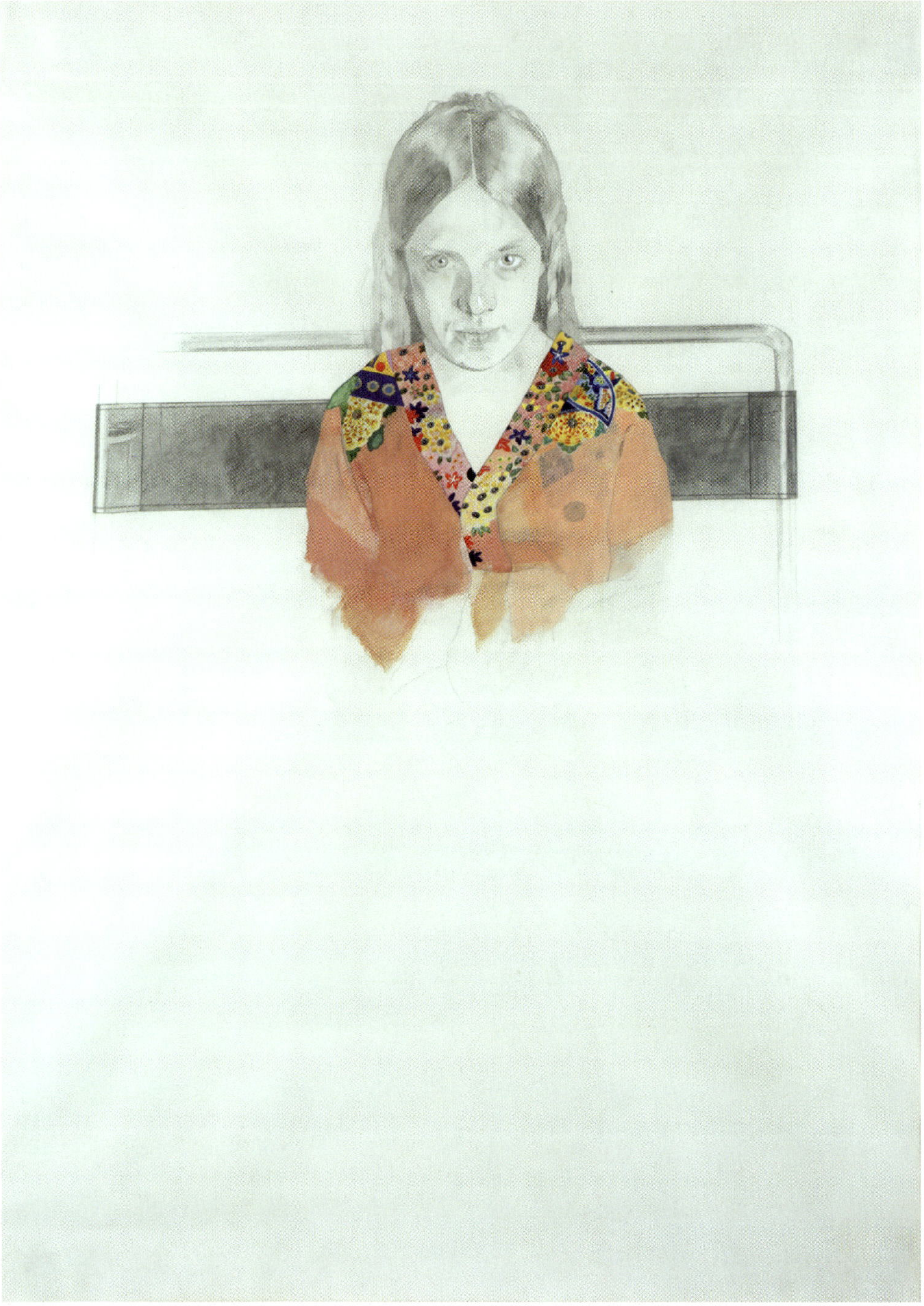

April en robe d'intérieur
1968
Watercolour and crayon

Girl in a Poppy Field
1974
Screenprint on paper

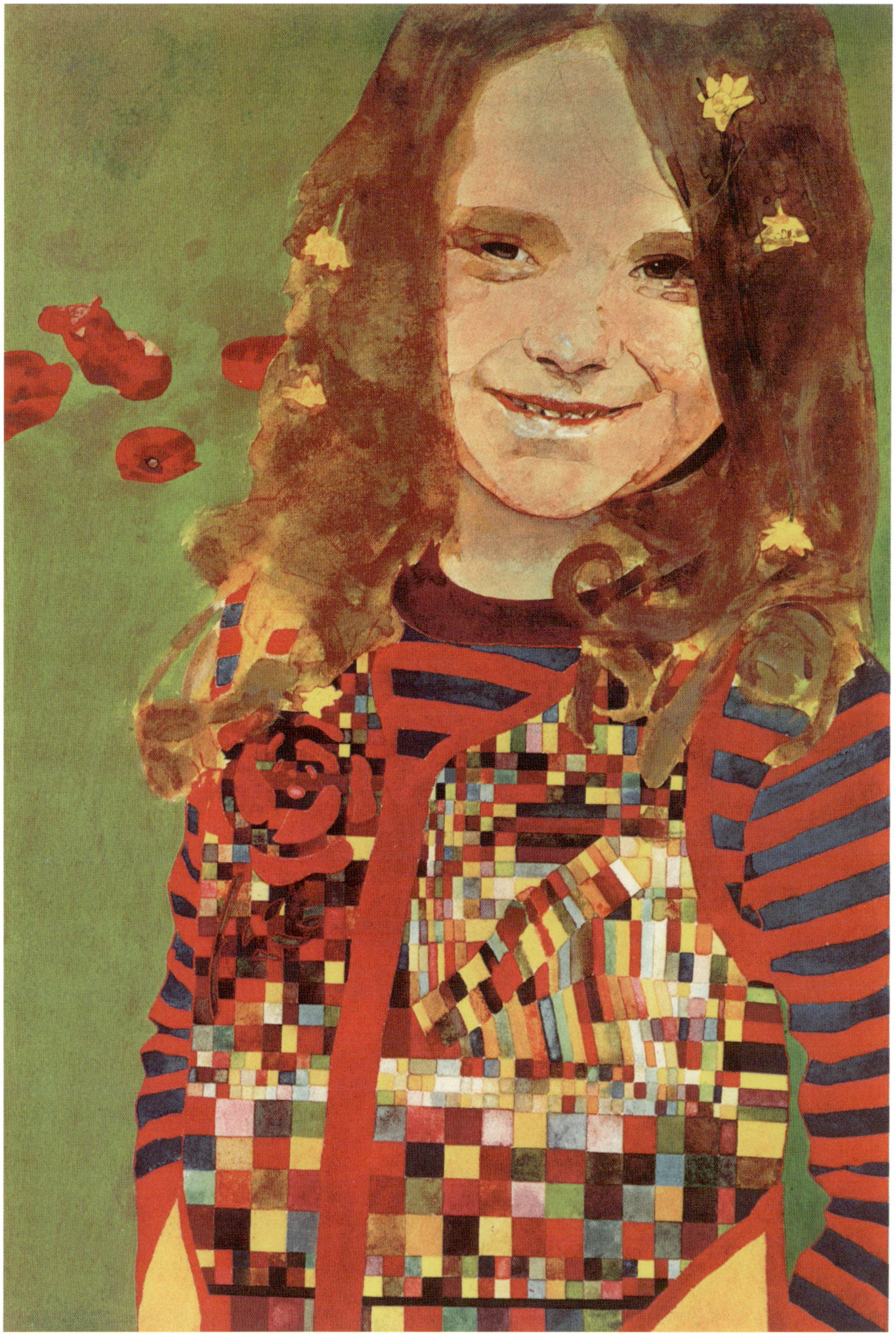

A Mad Tea Party at Watts Tower
1968 and 1992
Oil on canvas

and techniques. The courageous commitment to the ostensibly traditional can sometimes be far more explosive than the supposed provocations and outrages of the experimental vanguard. Ruralism is easily dismissed but in the long run has proven unpredictable and full of surprises, as changing tastes resurrect once unpopular styles and movements. By the end of the decade one of Blake's most vitriolic critics, Peter Fuller, had almost performed the ideological about-turn from Marxist to radical Ruskinite, painting was back in vogue and a triumphant celebration of Blake's oeuvre to date was on the horizon at the Tate Gallery. In many ways, his work captured the mood of the country better than some of the self-involved meditations on the role of art and the artist in society. It reflected a growing crisis of imagination, ecological concerns, economic decline and inner-city deprivation in a deep yearning for playful fantasies, engaging and emotive subject matter, authentic experiences and unspoiled nature. It might have lacked explicit criticality yet obviously did have a broader relevance, as the public reception of Blake's work confirmed.

The period is dominated by literary subjects drawn from the canon of English literature shared with the Victorians, with Shakespeare and Lewis Carroll featuring particularly strongly. *Alice's Adventures in Wonderland* is the theme of one of the earliest treatments of literary subject matter, Blake's A Mad Tea Party at Watts Tower 1968 and 1992, appropriately transporting Alice and her fellow guests to the fantastic architecture of Simon Rodia's Watts Tower in Los Angeles, which the artist had visited in 1963. In 1970, he and Graham Ovenden were invited to illustrate the Alice books, and Blake produced eight watercolours illustrating Through the Looking Glass which were later also published as prints.[15] The series concentrates on Alice, typically combining the fantastical world of the story with very real people and places. Blake worked with photographs, using a friend's children as models, as well as combining a wide range of source material from magazines, the work of other artists, personal and found photographs and the inspiration of Wellow and his children (his daughter's rainbow-coloured socks, for example, ending up on Tweedledum). *Alice* was an important introduction to the thematic universe of Ruralism *avant le lettre*, leading to the central subject of fairies that dominated the 1970s.

15
See Lewis Carroll, *Through the Looking-Glass and What Alice Found There*, illustrated by Peter Blake, preface by Marco Livingstone, London and New York, Merrell, 2006; and Natalie Rudd, *Peter Blake*, London, Tate Publishing, 2003, pp. 72–3.

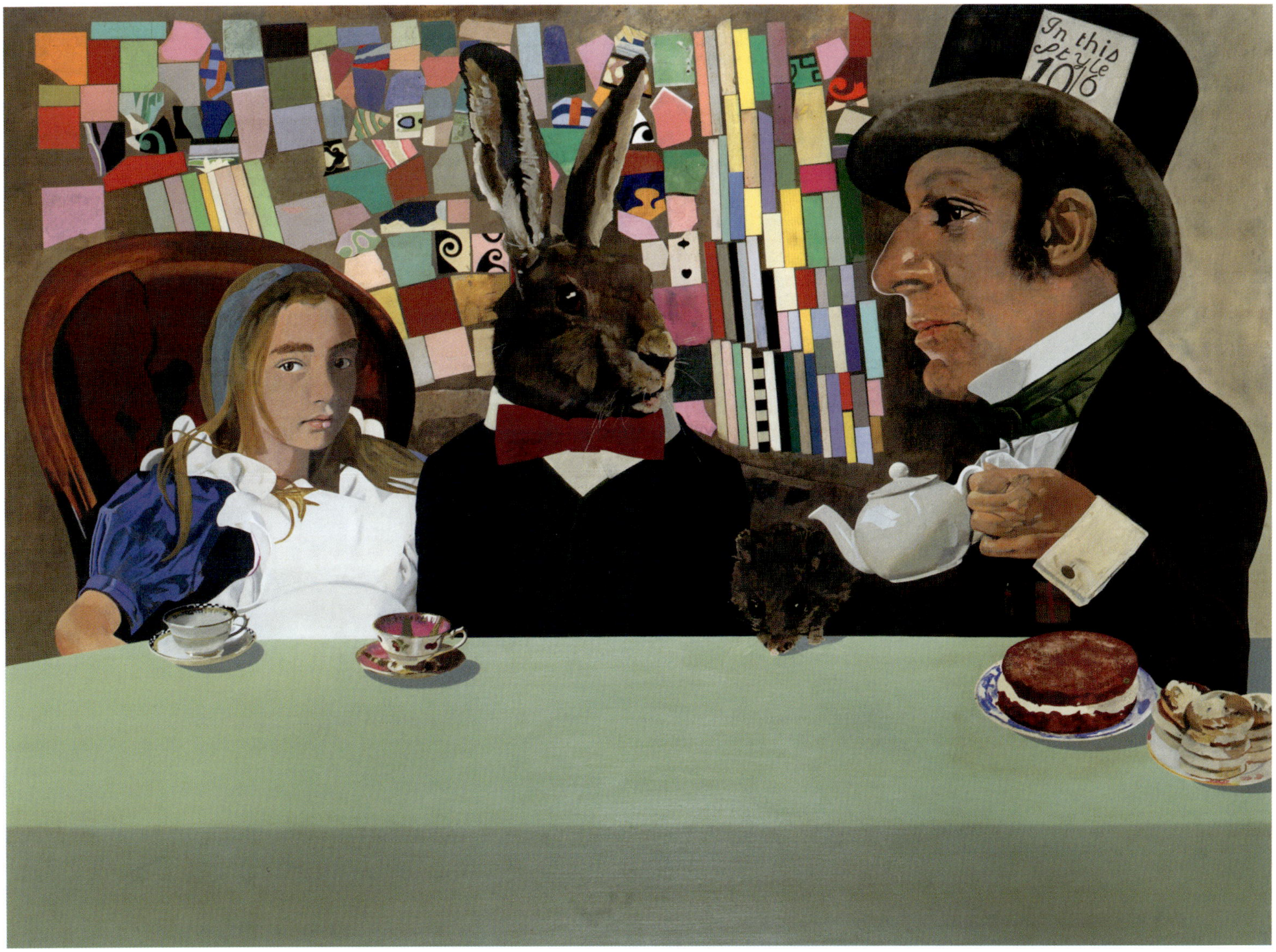
In this
style
10/6

'and to show you I'm not proud, you may shake hands with me!'
from *Illustrations to Through the Looking-Glass* 1970
Screen-print on paper

'and the two knights sat and looked at each other without speaking'
from *Illustrations to Through the Looking-Glass* 1970
Screen-print on paper

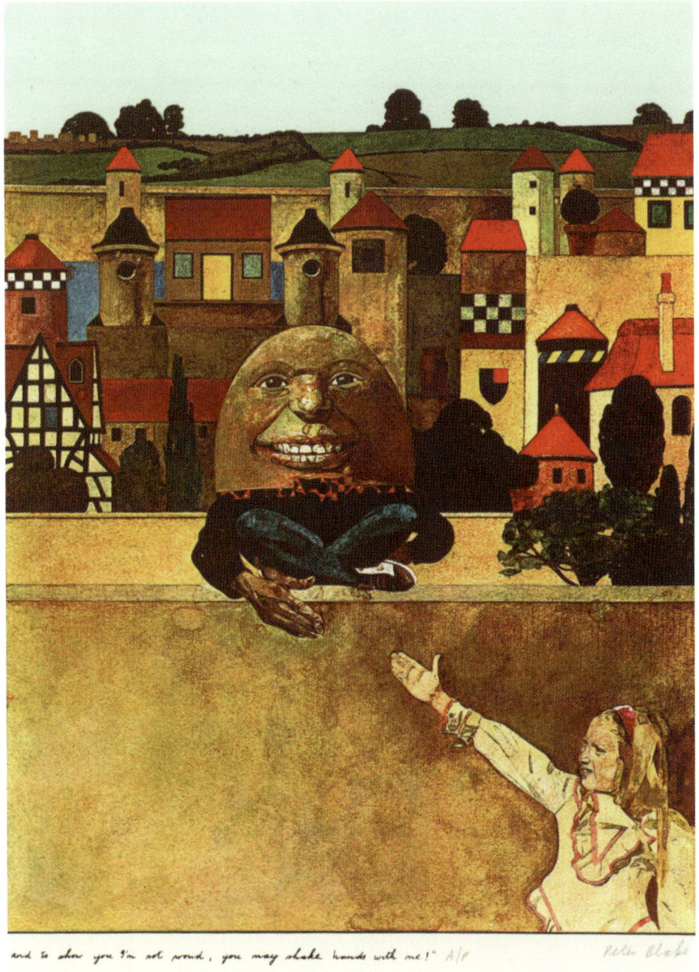

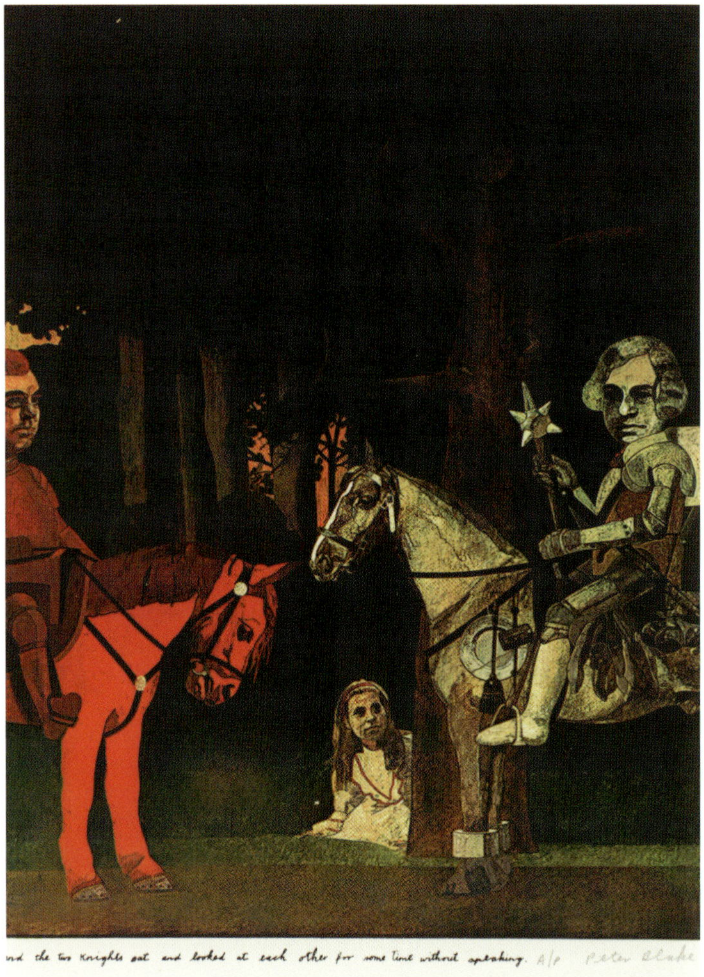

'But isn't it old!' Tweedledum cried
from *Illustrations to Through the Looking-Glass* 1970
Screen-print on paper

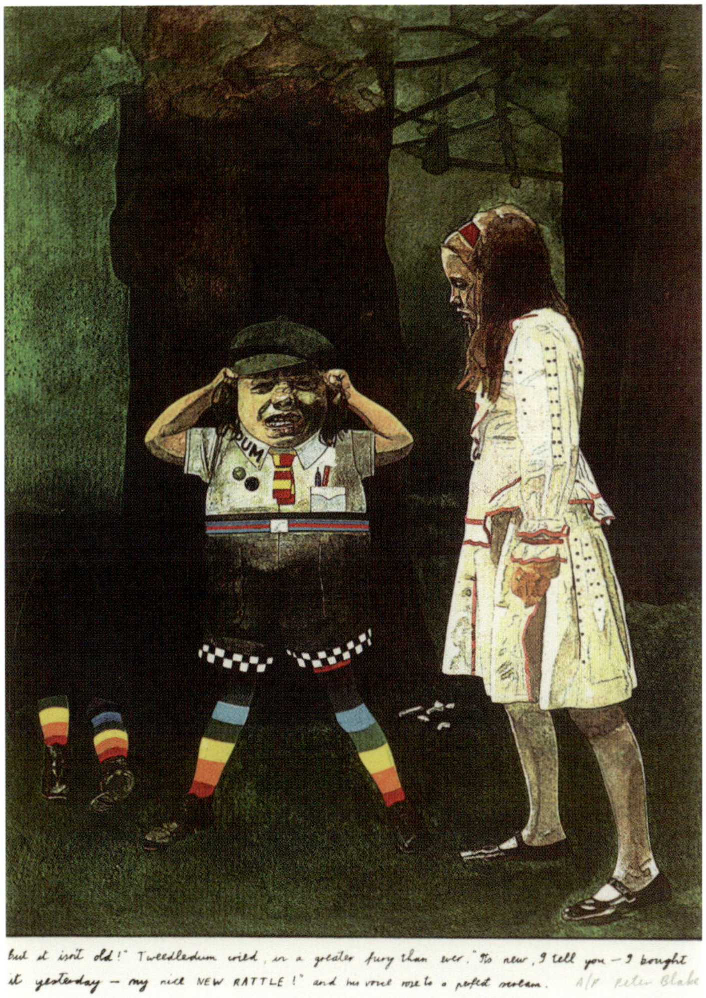

'It isn't manners for us to begin, you know', said the Rose
from *Illustrations to Through the Looking-Glass* 1970
Screen-print on paper

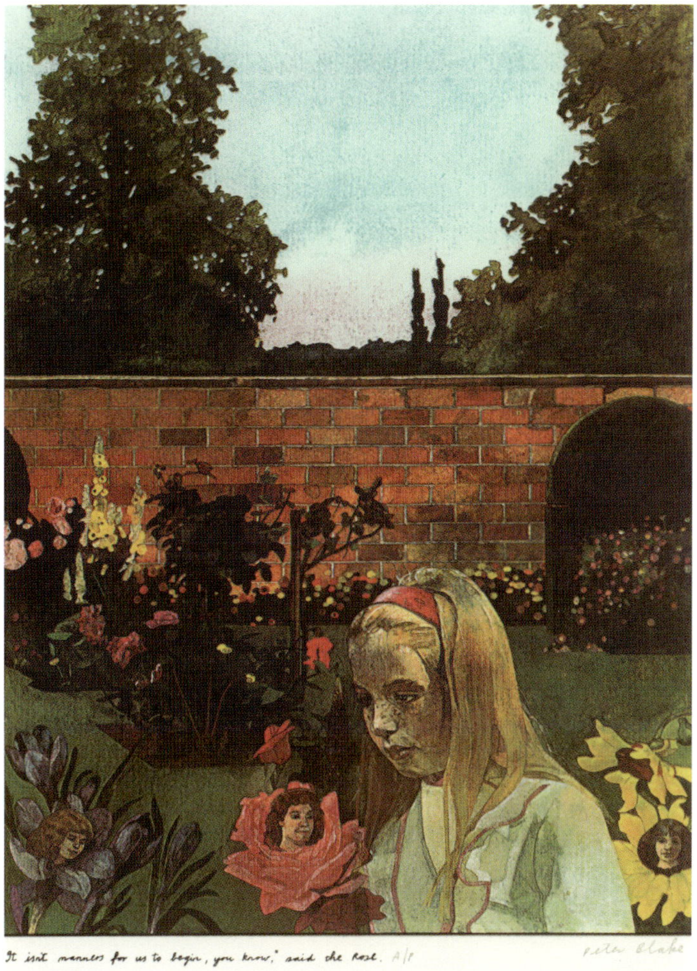

'For instance now, now there's the King's messenger'
from *Illustrations to Through the Looking-Glass* 1970
Screen-print on paper

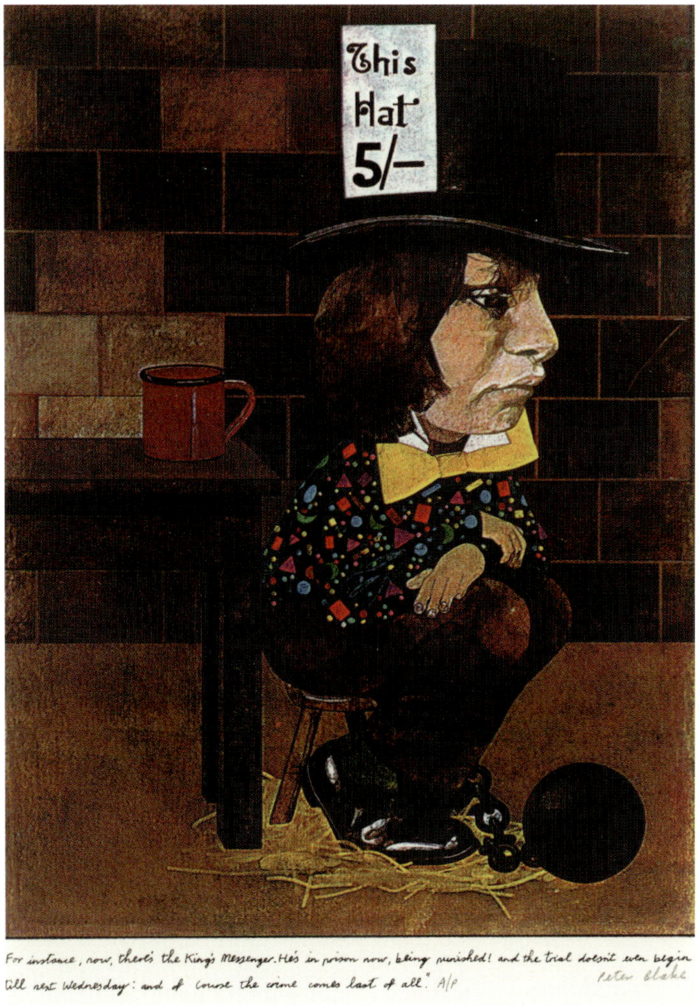

Just at this moment, somehow or other, they began to run
from *Illustrations to Through the Looking-Glass* 1970
Screen-print on paper

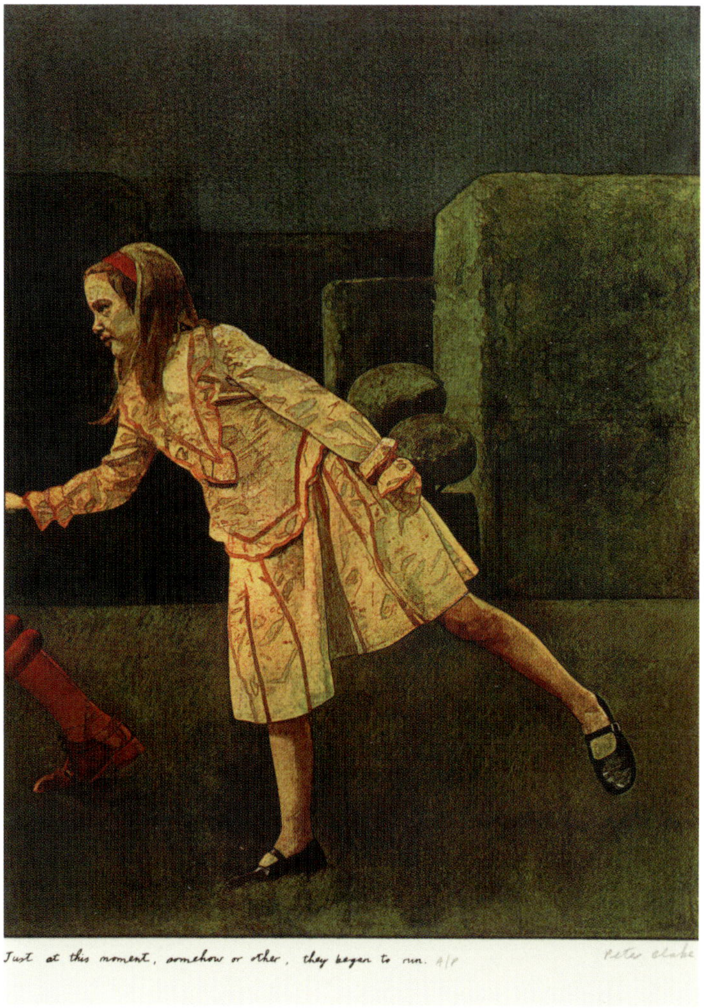

So Alice picked him up very gently
from *Illustrations to Through the Looking-Glass* 1970
Screen-print on paper

'Well, this is grand!' said Alice
from *Illustrations to Through the Looking-Glass* 1970
Screen-print on paper

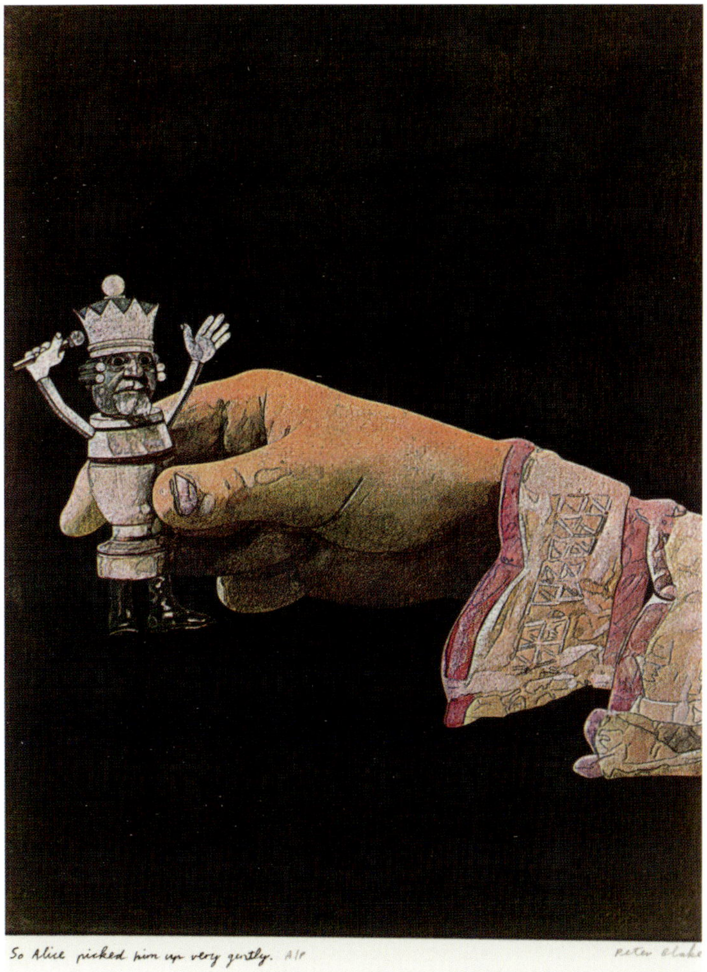

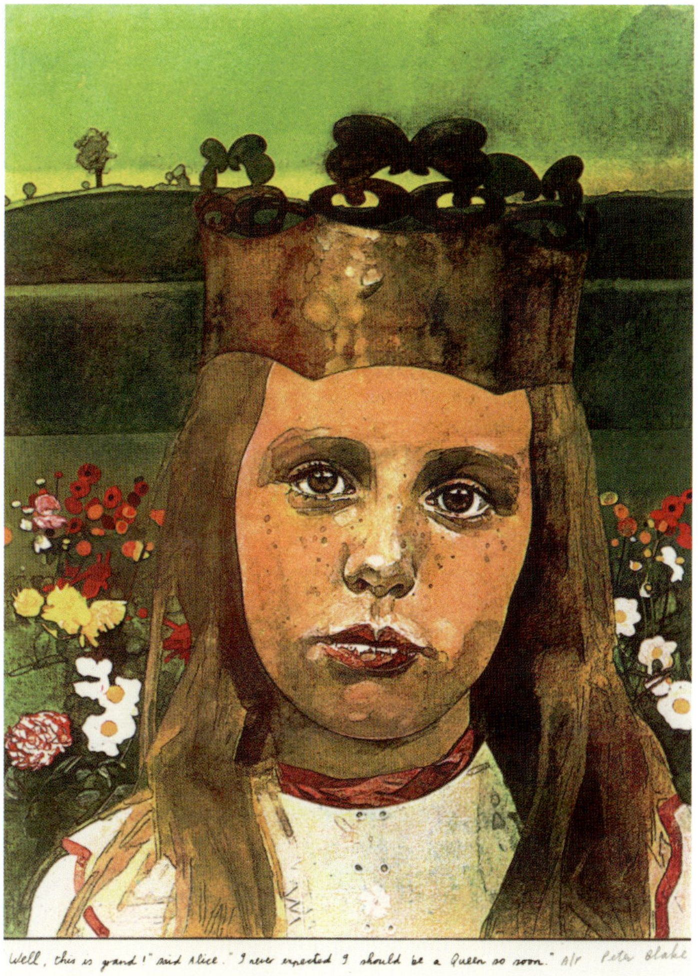

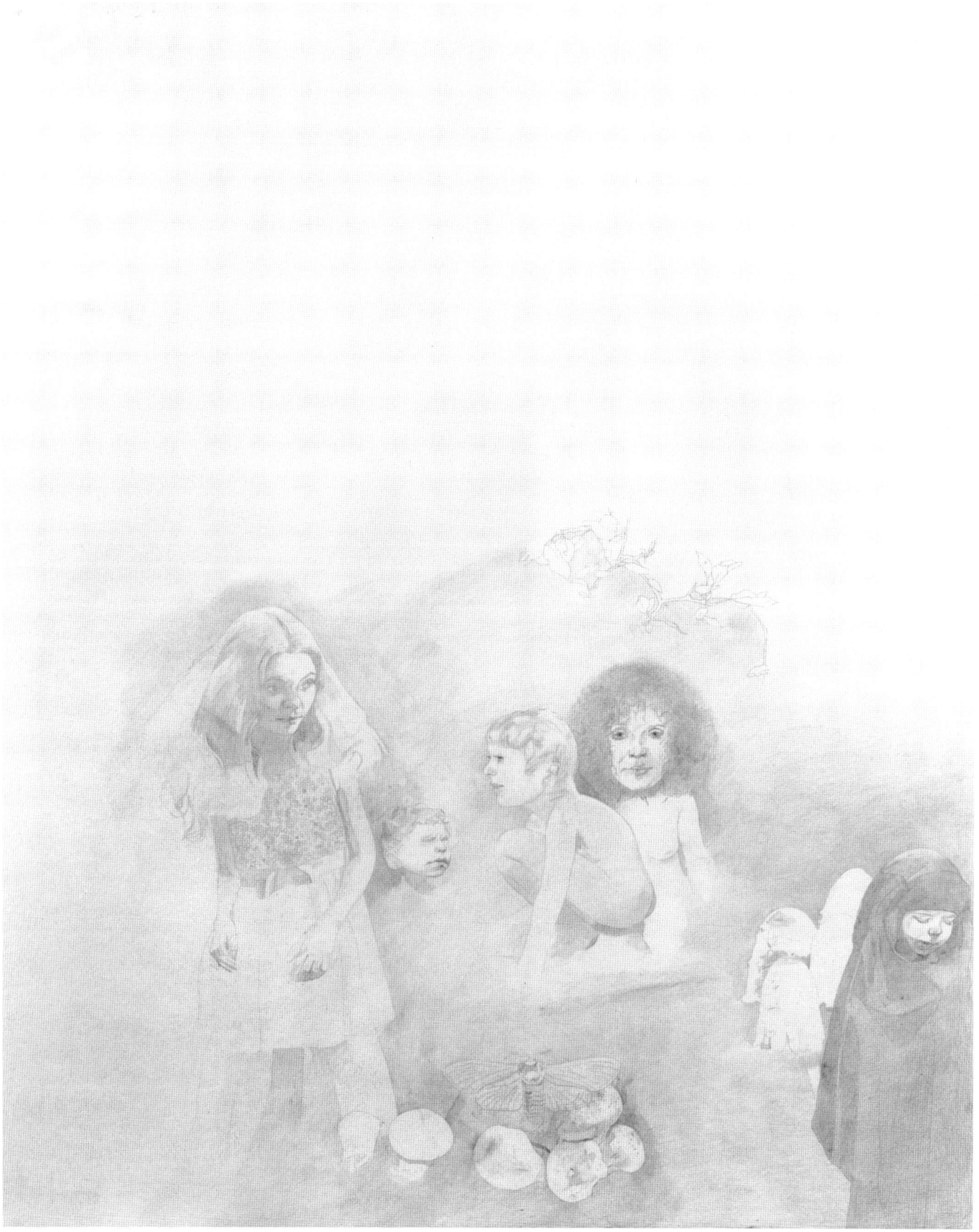

Death of a Moth
1972
Pencil on paper

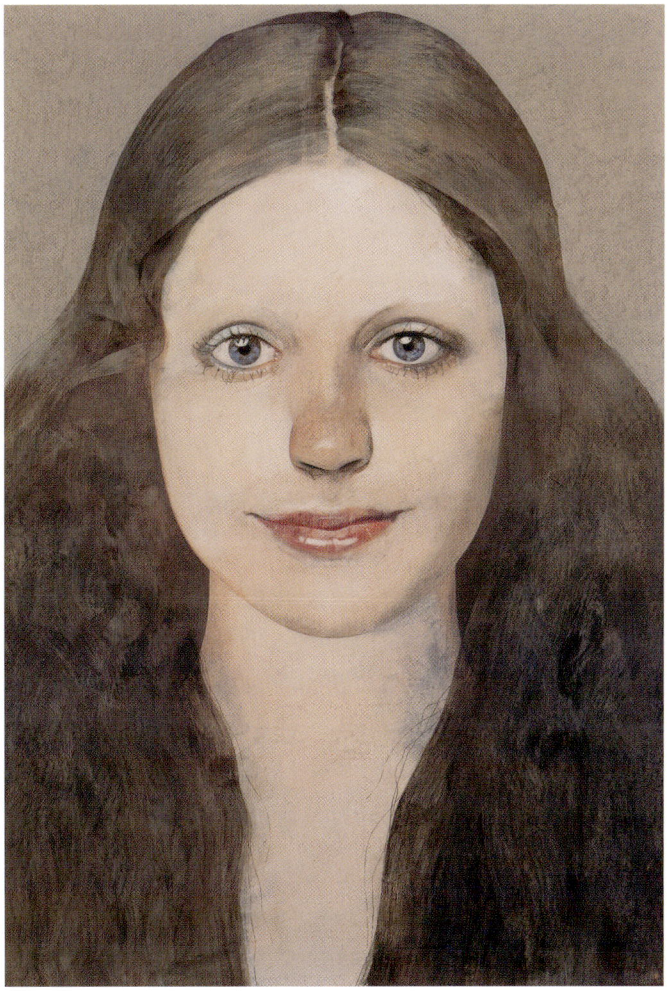

Titania
1972–4
Oil on board

Titania is a key theme of the period, treated in a number of important works during the 1970s, most prominently in the painting of the same title created between 1976 and 1983, its extended genealogy and serial reworking typical of Blake's working method. The highly sexualised pin-up girls of the previous decade have metamorphosed into the Queen of Fairies and wife of Oberon from Shakespeare's *A Midsummer Night's Dream*, an appropriately literary subject of central importance for the Ruralists during this period. The work continues the direct frontal confrontation with the subject found in so many of Blake's compositions, starting with Self Portrait in RAF Jacket c.1952–53 and On the Balcony 1955–57, here enhanced by the fragile nudity of the portrayed girl. Early versions of the work show a more stylised figure with a face surrounded by a flat and static aura of red hair, clearly inspired by ancient Egyptian sculpture, turning Titania into an animated Sphinx transported across millennia to the present. At this early stage, Titania seems to be standing in water and some of the dream figures blend into the brown background, while in the final version she wears boots made from leaves and is surrounded by a circus of fairies in blue. At the time of the 1983 retrospective, the work was shown in its nearly final stage, only missing some of the magic pendants around the neck and belly.

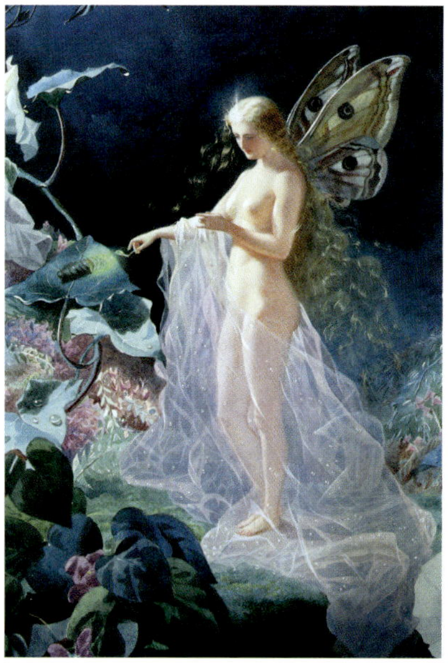

John Simmons
Titania 1866 (detail)
Watercolour and body colour

Blake's fairies are creatures firmly rooted in the present, not rarely seen mythical apparitions but very real people based on contemporary figures, including, among others, elements of the supermodel Twiggy, whom Blake portrayed in the 1960s. In this respect, Blake's Titania differs radically from, for example, John Simmons' watercolour of 1866, which presents a purified vision of a virginal, butterfly-winged creature symbolising innocence as much as unity with nature. Blake's Titania is a construct of closely observed models, photographs and fantasy beings, existing between dream and reality as the figure rises, not from an idyllic garden but from the dark waters of memory populated by attendant lesser fairies (described by Puck in the play as 'shadows' and 'visions' appearing in a 'dream'). Titania draws on the dramatic chiaroscuro of Fuseli's Gothic nightmares, as well as on the conventions of filmic representation as a form of dream imagery – animated projections of remembered moments in cinematic blue. Titania is depicted in a state of trance, intently staring ahead yet obviously taking in the apparitions

Titania
1976–83, work in progress
Oil on canvas

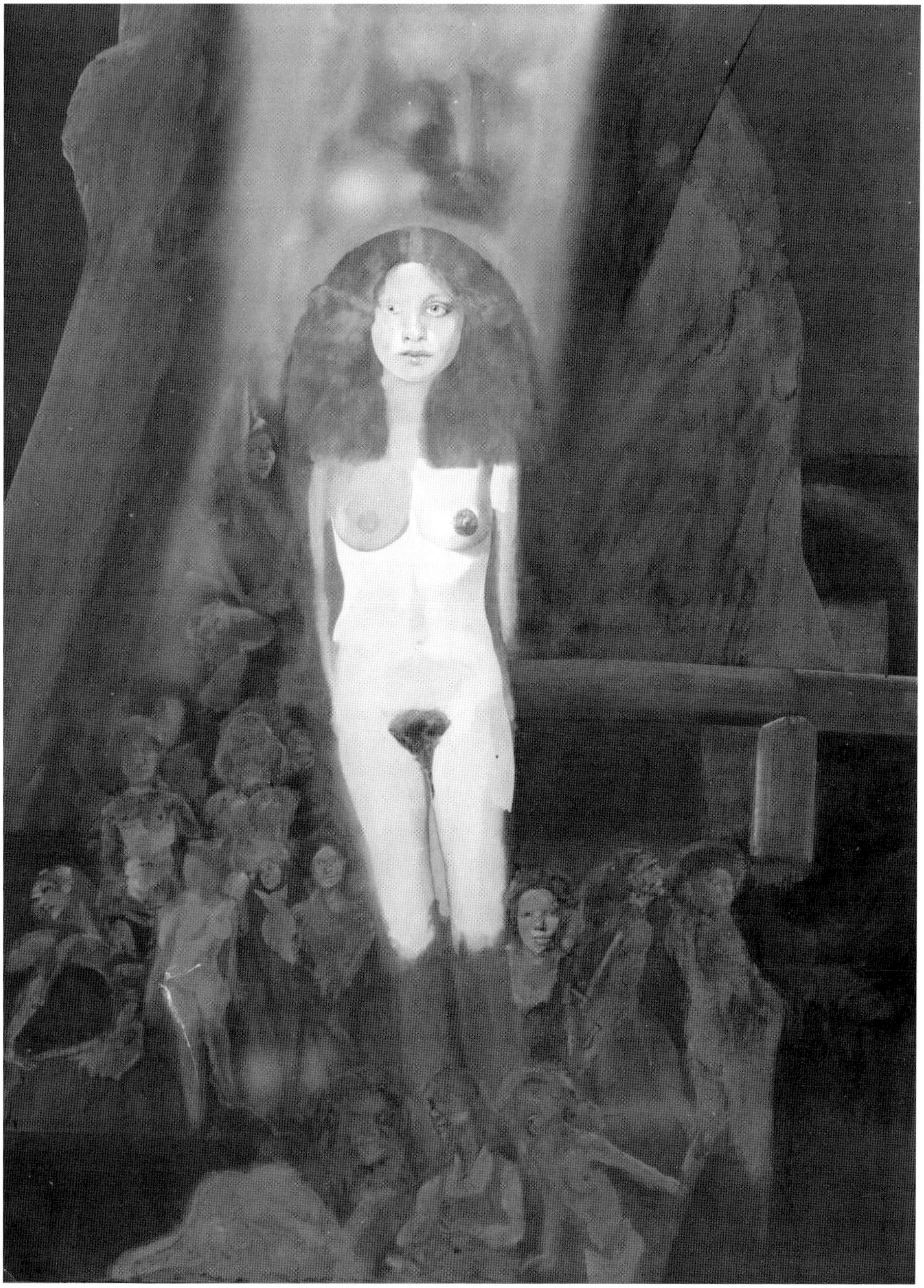

Titania
1976–83
Oil on canvas

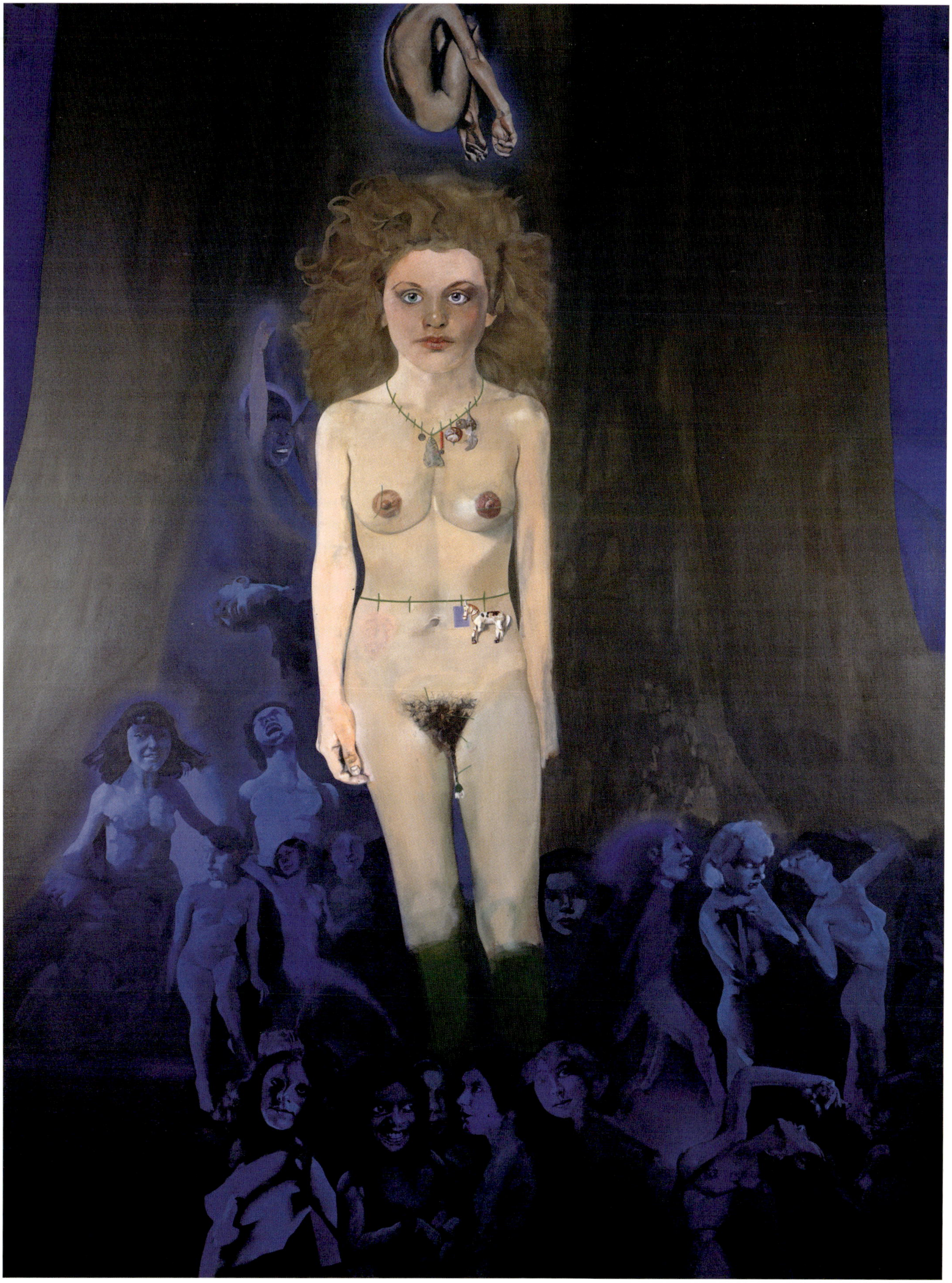

surrounding her. As in Fuseli and Victorian fairy painting, the dream state is here lived through with the intensity of real events, Titania existing in a simultaneous state of reality, vision and memory.

Blake had a long-standing interest in fairy literature and collected fairy books, an interest that was reawakened through reading to his daughter Liberty. *A Midsummer Night's Dream* was an extraordinarily popular subject from the Romantics onwards, with a proliferation of treatments in the second half of the nineteenth century. Blake's representation draws on the flowing gods, ghosts and spirits of William Blake and in particular Fuseli, who treated the subject several times, notably in *Titania and Bottom* c.1790, showing a varied assembly of fairies. Blake particularly admired Joseph Noël Patton, Richard Doyle and, above all, Richard Dadd and his obsessive-compulsive masterpiece *The Fairy Feller's Master Stroke* 1855–64.[16] At the same time, Titania follows the internal logic and personal mythology developed by Blake, who believed that, if fairies did indeed exist, they would live in the meadow below the stream near his house. Drawing on his long interest in the literary and visual Victorian fairy genre, he developed a fairy hierarchy that categorised the King and Queen of the fairies as half human scale, while lesser fairies would be smaller, down to a workman just half an inch tall. As no clothes exist in fairyland, Titania is dressed in a rather rudimentary outfit consisting of daisies in her pubic hair and green leaves for boots. Her 'non-functional' attire includes found objects and talismans: a shell, a stone, a conker, a spark plug and a toy horse. The action itself as depicted by Blake follows Shakespeare, with a column of fairies tumbling down in the background while others dance around Titania. The exalted fairies, including a coy Marilyn Monroe, with their exaggerated (almost formulaic) dancing gestures, leave the picture on the right-hand side to return moving into the opposite direction on the lower frame of the painting. Fairies at the feet of Titania discover the beholder, address him or her, laugh and run away, not unlike Puck talking directly to the audience in the finale of *A Midsummer Night's Dream*, extending the spell of this fantasy.

The enthusiasm for Shakespeare was shared by Blake's fellow travellers, and in 1980 the Ruralists decided to devote an entire exhibition to the subject of Ophelia. Blake's Ophelia 1977–2002 is a close relative to Titania, with a centrally

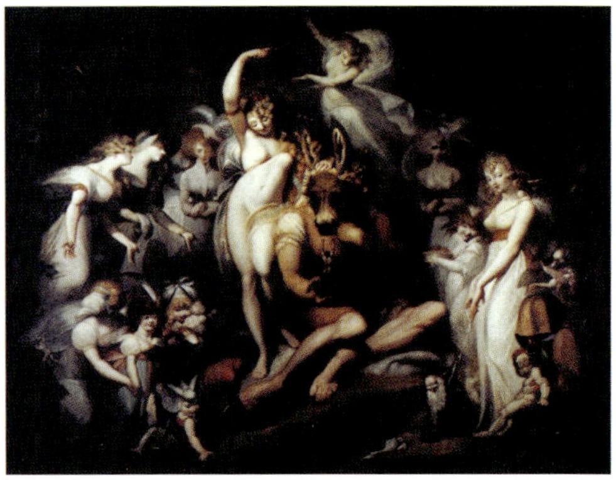

Johann Heinrich Fuseli
Titania and Bottom c. 1970
Oil on canvas

16
He tried several times, unsuccessfully, to acquire works by Richard Doyle. Interview with Peter Blake, 13 March 2007. See Jane Martineau (ed.), *Victorian Fairy Painting*, London, Merrell Holberton, 1997 for a comprehensive survey of the subject.

Richard Dadd
The Fairy Feller's Master Stroke
1855–64
Oil on canvas

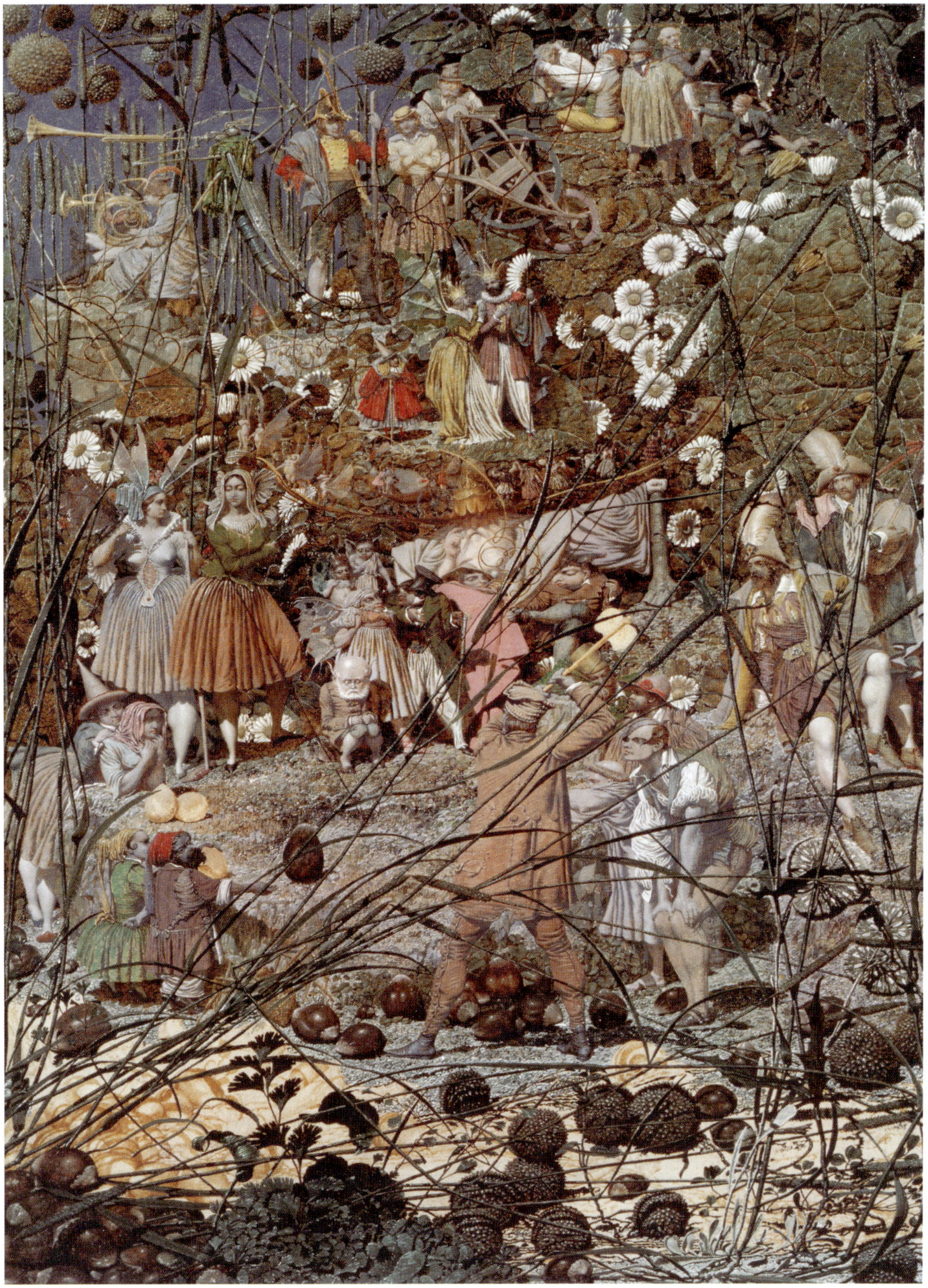

positioned, young, semi-naked figure directly confronting the viewer. The work originally lacked most of the iconographic attributes associated with the subject (in particular John Everett Millais' celebrated depiction of 1851–52), except for the half-immersion of the figure in water. As usual Blake developed his own, highly personal interpretations that breathe new life into well-known myths and narratives. As he explained, the depicted episode falls between Arthur Hughes and Millais' famous treatments in terms of its place in the narrative, reading between the lines of *Hamlet*. Originally, Ophelia was sitting on a branch, but in the course of Blake painting the work she 'fell off' into the pool of water and is now positioned in front of trees in the stream. Again, the fallen heroine is an all too real figure, approaching death as a vulnerable being with her soul and body literally laid bare, broken by her unrequited love. In a gesture of moving bathos, the flowers in Ophelia's hands are replaced by a bunch of naked branches, offered to the viewer in an act of pathetic fallacy. Following the principle of collage, Blake integrates isolated elements of classic interpretations of the subject (most importantly Arthur Hughes' painting of 1852), contemporary sources and his own inventions in a stripped-down composition that avoids all the appealing cuteness and absorbing proliferation of detail of the Victorian models. Blake's female protagonists of the Ruralist period are particularly delicate beings, mostly adolescent girls in various states of crisis, their frontal nudity and pale skin (perfectly captured in Blake's transparent layers of oil paint) exposing them remorselessly to the viewers' scrutiny.

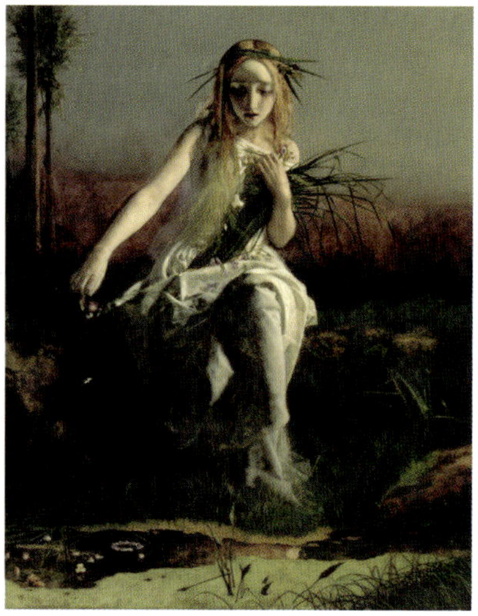

Arthur Hughes
Ophelia 1852 (detail)
Oil on panel

Blake executed a number of generic, usually small-scale fairy portraits during the period besides his literary treatments, transforming photographed and real subjects into youthful fairies. Flora – Fairy Child 1977 was based on a magazine photograph of a model named Florence, crowned with a wreath of flowers and elevated to the status of the Roman goddess of spring. Daisy Fairy 1981–82 takes Blake's daughter Daisy (born 1974) as inspiration and, again, by adorning the child with a wreath of daisies and a necklace of grass turns an earthly being into an otherworldly creature. Framing has always been a central compositional device to Blake, and he employed both painted and constructed frames as well as old-fashioned found frames, partly to create an architectural setting but also to achieve a spatial distancing between his revered subjects and the viewer. The use of

Ophelia
1977–2002, work in progress
Oil on board

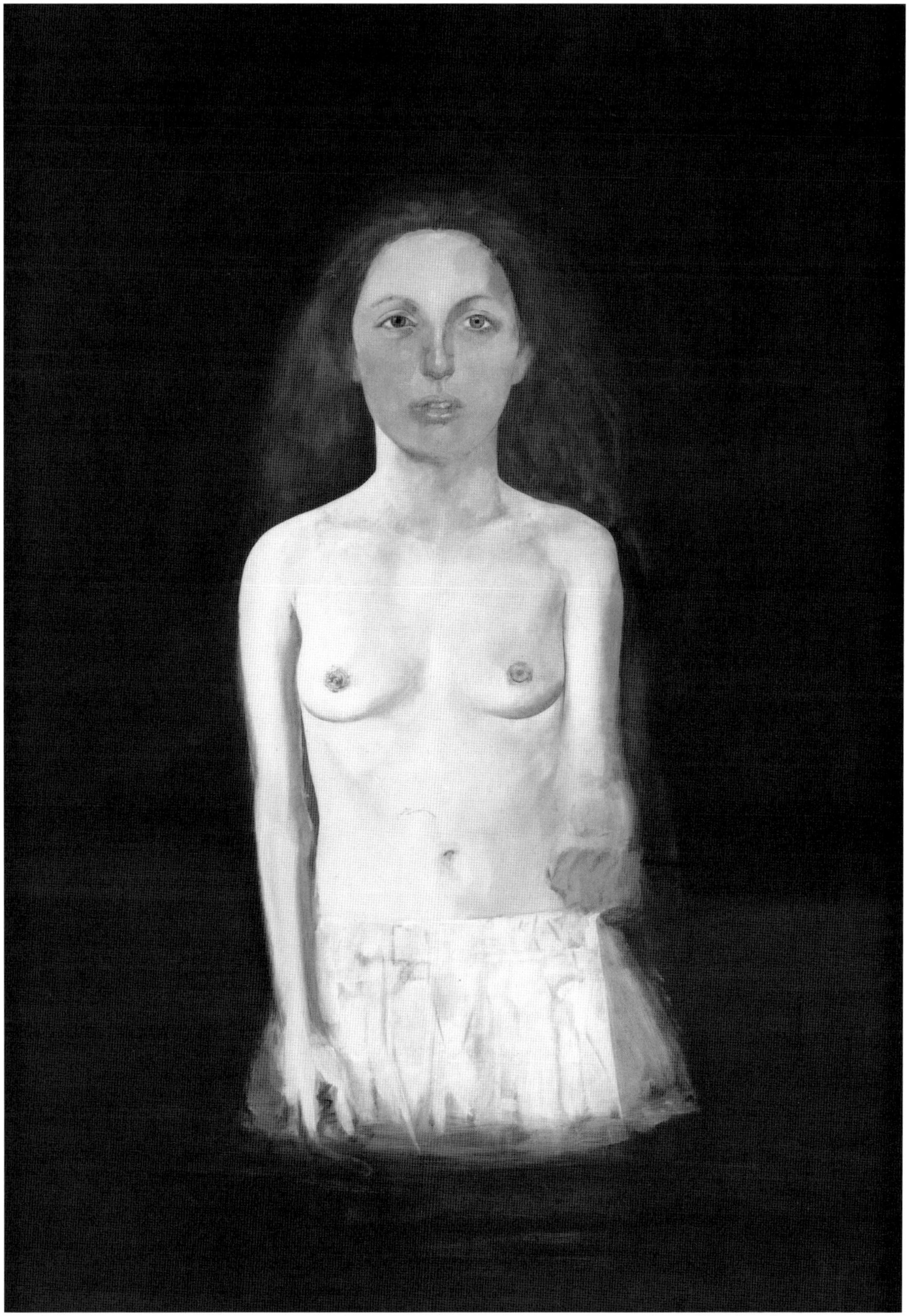

Ophelia
1977–2002
Oil on board

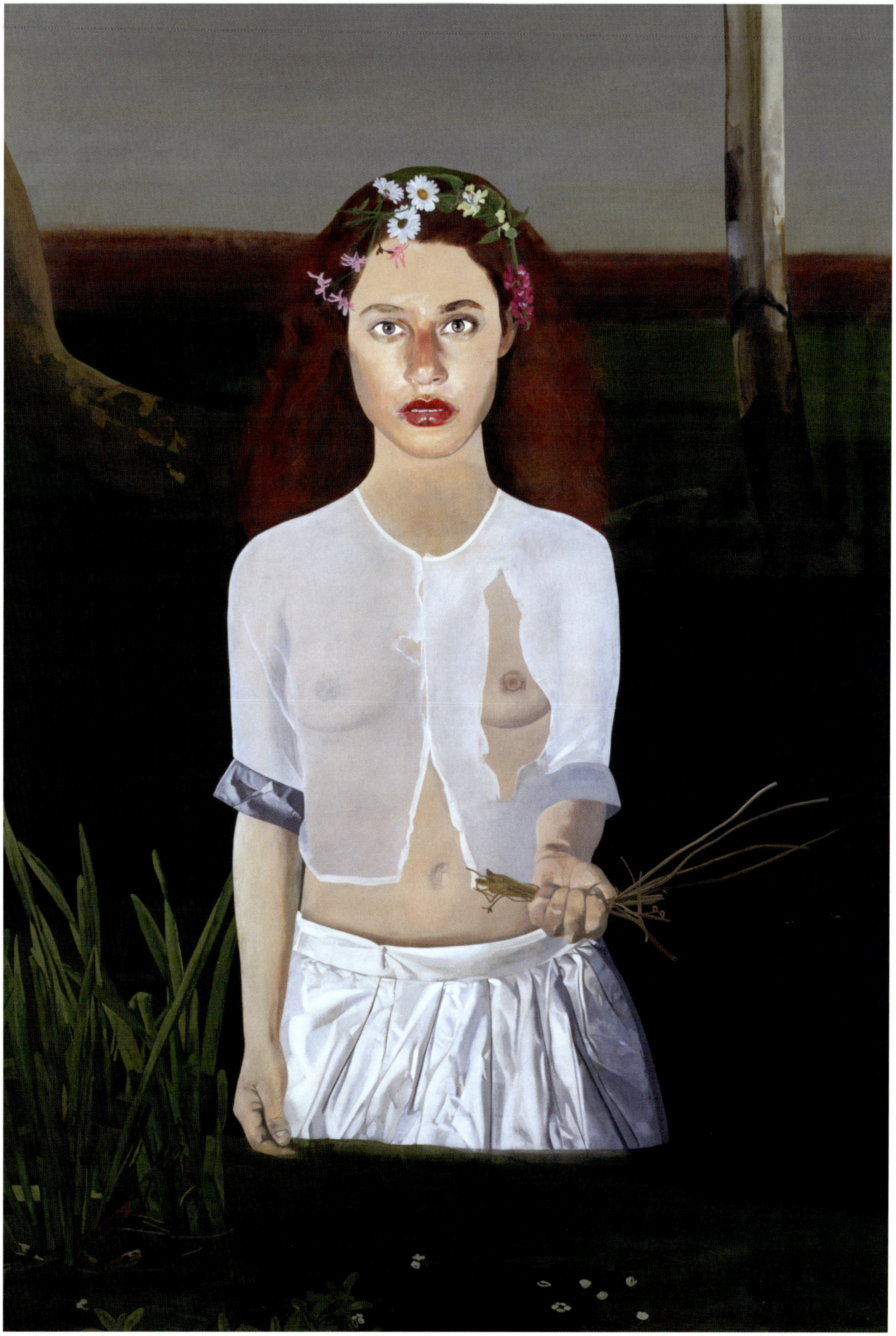

Daisy Fairy
1981–2
Oil on hardboard

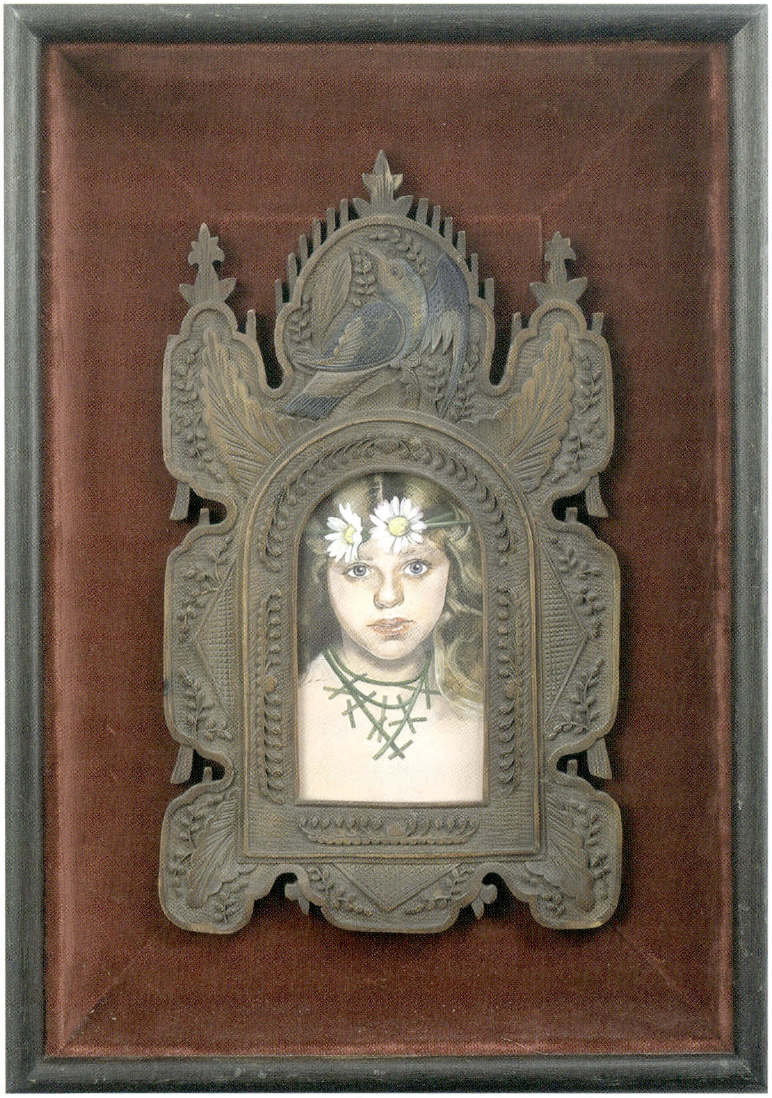

Flora – Fairy Child
1977
Oil on hardboard

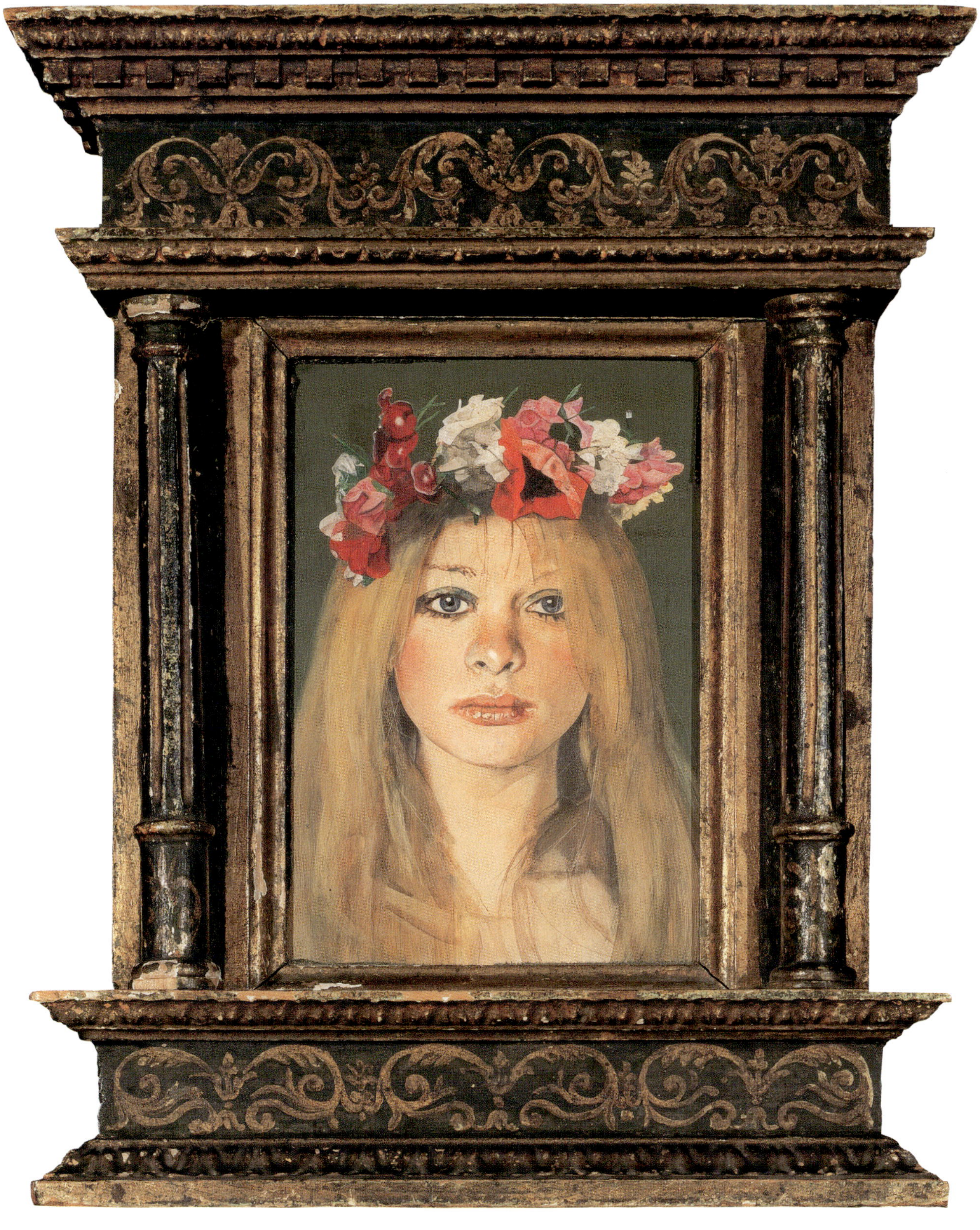

Nadia
1981
Oil on hardboard

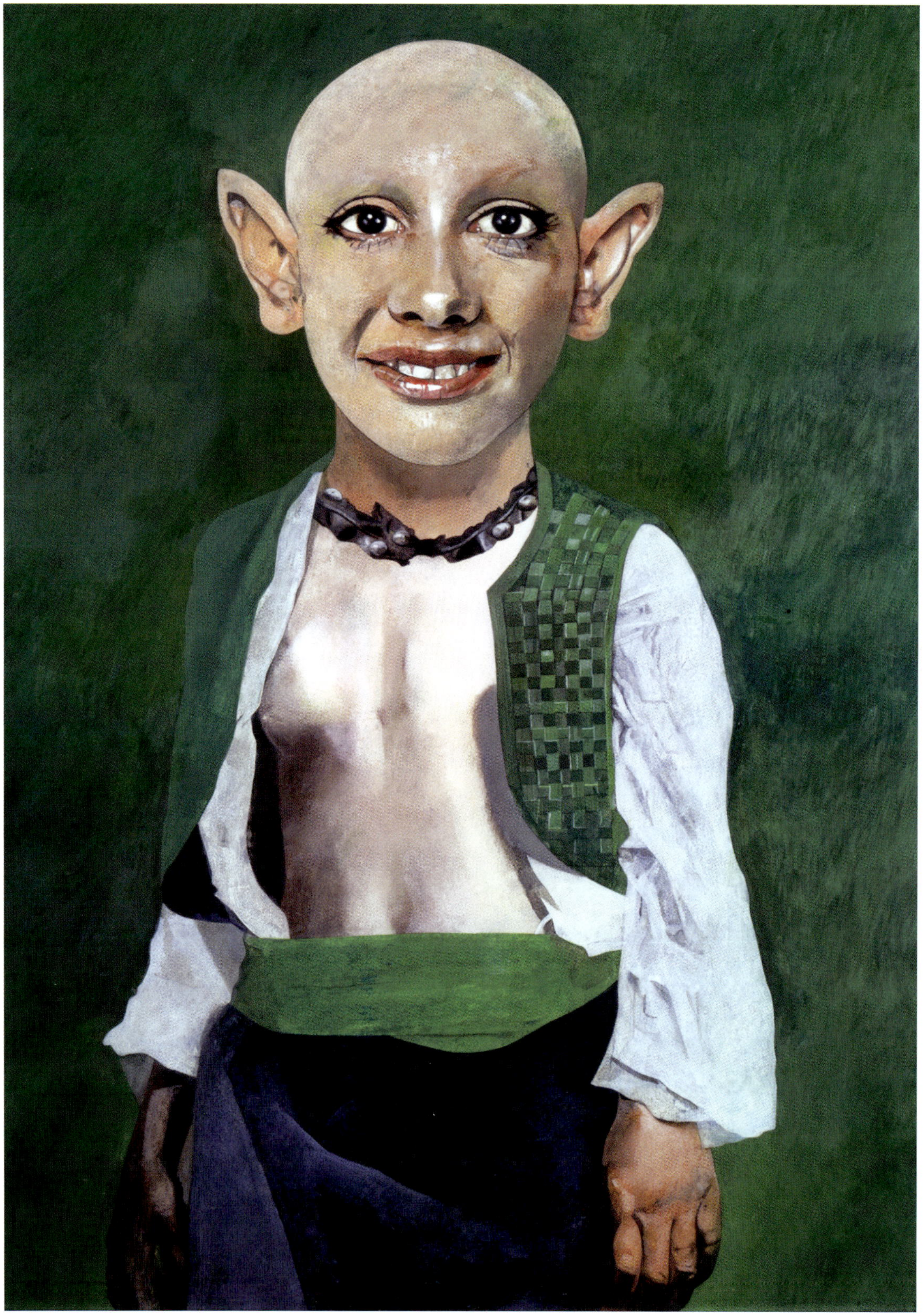

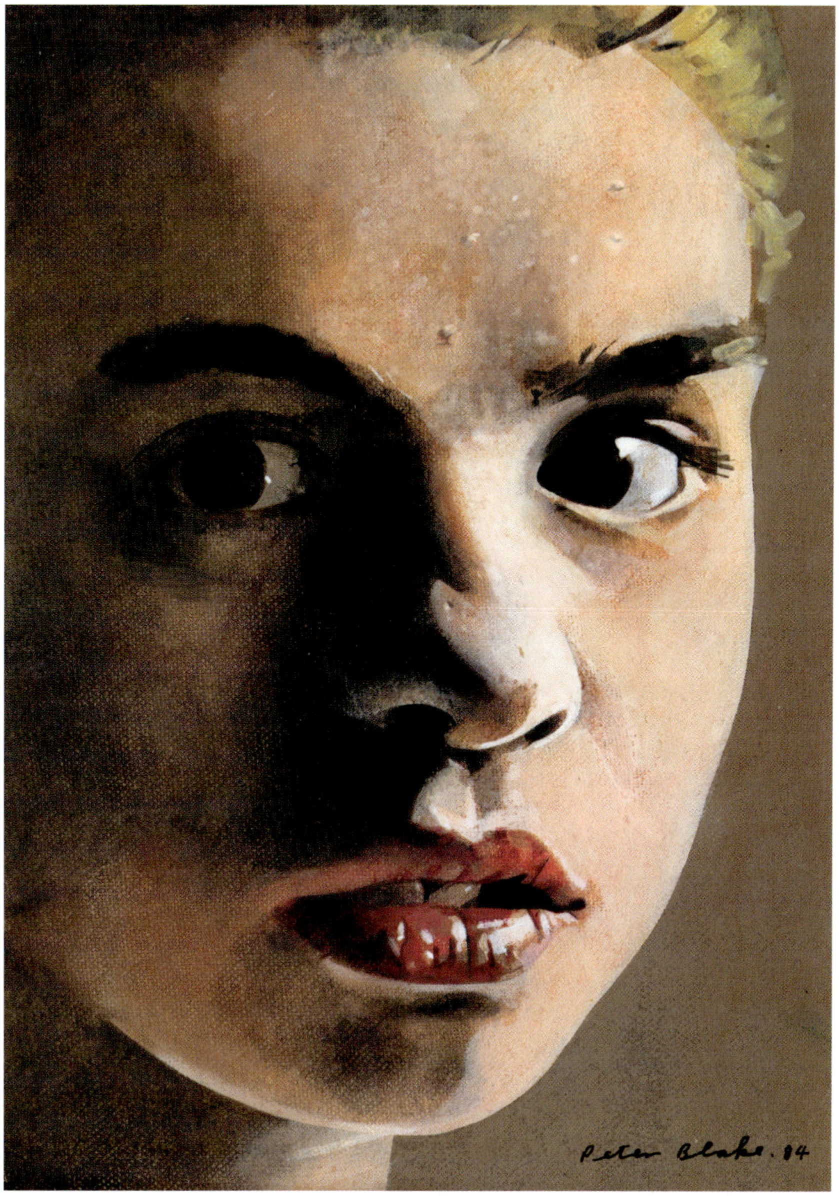

Boy Fairy VI
1984
Oil on canvas board

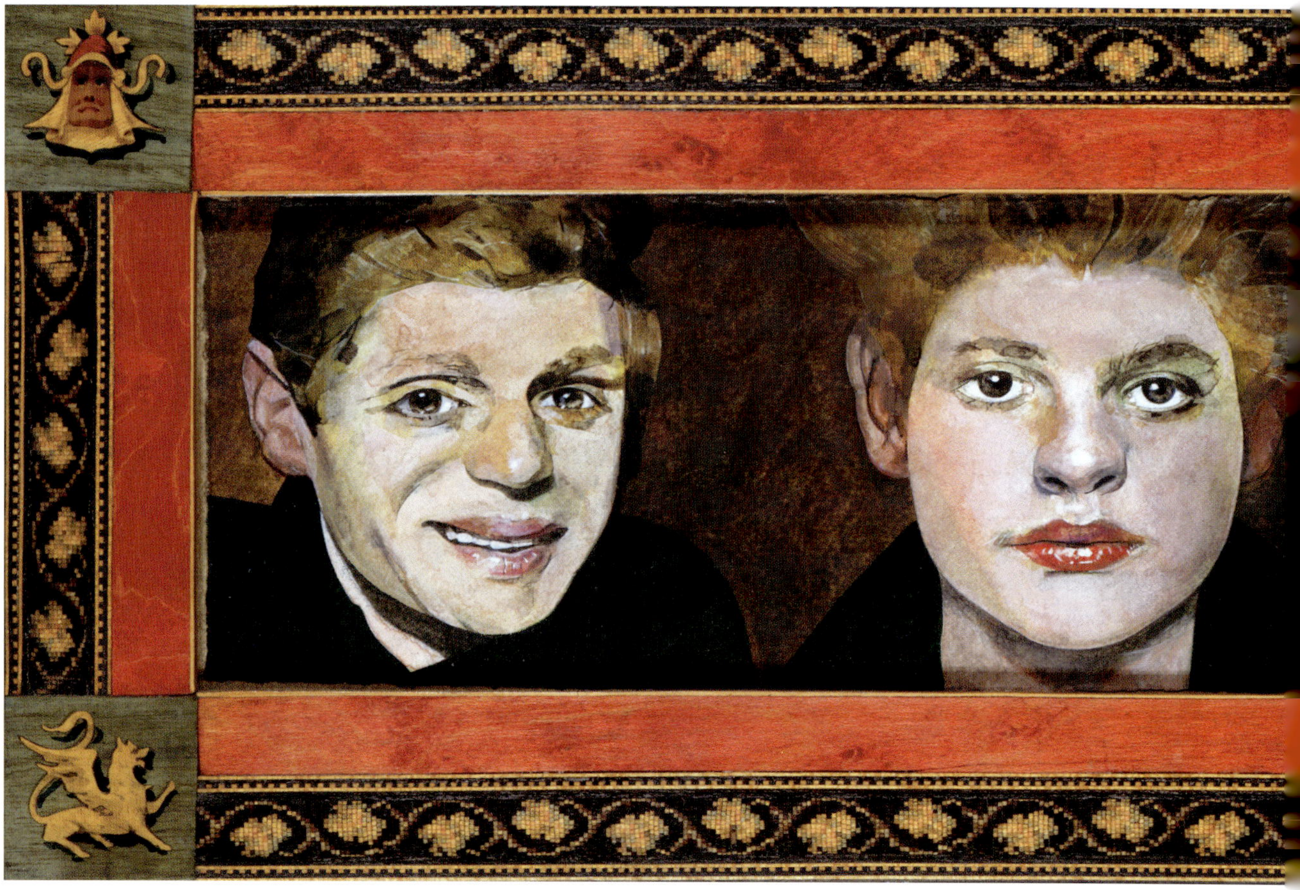

Hollywood Blondes v the Gilded Sluts
1977
Watercolour

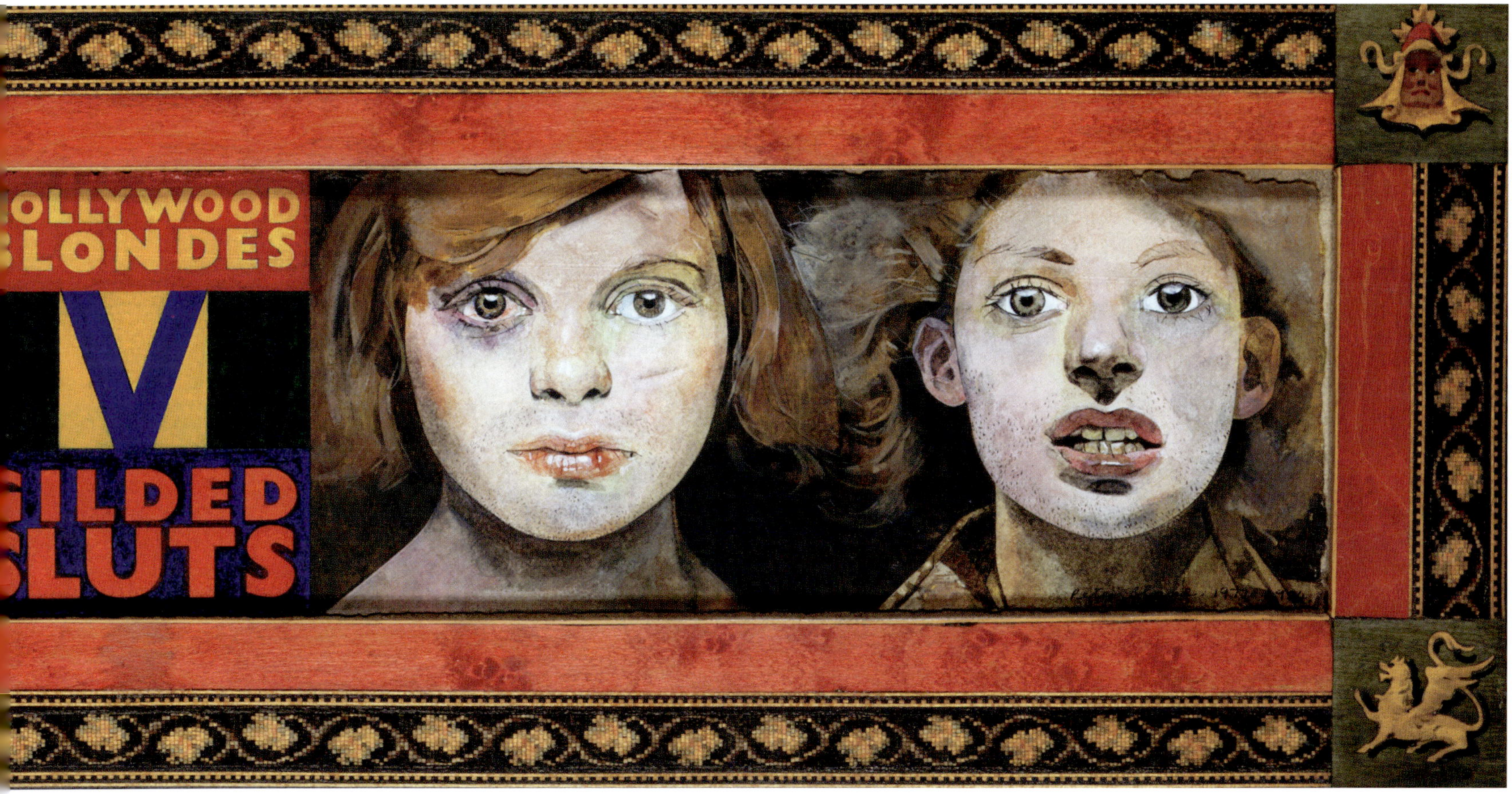

Ebony Tarzan
1972
Watercolour

Penny Black
1972
Watercolour

Pretty Boy Michael Angelo
1972
Watercolour

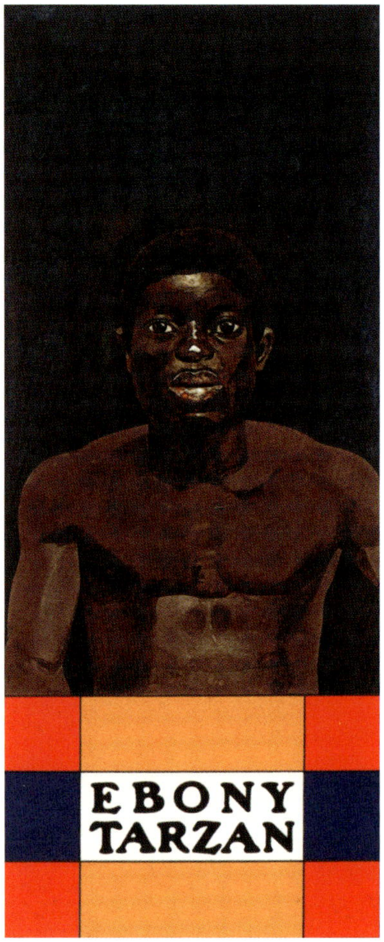

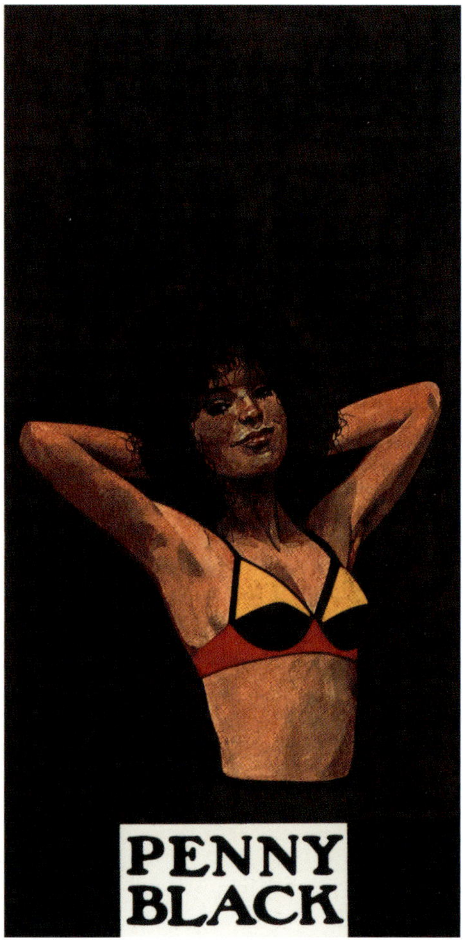

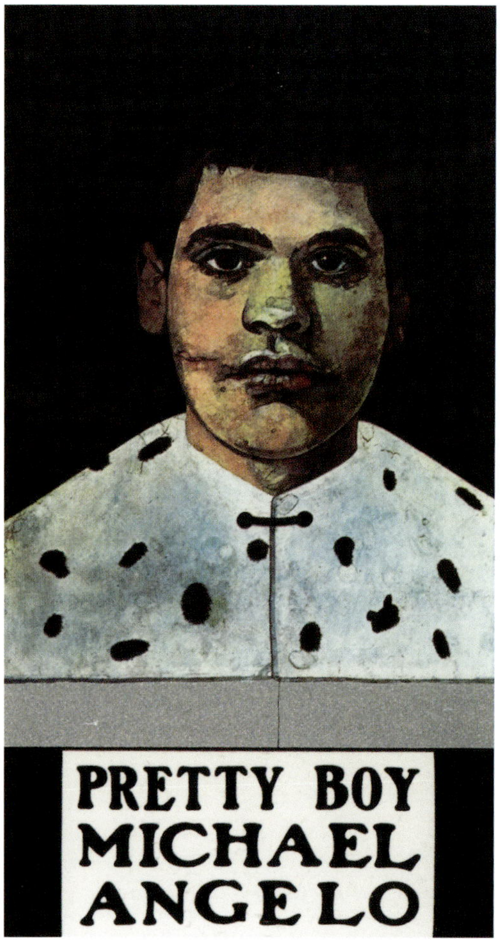

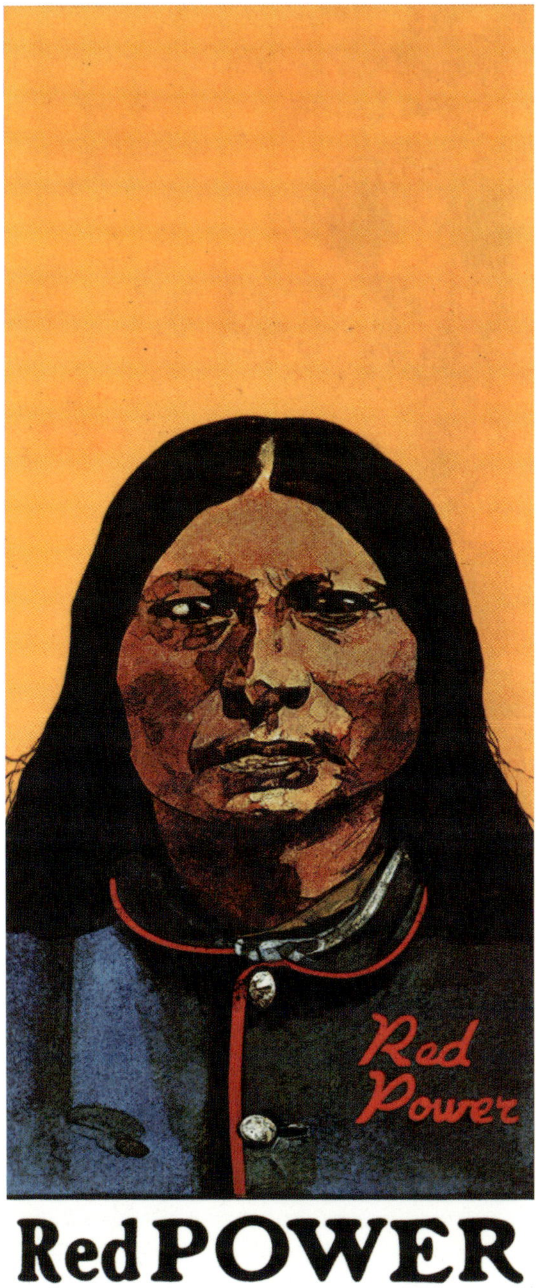

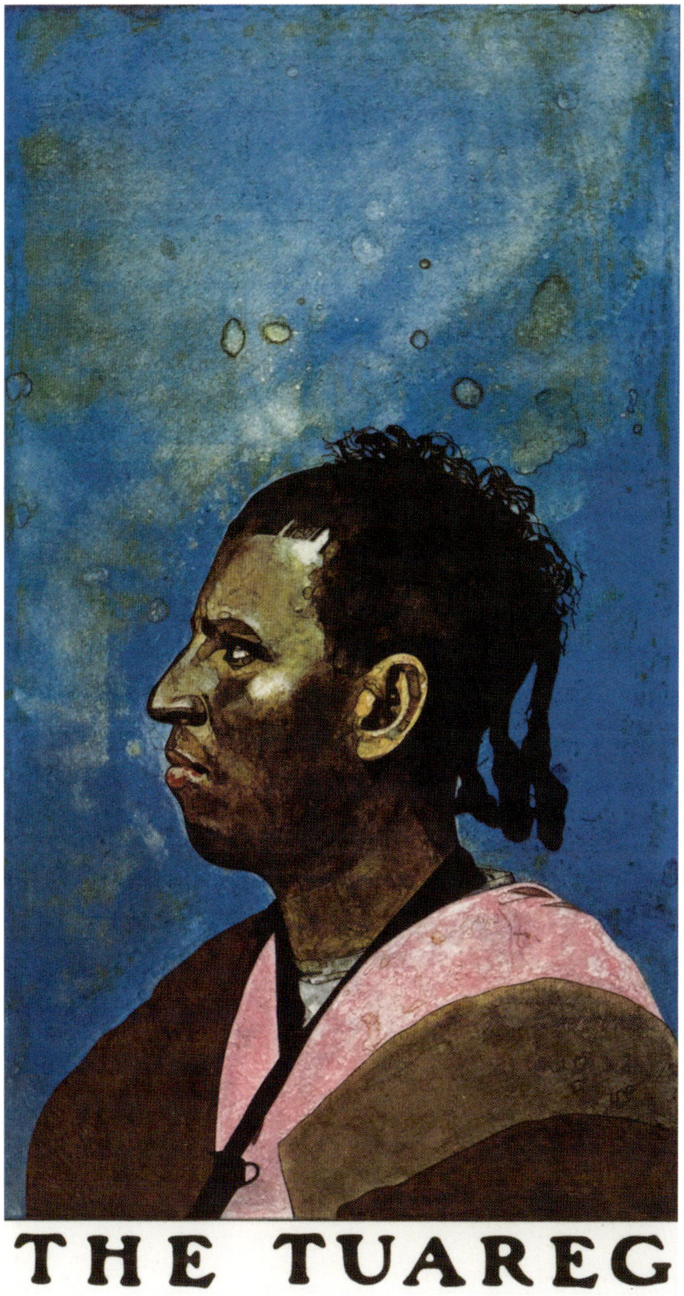

Red Power
1972
Watercolour

The Tuareg
1972
Watercolour

I may not be a Ruralist anymore but I saw a fairy in my garden in Chiswick
1982–91
Oil on canvas

ornate Italian Renaissance, intricate gilded Victorian and carved Asiatic frames during the 1970s represented a deliberate ploy to 'cock a snook', as Blake put it, at the reigning art practice of the time, for which framing had become all but irrelevant. These close-up portraits of children and adolescent girls in their precious surrounds confound their status as epitomes of innocence existing in a fantastic universe, parallel to our own. At the same time, Blake executed a series of drawings based on photographs discovered in an ethnographic book titled *Nature and Culture* (by Peter Landow, published in 1926), extracting the outdated and dangerously exploitative images of ethnic and racial typological classification and turning them into near-idyllic representations of nudes in natural environments and classical poses. Blake's cast of female figures are located between the extremes of saintly Madonna and 'Gilded Sluts', to appropriate one of his titles from the period. On the one hand, these representations are mediated archetypes of women in mythology, literature, art and the mass media. However, his imaginary ensemble of female figures transcends the schematic stereotypes and simple moral polarisations of female representation and presents them instead as a troupe of veritable tricksters – simultaneously saint and seductress, Madonna and pin-up girl, fairy and wrestler. It is their ambiguous personalities that rescue them from being mere types and subordinate objects of male desire and depict them instead as real and believable individuals, clearly strong but also fallible characters of the present.

Blake's return to London in 1979 and his major retrospective at the Tate Gallery in 1983 marked the end of his close engagement with Ruralism. His association with the Ruralists had always been an ambivalent one. While a founding and 'card-carrying' member of the Brotherhood, he also remained cautiously aloof, sometimes, it seems, secretly observing his fellow travellers with a degree of sympathetic amusement.[17] 'I didn't ever stop being an urbanist really', Blake stated, and he devoted himself to series of wrestlers and other urban subjects while living in the country. However, this return to London did not signal a total severance of his Ruralist ties, and in 1982 he created a work with the programmatic title I may not be a Ruralist anymore but I saw a fairy in my garden in Chiswick, confounding his critics who expected a more unambiguous Peter Blake. Unusually for a

17
Christopher Martin rightly suggests that Blake 'saw it all as a spontaneous, spur of the moment thing that just happened, rather magically, in the warmth of companionship that had been generated among those present. Even the name was arrived at casually, without much enthusiasm.' 'In the Secret Garden: Autumn with the Ruralists', *Art & Design*, no. 23, 1991, p. 15.

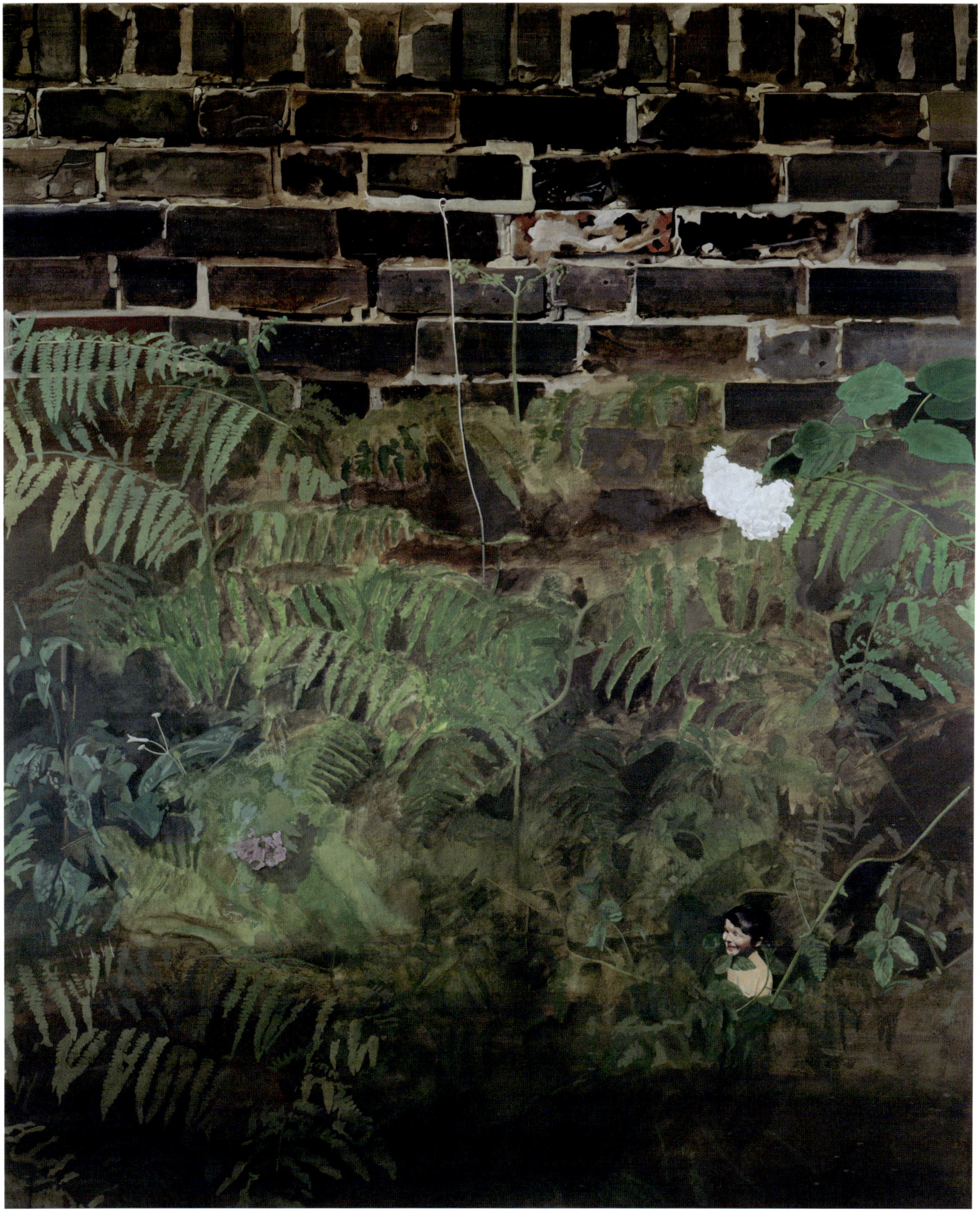

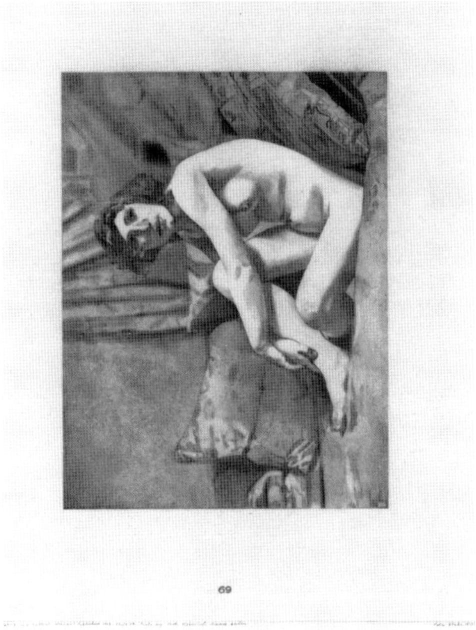

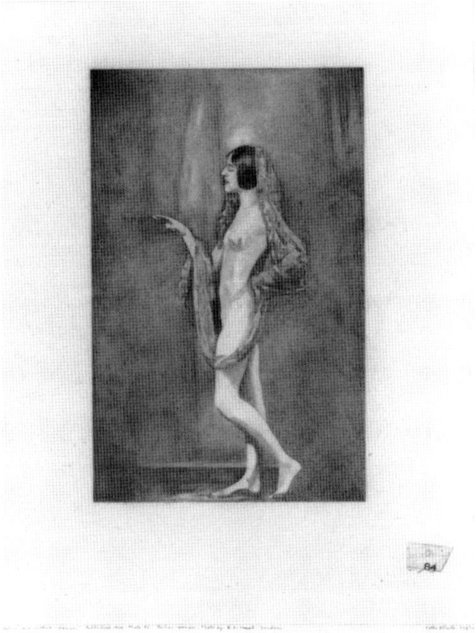

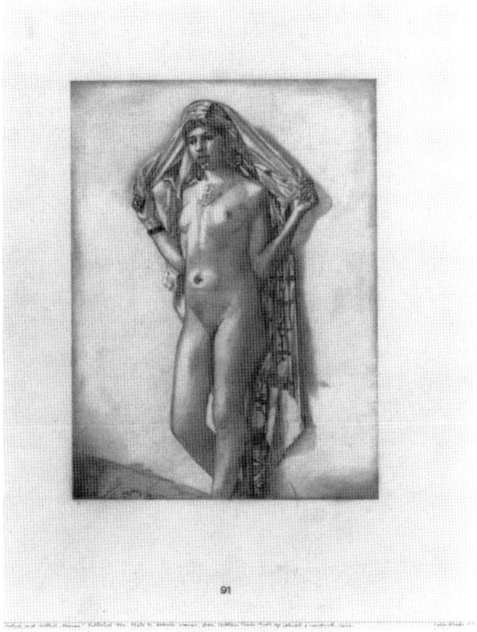

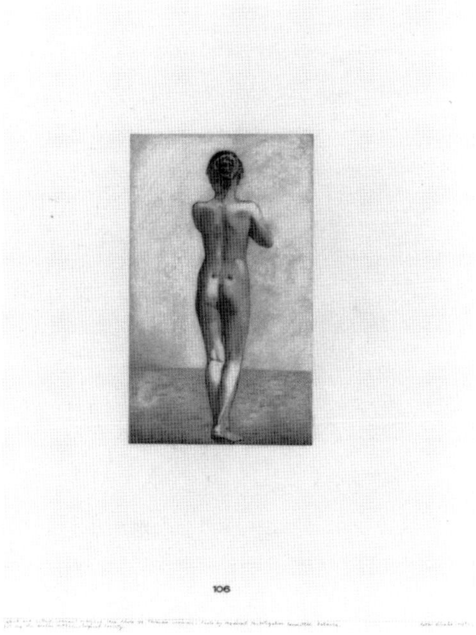

Plate 69. Czech Woman. Photo by Professor Henrich Maass Berlin
1973–7
Pencil on paper

Plate 84. Italian Woman. Photo by E.O. Hoppé, London
1973–7
Pencil on paper

Plate 91. Bedouin Woman from Southern Tunis. Photo by Lehnert and Landrock, Cairo
1973–7
Pencil on paper

Plate 106. Javanese Woman, Photo by Medical Investigation Committee Batavia
1973–7
Pencil on paper

Plate 113. Girl from the island of Bali. Photo by Dr. Krause, Bali. Lent by Dr. Karl With, Cologne
1973–7
Pencil drawing

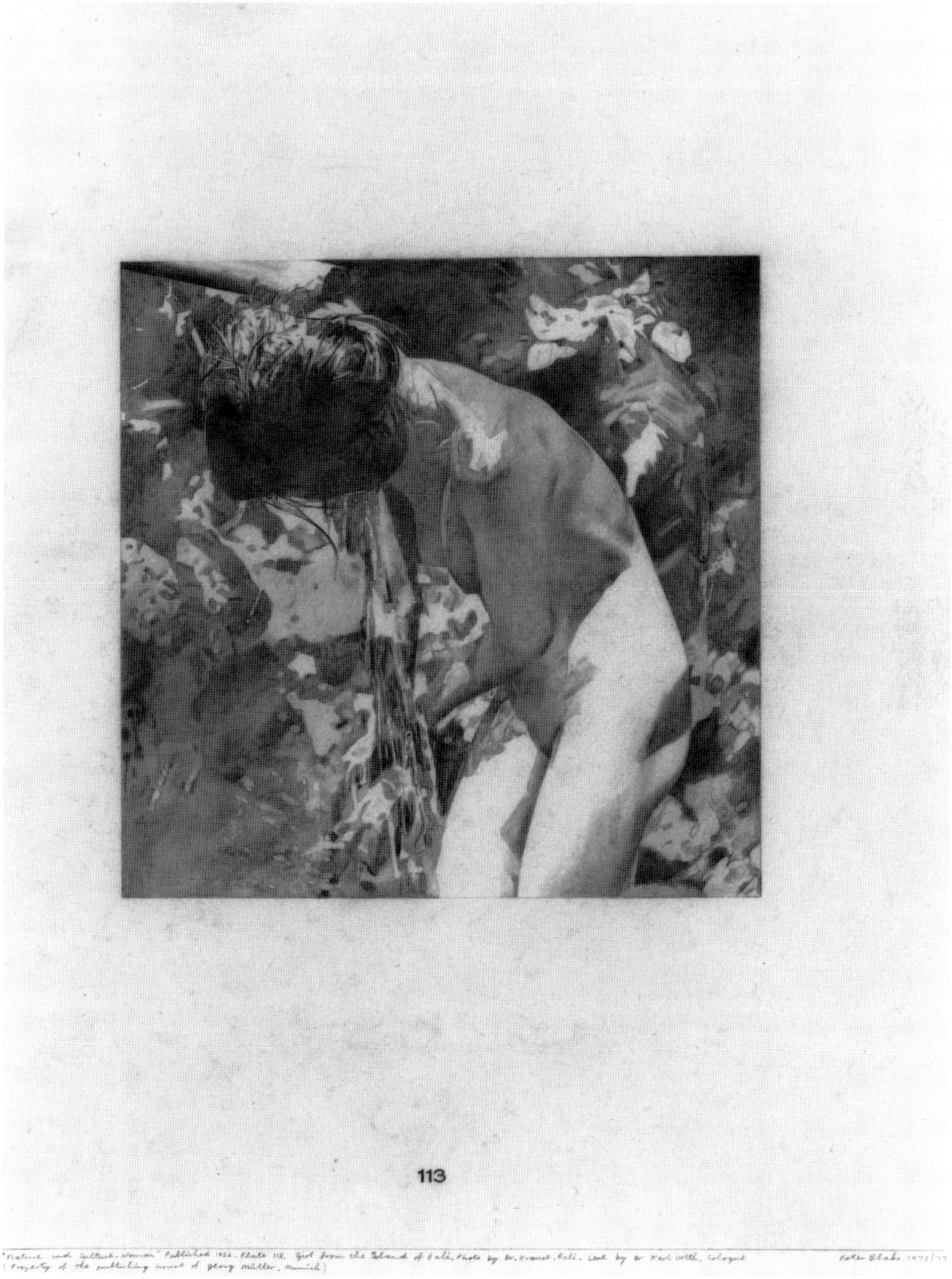

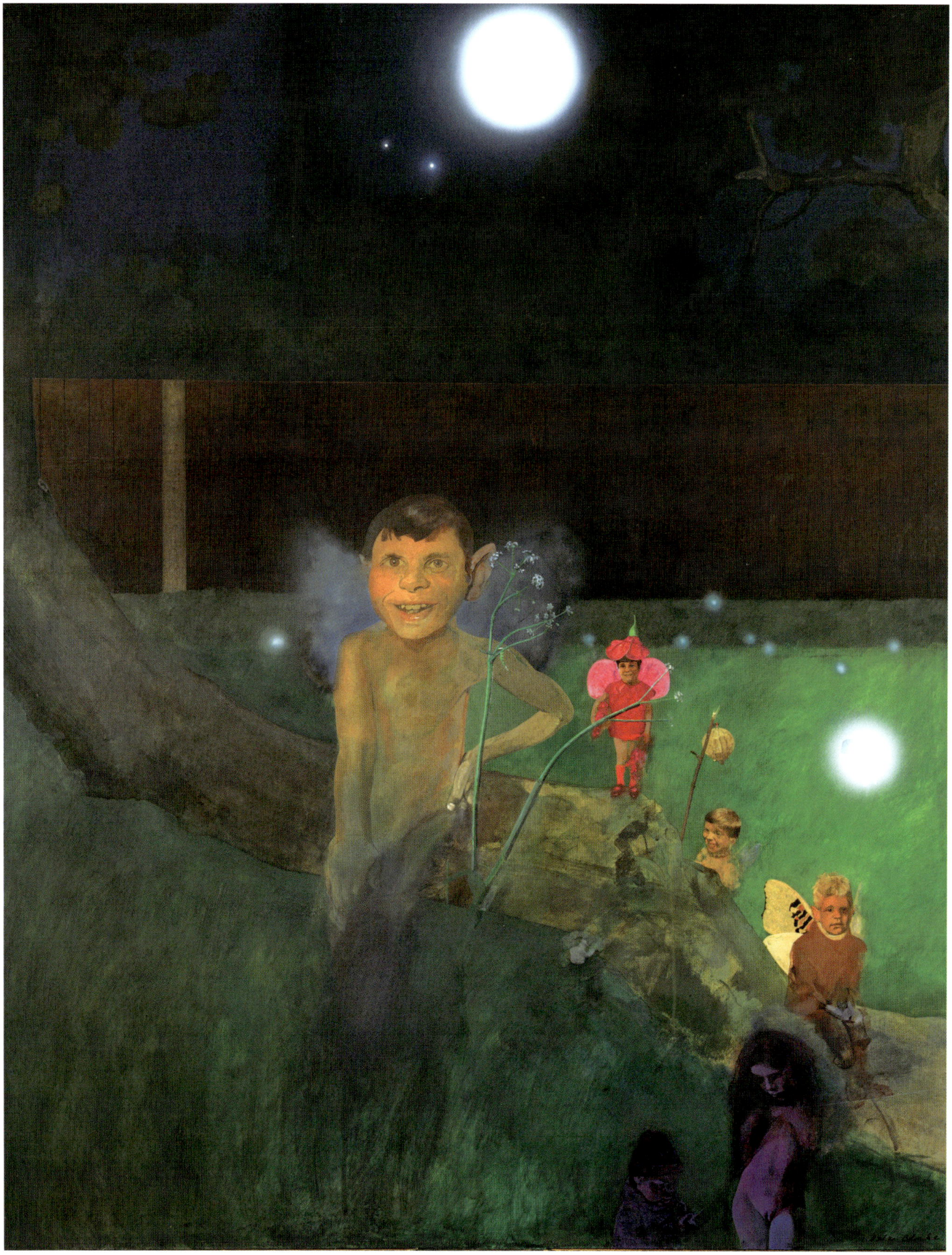

Puck, Peaseblossom, Cobweb, Moth and Mustardseed
1969–84
Acrylic on hardboard

retrospective, all the Ruralist members were invited to present their version of 'the Definitive Nude'.

Many critics celebrated Blake's return to London as the homecoming of the prodigal son, who had been lost in 'nooks and dingles of a moonlit land peopled by insufferably coy spirits'.[18] But to what extent was Blake's Ruralist period a break with his past as celebrated Pop artist? In terms of his painting style, the continuities were more prominent than the departures, as Blake remained true to his idiosyncratic realist style. What was lost were the strong graphic elements, the hard-edged patterns, framing devices and declamatory sign lettering. Blake's primary attention remained devoted to people even as his ensemble developed from the stars of stage, screen and circus tent to mythical and fairy-tale figures. In this respect, the shift from pronouncedly contemporary subject matter drawn from pop cultural sources to the evocation of fairies and literary fantasy figures was less of a rupture than might be imagined. Blake continued to evoke a dream world of distant heroes, stars and idols, near mythical figures surrounded by a supernatural aura and magic presence, seducing innocent mortals – whether star-struck teenagers or dreaming children – through their skills in music, acting or magic. Blake treated his subjects, as he phrased it himself, almost like a repertory company, and five years earlier the adolescent fairy Titania might have been a stripper or fearsome female wrestler. Puck, Peaseblossom, Cobweb, Moth and Mustardseed 1969–84 is one of the works in which the two obviously related spheres come together, as Puck is somewhat mischievously yet fittingly equipped with the face of American pop star Del Shannon.

Peter Blake's art has been called deeply nostalgic, an expression of longing for the innocence of childhood, the excitements of youth and the feeling of belonging of the fan. It is permeated by an atmosphere of persistent yearning for an idyllic refuge, manifested most pronouncedly in his Ruralist period but present throughout his work – from the meticulous assembly of mementos in On the Balcony 1955–57 to the fantastically artificial paradise of Venice Beach in 'The Meeting' or 'Have a Nice Day, Mr Hockney' 1981–83. Despite the free postmodern play with historical allusions and clever combinations of disparate stylistic elements strip-mined from the plentiful quarry of the past, nostalgia

18
Richard Cork, 'Happy Return of the Ruralist', *The Standard*, 10 February 1983, p. 20. See also Waldemar Januszczak, 'Blake's Progress,' *The Guardian*, 9 February 1983, p. 11; William Packer, 'Bewitched by fairies,' *The Financial Times*, 12 February 1983, p. 14.

3765
from *Six French Postcards* 1969
Screenprint on paper

J.A.
from *Six French Postcards* 1969
Screenprint on paper

Leo 153
from *Six French Postcards* 1969
Screenprint on paper

Leo 139
from *Six French Postcards* 1969
Screenprint on paper

Serie 83
from *Six French Postcards* 1969
Screenprint on paper

Leo 79
from *Six French Postcards* 1969
Screenprint on paper

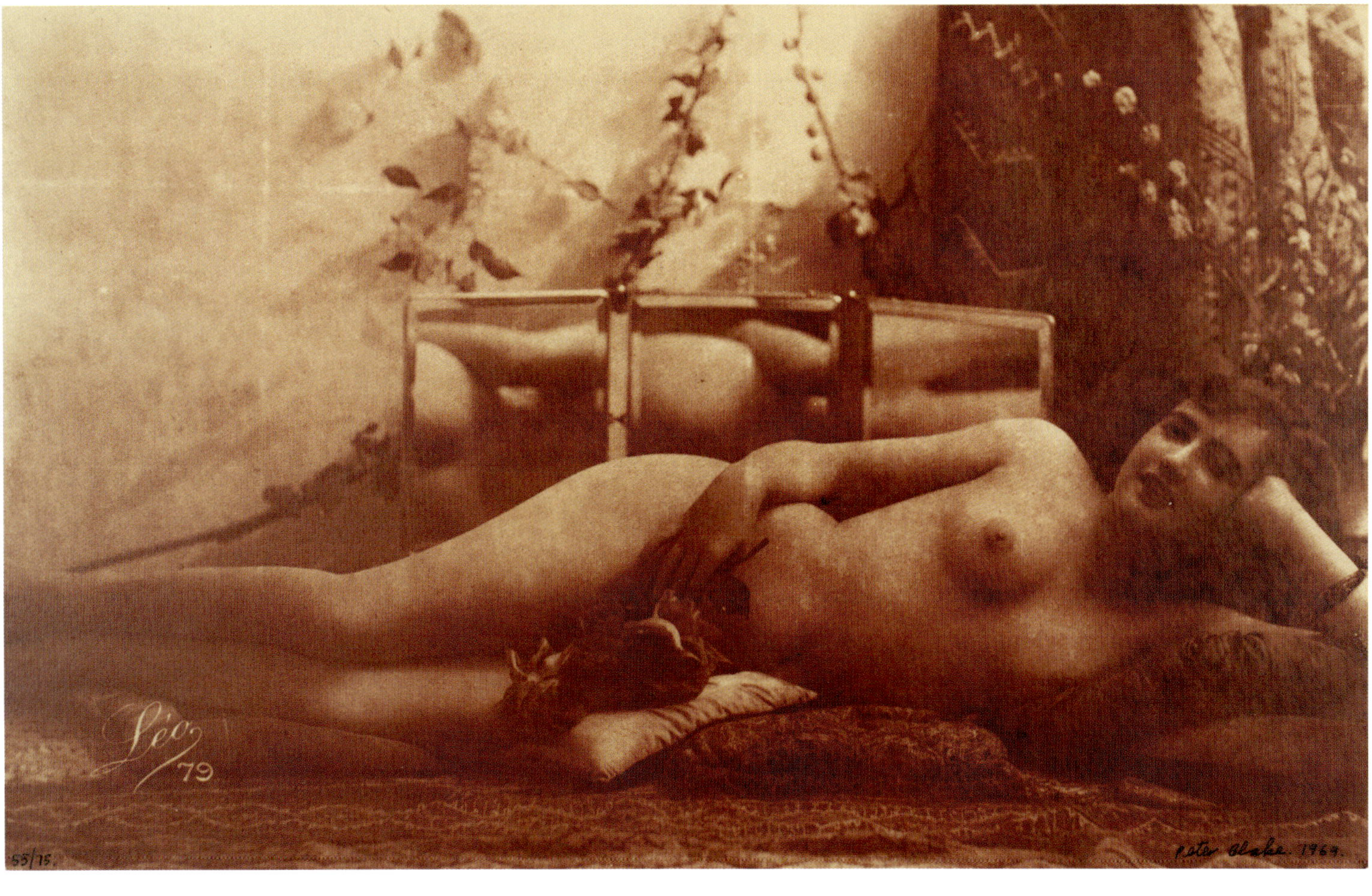

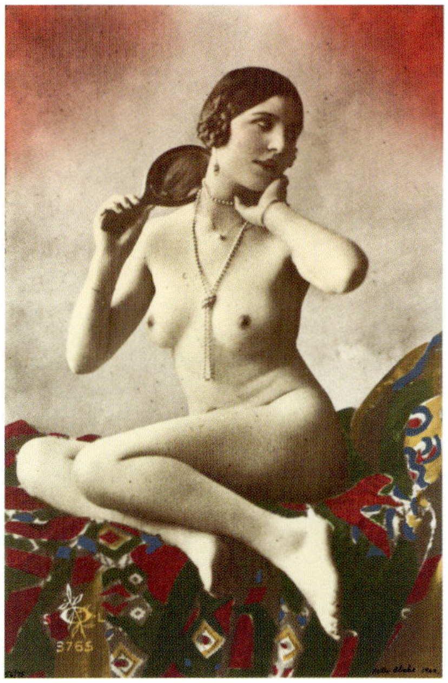
3765

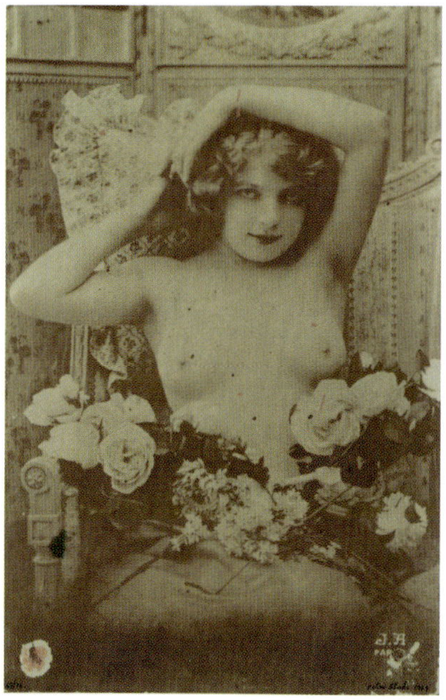
J.R.

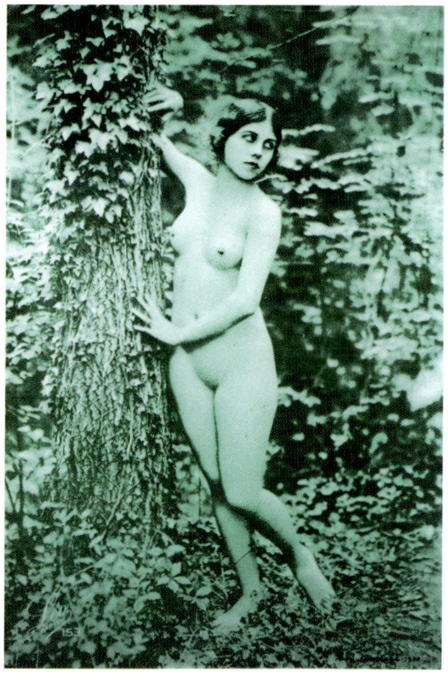

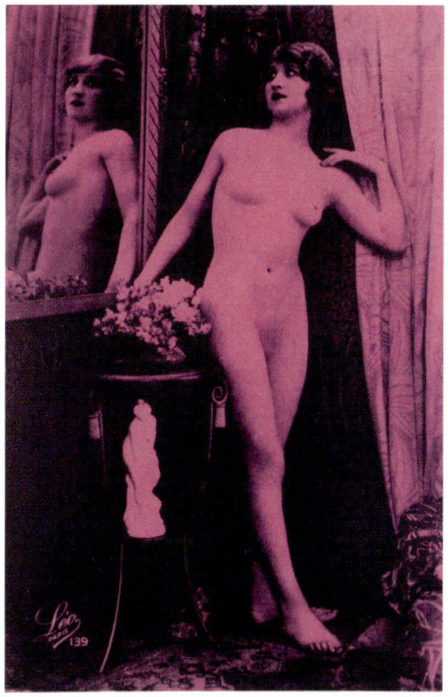
139

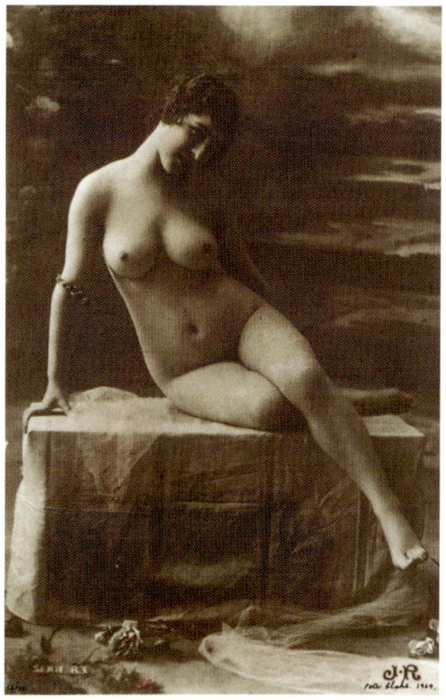
J·R

The Owl and the Pussycat
1981–3
Oil on hardboard

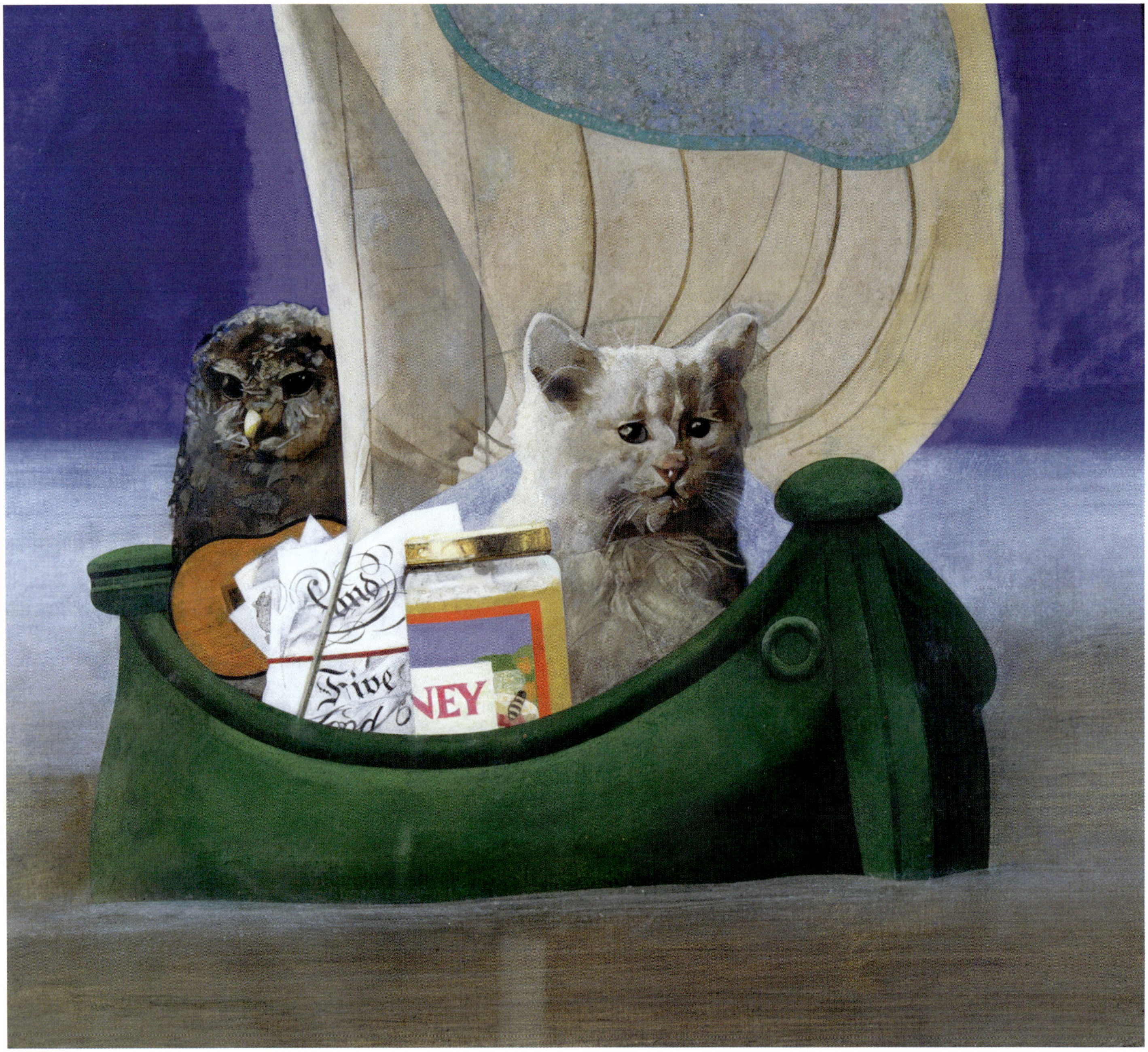

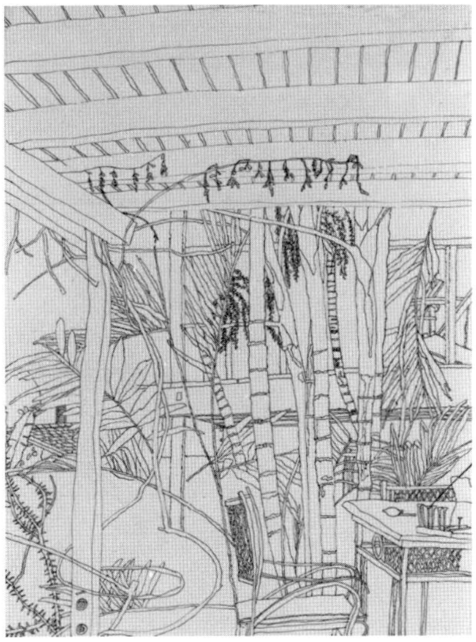

Barbados with Ian Dury
1979
Ink on paper

19
Jean Baudrillard, 'The Procession of Simulacra', in Brian Wallis (ed.), *Art after Modernism: Rethinking Representation*, New York, The New Museum of Contemporary Art; Boston, David R. Godine, 1984, p. 257.

20
Christian Thorne, 'The Revolutionary Energy of the Outmoded', *October*, no. 104, Spring 2003, p. 102.

21
Fredric Jameson, *Postmodernism, or, The Cultural Logic of Late Capitalism*, London and New York, Verso, 1991, pp. 19, 21.

22
Quoted in 'Editorial', *Art Monthly*, no. 302, December 2006–January 2007, p. 18

continues to be tainted by a whiff of treachery and a deceitful lack of authenticity. As Jean Baudrillard has suggested, 'When the real is no longer what it used to be, nostalgia assumes its full meaning.'[19] Unlike pastiche, nostalgia is perhaps not knowing enough in the witty conflation of ingredients from recent and distant periods. Nostalgic moments are also differentiated from 'retro as blank parody, the affectless recycling of alien styles, worn like so many masks'.[20] Fredric Jameson singles out the nostalgia film – or as the French call it, la mode rétro – as exemplary for approaching 'the "past" through stylistic connotation, conveying "pastness" by the glossy qualities of the image, and "1930s-ness" or "1950s-ness" by the attributes of fashion'. Jameson interprets this aesthetic appropriation of the past (and, therefore, by extension our experience of the present through the 'art language of the simulacrum, or the pastiche of the stereotypical past') as an 'elaborated symptom of the waning of our historicity'.[21] The issue then is one of distance, or the lack thereof, preventing a critical assessment of the past and an analytical engagement with the present, as well as a positive perspective on the future.

Above all, nostalgia remains permeated by sentiment or, as Clive Bell labelled it, 'false emotion'.[22] Is there then a place in art for enlightened nostalgia, free from the smokescreen of retrospective illusion and over-romantic yearning? The primary innovations that the fairy paintings of the 1970s introduced into Blake's oeuvre were narrative development and outright sentimentality. Blake's provocative choice of fairy paintings as an inspirational conduit was, in part, determined by the genre's unashamed display of exaggerated human emotions, almost completely absent in the art of the time. The Ruralist works capture an emotive moment that goes beyond the expressive limitations inherent in the static poses of the poster, signboard, advertisement and record cover. At the same time, Blake's nostalgic moments are always presented as artifice, spatially layered collages, carefully framed and labelled signs and constructs of memory with smudged limbs disturbing the perfect illusion. Further, they use the emotional power of archetypal myths and folk legends to convey universal lessons of tragedy, despair and hope. Blake trades in myths, but myths that are made of flesh and blood and are so real that they resist functioning purely as vehicles for escapist trips. There always remains an edge in his depictions of literary and mythical subjects, firmly rooting them in the present, however fantastic and otherworldly the setting might appear.

The desperate search for a better future in the past, in some faraway bucolic paradise, has been a constant in British culture since the Industrial Revolution and was described by Pevsner as the 'conservatism' in British art.[23] It has been argued that the return to Victorian values in 1970s' Britain 'can be understood only at the level of myth', the past offering 'stability and a system of codes and meanings which provide the illusion of an understandable world'.[24] In some ways, Blake filled a metaphorical vacuum with his Ruralist mythology, reflecting some primary trends and moods in British society in the 1970s. His Ruralist works were highly timely, mirroring a deep insecurity at a time of crisis, a shift towards conservative values but also a wider aesthetic and ideological immersion in the past. By the early 1970s, the ideals of the 1960s had faded and the belief in a futuristic technological utopia solving all of humankind's challenges had been superseded by the realities of global recession and political instability. The 1973 oil crisis paralysed the nation and in the following year the Heath government collapsed as the disintegration of the Britain's industrial heart led to violent clashes between striking miners (and other workers) and the authorities.

At the same time, design and fashion were caught in a neo-romantic nostalgia and heritage boom, rediscovering the Victorian and Edwardian era, with Laura Ashley successfully mass-marketing the new trend.[25] Exhibitions of Alphonse Mucha and Aubrey Beardsley at the Victoria and Albert Museum in 1963 and 1966 respectively rehabilitated and popularised the Art Nouveau style. *Sgt Pepper's Lonely Hearts Club Band* 1967 took listeners on an experimental trip down memory lane in search of a mythic childhood and a long-lost golden Victorian age. In the 1970s, not only was Victorian fairy painting rediscovered but numerous accounts of actual fairy sightings circulated. By now the fairies had moved far away from the overpopulated cities and countryside of central England and found a home in isolated Northern Scotland, in the mythical location of Findhorn, 'where the elemental world of plants and animals cooperates with fairies, elves, and gnomes in creating a land where nothing is impossible and legends are reborn'.[26] Their 'discovery' went hand in hand with the expanding ecological movement and wide-

23
Nikolaus Pevsner, *The Englishness of English Art: An Expanded and Annotated Version of the Reith Lectures Broadcast in October and November 1955*, Harmondsworth, Penguin, 1984, p. 195.

24
Robert Hewsion, *Too Much: Art and Society in the Sixties 1960–75*, London, Methuen, 1986, p. 305.

25
See Dominic Sandbrook, *White Heat: A History of Britain in the Swinging Sixties*, London, Little, Brown, 2006, pp. 420–30.

26
Quoted in Carole G. Silver, *Strange and Secret Peoples: Fairies and Victorian Consciousness*, Oxford, Oxford University Press, 1999, p. 208.

Postcard
1974, reworked 1988
Hand-coloured photograph

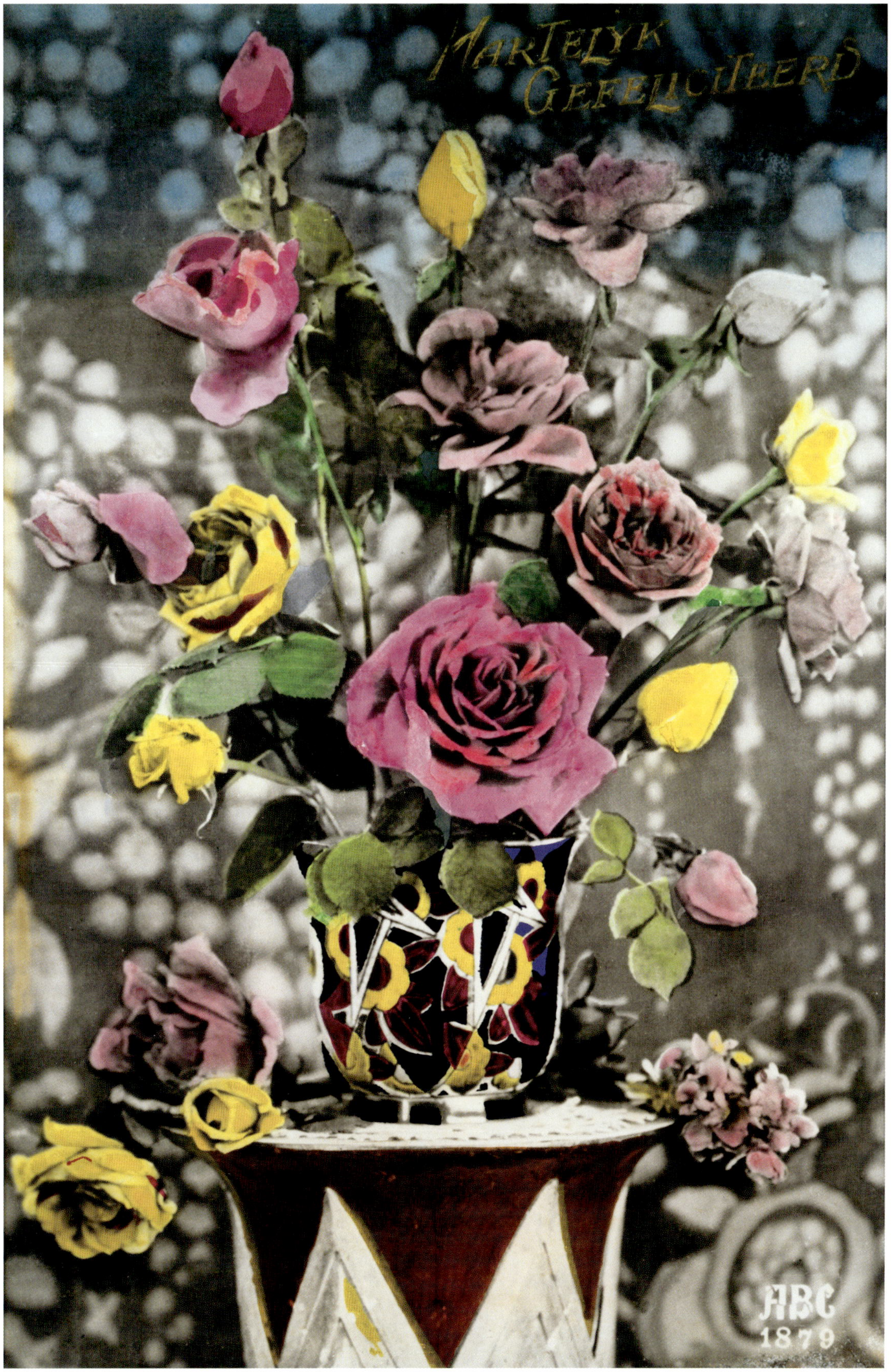

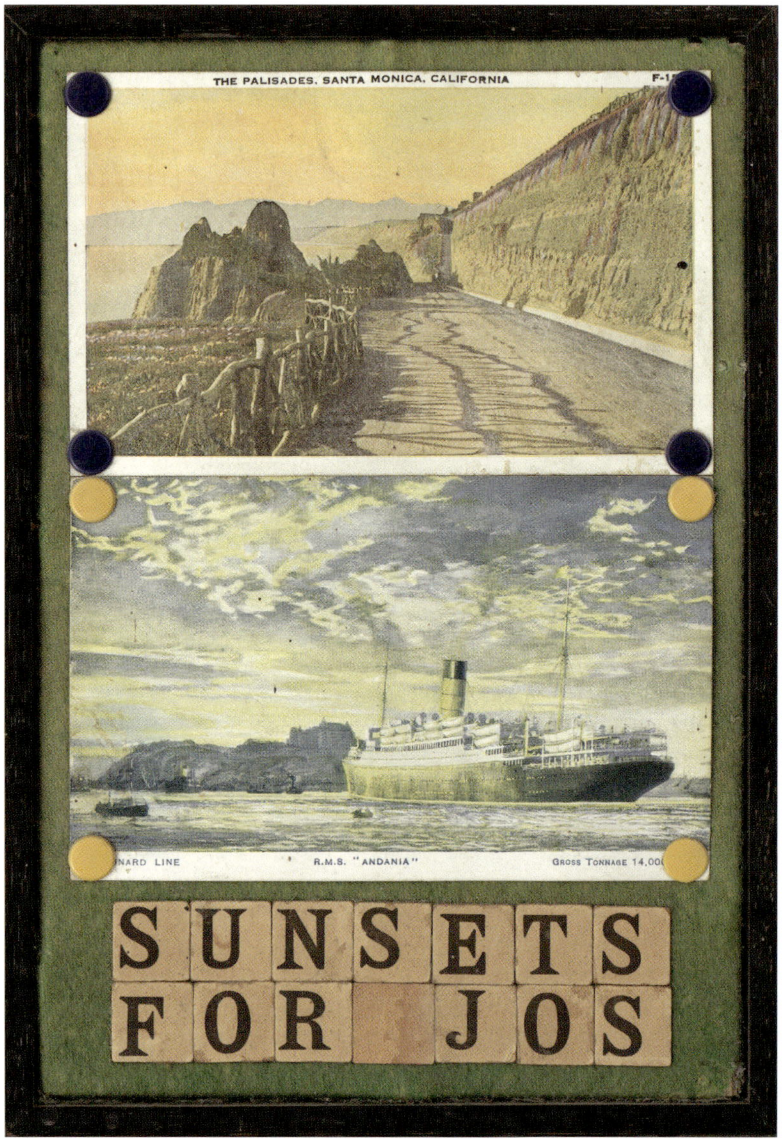

Souvenir for Jos
1974
Collage

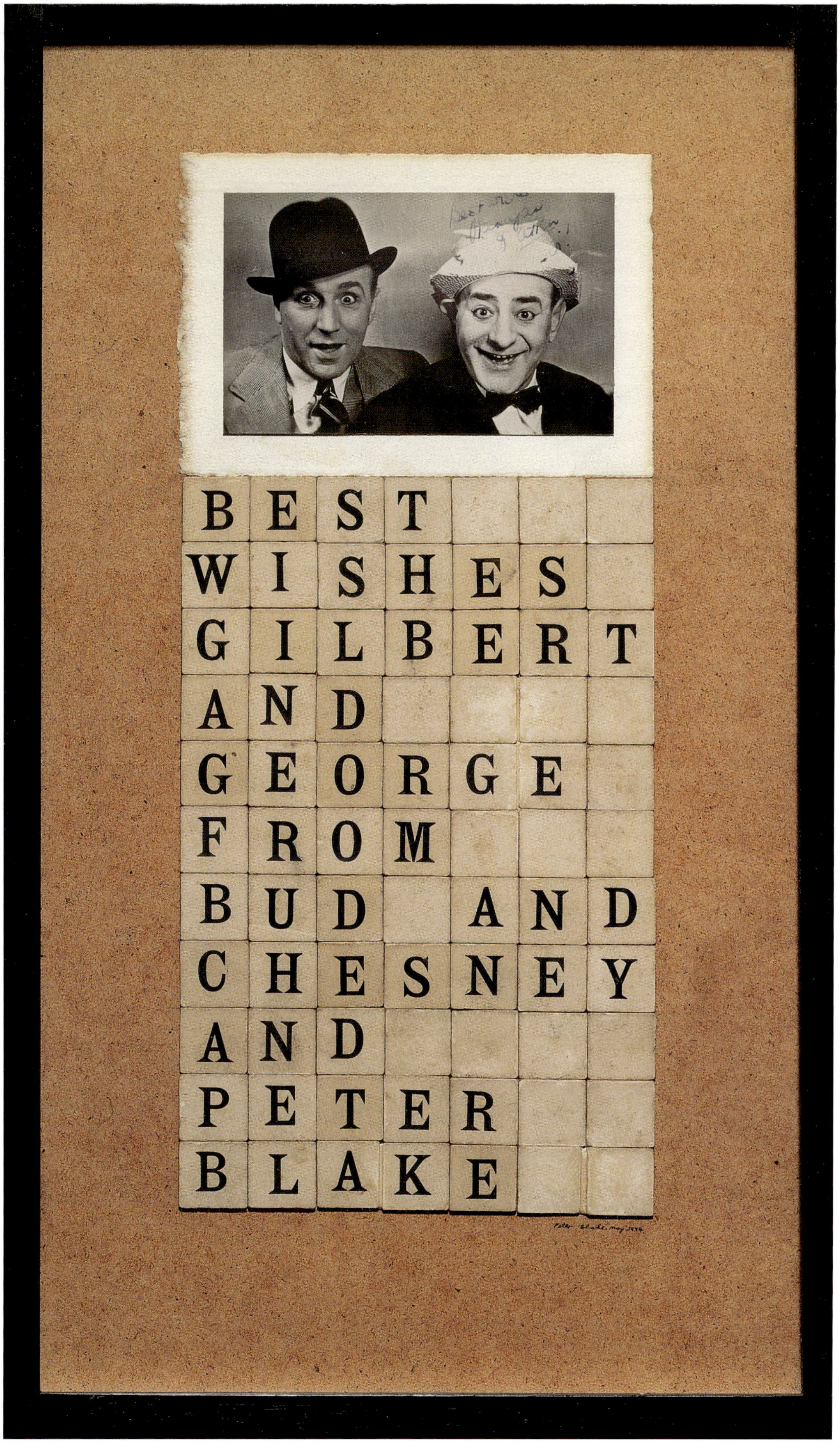

Souvenir for Gilbert and George
1974
Collage

Studio Tack-Board
1972
Screenprint on paper

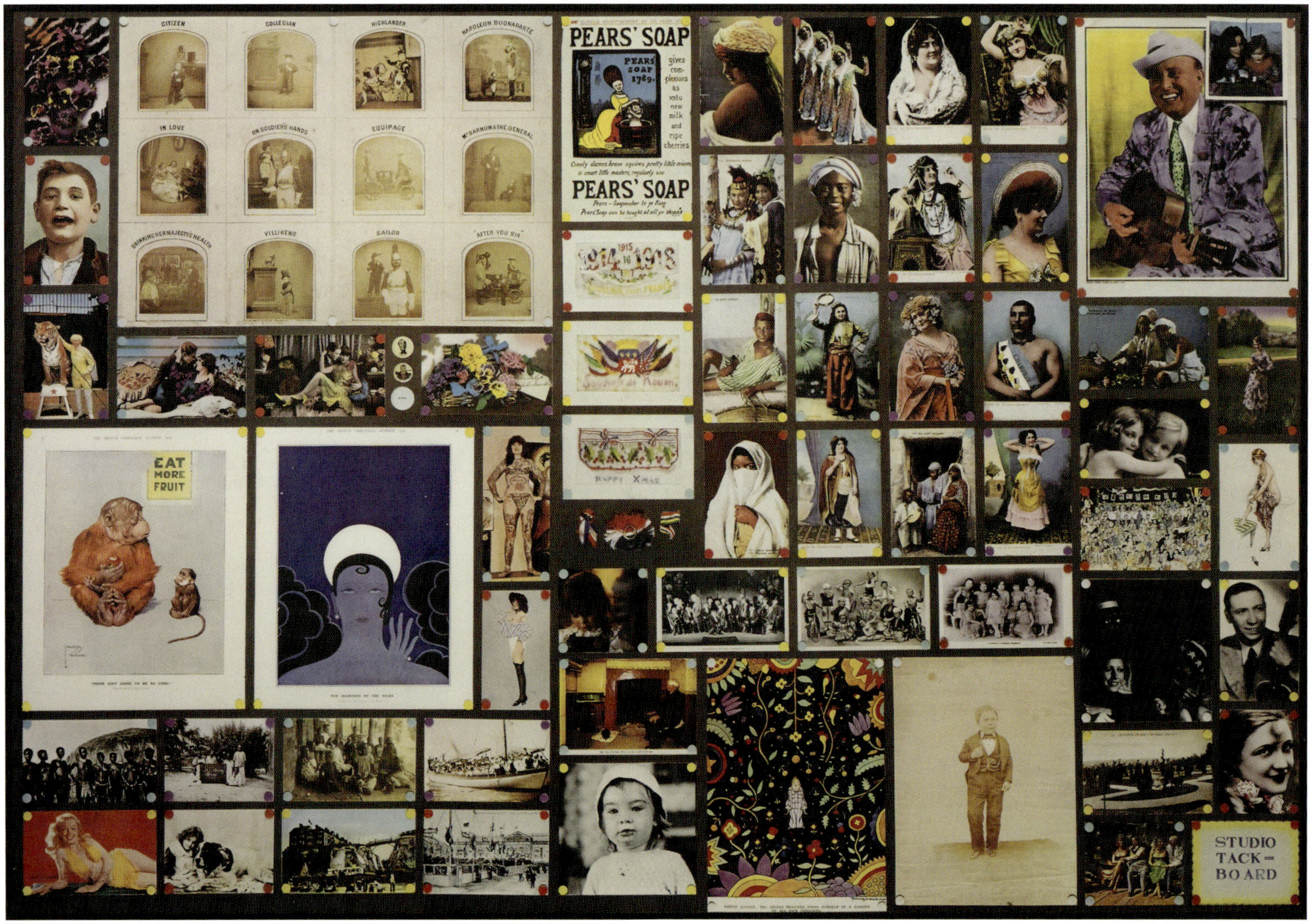

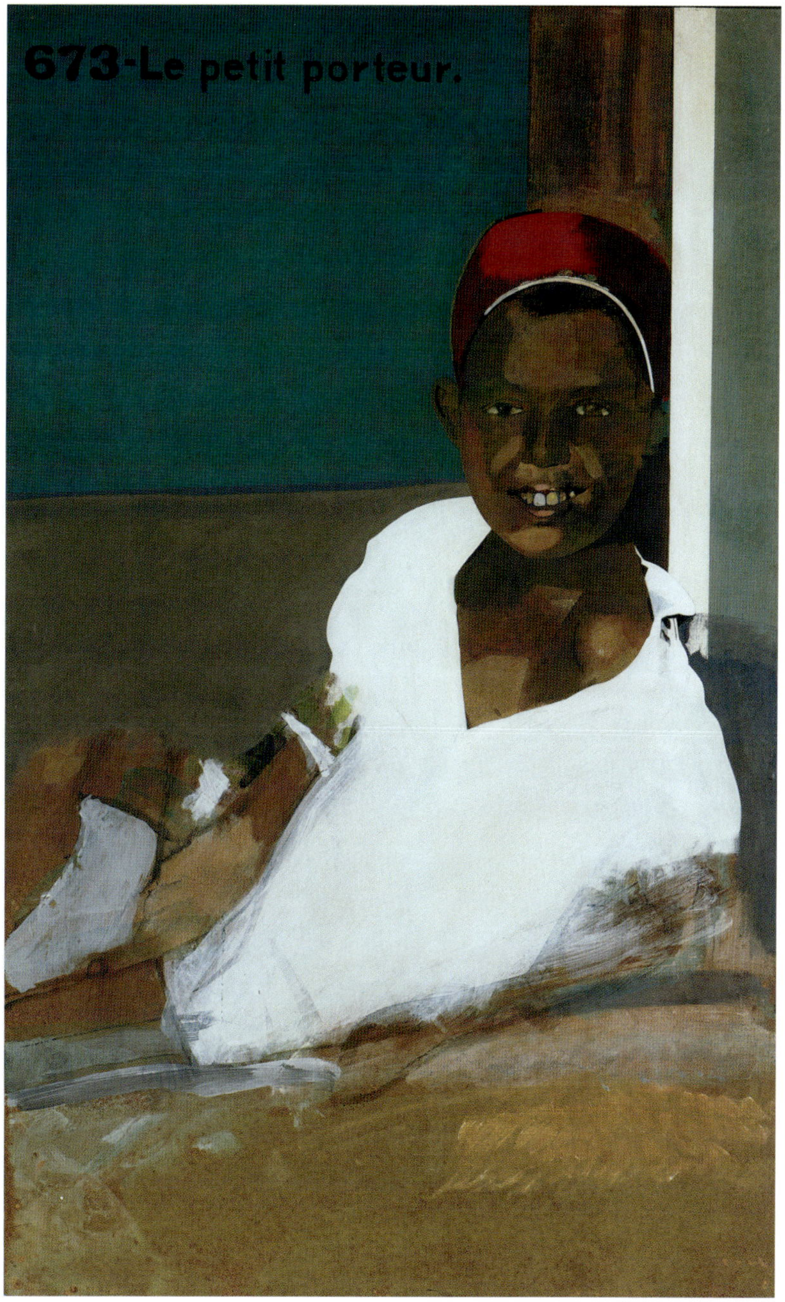

Le Petit Porteur
1964–5
Cryla on hardboard

The Twins in their Tea Garden
1991
Oil on board

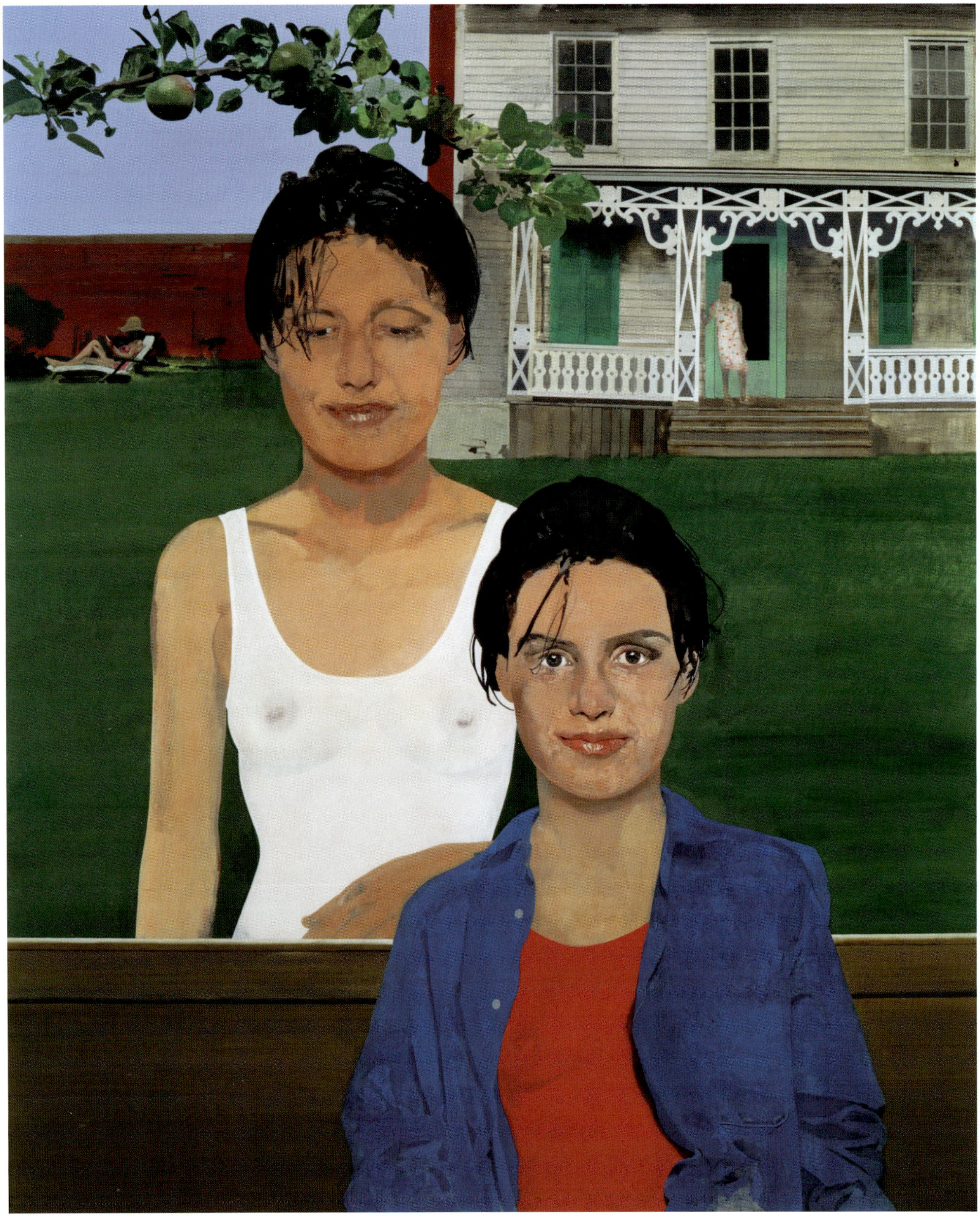

spread concern over the destruction of humankind's natural habitat. Rather than taking an eccentric turn and detaching himself from the realities of contemporary life, Blake's work of the 1970s chimed with the underlying frame of mind of the country. However, as much as Blake has always been a deeply nostalgic painter, his work has never provided a misty-eyed illusion of a mythical past that never was. On the contrary, rather than engaging in a form of retrogressive time travel and evoking a pastoral vision of pre-industrial England, Blake transported the ancient myths and literary heritage to the present, updating the universal meanings contained in these narratives and giving them a decidedly contemporary feel.

Almost three decades on, we find ourselves again in one of the periodic returns of the nostalgic and magical in painting. After the culture wars of the 1980s and 1990s, artists are again allowed to dream, and today there is a proliferation of painters, draughtsmen and draughtswomen who liberally exploit the history of fairy tales, book illustration and the art of the fantastic. Amy Cutler, Marcel Dzama, Ged Quinn and Mark Ryden, to name only a few, are equally devoted to variations on old-style realism and the exploration of the dark side of the Romantic. Perhaps their work is best described as whimsical, a critical term rediscovered in recent years as well as an intrinsic quality in Blake's art. It captures the somewhat quaint and eccentric nature of their work, their devotion to playful fancy and poetic improvisation, frequently suffused with a dark comical edge. As in Blake, pure nostalgic longing is forever tainted and the lost paradise is inevitably a broken one, frequently disturbed by acts of violence and psychological terror breaking through the allegorical surface of the fairy tale. These progeny of Blake demonstrate that *la mode rétro* is alive and kicking, constantly reinventing and metamorphosing itself, testament to the long shadow that Peter Blake's work of the 1970s continues to throw.

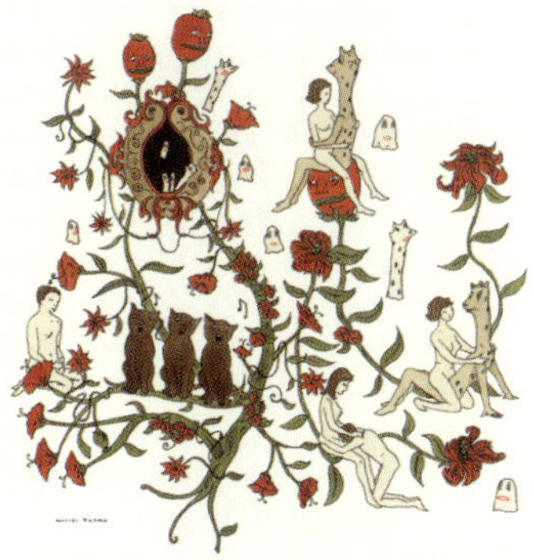

Marcel Dzama
Untitled 2003
Ink and watercolour on paper

The Twins in their Tea Garden (2nd version)
1995–9
Oil on panel

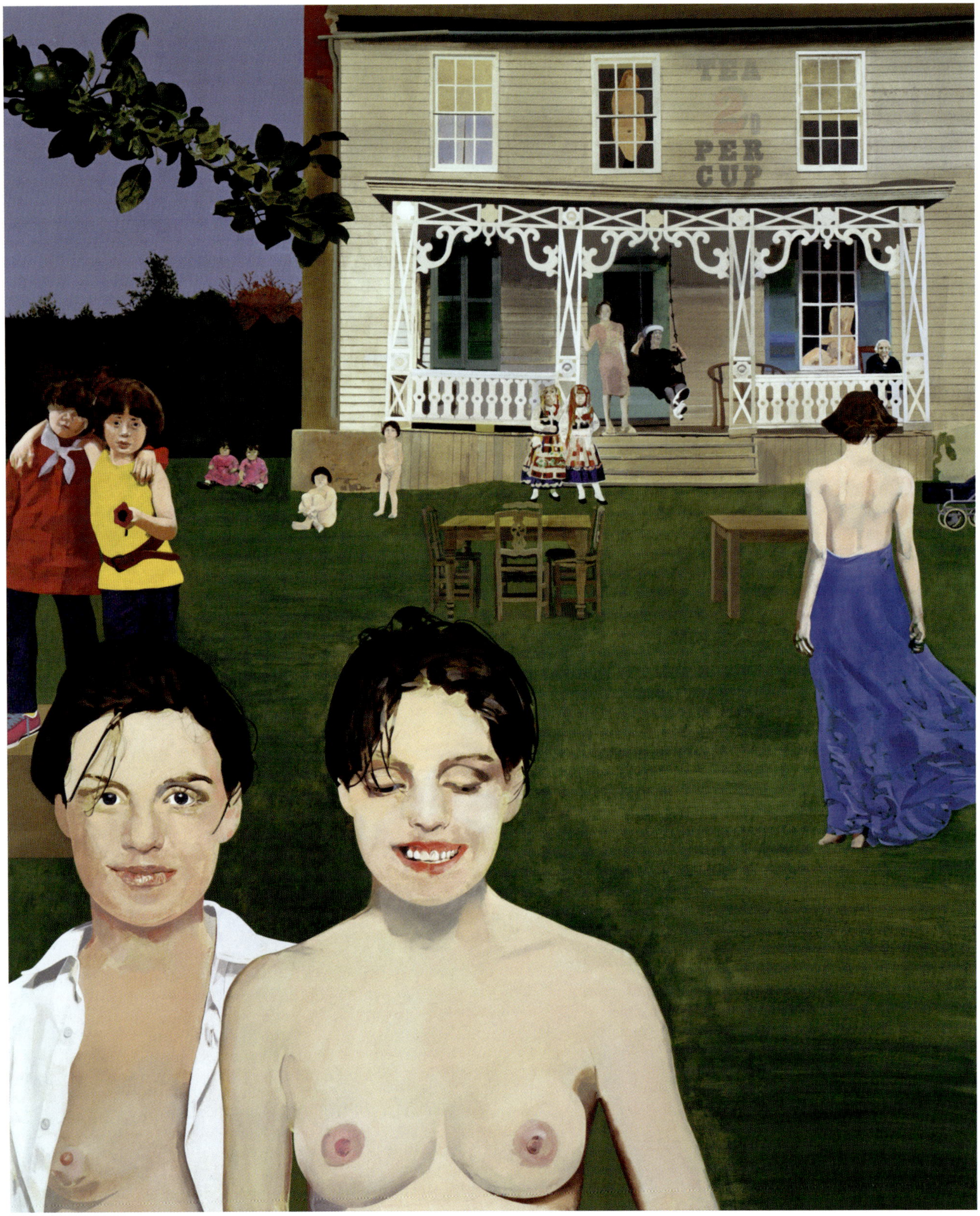

the 1980s to now

déjà vu

laurence sillars

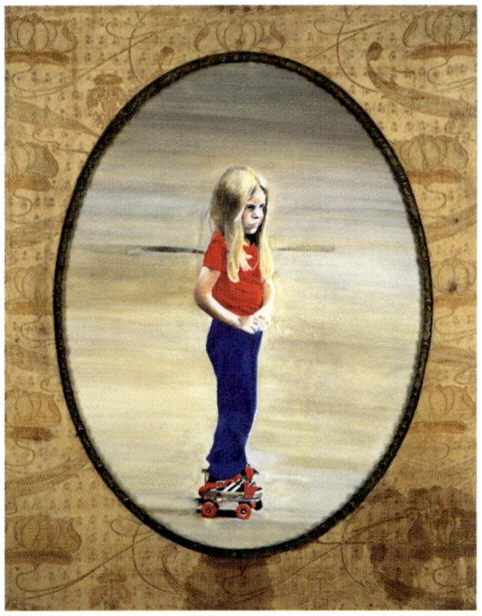

Daisy on Rollerskates
1983
Oil on canvas

Following the separation from his wife Jann Haworth in 1979 Peter Blake left his country life with the Ruralists and moved back to London. His return to the capital, once again placing him at the centre of the cultural world that had for so long provided a starting point for his work, did little to ease his spirits. Apart from his children, who remained in Avon, the artist struggled to find the ideas or the motivation to take him back to the easel. However, towards the end of the year a lifeline arrived in the form of an invitation from Peter Gould at the LA Louver Gallery in Los Angeles to attend the opening of *This Knot of Life* which was to include the work of Blake and several of his contemporaries. Blake travelled to California with his friend Howard Hodgkin, not yet realising that the journey would trigger a new direction in his work, marking the beginning of what was to become an increasingly conceptualised practice over the two and a half decades since then. In Los Angeles he stayed with David Hockney and when not sunbathing or sketching by the pool, spent his time as a 'voyeur of enormous goings-on', attending numerous parties, dinners and openings.[1]

The trip inspired a new series of paintings based on Venice Beach and its surroundings, the idea for at least one of which was finalised before his return to London. Hodgkin was similarly encouraged and the pair proposed to work on an exhibition together and show 'four pictures each, which we will hang alternately around the gallery'.[2] One memory in particular for Blake prompted a new work. A Remembered Moment in Venice, California 1981–91 depicts a scene in the early evening as Blake and Hodgkin were walking back to the gallery after a day on the beach. With the day-trippers gone and the evening crowds yet to arrive, few people were about as a girl on roller-skates passed them by. Blake had been struck by the quality of light and colours of California, and the painting, completed with his typical realist mastery, is unusually atmospheric for him, demonstrating a shift in palette – a tonal range adopted for several of his other 'Venice' paintings. Indeed Blake and Hodgkin's plan was for their exhibition to be in a gallery with 'bright LA lighting and sand on the floor'. Working from a photograph to create a portrait of Daisy, his daughter, Blake returned to Los Angeles the following year to take new photographs, to enable the painting to be finished in what was for him a typical fusion of fragments of his past, present, imagination and reality.

1
Quotations are from conversations with the artist in February and March 2007 unless otherwise noted.

2
'Peter Blake and Howard Hodgkin in California', *AMBIT 83*, 1983, p. 22.

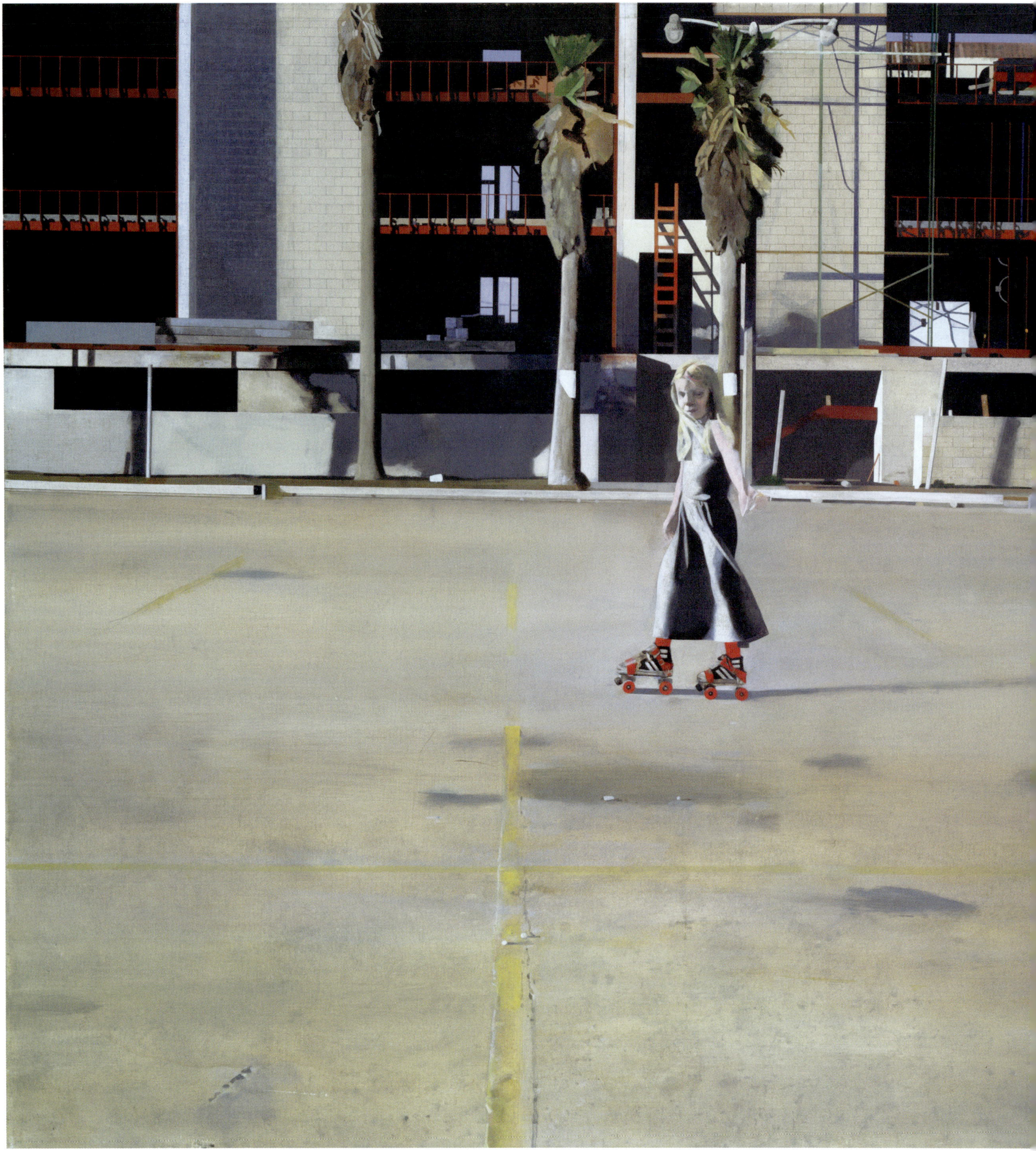

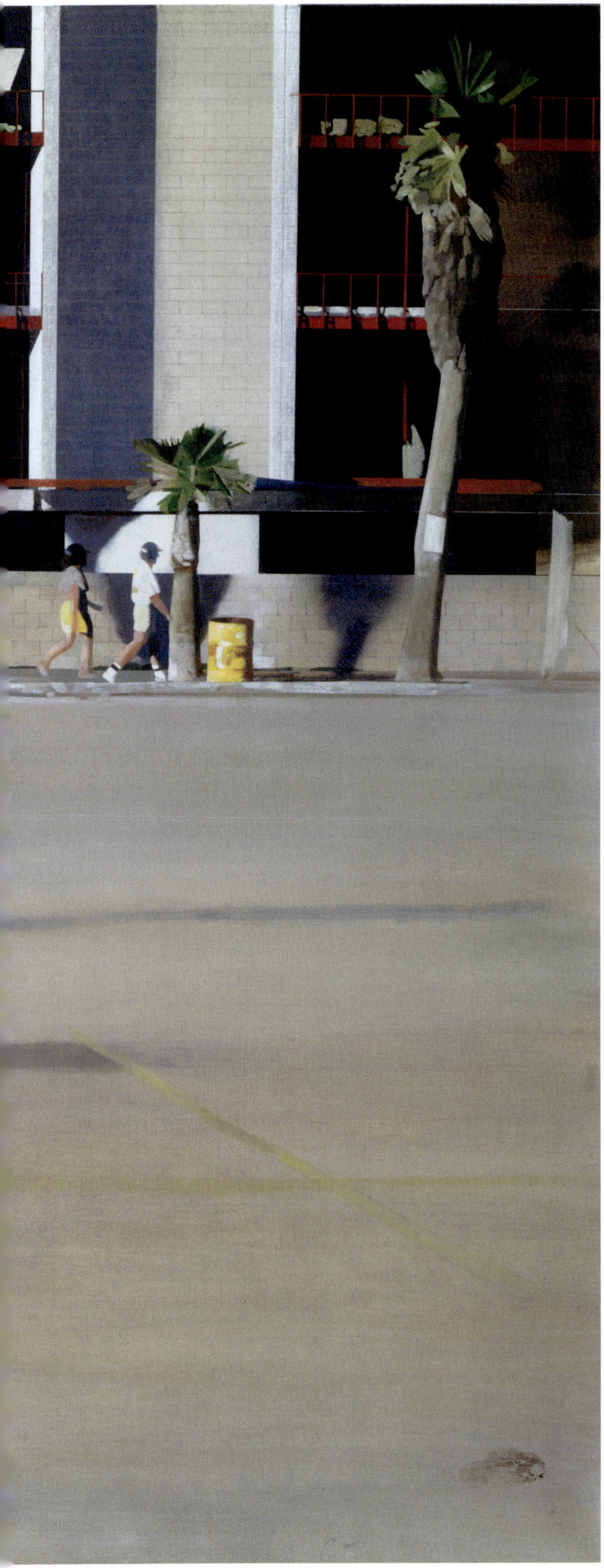

A Remembered Moment in Venice California
1981–91
Oil on canvas

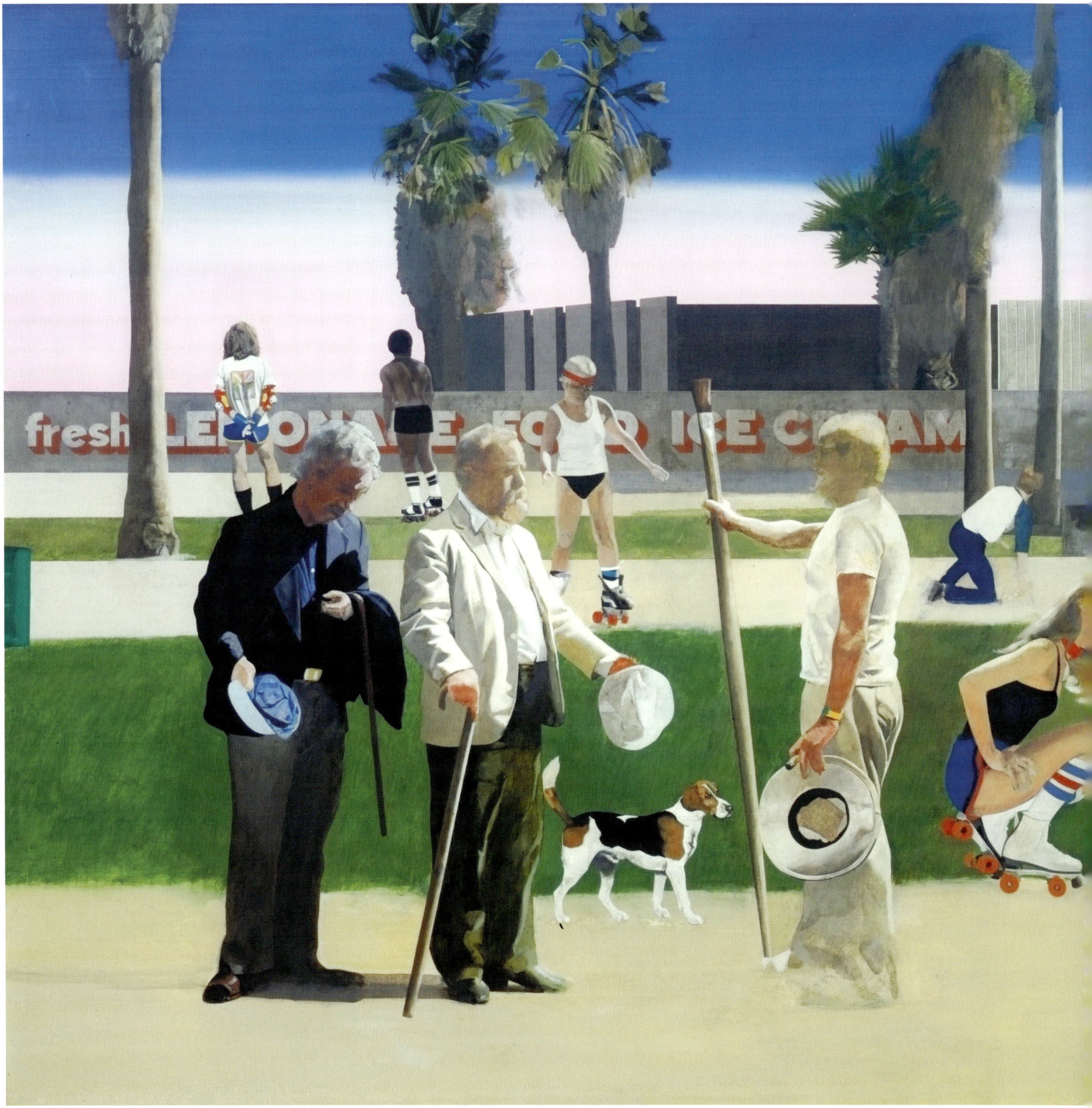
fresh
ICE

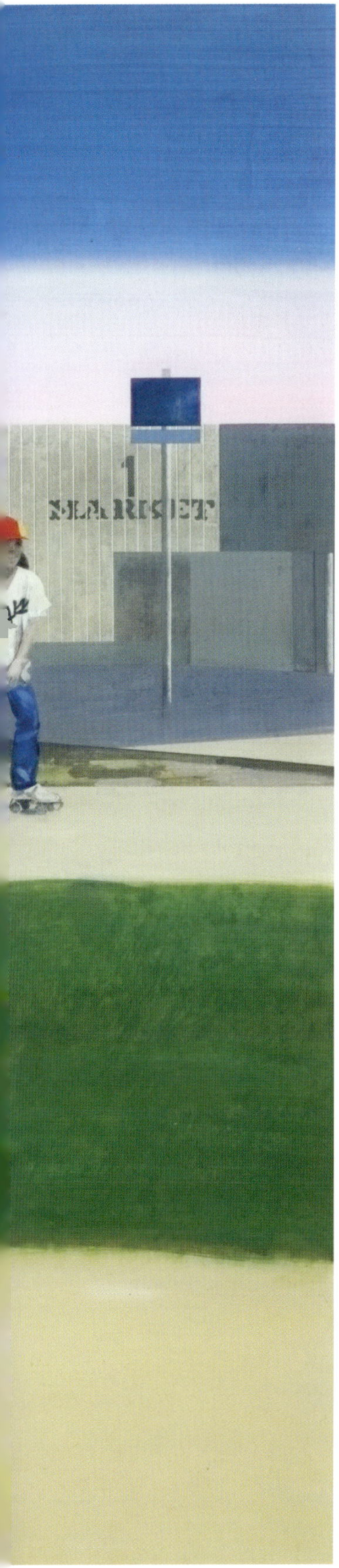

'The Meeting' or 'Have a Nice Day, Mr Hockney'
1981–3
Oil on canvas

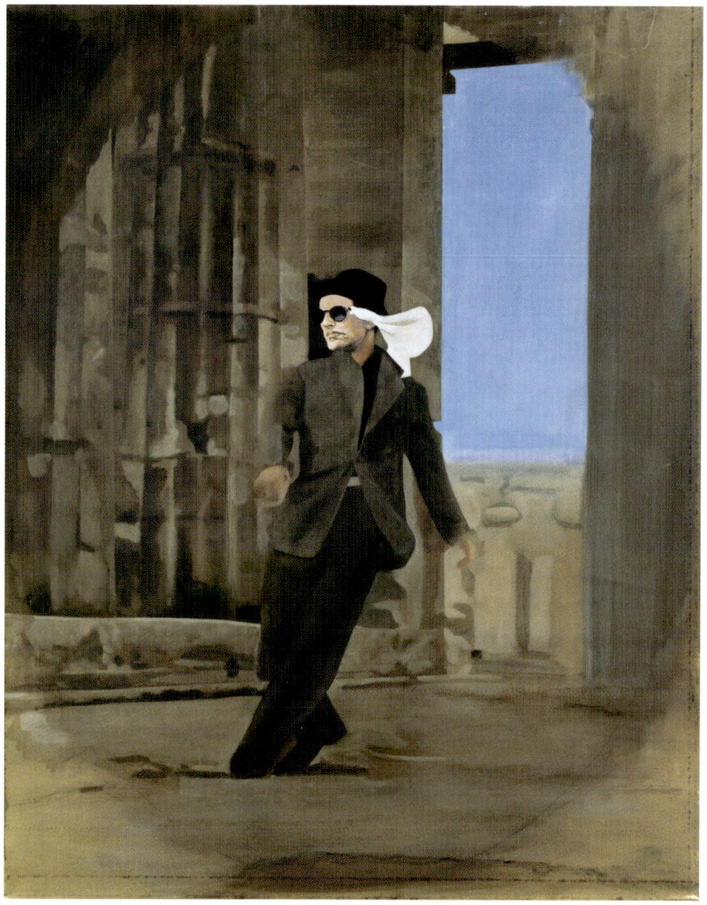

Montgomery Clift was a Twin
1981–3
Oil on canvas

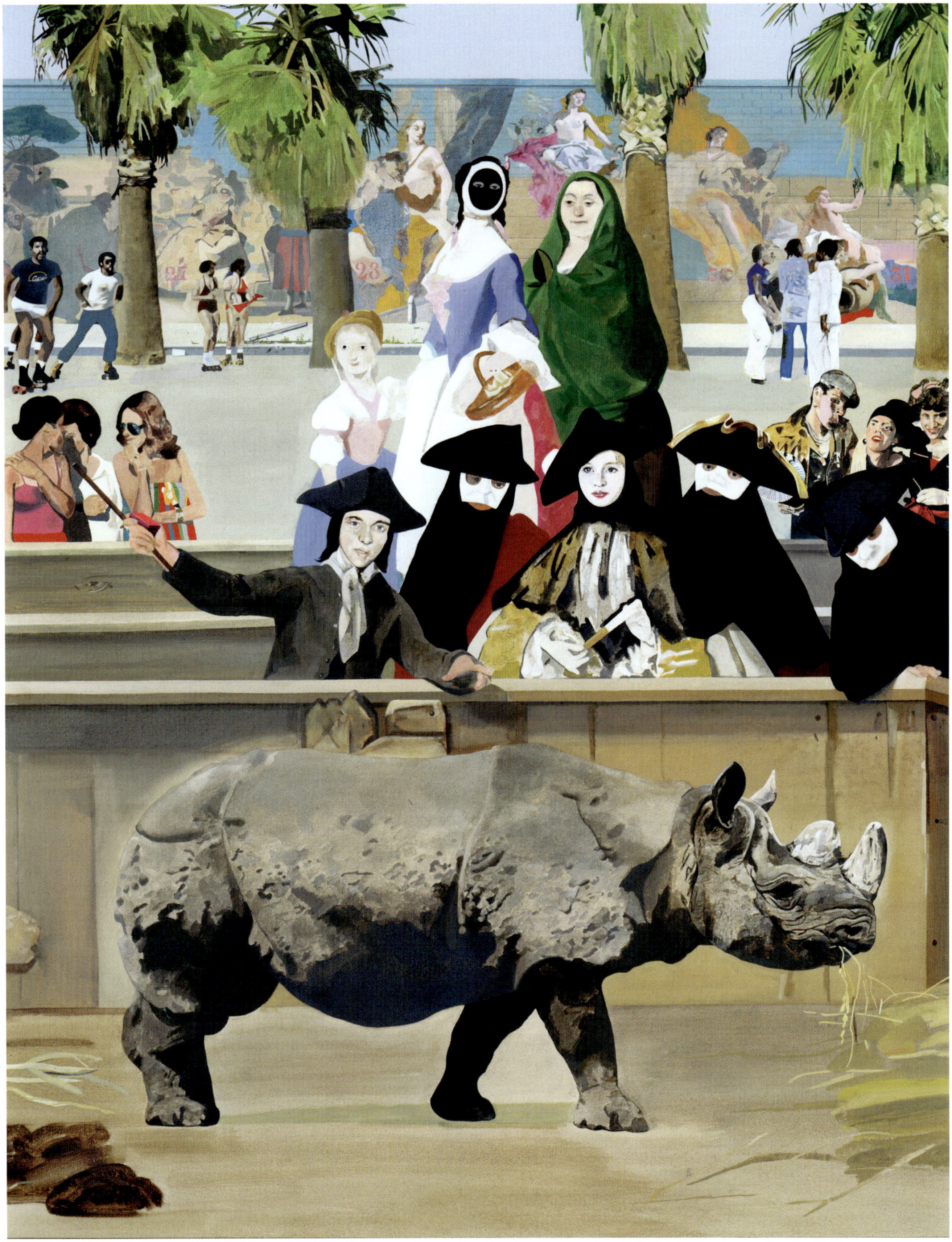

Exhibition of a Rhinoceros at Venice
1996
Oil on canvas

The remembered images of the events, sights and sounds of Los Angeles have remained firmly with Blake to this day. But this is what he does. He looks, memorises, recalls, reinterprets, borrows, and manipulates visual culture. Whether images derive from his memory or imagination, the ever-expanding realms of popular culture, the street or the walls of the National Gallery, they are all source materials and are treated with equal reverence. Cerebrating imagery rather than celebrating it, however manufactured, is what most distinguishes Blake's particular British rather than American Pop art sensibility. Within his disparate output, encompassing collage, painting, drawing, prints and sculpture, it is this approach that is the most consistently defining of Blake's career and is what keeps his work so fresh and appealing to so many audiences today. Whether or not the work he makes at any given time can be termed 'Pop art' in any traditional sense (he now self-consciously drifts in and out of the Pop style), it is his approach to, rather than the content of, a work that makes it exist as such. Blake's perennial critique of the world's images, coupled with the increasing role he has taken in the presentation of his work, has amounted to an increasingly conceptual bias in his output, particularly since the beginning of the 1980s.

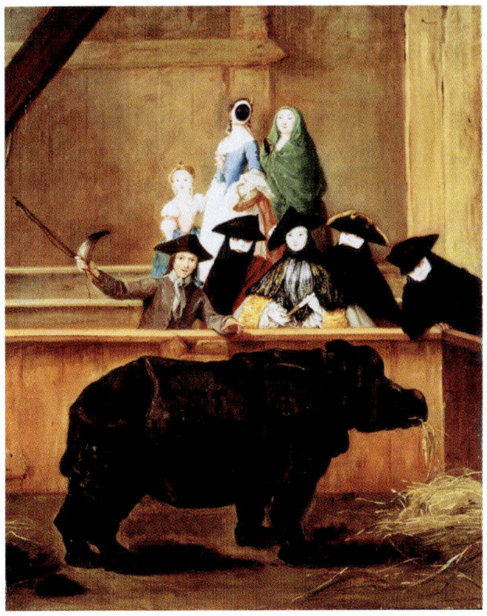

Pietro Longhi
Exhibition of a Rhinoceros at Venice
c.1751
Oil on canvas

Although far removed form the reductionist strategies so common in British practice in the late 1960s and the 1970s, conceptual play may certainly be identified in Blake's work. For two further works in the 'Venice' series, 'The Meeting' or 'Have a Nice Day, Mr Hockney' 1981–83 and Exhibition of a Rhinoceros in Venice (finished in 1996), Blake borrowed the compositions directly from art history: the former from Gustave Courbet's *Bonjour Monsieur Courbet* 1854 and the latter from Pietro Longhi's *Exhibition of a Rhinoceros at Venice* c.1751. Blake has appropriated art history in this way throughout his career, updating images and icons for his own purpose, one of the earliest examples being On the Balcony 1955–57 with its copy of Edouard Manet's *The Balcony* 1898–99. Blake's technique of pastiche, whether copying images in paint or incorporating real ones through collage, is interesting for several reasons. His eclectic borrowing is in part an homage to those he admires and from whom he has learnt. He found, for example, much in common with the realist approach of Courbet, who shunned the Salon and rejected the idealistic approaches of the Romantic and Neo-Classical schools in

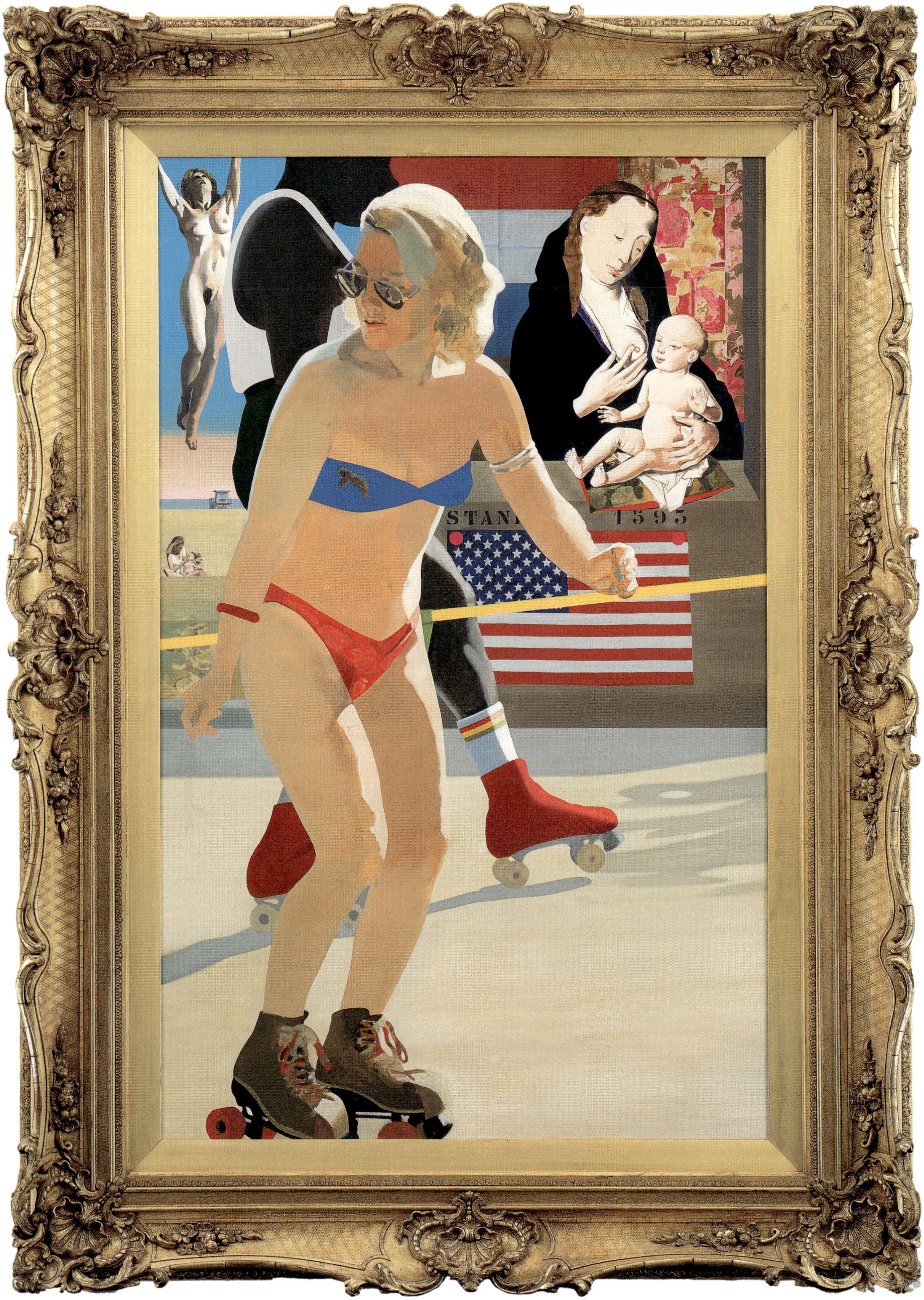
STAN
1593

Madonna of Venice Beach I
1994–6
Oil on canvas

favour of subjects taken from everyday life. Yet Blake's is also a ploy to locate himself within art-historical canons according to his own definitions. Keenly aware of the path of a successful artist, from first solo exhibition to mid-career retrospective to 'late period', Blake evaluates and positions himself within these terms and histories before any critic or curator can do it for him. At the time of writing he has just begun work on a new series of *Costume Life* paintings, revisiting some of his very early watercolours, which will be set against a highly decorative Klimt-esque background. When finished, which may or may not be in time for this exhibition, the paintings will be adorned with the legend 'Peter Blake Late Period'.

Exhibition of a Rhinoceros in Venice was still a work in progress in 1996 when included in Blake's *Now We Are 64* exhibition at the National Gallery, London, the culmination of his two-year residency there. Seventeen years after his visit to Los Angeles and the first of his Venice paintings, the theme was still preoccupying him. Whatever their source, it is typical for Blake to rework his images substantially over lengthy periods of time and, similarly, once he begins a thematic series, to return to it again and again. In the case of the rhinoceros painting, Blake saw the original Longhi hanging in the National Gallery and decided to 'transcribe' it: 'I had been working on a series about Venice, California, so I could simply relocate the painting there.'[3] Several other long-standing works were eventually finished and exhibited as a result of the residency – the prevalence of historical imagery surrounding him on a daily basis clearly had a profound effect. Much to the frustration of those trying to sell his work, Blake is renowned for taking years, if not decades, to complete a canvas, continually updating it or abandoning it for significant periods before returning it to the easel. In this way, and because of his unusual willingness to exhibit paintings in an unfinished state, Blake's work can become an ongoing commentary on the world and its preoccupations, aesthetic or otherwise. Like the picture of Dorian Gray, his paintings change over time, incorporating and reflecting new stories and experiences, real and imagined, as their lives echo that of their producer.

Given his innate fascination with all kinds of images, be they found or of his own making, it is not surprising that Blake concerns himself as much with the display of his work as with its production. From the 1980s he began to use the

3
Peter Blake, *Now We Are 64: Peter Blake at the National Gallery*, London, National Gallery Publications, 1996, p. 7.

Madonna of Venice Beach (California) No. IV
1995
Oil on wood panel

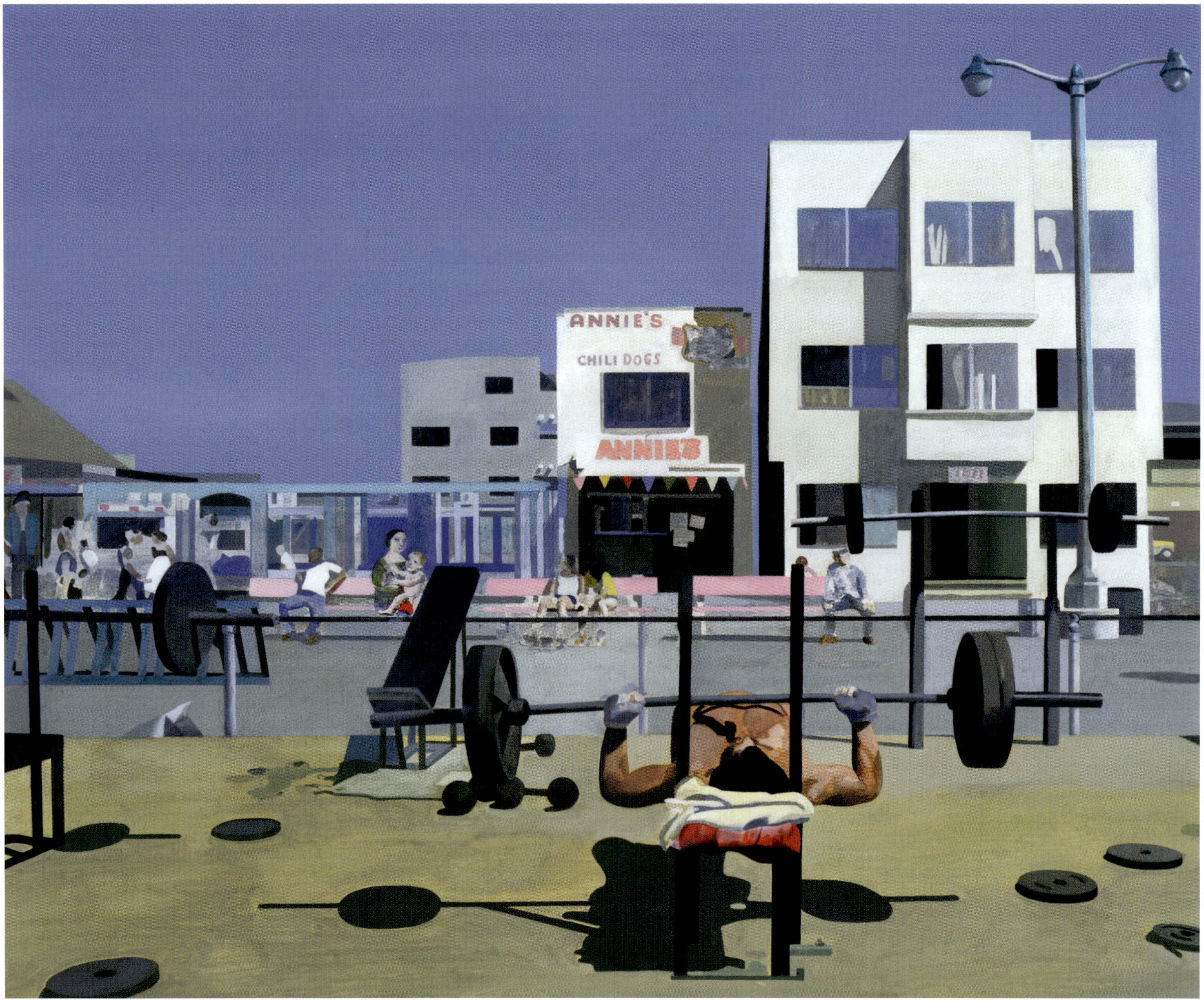

Madonna of Venice Beach II
1995
Oil on canvas

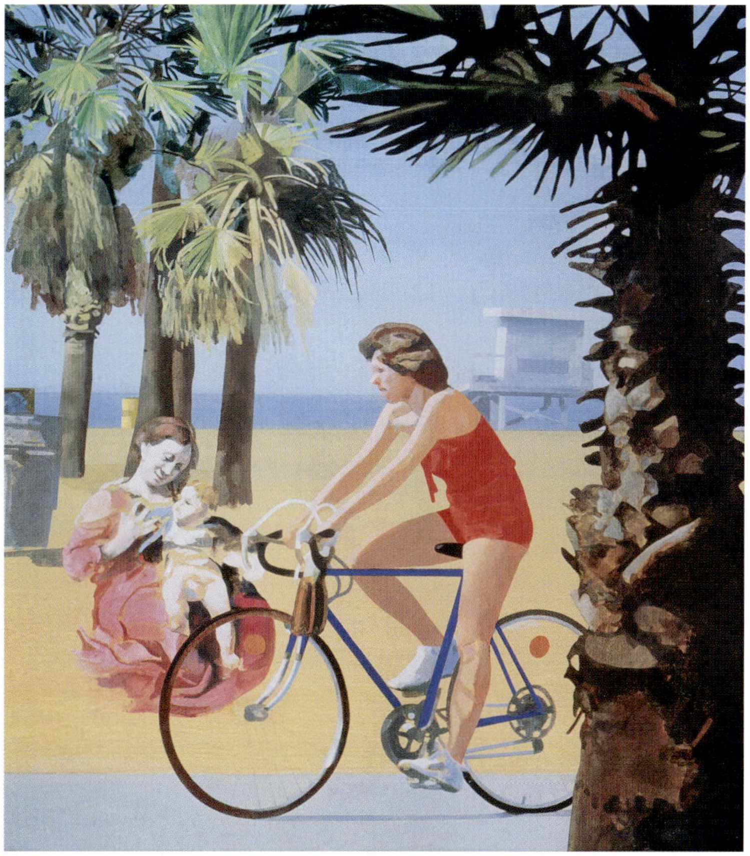

The National Gallery Madonna
1994–2000
Oil on canvas

Madonna of Venice Beach VI
1995
Oil on canvas

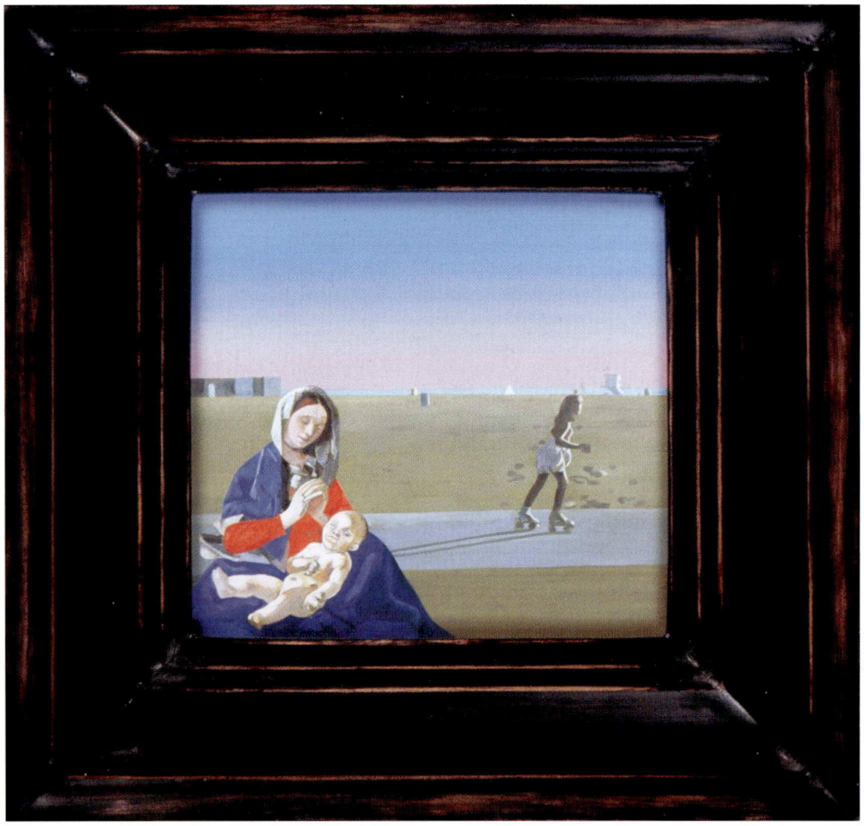

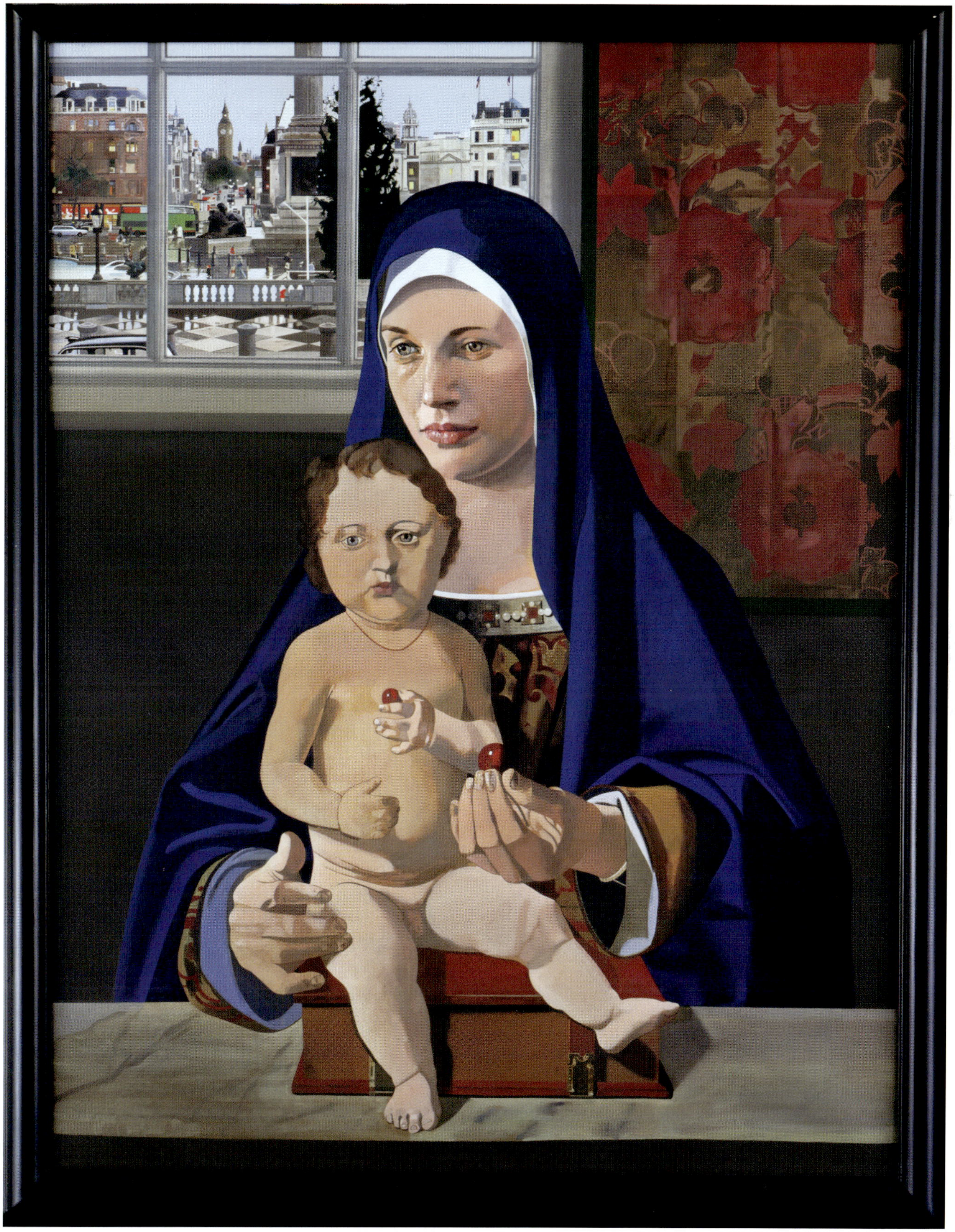

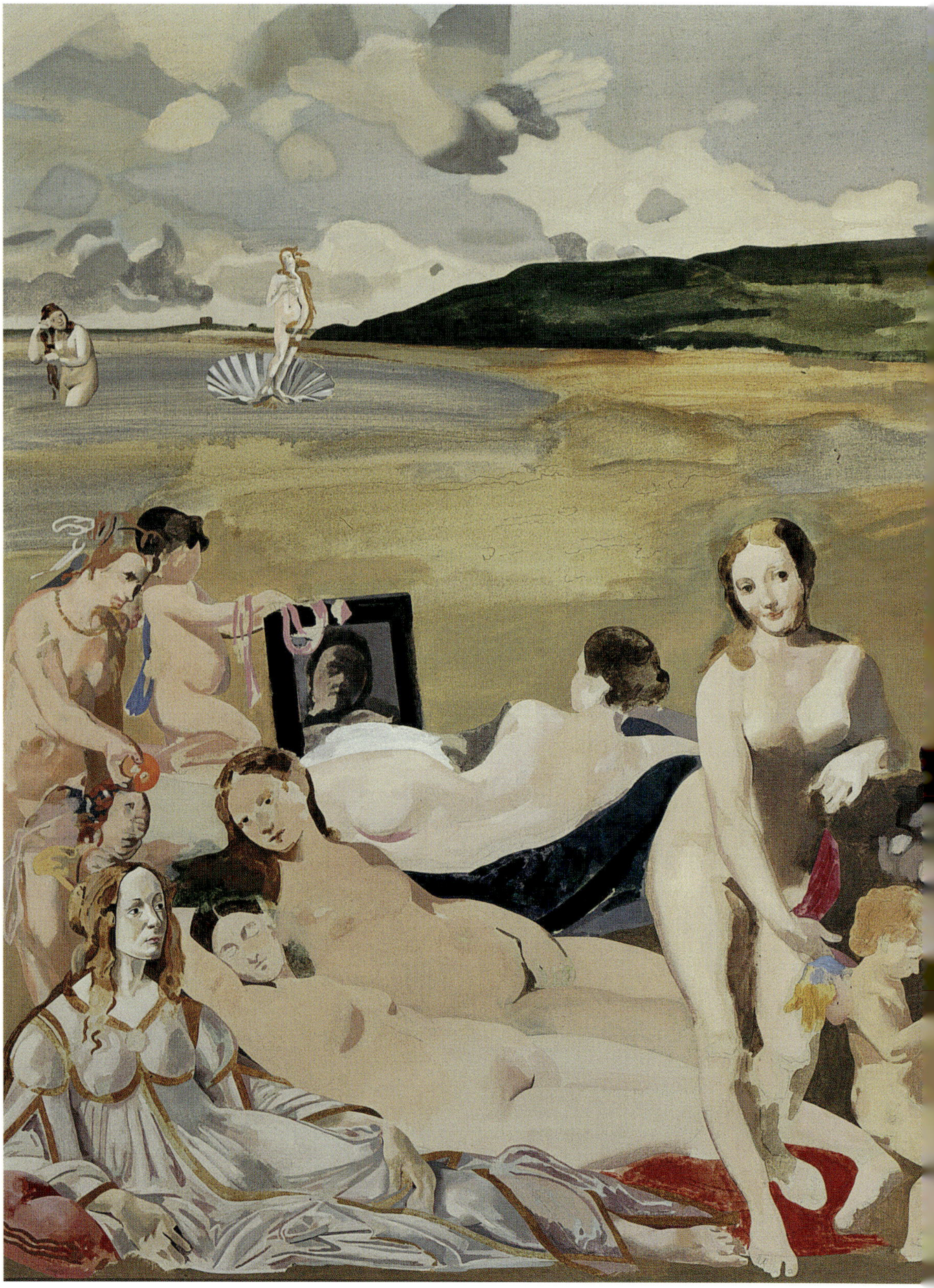

The Venuses' Outing to Weymouth
1994–2004
Oil on canvas

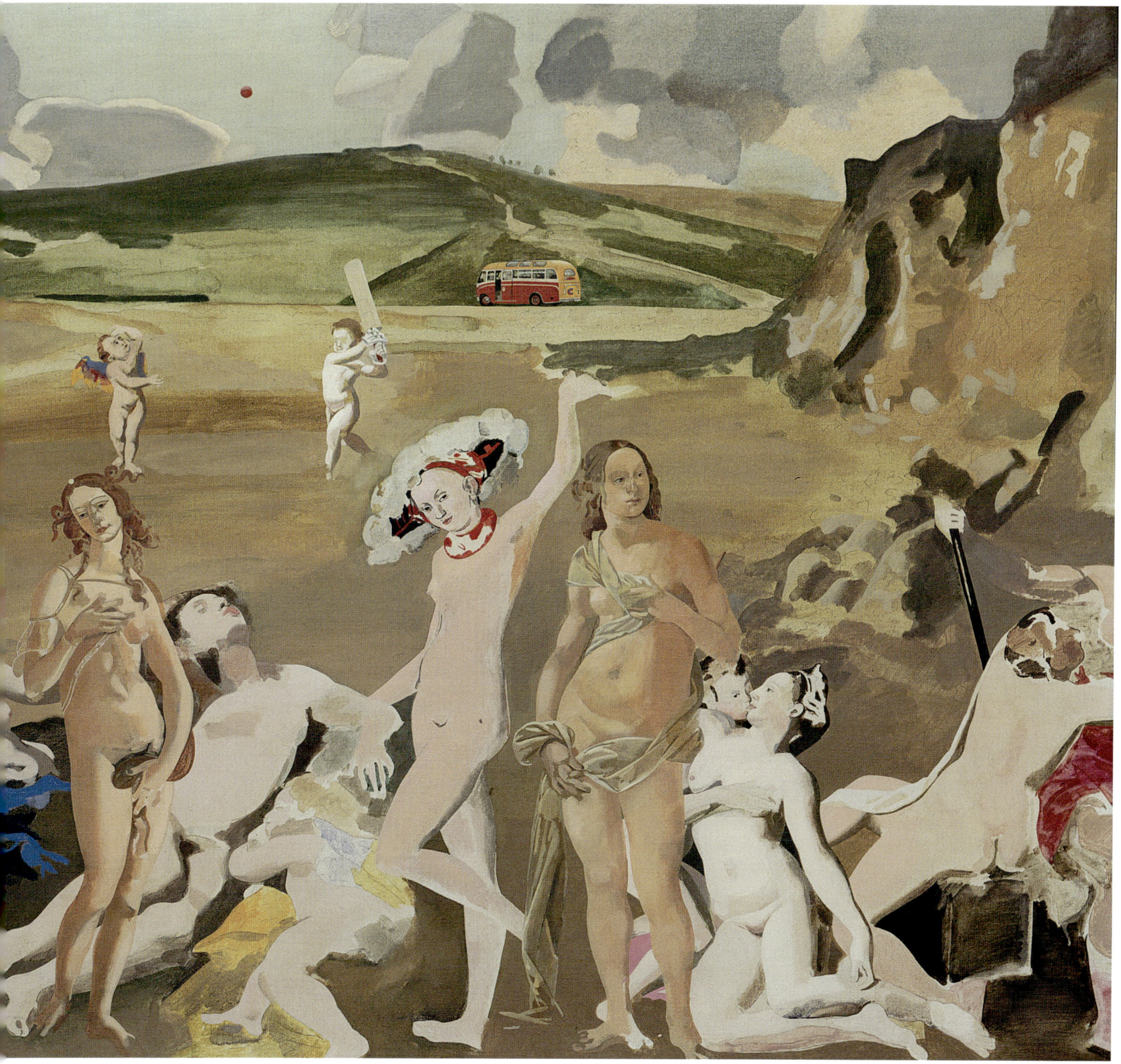

Still Life (I) (After van Os, Fruit and Flowers in a Terracotta Vase)
1996
Oil on canvas on board

Still Life (III) (After Fantin-Latour, The Rosy Wealth of June)
1996
Oil on canvas on board

Still Life (VI) (After Courbet, Still Life with Apples and a Pomegranate)
1996
Oil on canvas on board

Still Life (VIII) (After Steenwyck, Still Life: An Allegory of the Vanities of Human Life)
1996
Oil on panel

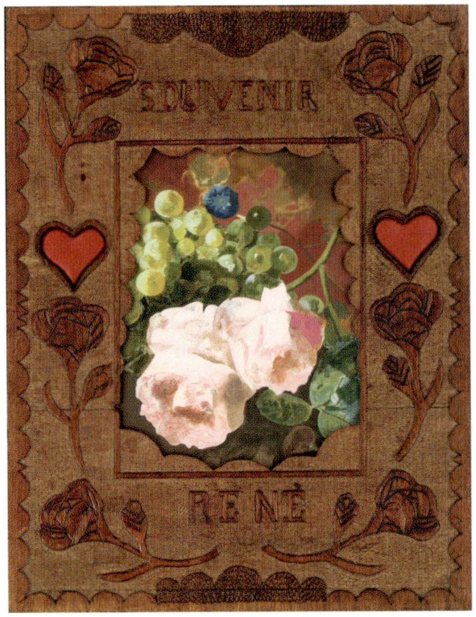

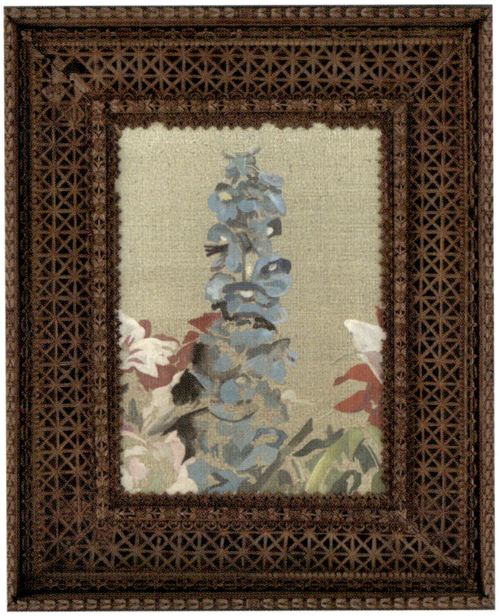

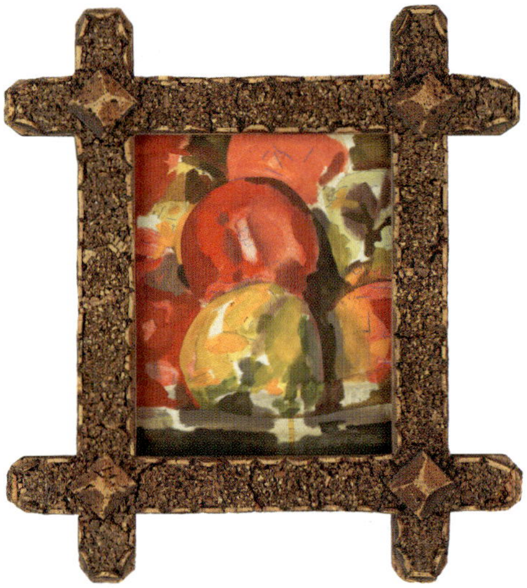

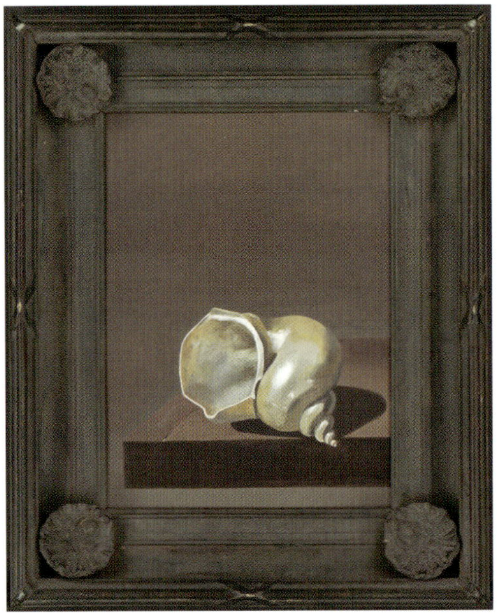

The Deer Park (After Velasquez, The Boar Hunt). In Memory of Michael Andrews
1996
Oil on canvas

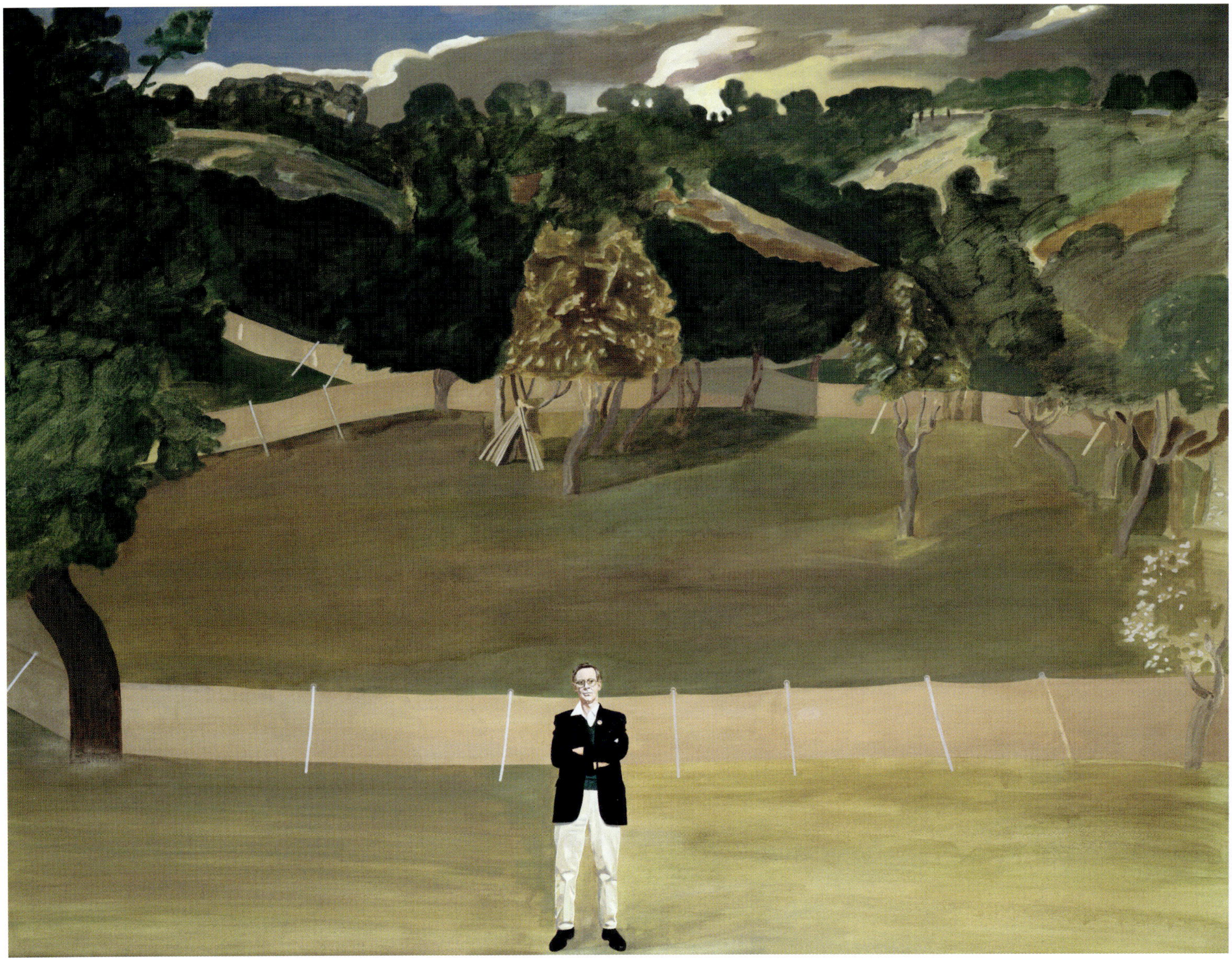

D'Aprés Luis Melendez: detail de 'Still Life with Oranges and Walnuts'
1996–2001
Oil on cardboard

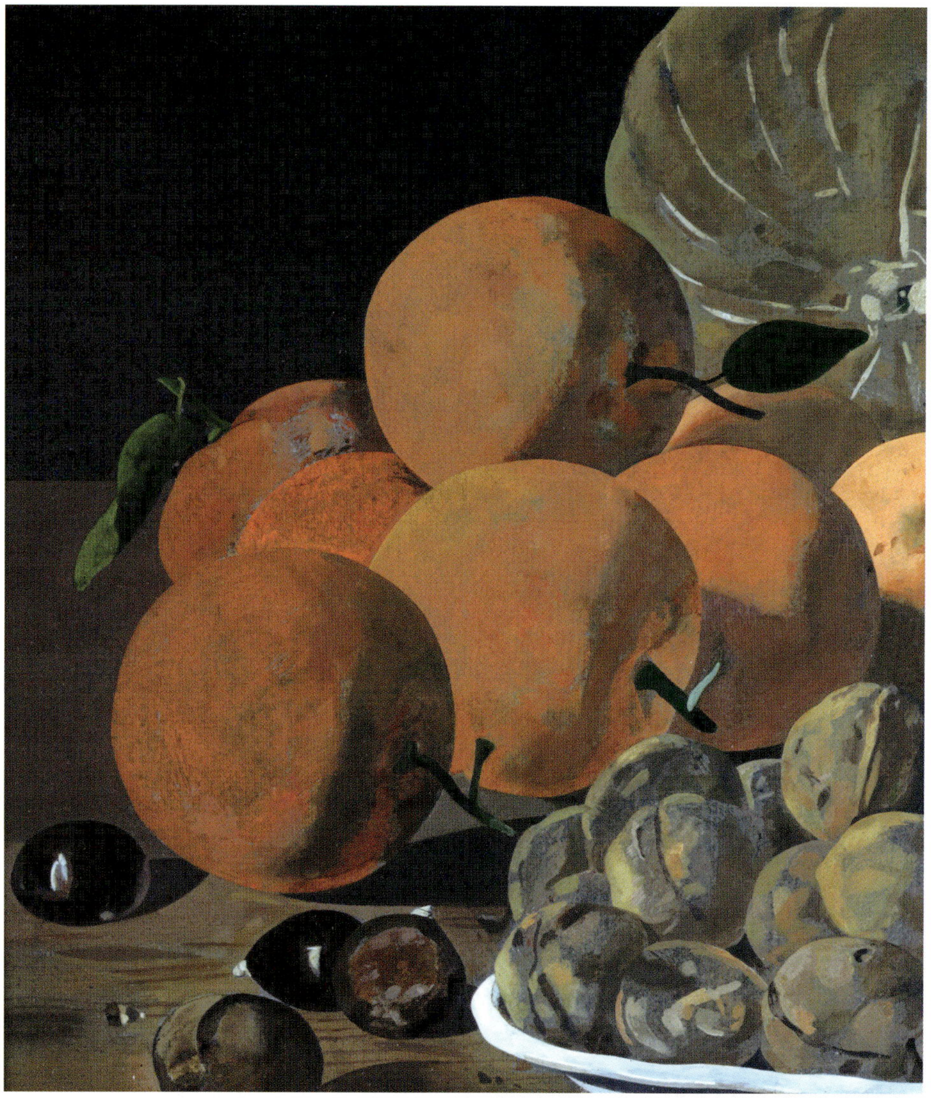

After Velasquez, Still Life II, Kitchen Scene with Christ in the House of Martha & Mary
1996–2001
Oil on wood

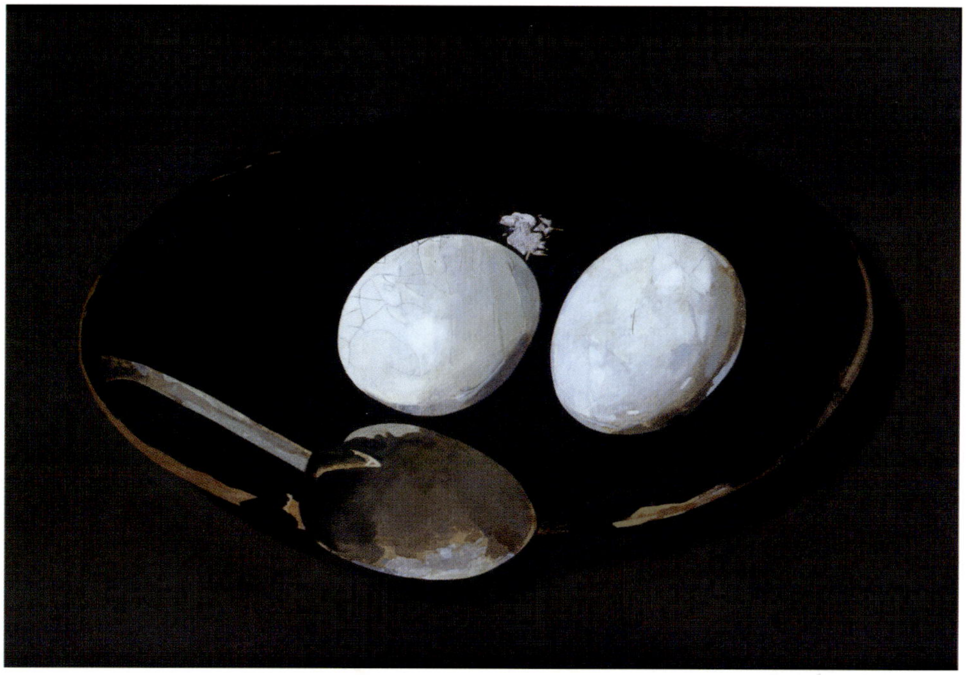

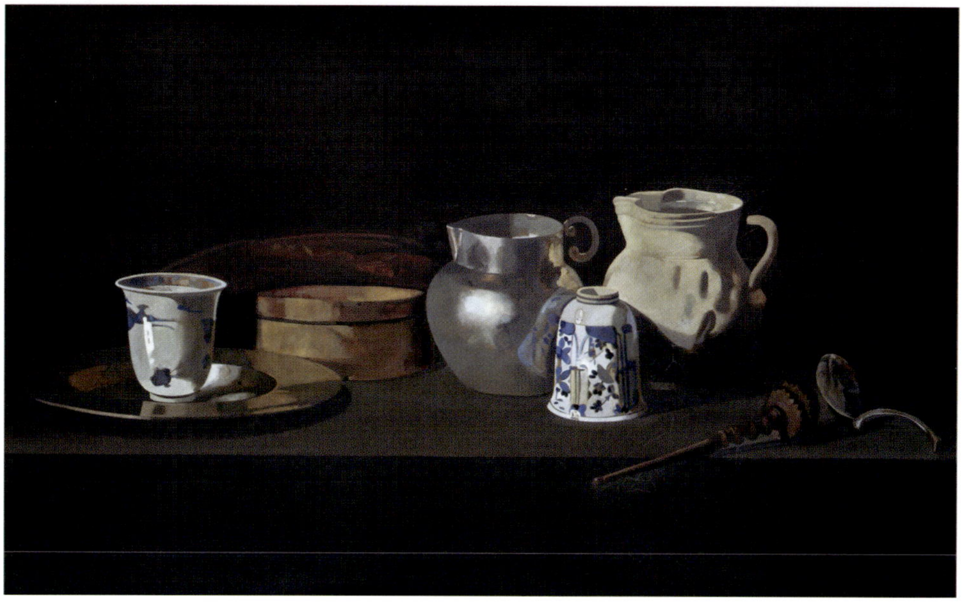

D'Aprés Juan de Zurbaran, 'Still Life with Chocolate Service'
1996–2001
Oil on wood

Tarzan and his Family at the Roxy Cinema, New York
1964–2002
Acrylic on canvas

exhibition almost as a conceptual device controlling the presentation of his work in a way that deliberately shaped how audiences received it, and as a means to evaluate his own practice. In 1981 he was invited to have a retrospective at the Tate Gallery, London, to open in February 1983. Working closely with the curators, he planned a series of environments, rather than straightforward galleries, which would best represent the development of his career to date. Blake has often likened his career to the form of a tree, its straight trunk representing the core of the artist's activity – traditional figurative painting. 'Where my art has left to go on different excursions there are branches like Pop Art, wood engraving, and Ruralism.'[4] His analogy may have gone some way to shaping the thinking behind the structure of his exhibition, presented almost as a series of rooms or branches, each one representing another thematic excursion.

At the entrance to the exhibition visitors were greeted by *Sculpture Park* 1981–83, Blake's most ambitious sculpture to date, made collaboratively with Chrissy Wilson (whom he married in 1987). The work consisted of found objects, some natural, some manufactured, collected over many years, often before the artist knew their ultimate purpose. Miniature figures, houses, cars, street furniture and a wealth of other peculiar forms were intricately arranged into a fantasy land complete with scaled-down copies of sculptures by, among others, Constantin Brancusi, Barbara Hepworth and Henry Moore. The work perhaps suggests Blake's approach to himself and art history as part of a growing self-consciousness of 'the artist' within the world of art-historical discourse, rather than focused on the idea of 'connoisseurship' which had previously been so strong. Blake planned a second version of the work 'with figures at Action Man size' but promptly abandoned the idea once he realised it would be over fifty feet long. *Sculpture Park* was accompanied by a group of works collectively entitled *Incident from a Sculpture Park*. These sculptures, with titles such as *Africans Looking at an Asian Sculpture* and *Asians Looking at an African Sculpture*, were wry comments on the ways in which not only objects but also the people looking at them are categorised. The two works, with their critique of the ways in which objects are presented, categorised and engaged with, thus functioned as an introduction to the exhibition and indeed to Blake's entire working ethos.

4
Peter Blake in Christopher Martin (ed.), 'The Ruralists', *Art & Design*, no. 23, 1991, p. 36.

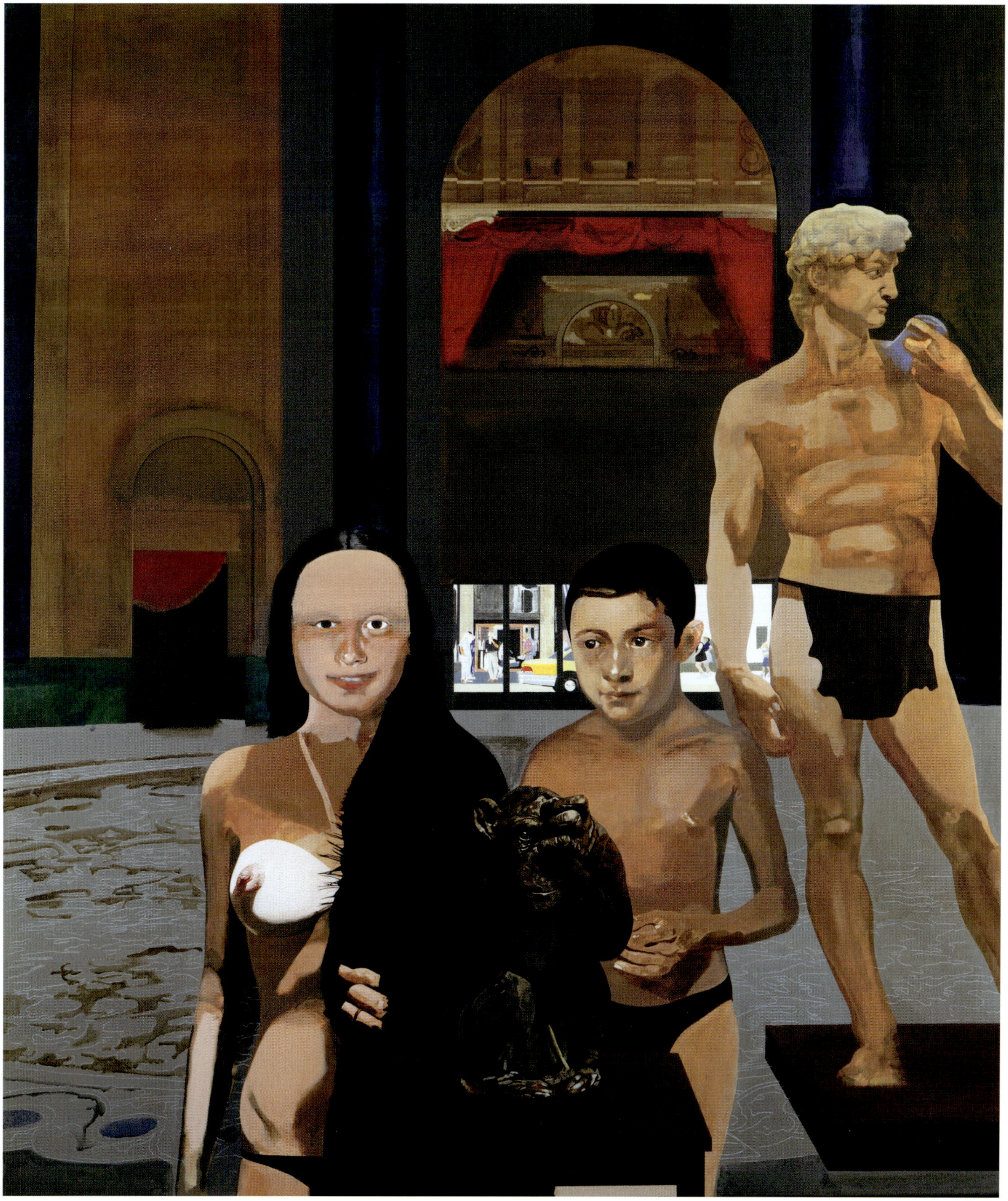

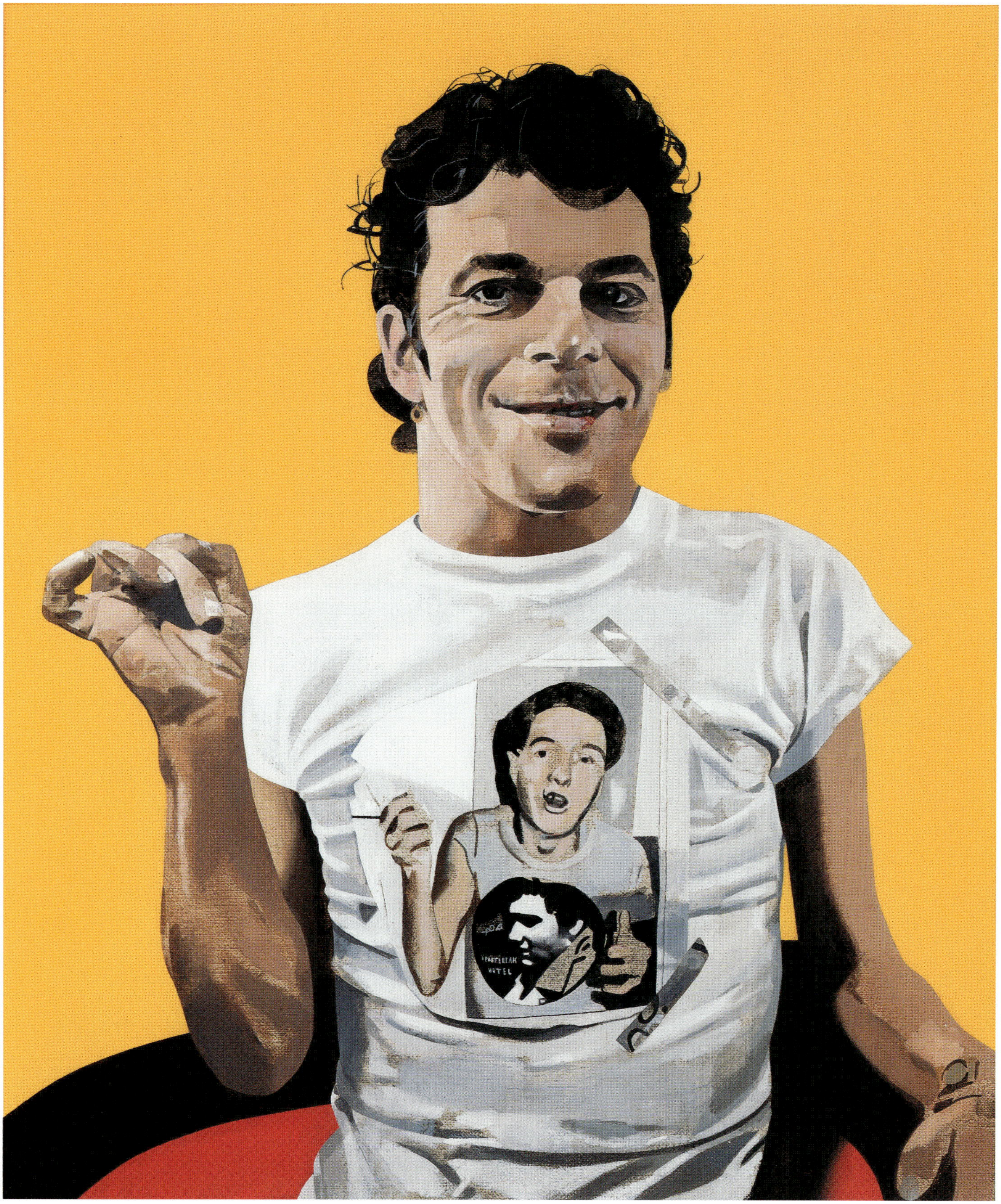

Ian Dury
2001
Acrylic on board

To further condition the audience the first room of the exhibition was, in Blake's words, something of an 'ante-room', complete with the theme tune 'Peter the Painter' written especially by Ian Dury, one of Blake's former students. The walls were painted in primary colours and the paintings that hung upon them were of Blake's celebrated pop heroes – The Beatles 1963–68, Bo Diddley 1963, Portrait of Sammy Davis Jr 1960 and others. The second room, appropriately accompanied by the lilting English Romanticism of Vaughan Williams and Edward Elgar, was dedicated to Blake's work with the Brotherhood of Ruralists. Although he continued (as indeed he still does) to contribute to the group's collective exhibitions, the Tate show provided something of a finale to Blake's time as a Ruralist, much to the relief of several critics who found his work of the period stilted in its unashamed nostalgia. Richard Cork shared the sentiment of a number of critics when he ended his review of the exhibition with the words 'I only hope that Blake's recent return to London, where he made all his best work, will help him recover the old infectious enthusiasm for contemporary life. He is too good an artist to dissipate his unique talents any longer.'[5] To mark the occasion Blake asked the members of the Ruralist group to each make a painting of the 'definitive nude', with set dimensions. Six different versions of this 'definitive' figure, uniform in size but of course not in content, ultimately hung side by side.

5
'Happy Return of the Ruralist', *London Evening Standard*, 10 February 1983.

Music also provided a framework for many other rooms. A collection of 'sentimental songs' accompanied the work Blake made during his divorce and the development of his relationship with Chrissy Wilson. Like the themes and personalities to which he continually returns in his painting, the endless repetition of familiar songs by Gladys Knight and the Pips and Elton John became entangled with the work itself, guiding visitors through the exhibition (if not in some cases hastening their exit). Long concerned to distribute his work within the widest possible context, preferably on terms comparable to the pop music that was now accompanying it, Blake saw the exhibition's catalogue as a further opportunity to circulate his work and make it physically accessible to as many people as possible. 12,500 copies of the publication included a free print of The Owl and the Pussycat 1981–83, each one signed by the artist.

Original artwork for the Band Aid single ‘Do They Know It’s Christmas?’
1984
Paper collage

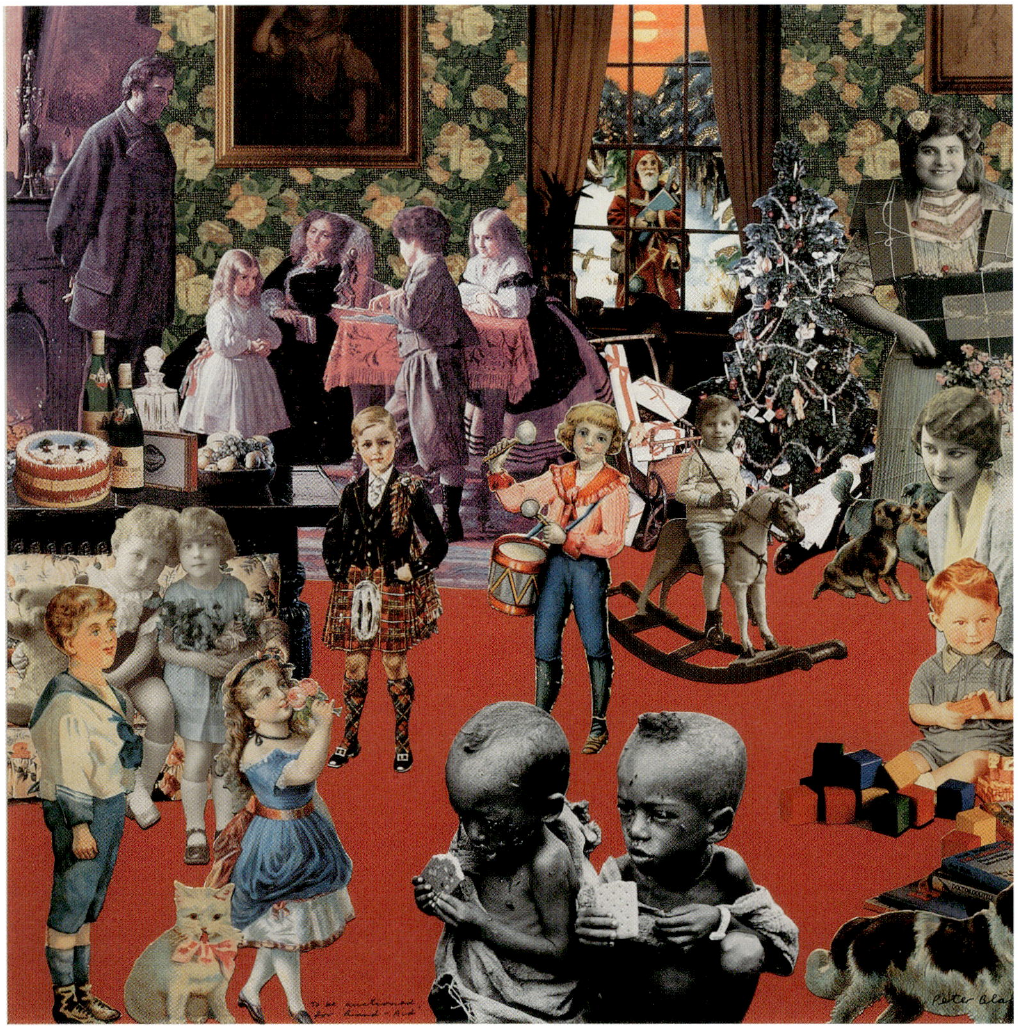

Toy Shop No. 2
1986–8
Mixed media

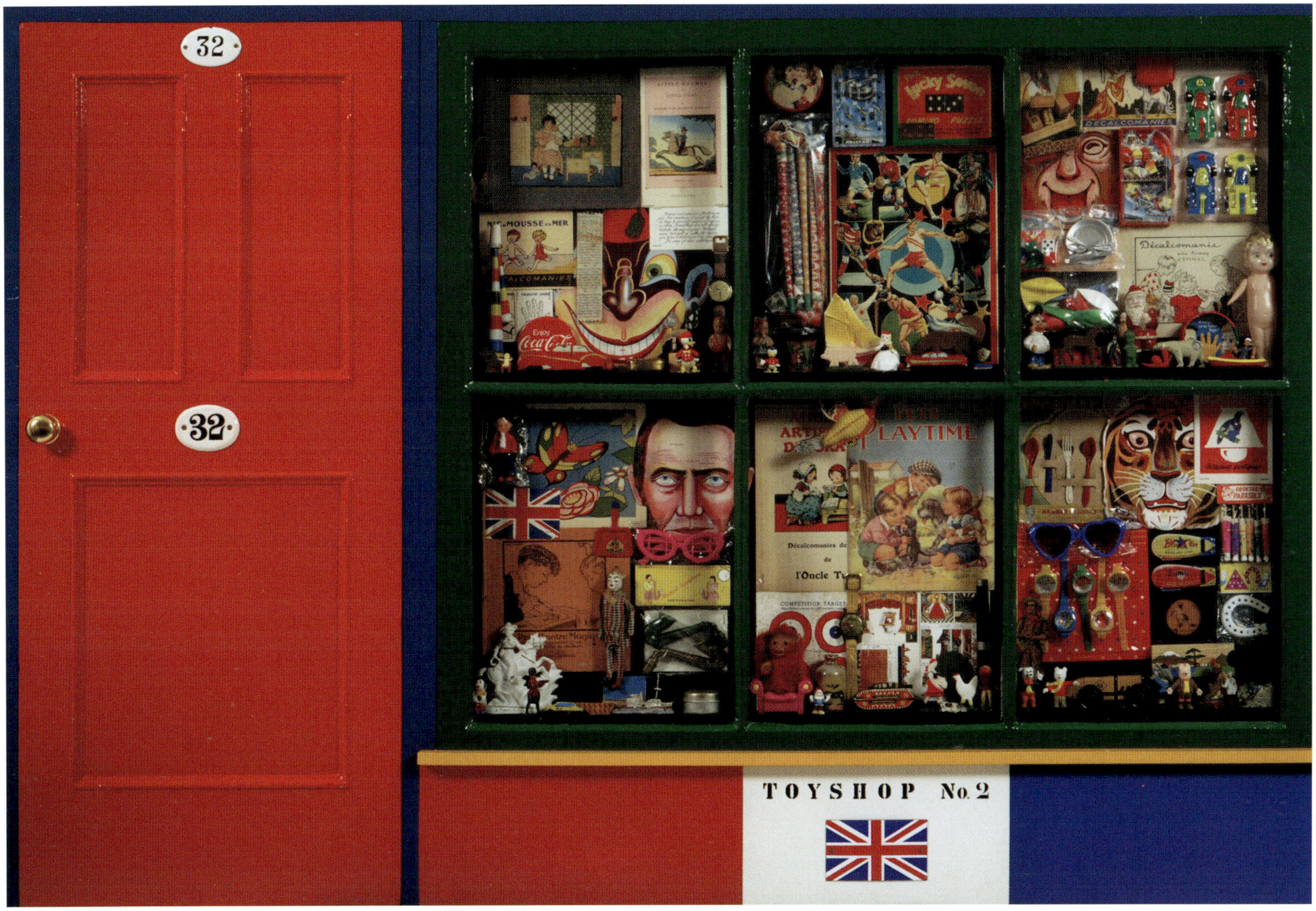

The 1980s progressed as a productive decade for Blake with his studio-based and commercial practices continuing to flourish, ensuring the distribution of his work through a variety of means and contexts. In 1984 he was commissioned by Bob Geldof to design the cover for the Band Aid single and went on to make the poster for the Live Aid concert the following year. Continuing his long-standing fascination with the world of entertainment, he made several important additions to ongoing series, perhaps most notably to his wrestlers, begun in 1961. To these extraordinary characters, Blake continued to bring his unique imagination, applying a narrative framework to solitary fictional figures through their names and titles, typically via text incorporated as a graphic device within the work itself, and facial expressions and poses that mimicked film-stills or publicity shots. Yet despite his consistent output and the success of the Tate exhibition, the 1980s were a critically hostile background for Blake, the prevailing tastes of the decade jarring with the Pop sensibility that consistently remained at the core of his work. Despondent about the cultural world that now surrounded him, Blake accepted an invitation for an exhibition from the Nishimura Gallery in Tokyo as another opportunity to do more than simply show pre-existing work.

With *Déjà Vu* (9–31 May 1988) Blake set out 'to recreate his high point in Pop art… to do it all again'. Rather than embark on a new thematic approach, he copied previous versions of his own classic Pop paintings, using the idiom's own technique to initiate a critique of Pop art within its own terms. Plundering the history of his own practice was arguably a logical step for one who has so consistently transmediated the imagery of others. The exhibition included around thirty works, such as Toy Shop No. 2 1986–88, *The Beatles* 1987 and *Everly Wall* 1987. Blake not only sought to jump-start the re-emergence and appreciation of Pop art but also used the process to question its position within art history and to re-access his own practice. Furthermore, with works such as *The Second Real Target 25 Years Later*, just as with the first version, he probed the disparities between British and American Pop by questioning the use of the icon so prevalent within the latter by artists such as Jasper Johns. Yet with the Tokyo exhibition far removed from the British art world, it was only the keenest of critics in the UK who took note, and so it did little to raise the debate Blake felt was long overdue.

By the start of the next decade the cultural territory that surrounded Blake had become more accepting, and in fact before too long it was as though many of the tastes and preoccupations that had been so celebrated in the 1960s during his high Pop period had come full circle. For Blake, many of the characters who had played such an important part in his life at that time had 1990s' counterparts. Robert Fraser, the celebrated dealer and one-time sharer of Mick Jagger's handcuffs became Jay Jopling; the influential collector Ted Power became Charles Saatchi; Terence Stamp became Jude Law; Twiggy became Kate Moss; and the rivalry between the Beatles and the Stones was matched by that of Blur and Oasis. Wherever Blake looked, the swinging sixties were being recalled and slowly morphing into the 'Cool Britannia' (itself a sixties' term) that was soon to be so heavily promoted by Tony Blair's New Labour.

In art-world terms, the launch pad for this particular cultural renaissance came in the form of Marco Livingstone's important *Pop Art* exhibition held at London's Royal Academy in 1991. Leading to a critical reassessment of Blake's work, the exhibition also introduced it to a younger generation of British artists, just as Blake and his contemporaries had been struck by *Modern Art of the United States* at the Tate Gallery in 1956. Blake was to become something of a grandfather to the 'Young British Artists', going out of his way to support them and attend their exhibition openings, and many have acknowledged his impact upon them. As Blake had always done, it was once again OK to celebrate and examine the often more quirky elements of a peculiarly British culture, just as artists such as Sarah Lucas, Gavin Turk and even Gary Hume began to do. Tracey Emin's incorporation of text, autobiography and references to childhood memory in her work also seems to owe much to Blake, as do, although to a lesser extent, Damien Hirst's categorisations of manufactured and natural objects.[6] Hirst also shares with Blake a passion for collecting (they have been known to bid for the same object at auction), and indeed for presenting self-curated selections of their collections in public.

In a reprise of his 1960s' social sphere Blake became friends with many important figures in the British music world of the 1990s and received commissions for several album covers, including Paul Weller's *Stanley Road* 1999,

6
Hirst has on a number of occasions mentioned his fascination with Blake's *Girl at a Window* 1962, which he saw on display in Leeds, his home town.

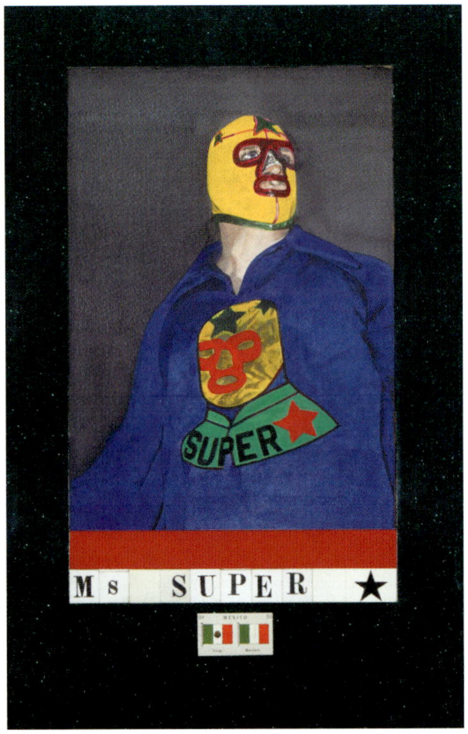

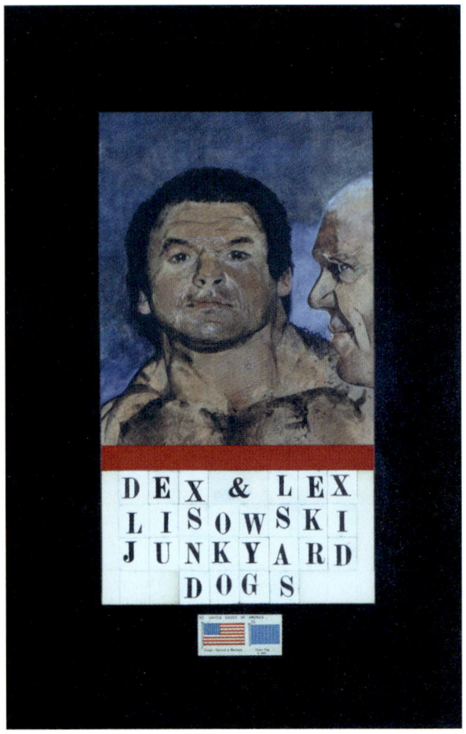

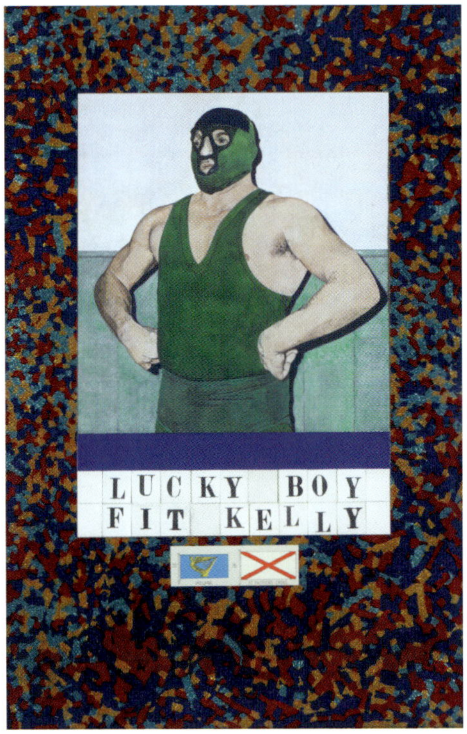

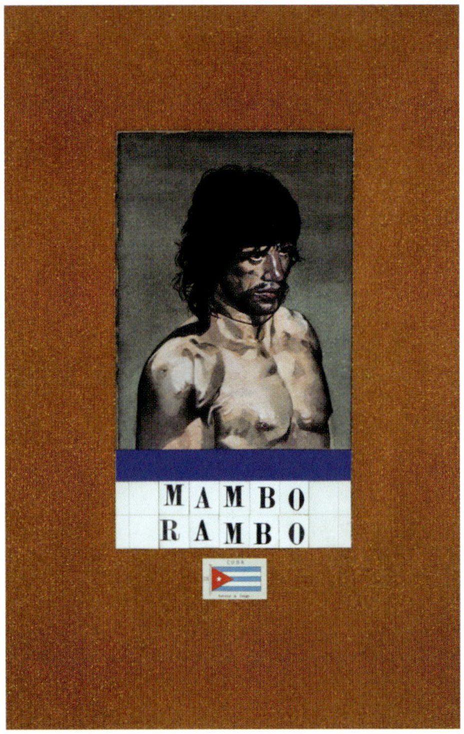

Ms. Super
1985
Watercolour and mixed media

Dex and Lex Lisowski Junkyard Dogs
1986
Watercolour and mixed media

Lucky Boy Fit Kelly
1987
Watercolour and mixed media

Mambo Rambo
1987
Watercolour and mixed media

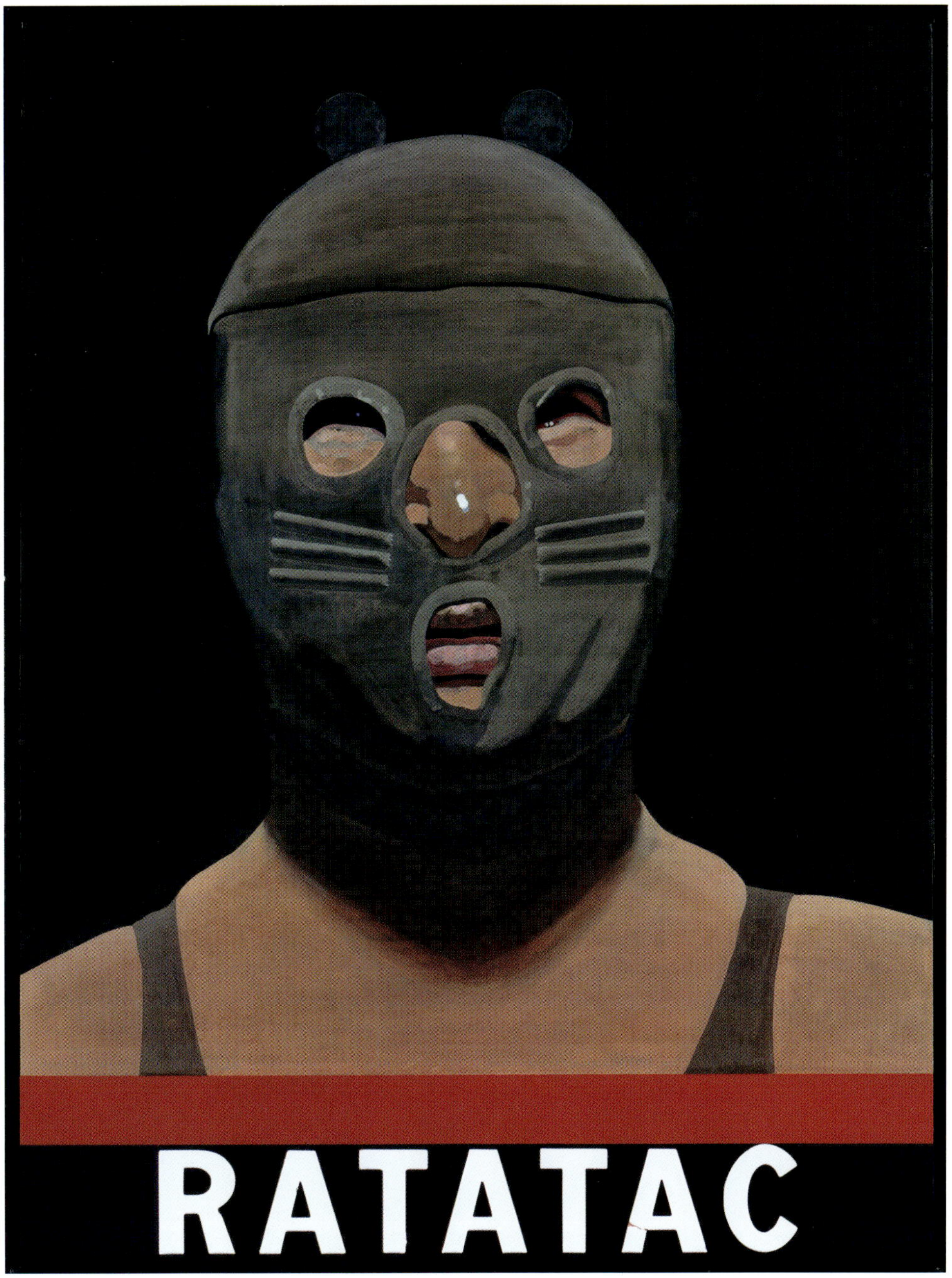

Ratatac
1997–2003
Oil on hardboard

Blanche Neige and Bet Noir
1976–81
Oil on panel

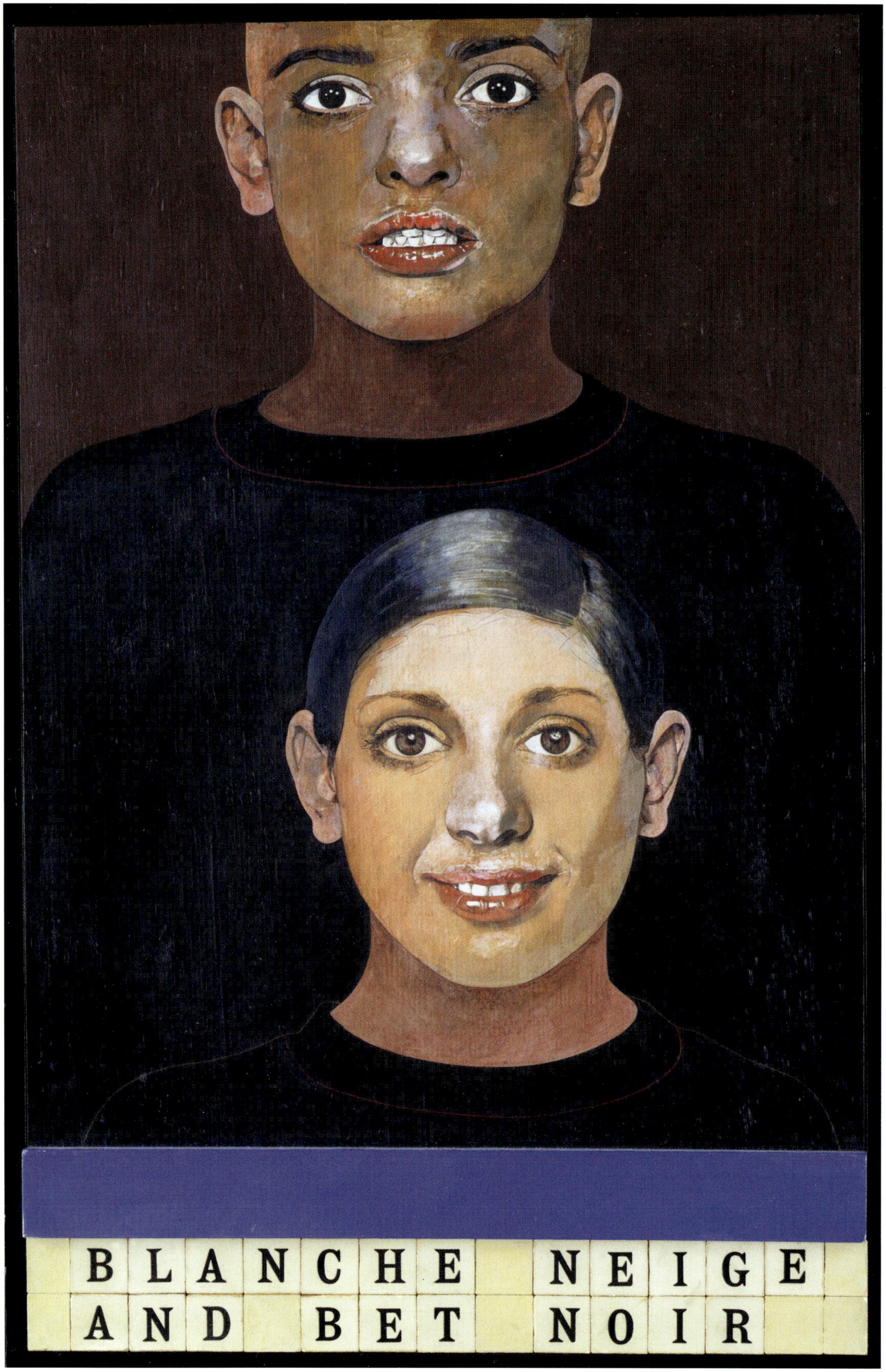

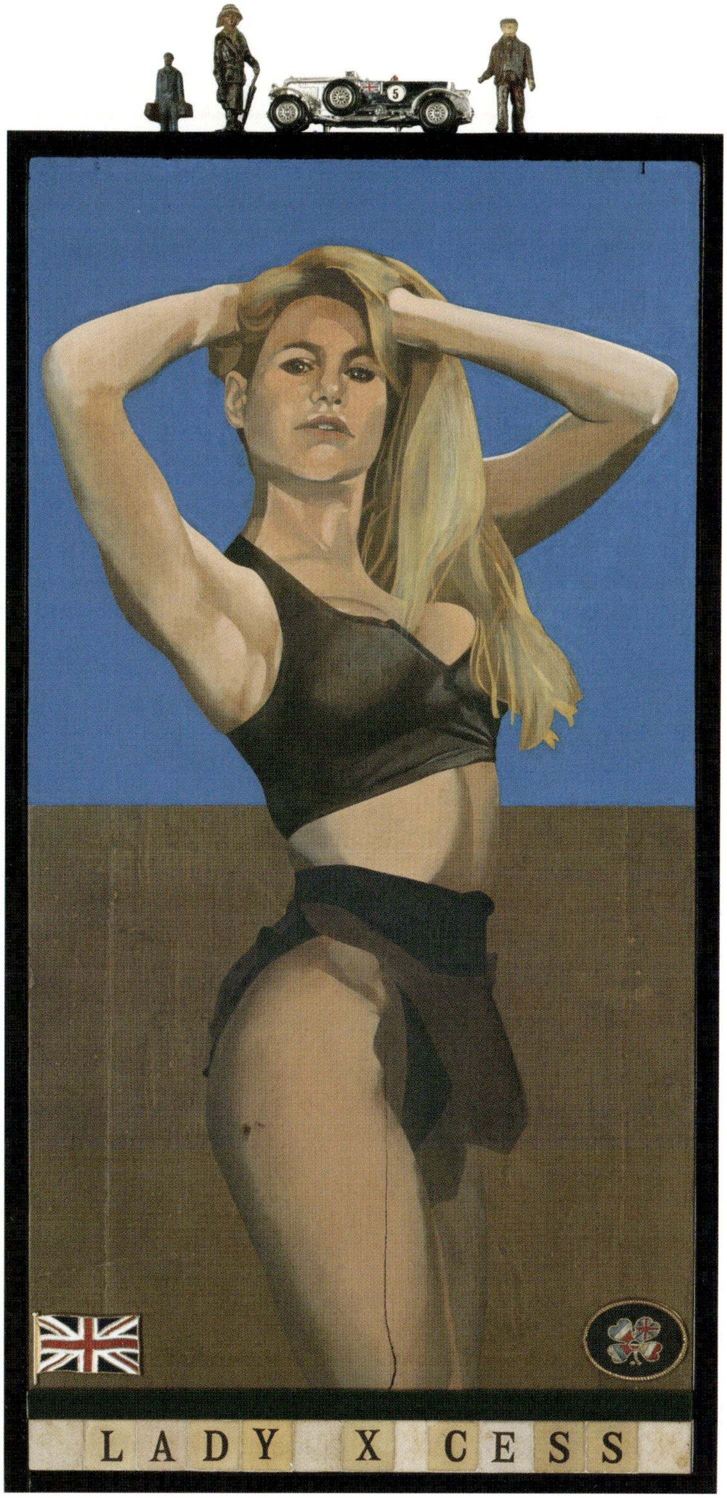

Lady X Cess
2002–3
Oil on wooden panel

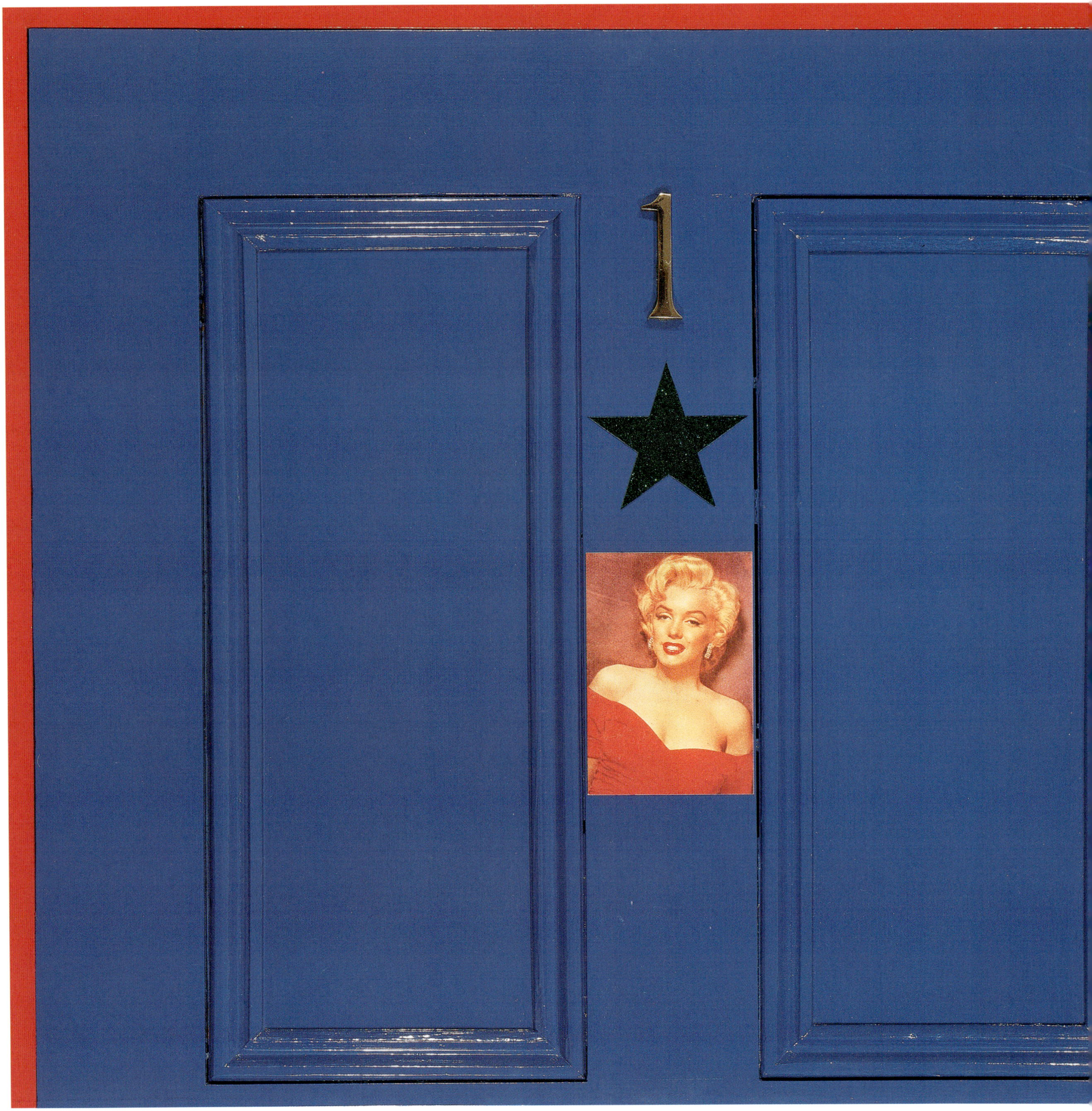
1

Untitled, from 'In Homage to Marilyn Monroe'
1990
Gloss paint and mixed media on wood

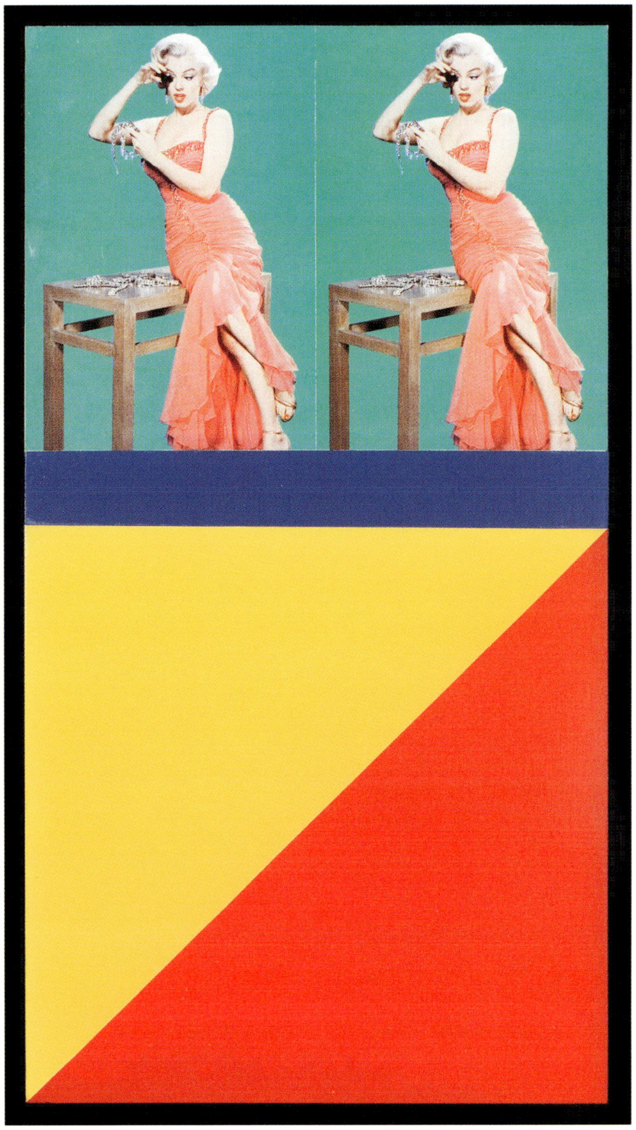

M.M. Yellow and Red
1990
Photographs and enamel paint on wood

Marilyn Monroe over a Painting No.1
1989–90
Photographs and enamel paint on wood

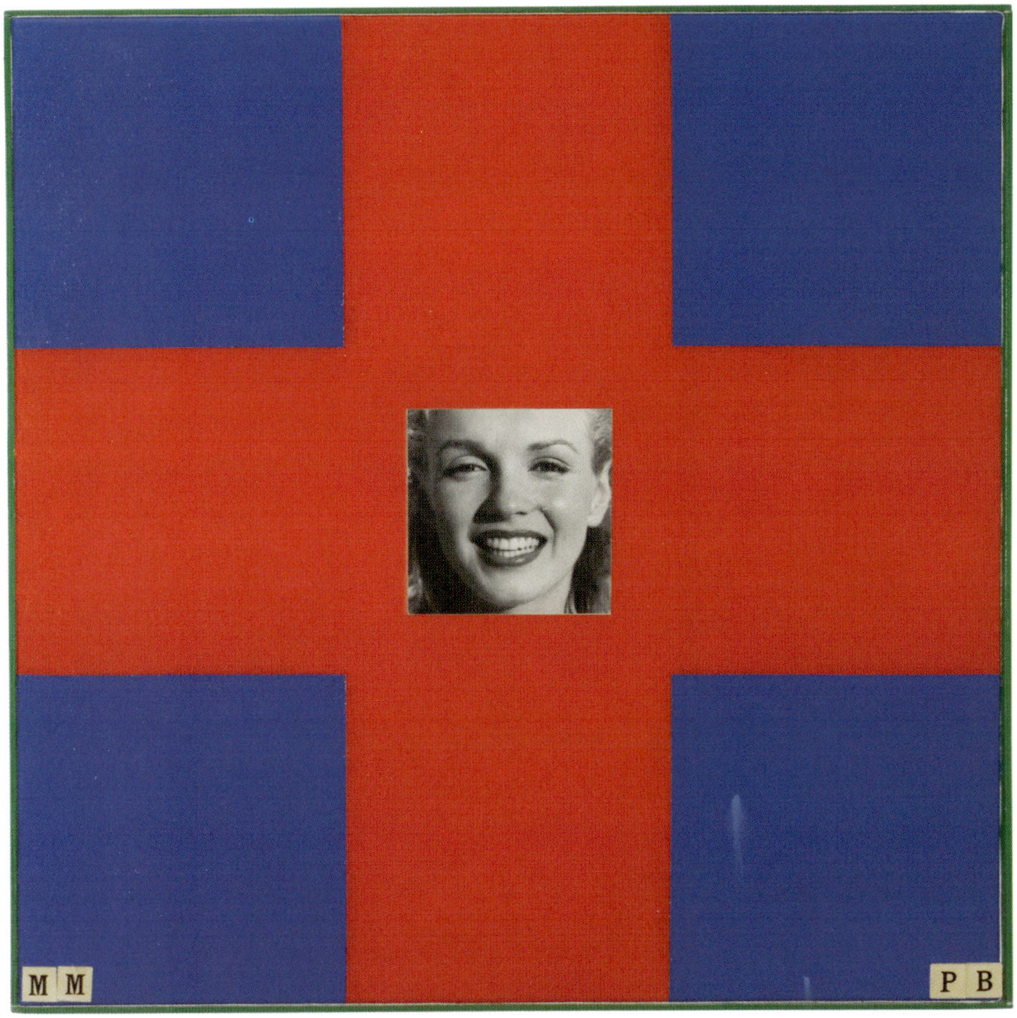

Marilyn Monroe: Red Cross
1989–90
Oil and photograph on canvas

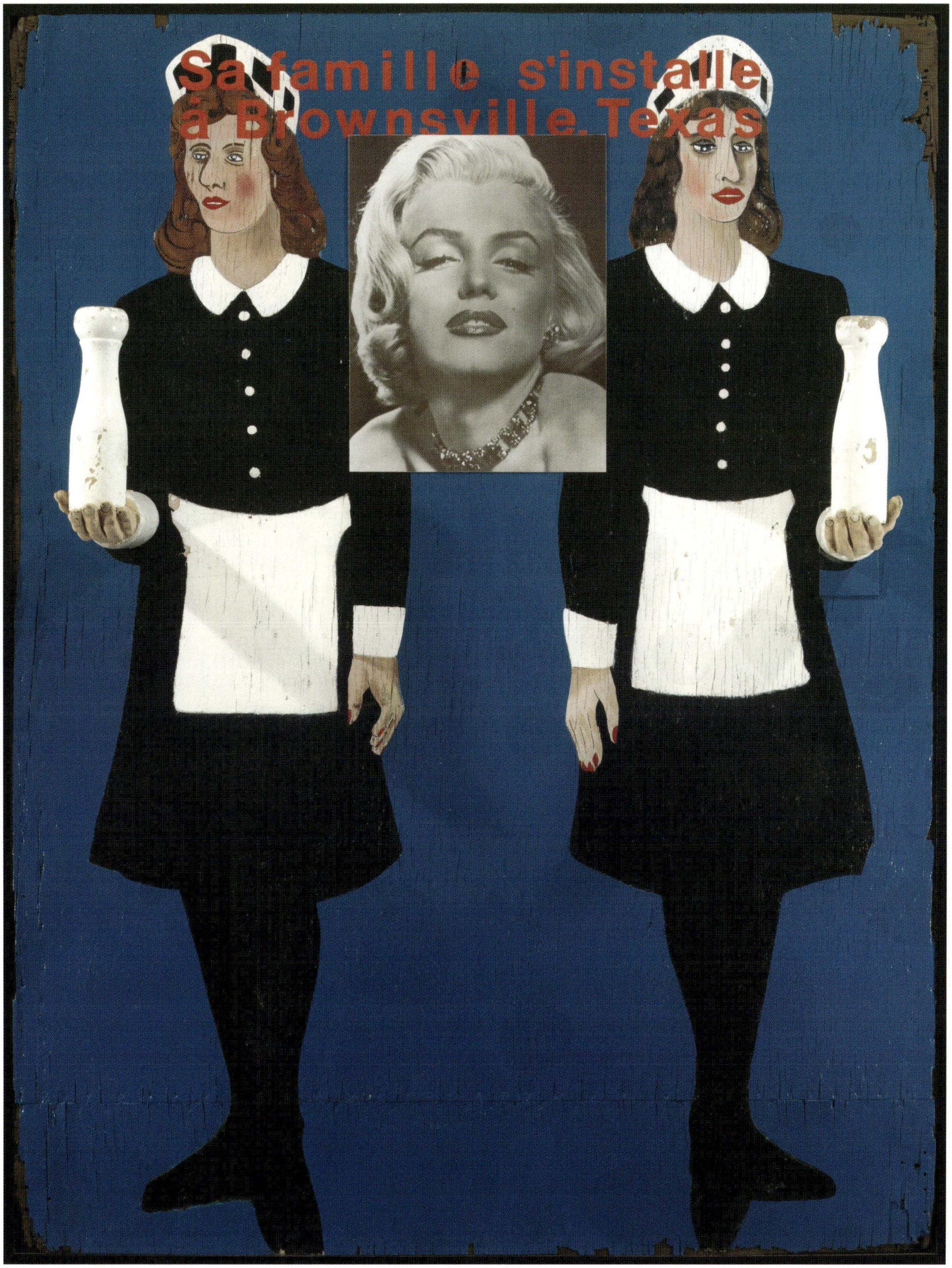
Sa famille s'installe
à Brownsville, Texas

Norma Jean Baker 1926–1962
1988
Photographs and black enamel on wood

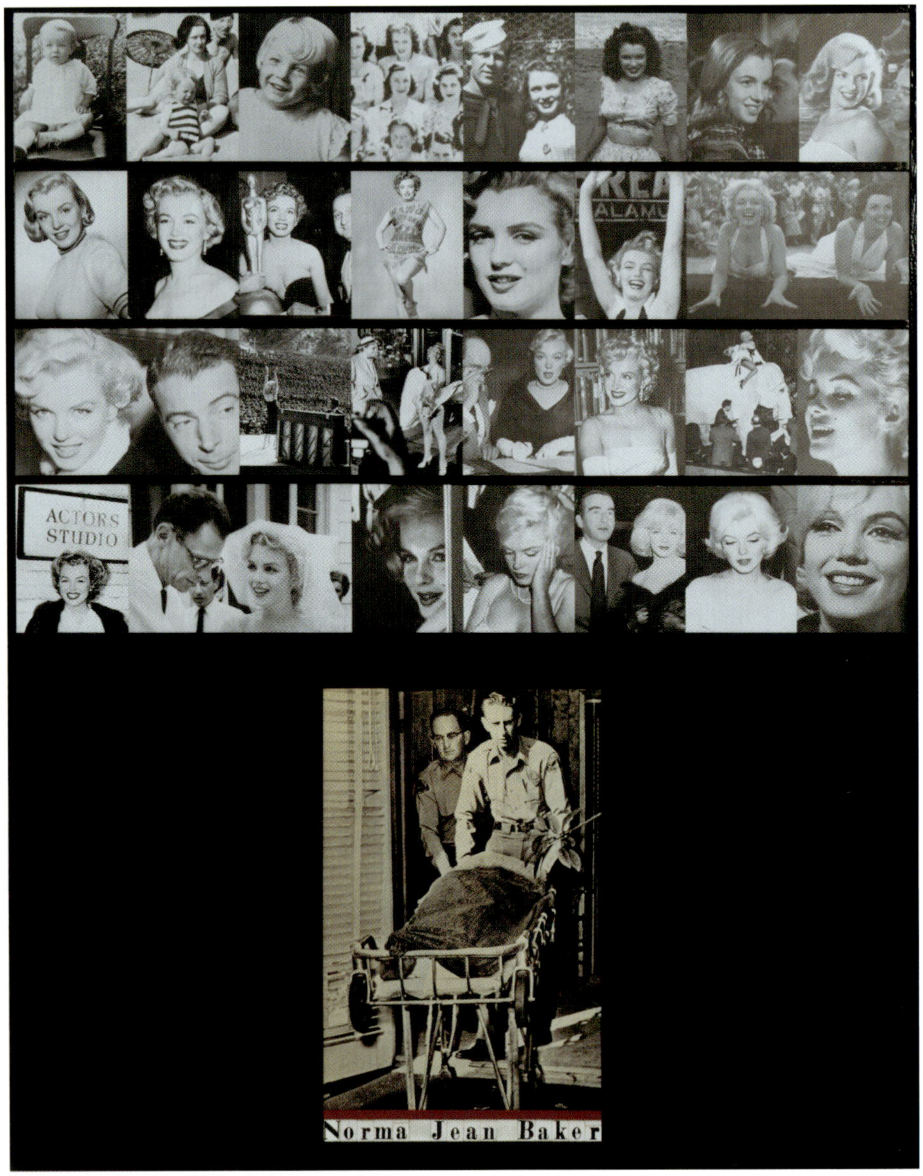

Blake's *Elvis Shrine* in his studio
London 2003

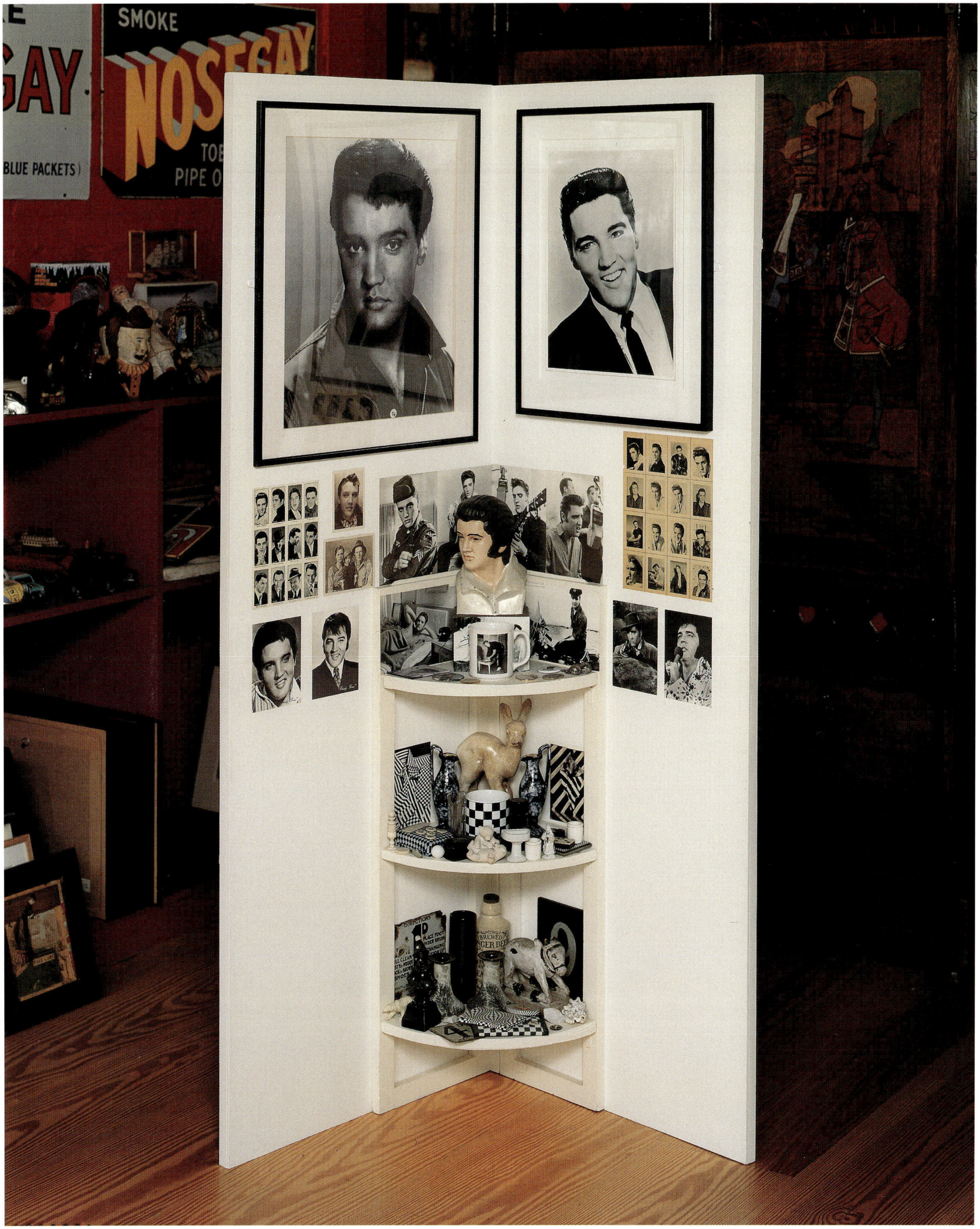
SMOKE
NOSEGAY
GAY
BLUE PACKETS)

A Museum for Myself
1982
Oil on hardboard

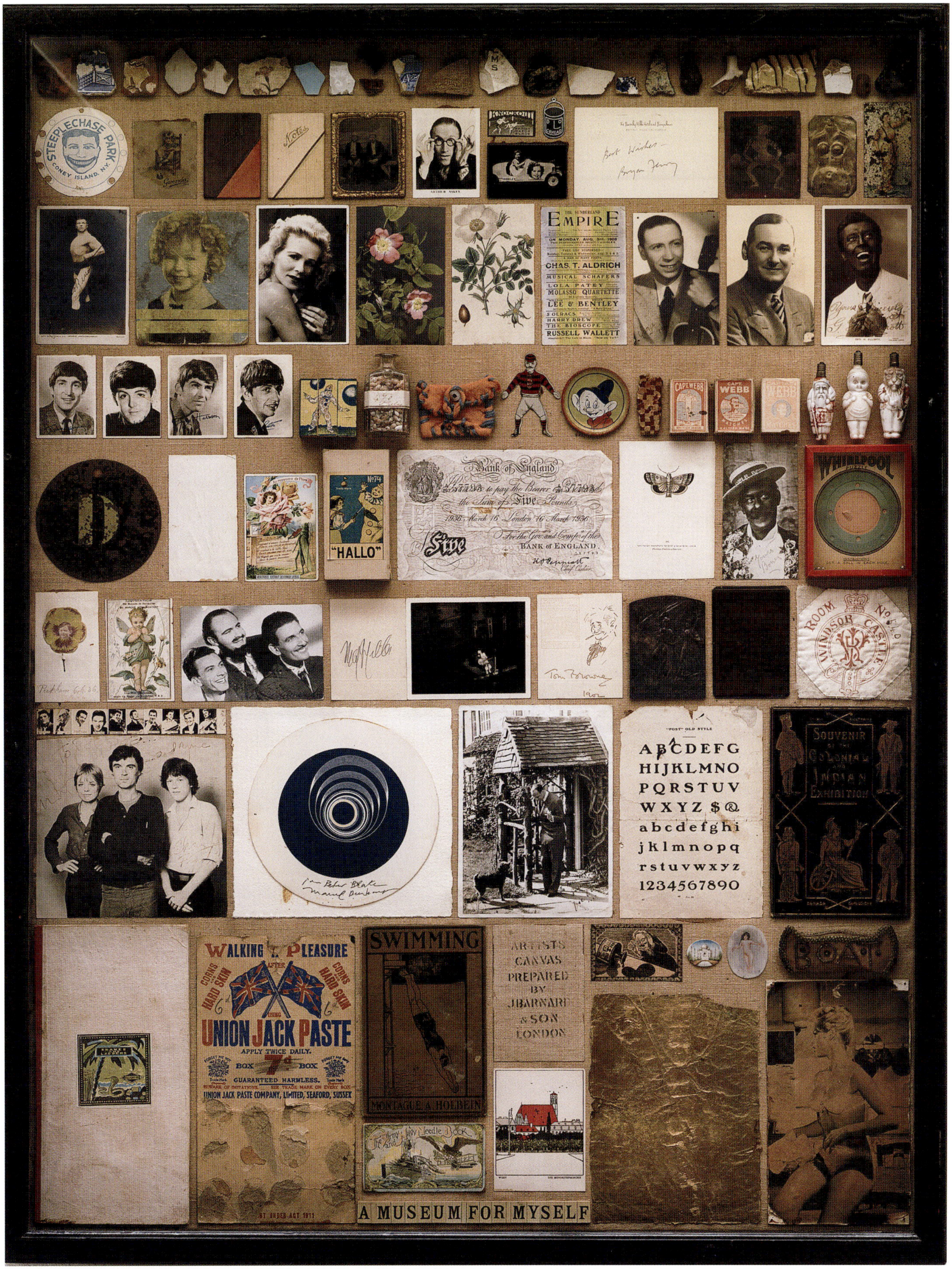
STEEPLECHASE PARK
CONEY ISLAND, N.Y.
EMPIRE
CHAS. T. ALDRICH
CAPT WEBB
"HALLO"
Bank of England
Five
WHIRLPOOL
ROOM No.
WINDSOR CASTLE
ABCDEFG
HIJKLMNO
PQRSTUV
WXYZ $&
abcdefghi
jklmnopq
rstuvwxyz
1234567890
SOUVENIR OF THE COLONIAL AND INDIAN EXHIBITION
WALKING PLEASURE
UNION JACK PASTE
APPLY TWICE DAILY.
GUARANTEED HARMLESS.
UNION JACK PASTE COMPANY, LIMITED, SEAFORD, SUSSEX
SWIMMING
MONTAGUE A. HOLBEIN
ARTISTS CANVAS PREPARED BY J.BARNARD & SON LONDON
A MUSEUM FOR MYSELF

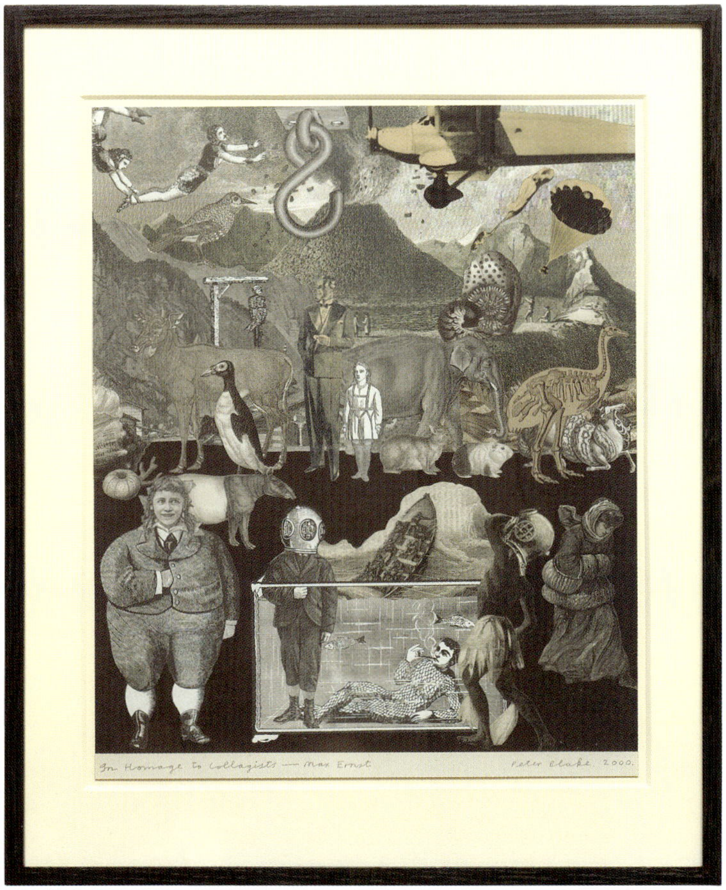

In Homage to Collagists
2000
Collage

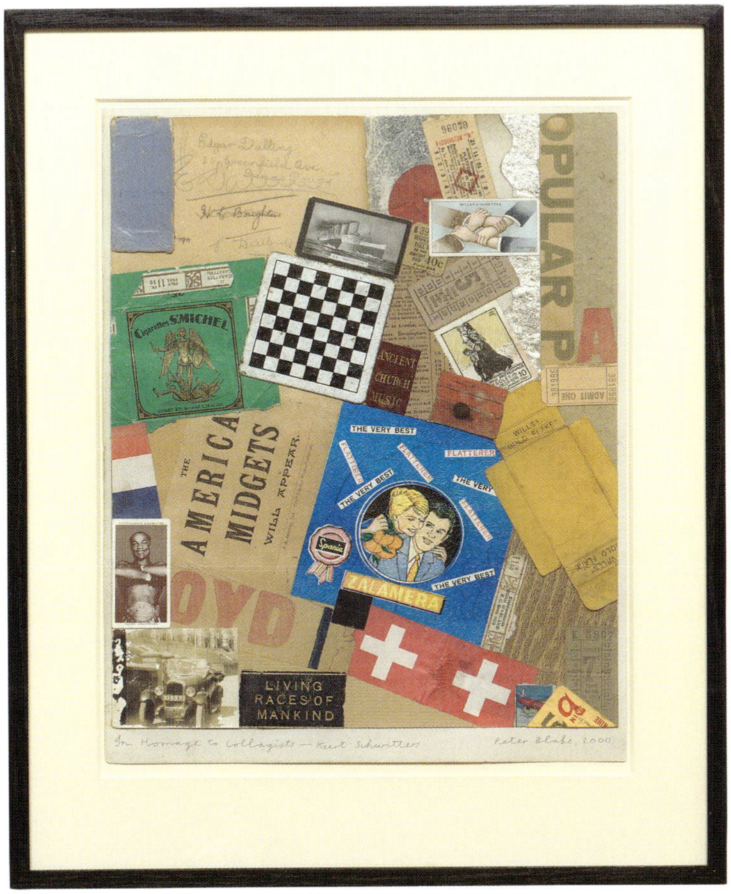
OPULAR P
THE VERY BEST
FLATTERER
ZALAMERA
ANCIENT CHURCH MUSIC
ADMIT ONE
THE AMERICA MIDGETS WILL APPEAR.
LIVING RACES OF MANKIND
In Homage to Collagists – Kurt Schwitters
Peter Blake, 2000

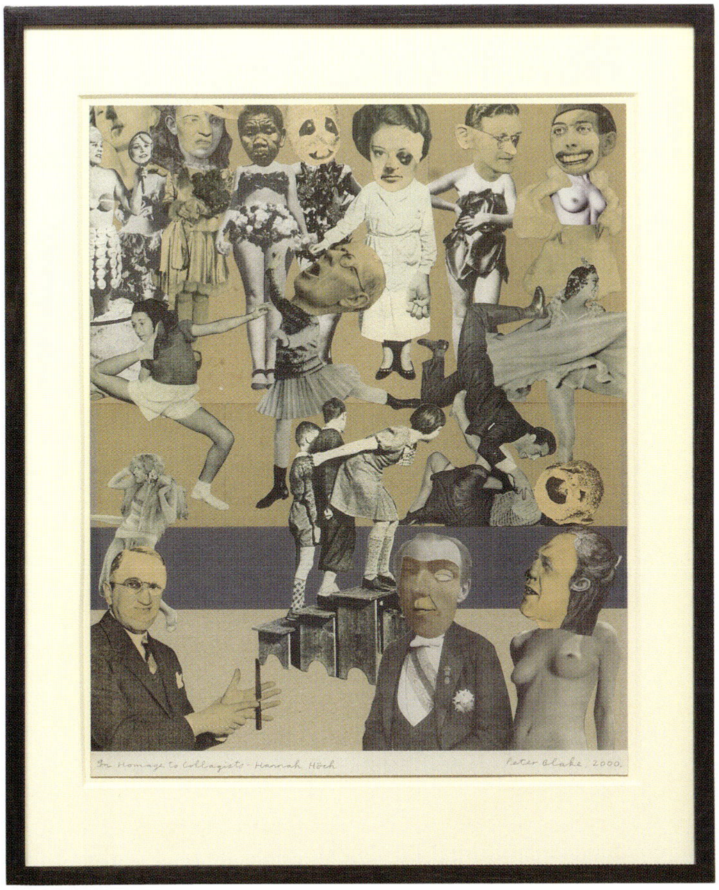
In Homage to Collagists – Hannah Höch
Peter Blake, 2000

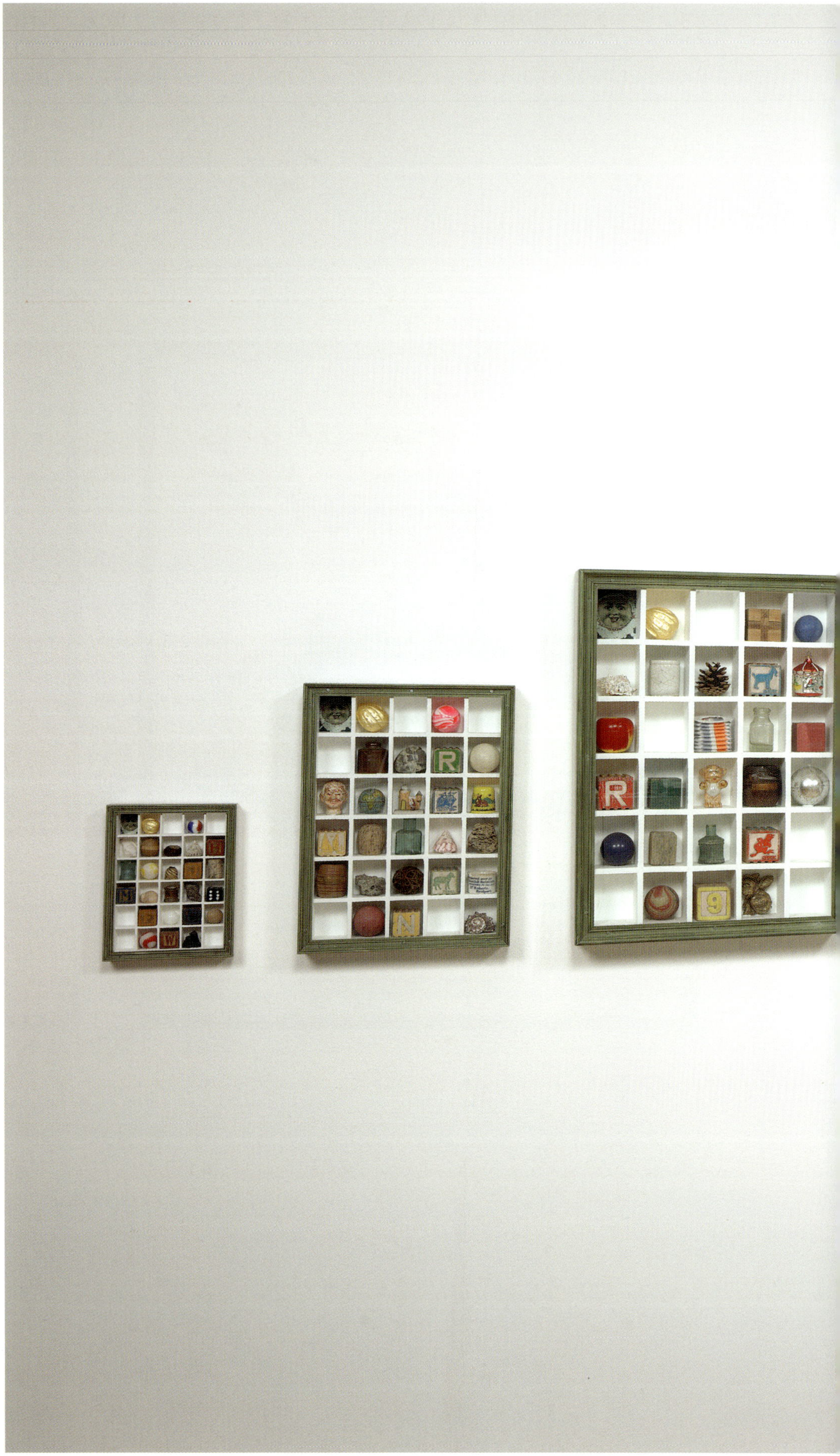

In Homage to Joseph Cornell
2005
Mixed media

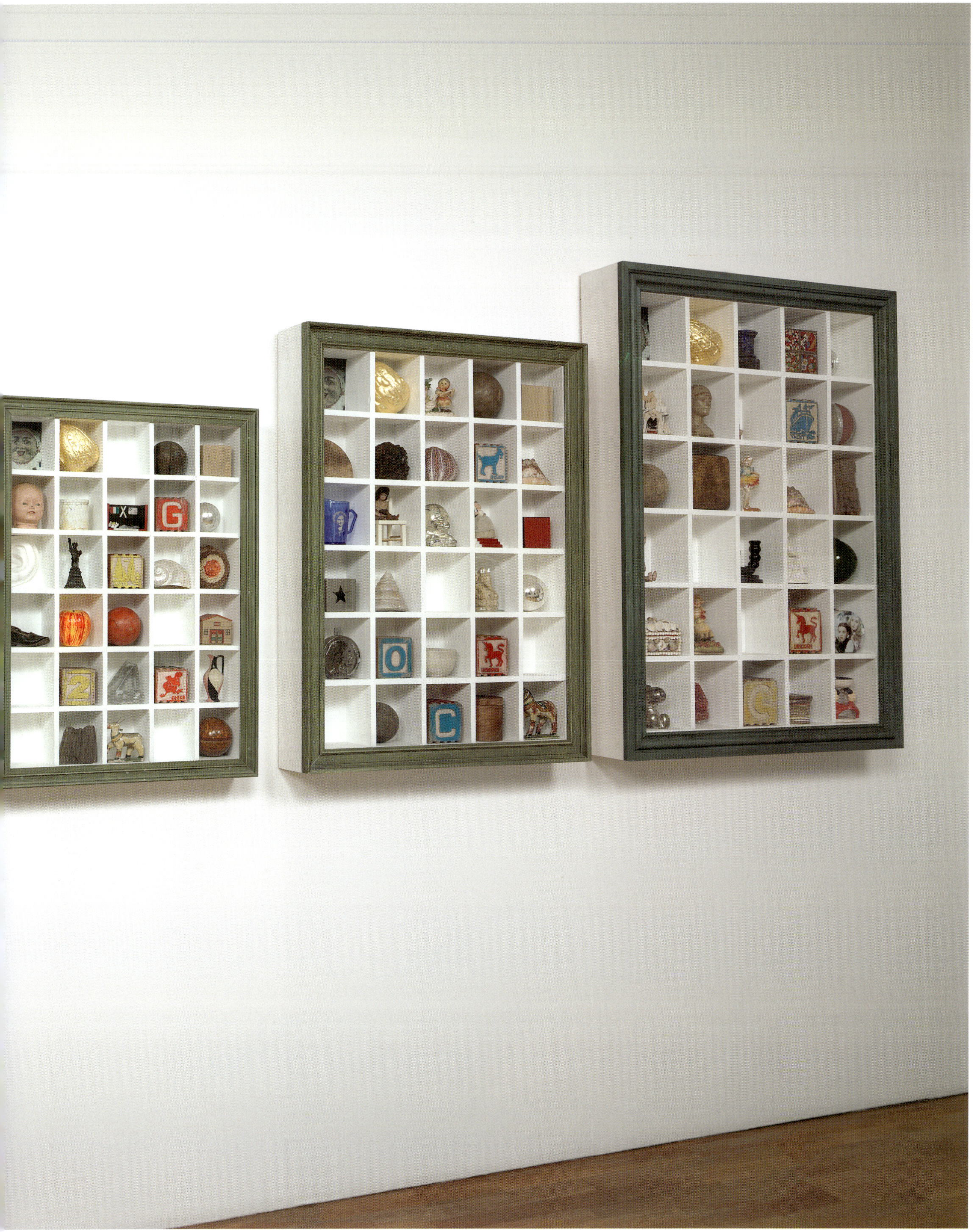

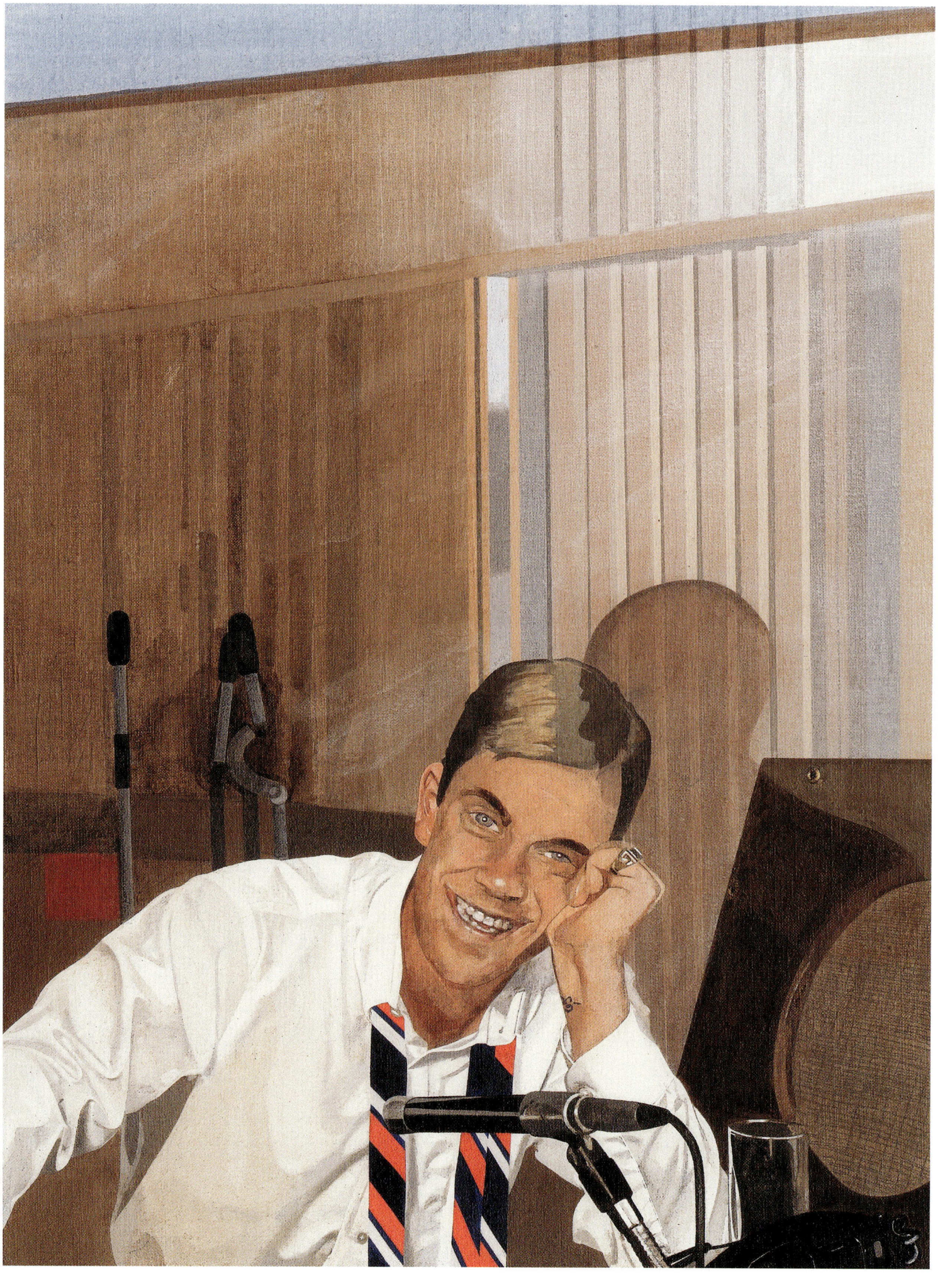

Robbie Williams
2002
Acrylic on board

Robbie Williams' Swing When You're Winning 2001 (Blake's design was later dropped by the record company despite being favoured by Williams himself), the posthumously compiled *John Peel – Right Time Wrong Speed* 2006 and, somewhat predictably, Oasis's *Stop the Clocks* 2006. Just as it had with his Sgt Pepper's Lonely Hearts Club Band cover, Blake's work had once again seamlessly merged with contemporary popular culture and was entering the homes of millions worldwide. Much admired by a younger generation of visual and performing artists, Blake continued to pay tribute to his own heroes, remaining true to the passions that have now driven his work for over fifty years. In his 1990 exhibition *In Homage to Marilyn Monroe* Blake presented a series of constructed 'shrines' to his all-time favourite pin-up, and has since been working on a similar monument to Elvis Presley.

Yet it is the continuing celebration of his art-historical precedents that has led Blake's richest output in recent years. In Homage to Collagists 2000 and Homage to Joseph Cornell 2005, rather than directly incorporate the work of another artist within his own, as he had so frequently done in the past, with remarkable artistry Blake mimicked the style and technique of Max Ernst, Hanna Höch, Kurt Schwitters and Cornell to produce three collages (one for each artist) and a series of six constructions, each proportionately bigger than the last, for Cornell. Existing as a kind of simulacrum, the works aren't copies and yet, disconcertingly recognisable both as 'Peter Blakes' and as works of the earlier artists, neither are they originals. This playful and perhaps even self-indulgent manipulation of art history is a way once again of assessing the contribution of these artists to the canon and Blake's own position within it. Perhaps his most flamboyant celebration of art history to date is *Marcel Duchamp's World Tour*, a series that has occupied the artist most recently. The motivation for these paintings was quite simply Blake's desire to thank Duchamp for his ground-breaking gesture with a urinal that henceforth gave artists the freedom to define what could become art – a philosophy that has informed all branches of Blake's practice.[7] The paintings, five of which have been completed, depict Marcel Duchamp in an American tour bus travelling around the world meeting real and fictional figures from the worlds of art and popular entertainment. The first, The Marcel Duchamp World Tour: The Tarzan Family

7
Duchamp placed his urinal, signed 'R Mutt', on its back in an exhibition in New York in 1917. In an anonymous article, generally attributed to Duchamp and published the same year in *The Blind Man*, the author wrote of three important points revealed by the gesture that have all informed Blake's practice: first, that the act of choosing a found or 'readymade' object is a creative undertaking in itself; secondly, that by displacing it from its original context it ceases to have a 'useful' function and becomes art; and thirdly, that its re-presentation and the addition of a title gives it a new thought and meaning.

Marcel Duchamp's World Tour: The Artists' Fancy Dress Ball
2004
Oil on canvas

1995–2005, shows a cigar-smoking Duchamp standing alongside Tarzan and his family (including Cheeta, whom Blake discovered is exactly the same age as him and also likes to paint). He travels on in other works to meet Elvis and the Spice Girls, has a game of chess (what else?) with Tracey Emin, goes to the Congress of Unusual People and attends The Artists' Fancy Dress Ball, hosted by Damien Hirst dressed as Watteau's 'Pierrot', Picasso as Touchstone from Shakespeare's *As You Like It* taken from a John Zoffany painting, and Edward Hopper. Duchamp makes his impact wherever he stops, regardless of whether his newfound context be culturally high, low, or a fusion of the two.

The characters who populate these paintings exist as a roll-call of those who have starred in Blake's work since the mid-1950s, a mapping of all that has been important to him in the time that has since elapsed – perhaps really marking this as Blake's authentic 'late work'. Despite his constant engagement with art history, it is difficult to relate any of Blake's work since the 1980s to that of his contemporaries. Rather, he views it just as he does images from popular culture: as part of a social milieu that he records and criticises. Blake's style is unique: whatever he produces, be it a children's book, his recent poster for the Victoria & Albert Museum's Toy Museum, an album cover, or even a painting, is instantly recognisable. Whether on the front of a Beatles LP or on the walls of a national collection, Blake's images, just like the ones he incorporates within them, are in mass circulation. This is why Blake has, after six decades (and counting) of making work, such universal appeal, and why he has truly realised his most long-standing aim: to make his art 'the visual form of pop music'.[8]

8
Peter Blake, 'The Bigger Picture', *The Guardian*, 21 January 2006.

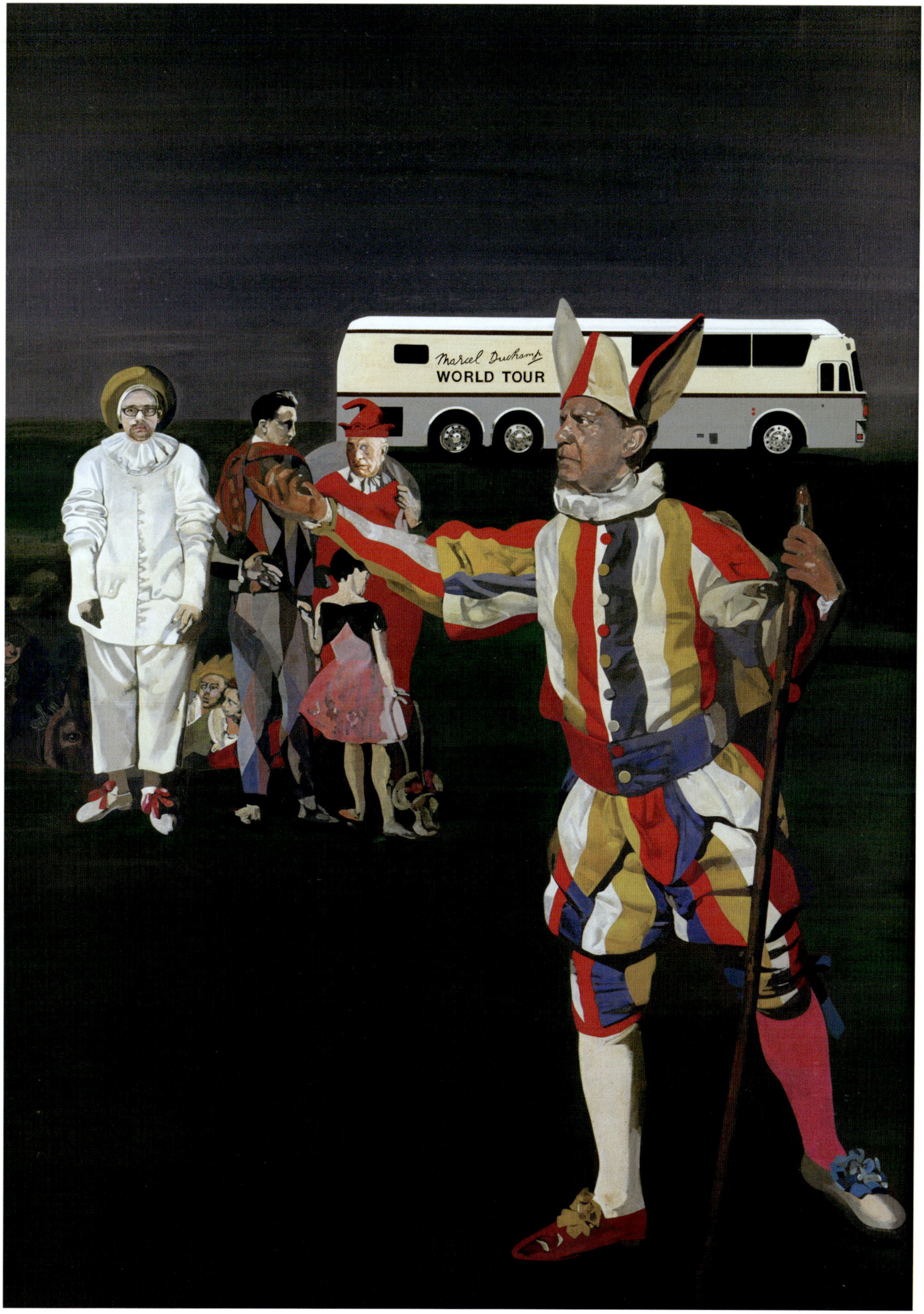
Marcel Duchamp
WORLD TOUR

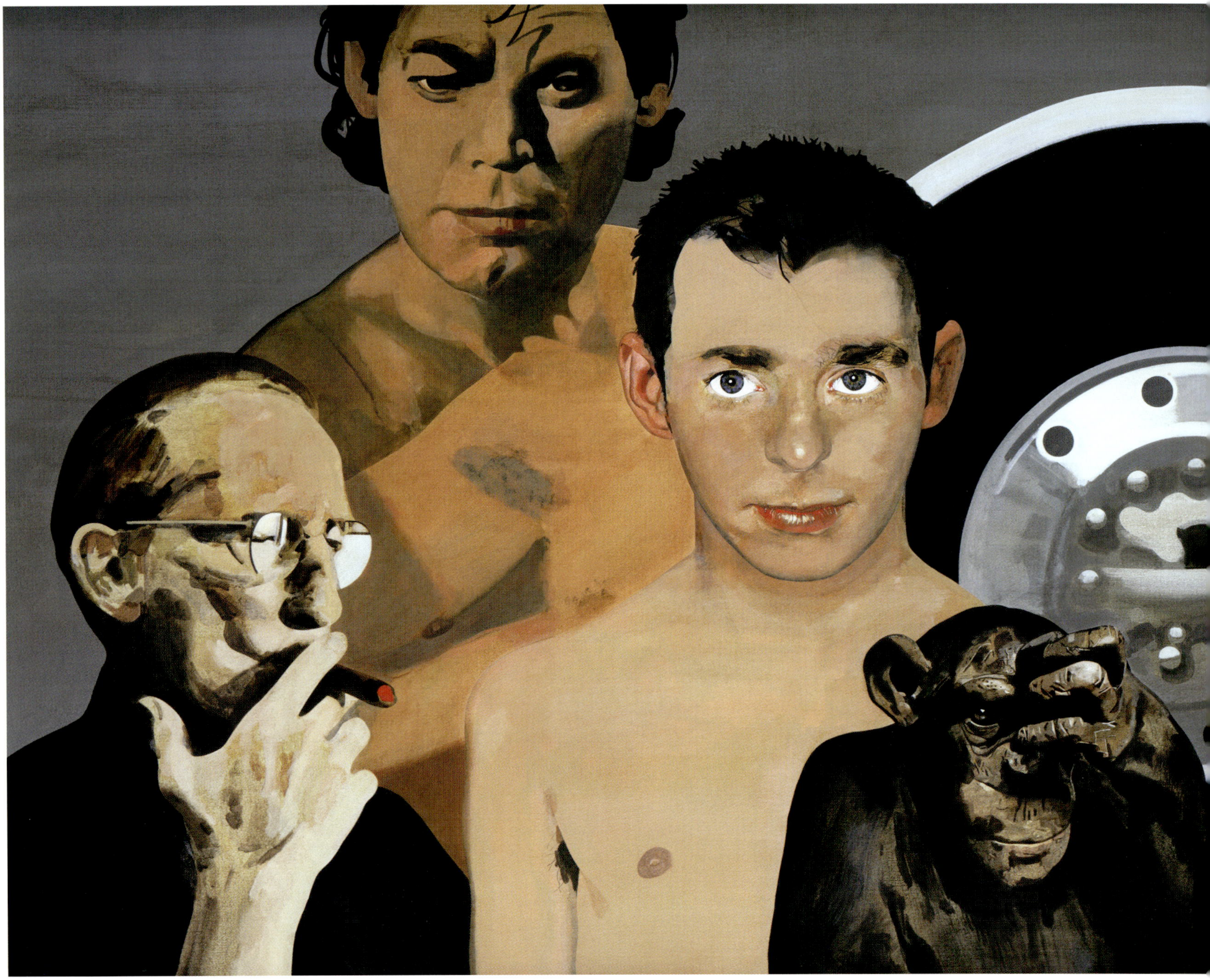

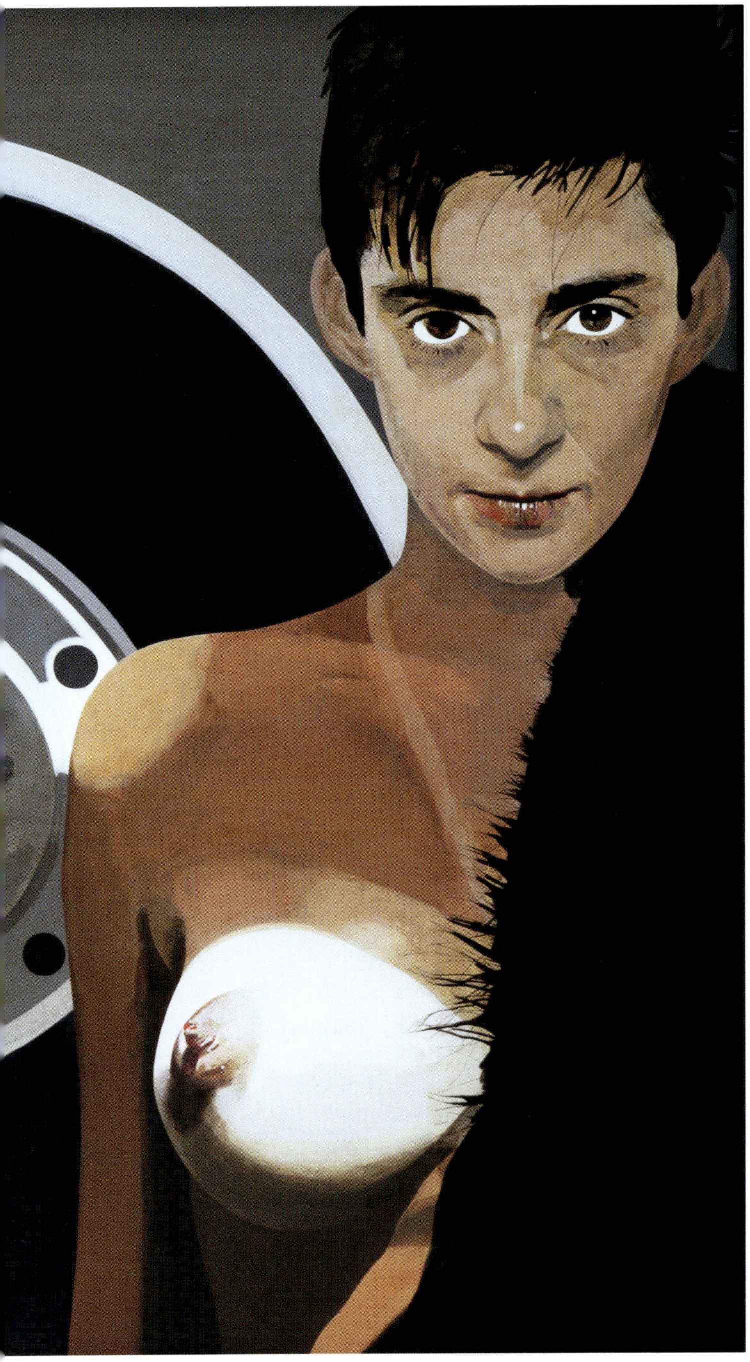

Marcel Duchamp's World Tour: The Tarzan Family
1995–2005
Acrylic on canvas

Marcel Duchamp's World Tour: Playing Chess with Tracey
2003–5
Acrylic on canvas

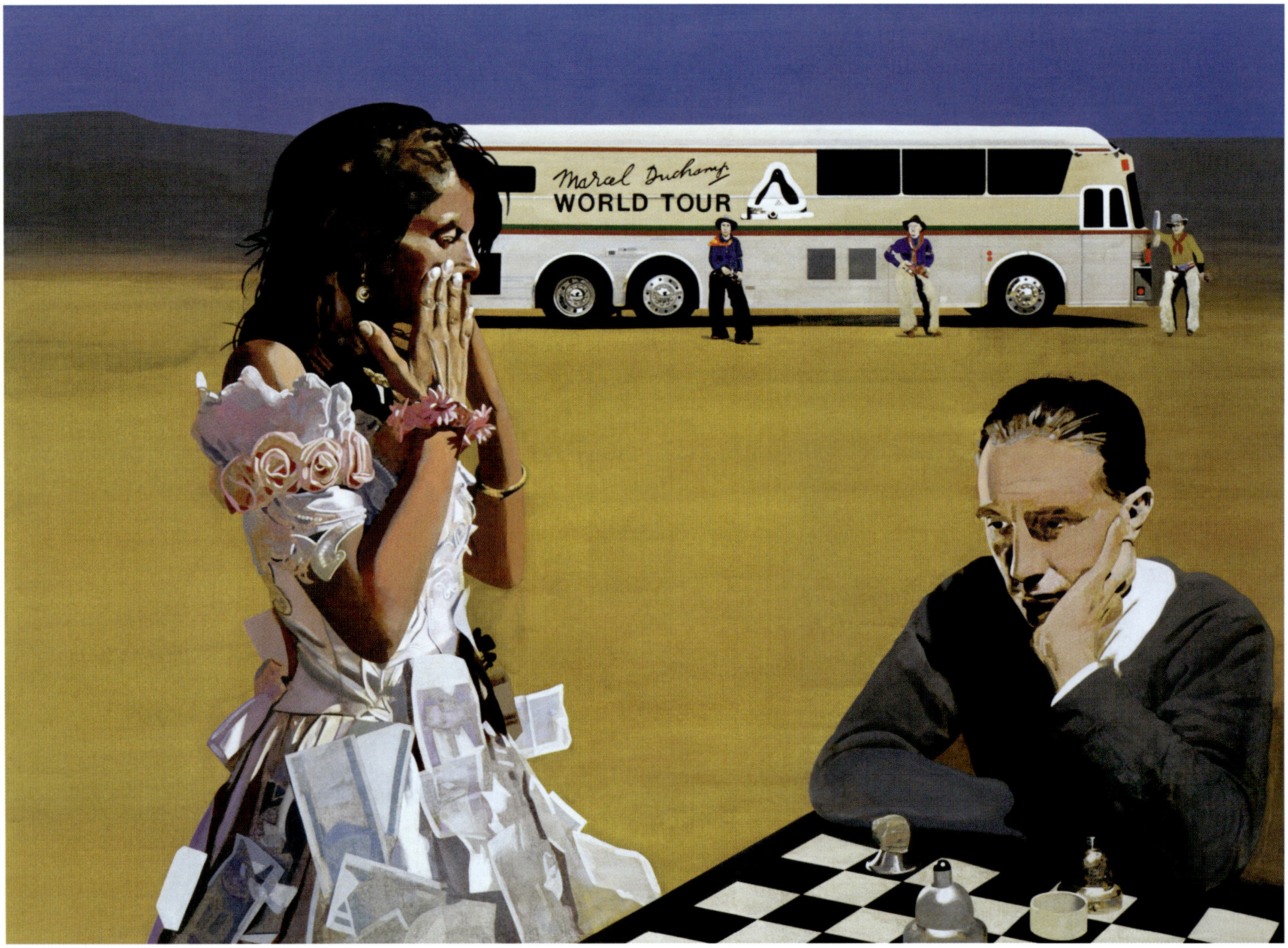

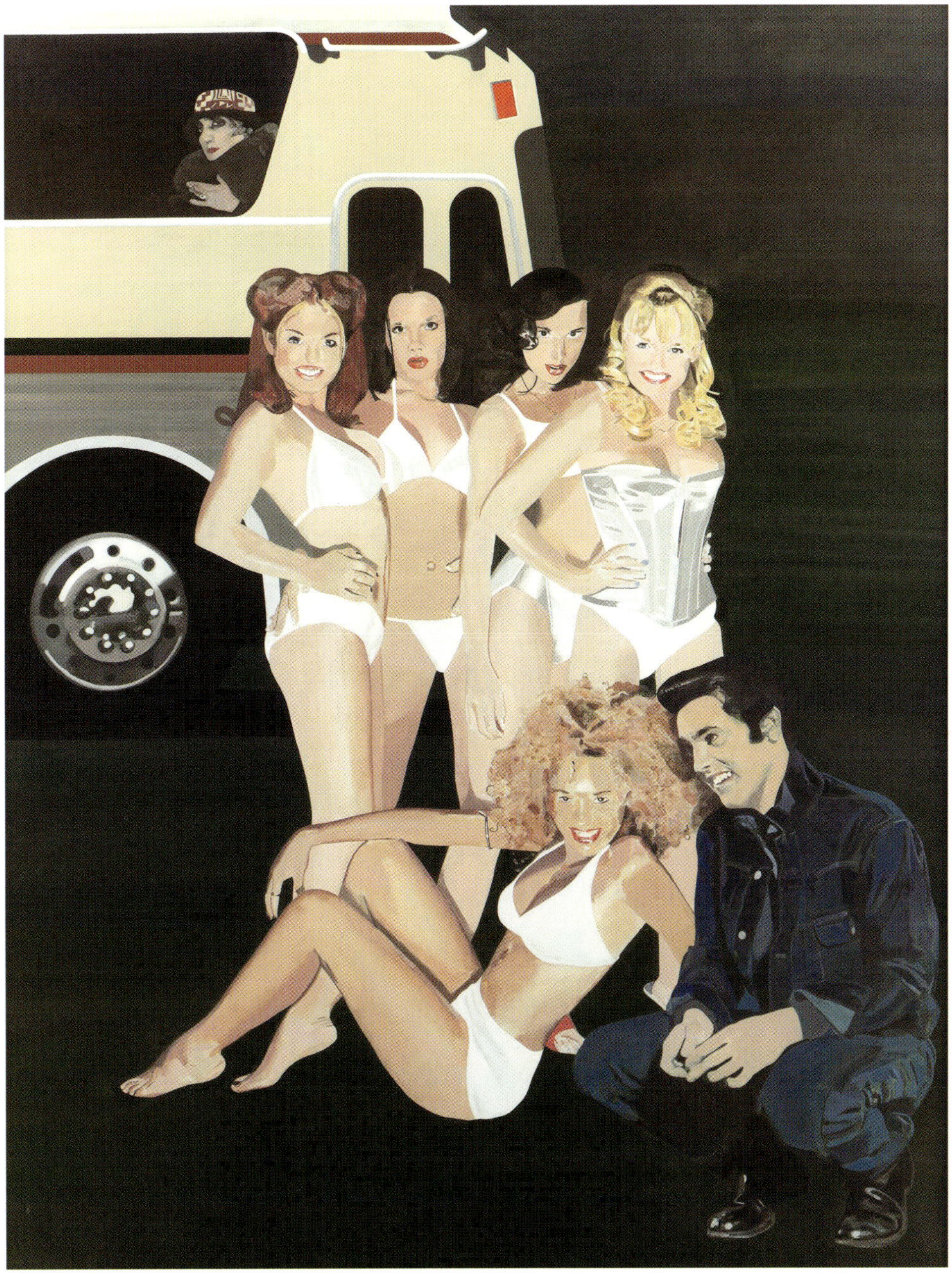

**Marcel Duchamp's World Tour:
He meets the Spice Girls and Elvis**
2000–5
Acrylic on canvas

Marcel Duchamp's World Tour: He meets the Congress of Unusual People with the Ringling Brothers and Barnum and Bailey (Combined) Circus Season – 1929
(detail and overleaf)
2004–5
Acrylic on canvas

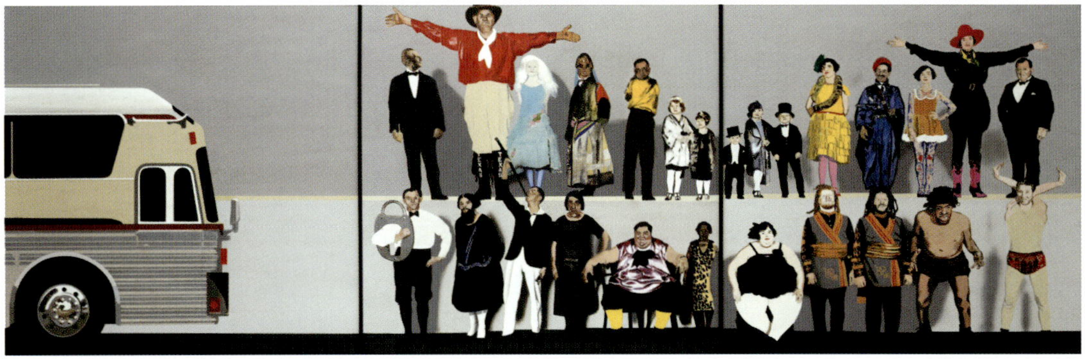

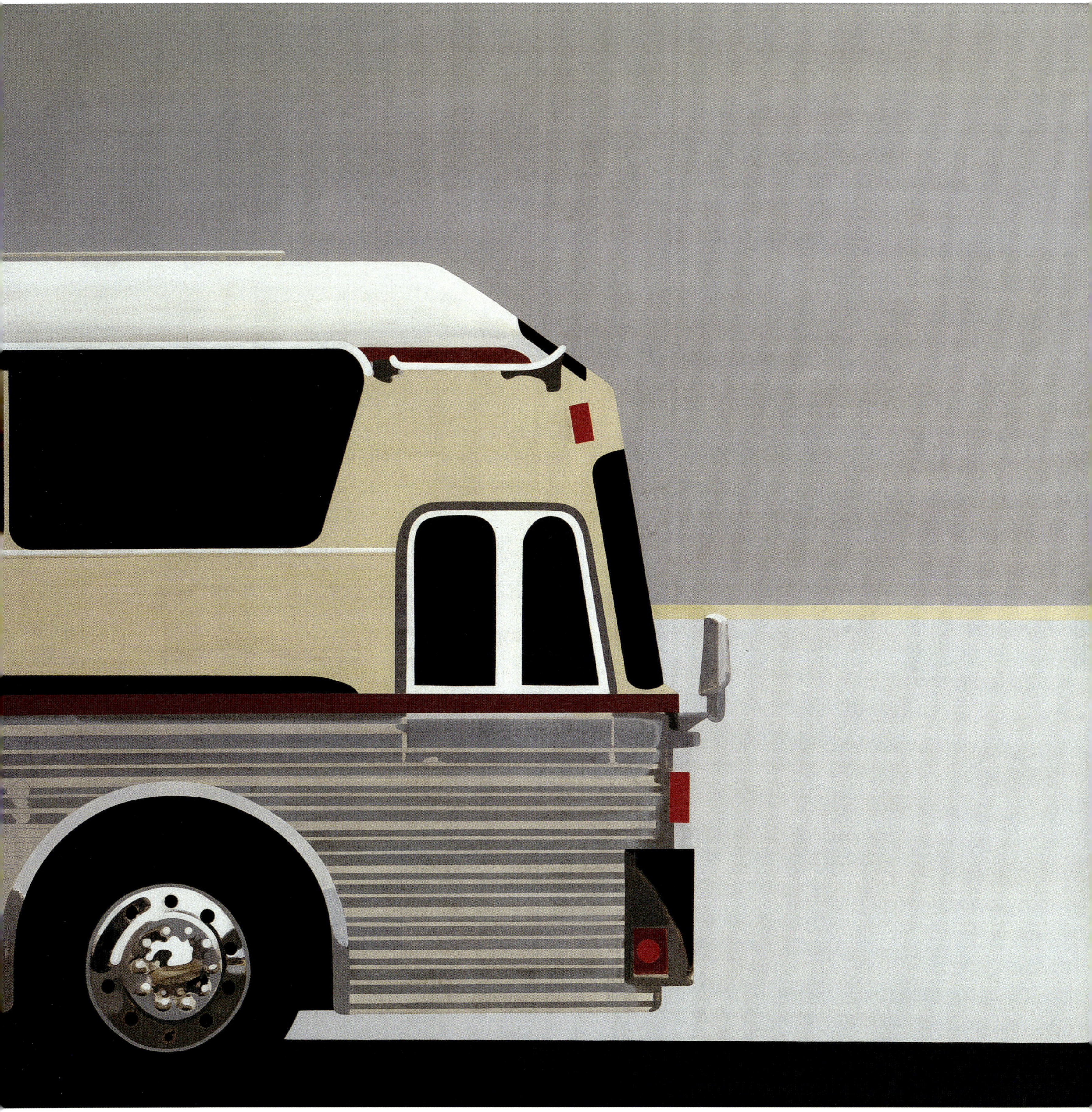

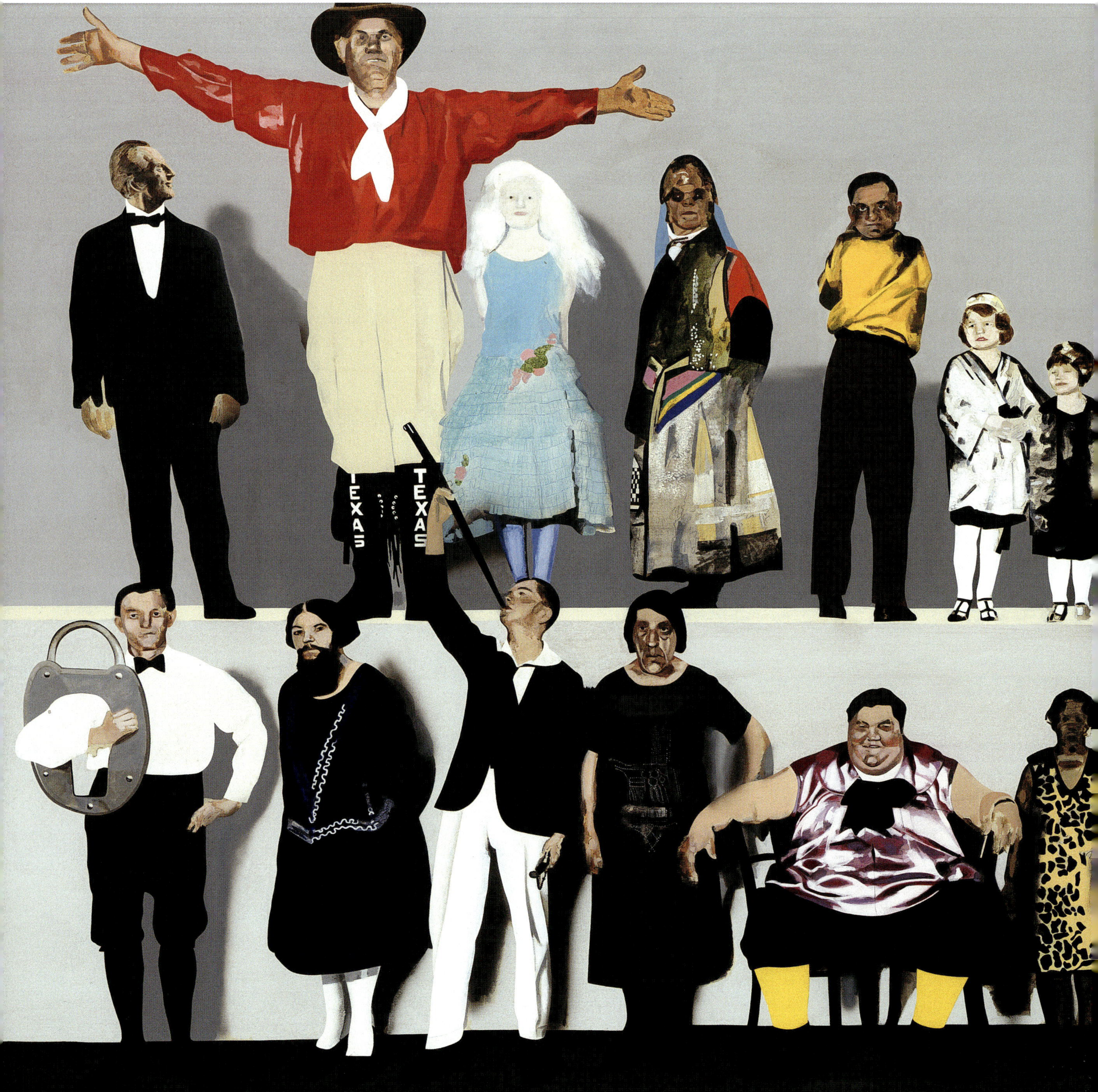
TEXAS
TEXAS

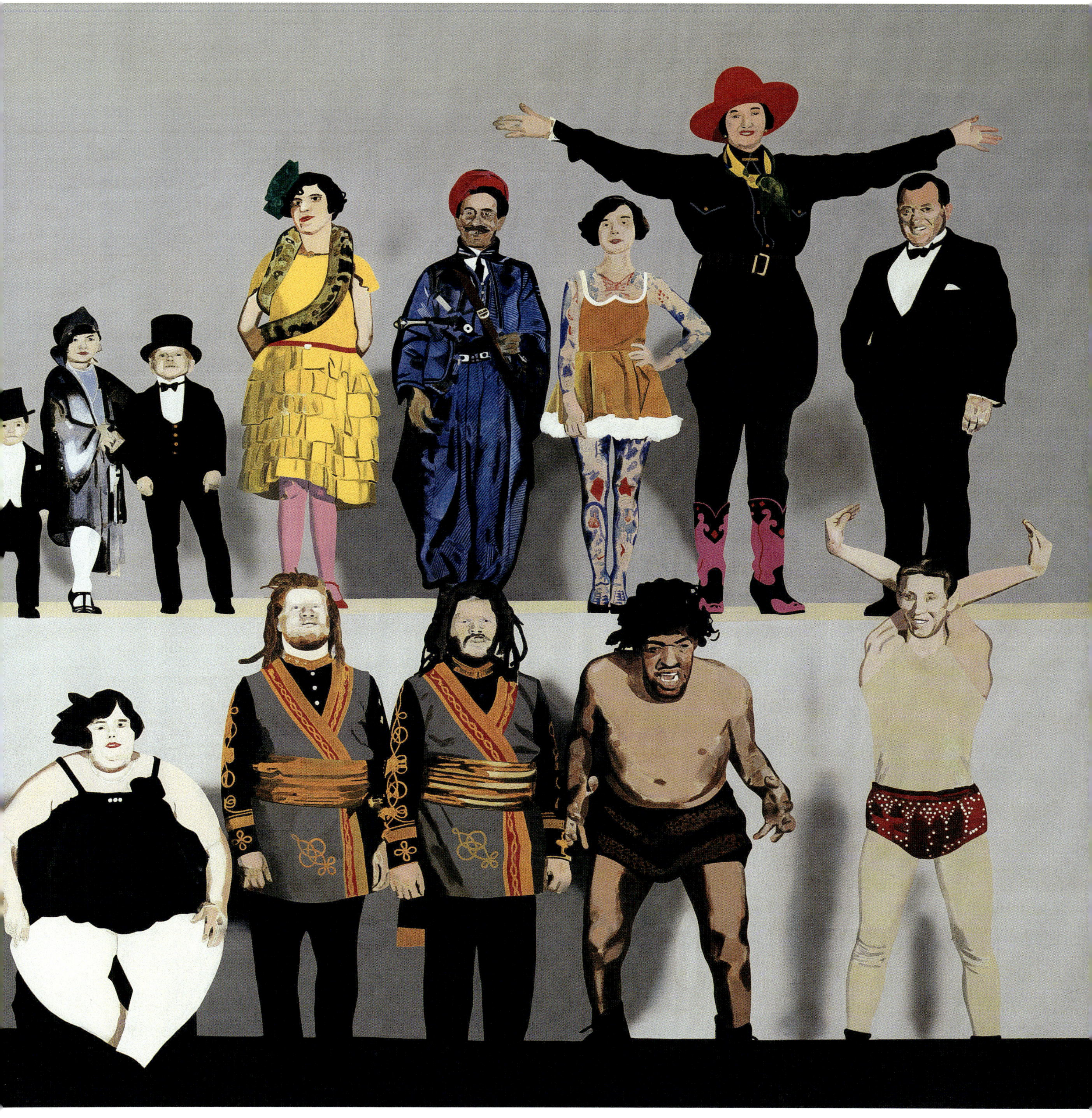

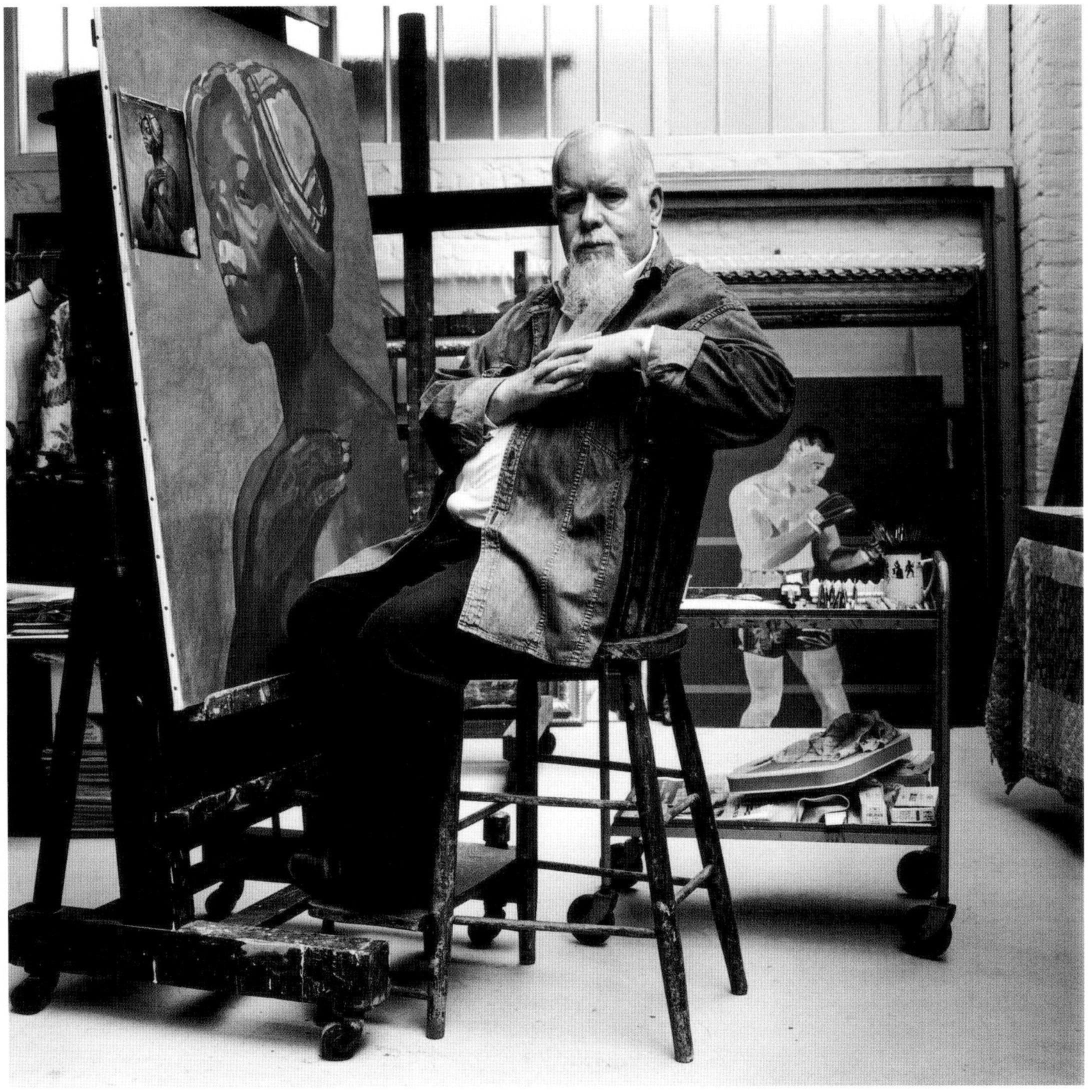

List of exhibited works

Height precedes width followed by depth

Self Portrait 1949
Oil on hardboard
29.9 x 22.8 cm (11¾ x 9 in)
Collection Burghard Freiherr von Cramm

The Deluge 1953–4
Oil on board
35 x 45.7 cm (13¾ x 18 in)
Hazlitt Holland-Hibbert, London

Boy and Pigeons c.1954
Oil on hardboard
48.3 x 26 cm (19 x 10¼ in)
Private Collection, London

Children Reading Comics 1954
Oil on hardboard
36.9 x 47 cm (14½ x 18½ in)
Tullie House Museum and Art Gallery, Carlisle

ABC Minors 1955
Oil on hardboard
76 x 49 cm (29 15/16 x 19 5/16 in)
Museum Ludwig, Cologne

Loelia, World's Most Tattooed Lady 1955
Oil and collage on panel
74.9 x 26.7 cm (29½ x 10½ in)
Collection Fleur Cowles

On the Balcony 1955–7
Oil on canvas
121.3 x 90.8 cm (47¾ x 35¾ in)
Tate. Presented by the Contemporary Art Society '63

Children Reading Comics 1956
Oil on hardboard
39.4 x 29.2 cm (15½ x 11½ in)
Royal College of Art Collection

Still Life of Apples 1956
Oil on wood panel
21 x 15.2 cm (8¼ x 6 in)
Collection Fleur Cowles

Shoe on the Beach at Nice 1956
Oil on hardboard
18.4 x 15.2 cm (7¼ x 6 in)
Private Collection, London

Siriol, She-Devil of Naked Madness 1957
Oil and collage on panel
74.9 x 21.6 cm (29½ x 8½ in)
Pallant House Gallery, Chichester (Wilson Loan)

Everly Wall 1959
Collage on hardboard
91.4 x 61 cm (36 x 24 in)
Collection Terry Blake

The Fine Art Bit 1959
Enamel, wood relief and collage on board
91.4 x 61 x 2.5 cm (36 x 24 x 1 in)
Tate. Purchased 1970

Girlie Door 1959
Collage and assemblage on hardboard
121.9 x 59.1 cm (48 x 23¼ in)
Private Collection

Gold Painting 1959
Gold leaf on canvas
76.2 x 61 x 1.9 cm (31 x 21 x ¾ in)
Property of Mrs. G. M. Sumner

Portrait of Sammy Davis Jr 1960
Oil on hardboard
36.8 x 31.7 cm (14½ x 12½ in)
Magda Archer and Harry Hill

Got a Girl 1960–1
Oil paint, wood, photo-collage and vinyl record on hardboard
94 x 154.9 x 4.2 cm (37 x 61 x 1⅝ in)
The Whitworth Art Gallery, University of Manchester

Boy with Hot Dog 1960–5
Acrylic on hardboard
36.5 x 40.7 cm (14⅜ cm x 16 in)
Arts Council Collection, Hayward Gallery, South Bank Centre, London

Kim Novak 1960 and 1987
Postcards and enamel print on hardboard
47.6 x 36.5 cm (18 11/16 x 14⅜ in)
Private Collection

The First Real Target 1961
Enamel on canvas and collage on board
53.7 x 49.3 cm (21¼ x 19⅜ in)
Tate. Purchased 1982

Love Wall 1961
Collage construction
125.7 x 205.7 cm (49½ x 81 in)
Fundação Calouste Gulbenkian

Self Portrait with Badges 1961
Oil on board
174.3 x 121.9 cm (68⅝ x 48 in)
Tate. Presented by the Moores Family Charitable Foundation to celebrate the John Moores Liverpool Exhibition 1979

Tattooed Lady 1961
Pen, ink and watercolour with collage
94.6 x 52.4 cm (37¼ x 20⅝ in)
Private Collection, Courtesy of Hazlitt Holland-Hibbert, London

Tuesday 1961
Enamel, wood relief and collage on board
47.6 x 26.7 x 38 cm (18¾ x 10½ x 1½ in)
Tate. Presented by E. J. Power through the Friends of the Tate Gallery 1974

Baron Adolf Kaiser 1961–3
Oil on panel
61 x 51 cm (24 x 20$\frac{1}{16}$ in)
Arts Council Collection, Hayward Gallery, South Bank Centre, London

Kid McCoy 1961–5
Cryla and collage on hardboard
58.4 x 29 x 5.7 cm (23 x 11⅜ x 2¼ in)
Zabludowicz Collection

Pin-up Girl 1962
Drawing on paper
27 x 21 cm (10⅝ x 8¼ in)
Private Collection, London

The Toy Shop 1962
Mixed media, glass and painted wood
156.8 x 194 x 34 cm (60½ x 75½ x 13⅜ in)
Tate. Purchased 1970

Piece of Marilyn Monroe's Dressing Room Door 1962 reworked 1987
Enamel paint, postcard, lettering and silver-star on wooden door
49.5 x 60.3 cm (19½ x 23¾ in)
Private Collection, Tokyo

Bo Diddley 1963
Acrylic on hardboard
122.6 x 78.4 cm (48¼ x 30⅞ in)
Museum Ludwig, Cologne

The Lettermen 1963
Oil on hardboard
124.5 x 185.4 cm (49 x 73 in)
Ferens Art Gallery: Hull Museums & Art Gallery

Kandy 1963–5
Acrylic and collage on hardboard
29.2 x 15.2 cm (11½ x 6 in)
Private Collection, London

The Beatles 1963–8
Acrylic emulsion on board
121.9 x 91.4 cm (48 x 36 in)
Pallant House Gallery, Chichester (Wilson Gift through the National Art Collections Fund, 2004)

Klarence Haus 1963–89
Oil on panel and enamel on wood with letters and toys
55.9 x 38.1 x 7 cm (22 x 15 x 2¾ in)
Magda Archer and Harry Hill

Beach Boys 1964
Screen-print on paper
53 x 30.8 cm (20⅞ x 12⅛ in)
Tate. Presented by Rose and Chris Prater through the Institute of Contemporary Prints 1975

Jean Harlow 1964
Acrylic on hardboard
44.5 x 36.8 cm (17½ x 14½ in)
Mr and Mrs Terry Blake

Battle begun 1964 (work in progress)
Cryla on canvas
182.9 x 284.5 cm (72 x 112 in)
Collection Peter Blake

Once Upon a Time 1964 (work in progress)
Oil on canvas
182.9 x 284.5 cm (72 x 112 in)
Collection Peter Blake

Kamikaze 1965
Acrylic and collage on hardboard
78.7 x 47.6 cm (31 x 18¾ in)
Amgueddfa Cymru – National Museums Wales. Purchased 2006 with the assistance of the Art Fund and the Derek Williams Trust

The Masked Zebra Kid 1965
Acrylic, enamel, collage and assemblage on wood
55.2 x 26.7 x 3.8 cm (21¾ x 10½ x 1½ in)
Tate. Purchased 1974

Portrait of David Hockney in a Hollywood Spanish Interior 1965
Acrylic on canvas
182.8 x 152.8 x 2.1 cm (72 x 60 x $\frac{13}{16}$ in)
Tate. Presented by David Hockney 2002

Simon Rodia 1965
Acrylic on hardboard
30.5 x 35.6 cm (12 x 14 in)
The Agnes and Frits Becht Collection, Naarden, Holland

Tarzan, Jane, Boy and Cheeta 1966–75
Acrylic on canvas
121.9 x 91.4 cm (48 x 36 in)
Astrup Fearnley Collection, Oslo

April en robe d'intérieur 1968
Watercolour and crayon
115.6 x 82.5 cm (45½ x 32½ in)
Private Collection, Paris

A Mad Tea Party at Watts Tower 1968–92
Oil on canvas
91.4 x 121.9 cm (36 x 48 in)
Private Collection

J.A. 1969
from *Six French Postcards*
Screenprint on paper
43 x 27.2 cm (16$\frac{15}{16}$ x 10$\frac{11}{16}$ in)
Tate. Presented by Waddington Galleries through the Institute of Contemporary Prints 1975

Leo 79 1969
from *Six French Postcards*
Screenprint on paper
27.3 x 42.6 cm (10¾ x 16¾ in)
Tate. Presented by Waddington Galleries through the Institute of Contemporary Prints 1975

Leo 139 1969
from *Six French Postcards*
Screenprint on paper
43.1 x 27.5 cm (16$\frac{15}{16}$ x 10$\frac{13}{16}$ in)
Tate. Presented by Waddington Galleries through the Institute of Contemporary Prints 1975

Leo 153 1969
from *Six French Postcards*
Screenprint on paper
43.2 x 28 cm (17 x 11 in)
Tate. Presented by Waddington Galleries through the Institute of Contemporary Prints 1975

Serie 83 1969
from *Six French Postcards*
Screenprint on paper
43.1 x 27.6 cm (16$\frac{15}{16}$ x 10⅞ in)
Tate. Presented by Waddington Galleries through the Institute of Contemporary Prints 1975

3765 1969
from *Six French Postcards*
Screenprint on paper
42.5 x 27.2 cm (16¾ x 10$\frac{11}{16}$ in)
Tate. Presented by Waddington Galleries through the Institute of Contemporary Prints 1975

Puck, Peaseblossom, Cobweb, Moth and Mustard Seed 1969–84
Acrylic on hardboard
100.3 x 77.8 cm (39½ x 30⅝ in)
Galerie Claude Bernard, Paris

Tarzan Meets the Jungle Goddess 1969–94
Oil on canvas
91.4 x 121.9 cm (72 x 60 in)
Private Collection

'and to show you I'm not proud, you may shake hands with me!'
from *Illustrations to Through the Looking-Glass* 1970
Screen-print on paper
24.2 x 18 cm (9½ x 7$\frac{1}{16}$ in)
Tate. Presented by Rose and Chris Prater through the Institute of Contemporary Prints 1975

'and the two knights sat and looked at each other without speaking'
from *Illustrations to Through the Looking-Glass* 1970
Screen-print on paper
24.3 x 18.1 cm (9 9/16 x 7 1/8 in)
Tate. Presented by Rose and Chris Prater through the Institute of Contemporary Prints 1975

'But isn't it old!' Tweedledum cried
from *Illustrations to Through the Looking-Glass* 1970
Screen-print on paper
24.4 x 18.1 cm (9 5/8 x 7 1/8 in)
Tate. Presented by Rose and Chris Prater through the Institute of Contemporary Prints 1975

'It isn't manners for us to begin, you know', said the Rose
from *Illustrations to Through the Looking-Glass* 1970
Screen-print on paper
24.1 x 17.8 cm (9 1/2 x 7 in)
Tate. Presented by Rose and Chris Prater through the Institute of Contemporary Prints 1975

'For instance now, now there's the King's messenger'
from *Illustrations to Through the Looking-Glass* 1970
Screen-print on paper
24.1 x 17.8 cm (9 1/2 x 7 in)
Tate. Presented by Rose and Chris Prater through the Institute of Contemporary Prints 1975

Just at this moment, somehow or other, they began to run
from *Illustrations to Through the Looking-Glass* 1970
Screen-print on paper
24.3 x 18 cm (9 9/16 x 7 1/16 in)
Tate. Presented by Rose and Chris Prater through the Institute of Contemporary Prints 1975

So Alice picked him up very gently
from *Illustrations to Through the Looking-Glass* 1970
Screen-print on paper
24.5 x 18.1 cm (9 5/8 x 7 1/8 in)
Tate. Presented by Rose and Chris Prater through the Institute of Contemporary Prints 1975

'Well, this is grand!' said Alice
from *Illustrations to Through the Looking-Glass* 1970
Screen-print on paper
24.2 x 17.9 cm (9 1/2 x 7 1/16 in)
Tate. Presented by Rose and Chris Prater through the Institute of Contemporary Prints 1975

Costume Life Drawing 1971
Screenprint on paper
43.2 x 22.5 cm (17 x 8 7/8 in)
Tate. Presented by Rose and Chris Prater through the Institute of Contemporary Prints 1975

Liberty Blake in a Kimono 1971
Watercolour
50.1 x 30.5 cm (19 3/4 x 12 in)
Private Collection, London

Death of a Moth 1972
Pencil on paper
57.7 x 45.7 cm (22 3/4 x 18 in)
Collection Peter Blake

Flowers in a Vase or a Posy for Liberty 1972
Watercolour
22.9 x 19 cm (9 x 7 1/2 in)
Penelope Govett

Studio Tack-Board 1972
Screenprint on paper
97.2 x 136.8 cm (38 1/4 x 53 7/8 in)
Tate. Presented by Robert Simon 1975

Titania 1972–4
Oil on board
17.8 x 11.7 cm (7 x 4 5/8 in)
Private Collection

Souvenir for Judith 1973
Collage
24.8 x 18.4 cm (9 3/4 x 7 1/4 in)
Collection Peter Blake

Girl in a Poppy Field 1974
Screenprint on paper
41.3 x 27.3 cm (16 1/4 x 10 3/4 in)
Tate. Presented by Waddington Galleries through the Institute of Contemporary Prints 1975

Souvenir for Jim Dine 1974
Collage
35.6 x 51.1 cm (14 x 20 1/8 in)
Collection Peter Blake

Souvenir for Gilbert and George 1974
Collage
45.1 x 24.7 cm (17 3/4 x 9 3/4 in)
Collection Peter Blake

Souvenir for Hockney 1974
Collage
29.8 x 35.2 cm (11 3/4 x 13 7/8 in)
Collection Peter Blake

Souvenir for Jos 1974
Collage
24.1 x 16.5 x 1.9 cm (9 1/2 x 6 1/2 x 3/4 in)
Joslyn Tilson

Souvenir for Kitaj 1974
Collage
118.8 x 46.4 cm (46 3/4 x 18 1/4 in)
Collection Peter Blake

Postcard 1974–88
Hand-coloured photograph
123.5 x 81.3 cm (48 5/8 x 32 in)
Private Collection

Liberty as a 'Suffolk Child by John Constable R.A.'
from *For John Constable* 1976
Print and mixed media on paper
66.4 x 49.8 cm (26 1/8 x 19 5/8 in)
Tate. Presented by Bernard Jacobson Gallery 1976

Titania 1976–83
Oil on canvas
121.9 x 91.4 cm (48 x 36 in)
Courtesy of Michel Soskine, Inc., New York

Fairy with Toad stools c.1977
Oil on hardboard
14 x 10.1 cm (5 1/2 x 4 in)
Private Collection, Courtesy of Hazlitt Holland-Hibbert

Flora – Fairy Child 1977
Oil on hardboard
15.9 x 11.4 cm (6 1/4 x 4 1/2 in)
Penelope Govett

A Little Museum for Tom Phillips 1977
Collage
38.7 x 24.2 cm (15 1/4 x 9 1/2 in)
Collection Tom Phillips

Ophelia 1977–2002
Oil on board
139.1 x 96.8 cm (76 x 38 1/8 in)
Private Collection

Daisy Fairy 1981–2
Oil on hardboard
28 x 16.5 cm (11 x 6 1/2 in)
Private Collection, Madrid, Courtesy of Michael Soskine, Inc., New York

Eglentyne 1981–2
Oil on hardboard
8.9 x 8.9 cm (3 1/2 x 3 1/2 in)
Private Collection

'The Meeting' or 'Have a Nice Day, Mr Hockney' 1981–3
Oil on canvas
99.2 x 124.4 cm (39 1/16 x 49 in)
Tate. Presented by the Friends of the Tate Gallery out of funds bequeathed by Miss Helen Arbuthnot 1983

Montgomery Clift was a Twin 1981–3
Oil on canvas
88.9 x 68 cm (35 x 26¾ in)
Museo de Bellas Artes de Bilbao

The Owl and the Pussycat 1981–3
Oil on hardboard
27.3 x 31.8 cm (10¾ x 12½ in)
Bristol City Museum and Art Gallery

A Remembered Moment in Venice California 1981–91
Oil on canvas
79.4 x 105.4 cm (31¼ x 41½ in)
Galerie Claude Bernard, Paris

I may not be a Ruralist anymore but I saw a fairy in my garden in Chiswick 1982–91
Oil on canvas
126 x 100 cm (49⅝ x 39⅜ in)
Private Collection

Daisy on Rollerskates 1983
Oil on canvas on board
97.8 x 77.5 cm (38½ x 30½ in)
Nishimura Gallery, Tokyo

Boy Fairy II 1984
Oil on cardboard re-mounted on linen
17.8 x 12.7 cm (7 x 5 in)
Courtesy of Michel Soskine, Inc., New York

Little Jack Horner 1984
Oil on cardboard pasted on canvas
15.2 x 15.2 cm (6 x 6 in)
Private Collection, Courtesy of Galerie Claude Bernard, Paris

Prince 1984
Oil on cardboard re-mounted on linen
18 x 13 cm (7 1/16 x 5⅛ in)
Private Collection, Courtesy of Michel Soskine, Inc., New York

Bristol Bicycle Race 1985
Watercolour on paper
45.1 x 32.7 cm (17¾ x 12⅞ in)
Private Collection

Ms. Super 1985
Watercolour and mixed media
45 x 29.8 cm (17 11/16 x 11¾ in)
Galerie Claude Bernard, Paris

Dex and Lex Lisowski Junkyard Dogs 1986
Watercolour and mixed media
45.7 x 30.5 cm (18 x 12 in)
Galerie Claude Bernard, Paris

Cherry Bomb 1987
Watercolour and mixed media
44.8 x 29.5 cm (17⅝ x 11⅝ in)
Private Collection

Lucky Boy Fit Kelly 1987
Watercolour and mixed media
44.8 x 29.8 cm (17⅝ x 11¾ in)
Galerie Claude Bernard, Paris

Mambo Rambo 1987
Watercolour and mixed media
45.7 x 30.5 cm (18 x 12 in)
Galerie Claude Bernard, Paris

Norma Jean Baker 1926–1962 1988
Photographs and black enamel on wood
80.3 x 62.9 cm (31⅝ x 24¾ in)
Private Collection, Tokyo

Marilyn Monroe over a Painting No.1 1989–90
Photographs and enamel paint on wood
167 x 123.7 x 33.2 cm (65¾ x 49¾ x 13 in)
Mr and Mrs Anders Tuvlind, Sweden

Marilyn Monroe: Red Cross 1989–90
Oil and photograph on canvas
60.9 x 60.9 cm (24 x 24 in)
Private Collection, Sweden

Madonna of Venice Beach 1990
Oil on canvas
111.8 x 90.2 cm (44 x 35½ in)
Private Collection

M.M. Yellow and Red 1990
Photographs and enamel paint on wood
39.7 x 21.9 cm (15⅝ x 8⅝ in)
Private Collection

The Twins in their Tea Garden 1991
Oil on board
127 x 101.6 cm (50 x 40 in)
Nishimura Gallery, Tokyo

Madonna of Venice Beach I 1994–6
Oil on canvas
137 x 84 cm (53 15/16 x 33 1/16 in)
Private Collection

The National Gallery Madonna 1994–2000
Oil on canvas
121.9 x 91.4 cm (48 x 36 in)
Private Collection, Courtesy of Waddington Galleries, London

The Venuses' Outing to Weymouth 1994–2004
83.8 x 139.7 cm (33 x 55 in)
Oil on canvas
Mr and Mrs Theodore B. Baum

Madonna of Venice Beach (California) IV 1995
Oil on wood panel
28 x 34 cm (11 x 13⅜ in)
Private Collection

The Twins in their Tea Garden (Second Version) 1995–9
Oil on panel
127 x 101.6 cm (50 x 40 in)
Waddington Galleries, London

Marcel Duchamp's World Tour: The Tarzan Family 1995–2005
Acrylic on canvas
69 x 124.8 cm (27 3/16 x 49⅛ in)
Private Collection, Courtesy of Waddington Galleries, London

Still Life (I) (After van Os, Fruit and Flowers in a Terracotta Vase) 1996
Oil on canvas on board
48.7 x 36.7 x 2.7 cm (19⅛ x 14½ x 1⅛ in)
Collection Peter Blake

Still Life (III) (After Fantin-Latour, The Rosy Wealth of June) 1996
Oil on canvas on board
41 x 33.5 x 7 cm (16⅛ x 13¼ x 2¾ in)
Collection Peter Blake

Still Life (VI) (After Courbet, Still Life with Apples and a Pomegranate) 1996
Oil on canvas on board
45 x 41 x 4.5 cm (17¾ x 16⅛ x 1¾ in)
Collection Peter Blake

Still Life (VIII) (After Steenwyck, Still Life: An Allegory of the Vanities of Human Life) 1996
Oil on panel
38.5 x 31 x 6 cm (15⅛ x 12¼ x 2⅜ in)
Collection Peter Blake

The Deer Park (After Velasquez, The Boar Hunt). In Memory of Michael Andrews 1996
Oil on canvas
115 x 140 cm (45¼ x 55 in)
Waddington Galleries, London

After Velasquez, Still Life II, Kitchen Scene with Christ in the House of Martha & Mary 1996–2001
Oil on wood
30 x 42.5 cm (11 13/16 x 16¾ in)
Galerie Claude Bernard, Paris

D'Aprés Juan de Zurbaran, 'Still Life with Chocolate Service' 1996–2001
Oil on wood
47.5 x 74.5 cm (18 11/16 x 29 5/16 in)
Galerie Claude Bernard, Paris

D'Aprés Luis Melendez: detail de 'Still Life with Oranges and Walnuts' 1996–2001
Oil on cardboard
17.1 x 15.2 cm (6 3/4 x 6 in)
Galerie Claude Bernard, Paris

Ratatac 1997–2003
Oil on hardboard
94 x 69.2 cm (37 x 27 1/4 in)
Magda Archer and Harry Hill

Marcel Duchamp's World Tour: Meets the Spice Girls and Elvis 2000–05
Acrylic on canvas
121.9 x 91.4 cm (48 x 36 in)
Private Collection

Ian Dury 2001
Acrylic on board
30.5 x 25.4 cm (12 x 10 in)
Magda Archer and Harry Hill

Joe Louis – The Brown Bomber 2001–6
Oil on canvas
122 x 76.2 cm (48 x 30 in)
Waddington Galleries, London

A Ficticious Lady Wrestler Ms Love 2002
Oil and collage on board
36.2 x 22.8 cm (14 1/4 x 9 in)
Private Collection, Courtesy of Michael Soskine, Inc., New York

Gender Benders 2002–3
Oil and acrylic on board
43.2 x 34.9 cm (17 x 13 3/4 in)
Wetterling Gallery, Stockholm

Lady X Cess 2002–3
Oil on wooden panel
61.3 x 29.8 cm (24 1/8 x 11 3/4 in)
Collection Christensen

Marcel Duchamp's World Tour: Playing Chess with Tracey 2003–5
Acrylic on canvas
91.4 x 121.9 cm (36 x 48 in)
Waddington Galleries, London

Marcel Duchamp's World Tour: The Artists' Fancy Dress Ball 2004
Oil on canvas
127 x 96.5 cm (50 x 38 in)
Private Collection

Marcel Duchamp's World Tour: He Meets the Congress of Unusual People with the Ringling Brothers and Barnum and Bailey (Combined) Circus Season – 1929 2004–5
Acrylic on canvas
102 x 306 cm (40 3/16 x 120 1/2 in)
David Roberts Collection

Kate 2006
Watercolour
30.5 x 22.8 cm (12 x 9 in)
Private Collection, Courtesy of Hazlitt Holland-Hibbert

Costume Life 1 2007 (work in progress)
Oil on canvas
183 x 91 cm (72 x 36 in)
Collection Peter Blake

Costume Life 2 2007 (work in progress)
Oil on canvas
183 x 91 cm (72 x 36 in)
Collection Peter Blake

Costume Life 3 2007 (work in progress)
Oil on canvas
183 x 91 cm (72 x 36 in)
Collection Peter Blake

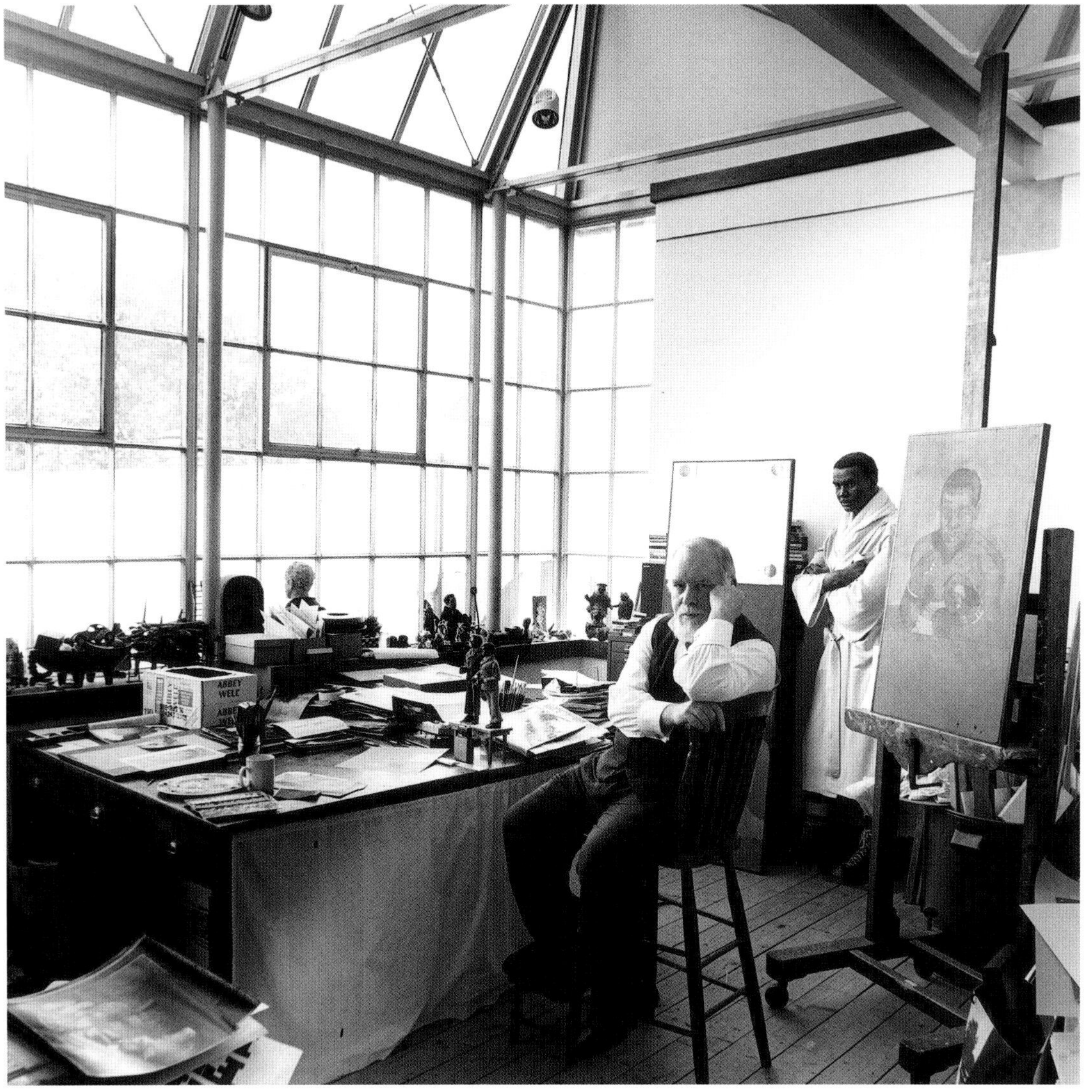

Biography

1932	Born 25 June, Dartford, Kent
1946–49	Gravesend Technical College and School of Art; Junior Art Department
1949–51	Gravesend School of Art
1950	Accepted by the Royal College of Art, London
1951–53	National Service in the R.A.F.
1953–56	Royal College of Art, London – First Class Diploma (1956)
1956–57	Leverhulme Research Award to study popular art; travelled in Holland, Belgium, France, Italy and Spain
1960–62	Taught at St. Martin's School of Art, London
1960–63	Taught at Harrow School of Art
1961	Featured in Ken Russell's B.B.C. 'Monitor' film *Pop goes the easel* / First Prize Junior Section, John Moores Liverpool Exhibition
1961–64	Taught at Walthamstow School of Art
1962	First One-Man exhibition, Portal Gallery, London
1963	Married Jann Haworth
1964–76	Taught at Royal College of Art, London
1968	Daughter, Juliette Liberty Blake, born
1969	Moved to Wellow, Avon / Retrospective exhibition at City Art Gallery, Bristol
1973–74	Retrospective exhibition; touring to Amsterdam; Hamburg; Brussels; Arnhem
1974	Daughter, Daisy Blake, born / Elected A.R.A. (Associate Member of the Royal Academy of Arts, London)
1975	Founding member of the Brotherhood of Ruralists, with Jann Haworth, Ann and Graham Arnold, David Inshaw, and Annie and Graham Ovenden
1979	Separated from Jann Haworth; returned to London
1980	Met Chrissy Wilson
1981	Elected R.A. (Member of the Royal Academy of Arts, London)
1983	Awarded C.B.E.
1985	Designed poster for Live Aid, world's largest ever multi-national pop concert on 13 July, in aid of African famine relief
1986	Publication of Marina Vaizey's monograph *Peter Blake*
1987	Marriage to Chrissy Wilson / Daughter, Rose Blake, born
1994	Third associate artist of the National Gallery
1998	Made Honorary Doctor, Royal College of Art, London
2002	Receives Knighthood
2005	Designed poster for the Live 8 concert 2nd July 2005 / Resigned from the Royal Academy of Arts, London
2006	Judge of *John Moores 24*, Liverpool

Solo exhibitions

1962 Portal Gallery, London

1965 Robert Fraser Gallery, London

1969 Leslie Waddington Prints, London / Robert Fraser Gallery, London / City Art Gallery, Bristol

1970 Ashgate Gallery, Farnham

1972 Waddington Galleries, London

1973–74 Stedelijk Museum, Amsterdam, touring to Kunstverein Hamburg; Gemeentemuseum, Arnhem; Palais des Beaux-Arts, Brussels

1974 Natalie Stern Gallery, London

1977 Waddington and Tooth Galleries, London

1978 Waddington Graphics, London

1979 Bohun Gallery, Henley-on-Thames

1980 Galleria Documenta, Turin

1983 Tate Gallery, London, touring to Kestner Gesellschaft, Hanover

1984 Galerie Claude Bernard, Paris

1986–87 Watermans Art Centre, Brentford, Middlesex, touring to Turnpike Gallery, Leigh

1988 Nishimura Gallery, Tokyo

1990 Waddington Galleries, London / Wetterling Gallery, Gothenburg, Sweden

1992 Govinda Gallery, Washington, D.C.

1993 The Tabernacle Cultural Centre, Machynlleth

1995 Galerie Claude Bernard, Paris

1996–97 *Now We Are 64: Peter Blake at the National Gallery*, National Gallery, London, touring to Whitworth Art Gallery, Manchester

1999 *A Cabinet of Curiosities from the Collections of Peter Blake*, Morley Gallery, London

2000 *Peter Blake: About Collage*, Tate Liverpool

2001–06 *Alphabet*, York College of Further and Higher Education, toured throughout Britain until 2006

2002 *Over the Rainbow*, Harley Gallery, Welbeck / *Sir Peter Blake/And Now We Are 70*, Paul Morris Gallery, New York

2003 *Peter Blake*, Artiscope (Zaira Mis), Brussels / *Peter Blake: Commercial Art*, The London Institute Gallery, London / *Peter Blake: Sculpture*, The London Institute Gallery, London

2005 *Peter Blake: 1-10 (Collages, Constructions, Drawings & Sculpture) & The Marcel Duchamp Paintings*, Waddington Galleries, London / *New Prints by Peter Blake*, The Charing X Gallery, London / *Peter Blake: Love*, Paul Stolper, London / *With a Little Help*, Spring Fine Art, Design & Antiques Fair, London

2006 *Peter Blake: 1975–2005*, Bjorn Wetterling Gallery, Stockholm / *Peter Blake Prints and Sculpture*, The Harley Gallery, Welbeck

Group exhibitions

1954 *Royal Academy Summer Exhibition*, Royal Academy of Arts, London

1955 *Paintings by Tutors and Students at the R.C.A.*, Exeter / *The Observer Exhibition of Portraits of Children*, R.W.S. Galleries, London / *Daily Express Young Artists' Exhibition*, New Burlington Galleries, London / *Summer Exhibition*, Royal Academy of Arts, London

1956 *Summer Selection*, Prospect Gallery, London

1958 *Five Painters*, Institute of Contemporary Arts, London / *The Guggenheim Painting Award 1958: British Section*, Whitechapel Art Gallery, London

1959 *Six from Now*, Cambridge

1960 *Theo Crosby: Sculpture, Peter Blake: Objects, John Latham: Libraries*, Institute of Contemporary Arts, London / *Grass by Tony Gifford, Gold by Peter Blake*, New Vision Centre, London / *Peter Blake, Roddy Maude-Roxby, Ivor Abrahams*, Portal Gallery, London / *The Mysterious Sign*, Institute of Contemporary Arts, London / *D.A.N.A.D. Design*, Portal Gallery, London

1961 *Young Commonwealth Artists Exhibition of New Art*, R.B.A. Galleries, London / *Momentum*, Raille Gallery, London / *Aspects of Collage*, Brook Street Gallery, London / *Drawings by Six Painters and Two Sculptors*, Rawinsky Gallery, London / *Pauline Boty, Peter Blake, Christine Porter, Geoffrey Reeve*, A.I.A. Gallery, London / *John Moores Liverpool Exhibition*, Walker Art Gallery, Liverpool

1962 *John Moores Prizewinners*, Institute of Contemporary Arts, London / *British Self Portraits from Sickert to the Present Day*, Laing Art Gallery, Newcastle-upon-Tyne (Arts Council touring exhibition) / *British Painting Today and Yesterday*, Arthur Tooth and Sons, London / *Summer 1962: A Selection of Paintings by Members of the A.I.A.*, A.I.A. Gallery, London / *Summer Exhibition*, Royal Academy of Arts, London / *Festival of Labour: Exhibition of New Art*, Congress House, London / *New Approaches to the Figure*, Arthur Jeffress Gallery, London / *Six Young Painters*, Cheltenham Art Gallery / *Towards Art?*, Royal College of Art, London / *New Realists*, Sidney Janis Gallery, New York

1962–63 *British Art Today*, San Francisco Museum of Art, touring to Dallas Museum of Contemporary Arts; Santa Barbara Museum of Art

1963 *1962: One Year of British Art*, Arthur Tooth and Sons, London / *Drawings by Artists of Two Generations*, Grabowsky Gallery, London / *Pop Art*, Midland Group, Nottingham / *Towards Art?*, Arts Council Gallery, Cambridge / *British Painting in the Sixties*, Whitechapel Art Gallery, London / *Obsession and Fantasy*, Robert Fraser Gallery, London / *Englische Malerei der Gegenwart*, Helmhaus, Zurich / *Dunn International Exhibition*, Beaverbrook Art Gallery, Fredericton, New Brunswick, touring to Tate Gallery, London / *Troisiéme Biennale de Paris*, Musée d'Art Moderne, Paris / *Drawings by Eight Artists*, Robert Fraser Gallery, London

1964 *The New Image*, Arts Council of Northern Ireland, Belfast / *Britische Malerei der Gegenwart*, Kunstverein für die Rheinlande und Westfalen, Dusseldorf / *Figuratie en Defiguratie*, Museum voor Schone Kunsten,

Ghent / *6 Young Painters*, Blackburn Art Gallery (Arts Council touring exhibition) / *New Painting 61–64*, Arts Council of Great Britain, London / *British Painting from the Paris Biennale 1963*, Royal College of Art, London / *Shakespeare Exhibition, 1954–1964*, Stratford-upon-Avon / *Englische Kunst der Gegenwart*, Städtische Kunstgalerie, Bochum / *Painting and Sculpture of a Decade: 1954–1964*, Tate Gallery, London / *Nieuwe Realisten*, Haags Gemeentemuseum, The Hague / *Summer Exhibition 1964*, Robert Fraser Gallery, London / *Pittsburgh International*, Carnegie Institute, Pittsburgh / *I.C.A. Screenprint Project*, Institute of Contemporary Arts, London / *Pick of the Pops*, National Museum of Wales, Cardiff / *Neue Realitäten & Pop Art*, Akademie der Kunst, Berlin

1965 *Café Royal Centenary Exhibition*, Café Royal, London / *Peter Stuyvesant Foundation: a Collection in the Making*, Whitechapel Art Gallery, London / *Pop Art: Nouveau Idealisme*, Palais des Beaux-Arts, Brussels / *London: The New Scene*, Walker Art Center, Minneapolis, touring to Washington; Seattle; Boston; Vancouver; Toronto; Ottawa / *Summer Exhibition*, Royal Academy of Arts, London / *Trends in Contemporary British Painting*, Bear Lane Gallery, Oxford / *Summer Show*, Robert Fraser Gallery, London / *La figuration narrative dans l'art contemporain*, Galerie Creuze, Paris / *Focus on Drawings*, Art Gallery of Toronto / *The English Eye*, Marlborough-Gerson Gallery, New York

1966 *European Drawings*, Solomon R. Guggenheim Museum, New York / *Work in Progress*, Robert Fraser Gallery, London / *Blake, Boshier, Caulfield, Hamilton, Paolozzi*, Studio Marconi, Milan / *Irish Exhibition of Living Art*, National College of Art, Dublin / *How They Started: Paintings By Some Former Students of the Royal College of Art*, Oxford University Press, London

1967 *British Drawings: The New Generation*, Museum of Modern Art, New York / *Work from 1956 to 1967 by Clive Barker, Peter Blake, Richard Hamilton, Jann Haworth and Colin Self*, Robert Fraser Gallery, London / *Le visage de l'homme dans l'art contemporain*, Musée Rath, Geneva / *Summer Exhibition 1967*, Robert Fraser Gallery, London / *Tribute to Robert Fraser*, Robert Fraser Gallery, London / *Jeunes Peintres Anglais*, Palais des Beaux-Arts, Brussels / *Englische Kunst*, Galerie Bischofberger, Zurich / *1967 Pittsburgh International*, Carnegie Institute, Pittsburgh / *Convocation Exhibition*, Royal College of Art, London / *Recent British Painting: Peter Stuyvesant Collection*, Tate Gallery, London / *Homage to Marylin Monroe*, Sidney Janis Gallery, New York

1967–68 *Three Painters/Peter Blake, Jim Dine, Richard Hamilton*, Midlands Arts Centre, Birmingham, touring to Arts Council Gallery, Cambridge

1968 *Holland Homage*, Galerie 20, Amsterdam / *Painting 1964–1967*, Hayward Gallery, London / *Old Testament Drawings*, Oxford University Press, London / *Britische Kunst Heute*, Kunstverein Hamburg / *Three Blind Mice, de Collecties: Visser, Peeters, Becht*, Stedelijk Van Abbemuseum, Eindhoven / *The Obsessive Image 1960–1968*, Institute of Contemporary Arts, London / *Group Show*, Robert Fraser Gallery, London / *L'Art Vivant 1965–1968*, Foundation Maeght, Saint Paul / *Summer Exhibition*, Royal Academy of Arts, London / *From Kitaj to Blake: Non-Abstract Artists in Britain*, Bear Lane Gallery, Oxford / *Menschenbilder: Ausstellung zum 10. Darmstädter Gespräch*, Kunsthalle Darmstadt

1969 *Pop Art*, Hayward Gallery, London / *John Moores Liverpool Exhibition*, Walker Art Gallery, Liverpool

1970 *Works on Paper*, Waddington Galleries, London / *Summer Exhibition*, Royal Academy of Arts, London / *Zeitgenossen: Das Gesicht unserer Gesellschaft im Spiegel der heutigen Kunst*, Städtische Kunsthalle, Recklinghausen / *Kelpra Prints*, Hayward Gallery, London / *Pop Art: Nieuwe Figuratie = Nouveau Réalisme*, Gemeentelijk Casino, Knokke / *Internationale der Zeichnung*, Mathildenhöhe, Darmstadt / *Contemporary British Art*, National Museum of Modern Art, Tokyo / *Pop '70*, Mayfair Gallery, London / *British Painting and Sculpture 1960–1970*, National Gallery of Art, Washington, D.C. / *An Exhibition of Paintings, Drawings and Screenprints by Peter Blake and Graham Ovenden Based on the Theme of Lewis Caroll's Alice*, Waddington Galleries, London

1970–71 *New Multiple Art*, Whitechapel Art Gallery, London

1971 *Group Show*, Mayfair Gallery, London / *Post Card Show*, Angela Flowers Gallery, London / *Works on Paper*, Waddington Galleries, London / *Critic's Choice*, selected by Robert Melville, Arthur Tooth and Sons Ltd /

Metamorphose de L'objet: Art et Anti-art 1910–1970, Palais des Beaux-Arts, Brussels

1972 *British Drawings 1952–1972*, Angela Flowers Gallery, London

1973 *Spring Collection*, Bear Lane Gallery, Oxford / *Estampes Anglaises Actuelles*, Galerie Stadler, Paris / *11 Englische Zeichner*, Staatliche Kunsthalle, Baden-Baden, touring to Kunsthalle, Bremen; I.C.C., Antwerp / *Earth Images*, Scottish National Gallery of Modern Art, Edinburgh / *Henry Moore to Gilbert and George: Modern British Art from the Tate Gallery*, Palais des Beaux-Arts, Brussels

1974 *Peter Blake*, Festival Gallery, Bath / *Peter Blake's Selection*, Festival Gallery, Bath / *British Painting '74*, Hayward Gallery, London / *Works on Paper*, Waddington Galleries, London

1975 *British Sculpture and Objects*, Kinsman Morison Gallery, London / *Realismus und Realität: Ausstellung zum 11. Darmstädter Gespräch*, Kunsthalle Darmstadt / *British Artists' Prints*, Queensland National Art Gallery, Brisbane

1975–76 *European Painting in the 70s*, Los Angeles County Museum of Art, touring to St. Louis Art Museum; Elvehjem Art Center, Madison, Wisconsin

1976 *Pop Art in England*, Kunstverein Hamburg, touring to Munich; York Art Gallery / *Arte Inglese Oggi 1960–76*, British Council exhibition, Palazzo Reale, Milan / *Peter Blake, Richard Hamilton, David Hockney, R.B. Kitaj, Eduardo Paolozzi*, Boymans-van Beuningen Museum, Rotterdam / *Summer Exhibition*, Royal Academy of Arts, London

1977 *Hayward Annual*, Hayward Gallery, London / *The Brotherhood of Ruralists*, Festival Gallery, Bath, touring to Edinburgh; Doncaster; Southampton / *British Painting 1952–1977*, Royal Academy of Arts, London

1978 *Groups*, Waddington Galleries, London / *The Brotherhood of Ruralists*, Bodmin Fine Arts Gallery, Bodmin / *Summer Exhibition*, Royal Academy of Arts, London

1979 *Groups II*, Waddington Galleries, London / *The Brotherhood of Ruralists*, Charleston Manor, Seaford, Sussex / *The Brotherhood of Ruralists*, Gainsborough's House, Sudbury, Suffolk / *This Knot of Life*, L.A. Louver Gallery, Los Angeles

1980 *Groups III*, Waddington Galleries, London / *Fairies*, Brighton Museum and Art Gallery / *Ophelia: Paintings and Drawings on the Theme of Ophelia by the Brotherhood of Ruralists*, City Museum and Art Gallery, Bristol / *Prints of the 70s by Six British Artists*, National Art Gallery, Wellington, touring to Wanganui; Auckland; Palmerston North; Christchurch; Dunedin / *Nudes*, Angela Flowers Gallery, London

1981 *Groups IV*, Waddington Galleries, London / *The Ruralists*, Arnolfini Gallery, Bristol, touring to Birmingham; Glasgow; London / *Six British Artists, Prints 1974–1981*, Waddington Graphics, London

1982 *Groups V*, Waddington Galleries, London / *British Drawings and Watercolours*, China Art Gallery, Beijing, touring to Shanyang; Hong Kong / *Summer Exhibition*, Royal Academy of Arts, London

1983 *Landscape*, Whitworth Art Gallery, Manchester / *Groups VI*, Waddington Galleries, London

1984 *Groups VII*, Waddington Galleries, London / *Works on Paper*, Waddington Galleries, London / *The Automobile and Culture*, Los Angeles Museum of Contemporary Art, touring to Detroit / *Look People*, National Portrait Gallery, London / *The Hard Won Image*, Tate Gallery, London

1985 *Groups VIII*, Waddington Galleries, London / *La Vie et l'Oeuvre de l'Ecrivain*, Galerie James Mayor, Paris / *Royal College of Art Printmaking Appeal Fund Exhibition*, Barbican Art Gallery, London

1985–86 *On Drawing: Aspects of Drawing from 1960–1985*, Frankfurter Kunstverein, Frankfurt

1986 *Studies of the Nude*, Marlborough Fine Art, London / *Heads*, Nicola Jacobs Gallery, London / *Little and Large*, Waddington Galleries, London / *Forty Years of Modern Art*, Tate Gallery, London / *American/European Painting and Sculpture*, L.A. Louver Gallery, Los Angeles

1987 *British Art in the 20th Century: The Modern Movement*, Royal Academy of Arts, London / *Pop Art U.S.A.–U.K.*, Odakyu Grand Gallery, Tokyo, touring to Daimaru Museum, Osaka; Funabashi Seibu Museum of Art, Funabashi; Sogo Museum of Art, Yokohama / *London Group Exhibition*, Royal College of Art, London / *Annual Exhibition of The Royal Glasgow Institute of Fine Arts*, McLellan Galleries, Glasgow

1987–88 *Comic Iconoclasm*, Institute of Contemporary Arts, London, touring to Douglas Hyde Gallery, Dublin;

Cornerhouse Gallery, Manchester, touring Europe

1988 *Mother and Child*, Lefevre Gallery, London / *Contemporary Art Auctions*, St. Peter's Church Hall, Portobello Road, London / *The British Picture*, L.A. Louver Gallery, Los Angeles / *Atlas 3 Exhibition*, Nigel Greenwood Gallery, London / *Contemporary Portraits*, Flowers East Gallery, London

1988–89 *Food*, Odette Gilbert Gallery, London

1988–90 *The New British Painting*, The Contemporary Arts Center, Cincinnati, Ohio, touring to Chicago Public Library Cultural Center; Haggerty Museum, Marquette University, Milwaukee, Wisconsin; Southeastern Center for Contemporary Art, Winston-Salem, North Carolina; Grand Rapids Art Museum, Michigan

1989 *Modern British Tapestries*, Bohun Gallery, Henley-on-Thames / *British Painting in the 1960s and 1970s*, Ramsgate Library Gallery / *Post-War British Prints*, Austin Desmond Fine Art, London / *Children and Childhood in British Art 1880–1989*, City Art Centre, Edinburgh / *Summer Exhibition*, Royal Academy of Arts, London / *Works on Paper*, Waddington Galleries, London / *Twentieth Century Works*, Waddington Galleries, London

1989–90 *The Secret Garden: The Work of The Brotherhood of Ruralists*, Piccadilly Gallery, London / *Picturing People*, British Council exhibition, touring to National Gallery, Kuala Lumpur; Museum of Art, Hong Kong; Empress Palace Gallery, Singapore

1990 *Pictures of Rock*, Kunsthallen Brandts Klaedefabrik, Odense, Denmark / *Three Ways*, Magyar Kepzomuveszeti, Budapest, touring to Istvankiraly, Szekessehervar; Pecf, Hungary / *Glasgow's Great British Art Exhibition*, McLellan Galleries, Glasgow / *Masterpieces from the Arts Council Collection: 20th Century British Paintings*, Ueno Royal Museum, Tokyo

1991 *British Art from 1930*, Waddington Galleries, London / *Summer Exhibition*, Royal Academy of Arts, London / *Art In Boxes*, England & Co, London / *Five Artists*, Waddington Galleries, London / *Pop Art 1960–1969*, Holm Gallery, London

1991–92 *Pop Art*, Royal Academy of Arts, London, touring to Museum Ludwig, Cologne; Centro de Arte Reina Sofia, Madrid

1992 *Ready, Steady, Go: Painting of the Sixties from the Arts Council Collection*, Royal Festival Hall, London, touring Britain / *Summer Exhibition*, Royal Academy of Arts, London / *Artificial Women*, Galerij Cotthem, Zottegem, Belgium / *Royal Academy Painters*, Galerie zur alten deutschen Schule, Thun / *The Painter in Glass*, Swansea Festival Exhibition, Glynn Vivian Art Gallery

1992–93 *Pop Art*, The Montreal Museum of Fine Arts

1993 *Kindred Spirits*, Bishops' Palace, Chichester / *Artist's Choice*, Boundary Gallery, London / *Beautiful Blooms*, Lamont Gallery, London / *The Sixties Art Scene in London*, Barbican Art Gallery, London

1994 *Summer Exhibition*, Royal Academy of Arts, London / *Peter Greenham Memorial Exhibition*, Friend's Room, Royal Academy of Arts, London / *Elvis + Marilyn: 2 x Immortal*, The Institute of Contemporary Art, Boston, touring the United States

1995 *Paintings from the 60s and 70s: Peter Blake, Patrick Caulfield and Howard Hodgkin*, Waddington Galleries, London / *Summer Exhibition*, Royal Academy of Arts, London / *Revolution: Art of the Sixties from Warhol to Beuys*, Museum of Contemporary Art, Tokyo

1995–96 *Marilyn Monroe*, Palazzo della Civilta Italiana, Rome

1996 *Football*, Gallery 27, London

1997 *Treasure Island*, Calouste Gulbenkian Foundation, Lisbon / *British Figurative Art, Part 1: Painting, The Human Figure*, Flowers East, London / *The Pop '60s: Transatlantic Crossing*, Fundaçáo das Descobertas, Lisbon / *Essence of Humour*, Crane Kalman, London

1998 *Self Portraits: 50 Faces of Contemporary Art*, Six Chapel Row Contemporary Art, Bath

1998–99 *Smakprov. Wetterling Gallery 1978–1998*, Wetterling Gallery, Stockholm / *POP-TASTIC!*, Wolverhampton Art Gallery, Wolverhampton

1999 *Collage: The Pasted-Paper Revolution*, Crane Kalman Gallery, London

2000 *Defining the Times*, Milton Keynes Gallery, Milton Keynes

2000–01 *The School of London and Their Friends: The Collection of Elaine and Melvin Merians*, Yale Center for British Art, New Haven, Connecticut, touring to Neuberger Museum of Art, Purchase College State University of New York, Purchase, New York

2001 *Pop Art U.S./U.K. Connections, 1956–1966*, The Menil Collection, Houston / *Summer Exhibition*, Royal Academy of Arts, London / *Les Années Pop*, Centre Pompidou, Paris / *Drawing Distinctions: Twentieth Century Drawings and Watercolours from the British Council Collections*, Milton Keynes Gallery / *Less is More, Large Works on a Small Scale*, Pallant House Gallery, Chichester

2002 *Transition: The London Art Scene in the Fifties*, Barbican Art Galleries, London / *United Kingdom United States*, Waddington Galleries, London / *Summer Exhibition*, Royal Academy of Arts, London / *POP-TASTIC*, The Shire Hall Gallery, Stafford / *British Pop Art*, Alan Cristea Gallery, London / *2001 A Space Oddity*, The Colony Room Club, A22 Projects, London

2002–03 *Blast to Freeze: British Art in the 20th Century*, Kunstmuseum Wolfsburg, touring to Les Abattoirs, Toulouse

2003 *Five in One: David Inshaw – Friends and Influences*, Royal West of England Academy, Bristol / *Marilyn Monroe – Life of a Legend*, County Hall Gallery, London / *Summer Exhibition*, Royal Academy of Arts, London / *Modern British Art*, Jonathon Clark Fine Art, London / *As Is When: A Boom in British Printmaking 1961–1972*, British Council, London

2004 *Naked*, Royal West of England Academy, Bristol / *An Artist's Choice: David Remfry Selects*, Bohun Gallery, Henley-on-Thames / *Diamond Dust Volume One*, Edinburgh Printmakers, Edinburgh / *These are a Few of My Favourite Prints*, Caroline Wiseman, London / *Design and Artists Copyright Society (DACS): Twenty Years*, The Mall Galleries, London / *Pop Art UK: British Pop Art 1956–1972*, Palazzo Santa Margherita, Palazzina dei Giardini, Modena / *Summer Exhibition*, Royal Academy of Arts, London / *Marilyn. Una vida de leyenda*, Reales Ataranzanes de Valencia, touring to Centro Cultural de la Villa Plaza de Colon, Madrid / *Art and the 60s: This Was Tomorrow*, Tate Britain, London, touring to Gas Hall, Birmingham Museums and Art Gallery; National Gallery of Victoria, Melbourne; Auckland Art Gallery

2005 *Collage: Signs and Surfaces*, Pavel Zoubok Gallery, New York / *The Brotherhood of Ruralists and the Pre-Raphaelites*, Peter Nahum at The Leicester Galleries, London / *Summer Exhibition*, Royal Academy of Arts, London / *British Pop*, Museo de Bellas Artes de Bilbao, Bilbao / *Bone Idle*, Charing X Gallery, London

2006 *Good Vibrations: le arti visive e il rock*, Papesse Centro Arte Contemporanea, Siena / *Shakespeare*, Methuen & Co., London

Donors and Sponsors

Copyrights and Credits

SPONSORS AND DONORS FOR TATE LIVERPOOL 2007

Arts Council England
BT
British Waterways
Bruntwood
Business in the Arts: North West
Caspar Schuebbe
DLA Piper
The Esmée Fairbairn Foundation
Frank Cohen
Galerie Urs Meile, Beijing-Lucerne
The Granada Foundation
The Guardian
The Henry Moore Foundation
Individual Restaurant Company plc
Inverforth Charitable Trust
Liverpool Culture Company
Liverpool Vision
The Marian Goodman Gallery, New York
Milligan
Nicolai Frahm
Northwest Regional Development Agency
P H Holt Foundation
Paul and Margrit Hahnloser-Ingold
The Paul Hamlyn Foundation
Pro Helvetia, Swiss Arts Council
The Red Mansion Foundation
ShangHart Gallery, Shanghai
The Sir Jules Thorn Charitable Trust
Tate Liverpool Members
Tate Members
United Utilities

TATE08 PARTNERS
Cains Brewery
DLA Piper
Manchester Airport Group

CORPORATE PARTNERS
David M Robinson Fine Jewellery & Watches
DLA Piper
DWF
Ethel Austin Property Group
Hill Dickinson
HSBC Bank Plc
Laureate Online Education
Liverpool Hope University
Liverpool John Moores University
Mason Owen & Partners
The University of Liverpool
Unilever UK

CORPORATE MEMBERS
Alliance & Leicester Commercial Bank
Andrew Collinge
Arup
Alder Hey Imagine Appeal, supported by Assura Group
Bank of Scotland Corporate
Barlows Plc
Beetham Organization Ltd
Bruntwood
Building Design Partnership
Community Foundation for Merseyside
Deloitte
Grant Thornton
Grosvenor
KPMG
Midas Capital Partners Ltd
Neptune Developments Ltd
Racquet Club
Royal Bank of Scotland
Ruia Group
Silverbeck Rymer
Taylor Young Ltd
Lime Pictures
Tilney Investment Management
The Works London Ltd
Toyota GB Plc

PHOTO CREDITS
pp. 23/25, 35, 68, 72, 117, 122, 125, 147, 148, 157, 165, 172, 191, 194, 195, 197–199 Photography by Prudence Cumming Associates, London

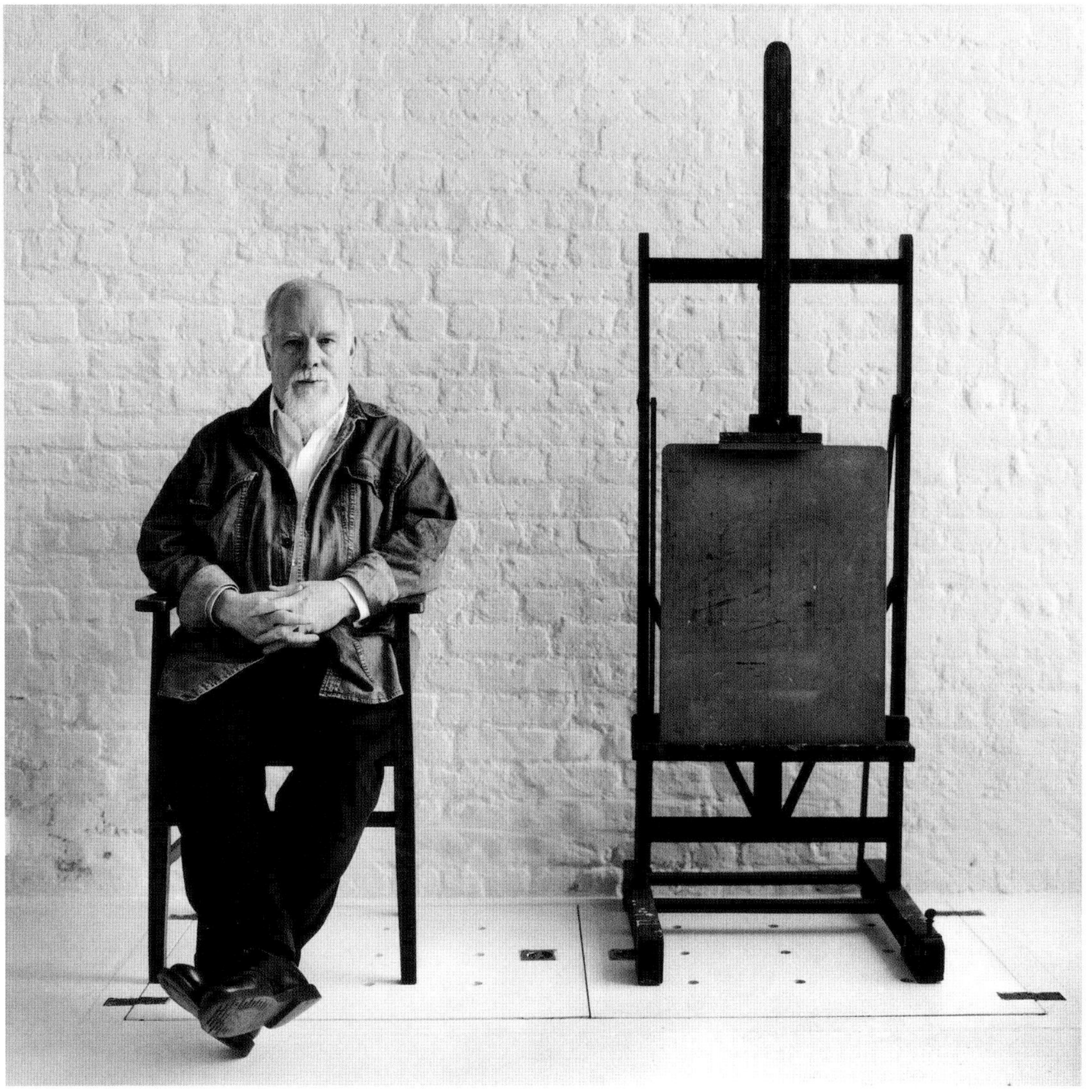

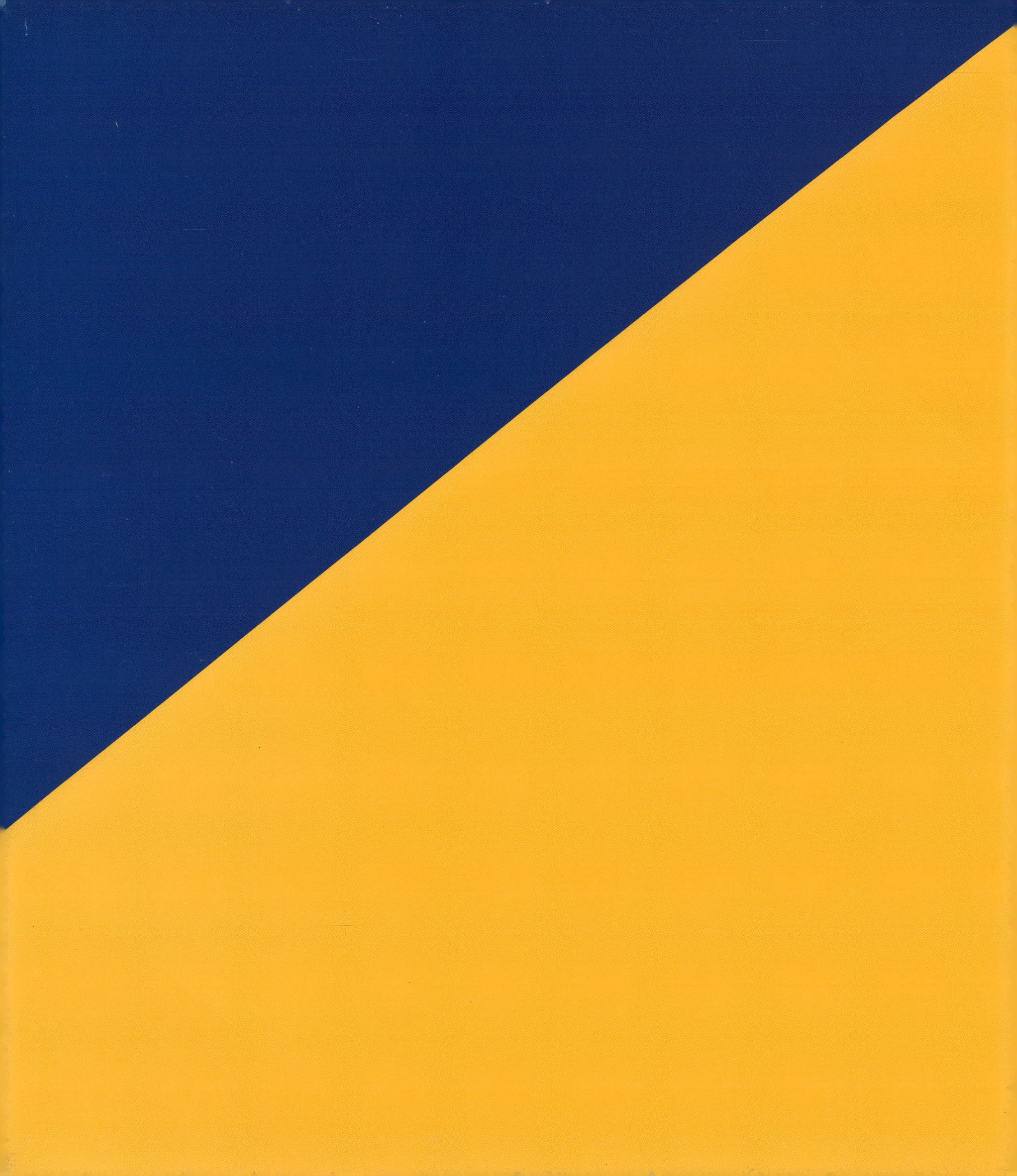